THE MARCH TO THE
SEA AND BEYOND

THE MARCH TO THE SEA AND BEYOND

Sherman's Troops in the Savannah and Carolinas Campaigns

JOSEPH T. GLATTHAAR

LOUISIANA STATE UNIVERSITY PRESS
BATON ROUGE

Copyright © 1985 by New York University and Joseph T. Glatthaar
Originally published by New York University Press
LSU Press edition published by arrangement with the author
All rights reserved
Manufactured in the United States of America

Designer: Ken Venezio

Louisiana Paperback Edition, 1995

04 03 02 01 00 99 98   5 4 3

Library of Congress Cataloging in Publication Data

Glatthaar, Joseph T., 1956–
The march to the sea and beyond.

Bibliography: p.
Includes index.
1. Sherman, William T. (William Tecumseh), 1820-1891.
2. Sherman's March to the Sea.   3. Sherman's March
through the Carolinas. I. Title.
E476.69.G53   1985   973.7′37   84-29496

ISBN 0-8071-2028-6 (pbk.)

The paper in this book meets the guidelines for permanence and dura-
bility of the Committee on Production Guidelines for Book Longevity
of the Council on Library Resources. ∞

For my grandmother, Mrs. Mary J. O'Sullivan,
and for my friends

Contents

CONTENTS

Illustrations

Preface

Only one scholar, Bell Irvin Wiley, has written an extensive social history of the Civil War participants. In twin volumes, one devoted to the Confederates and the other to the Federals, Wiley relied primarily upon letters, diaries, and reminiscences in attempt to "present soldier life as it really was."[1] No doubt, this is the starting point for all work on the common soldier, yet a thorough examination of his classic *The Life of Billy Yank* has produced some interesting results. There are fewer than two dozen references in the text about men in Sherman's army who marched from Atlanta to Savannah and through the Carolinas, and barely more than a dozen footnote citations are from these men. Wiley concentrated his research on soldiers from the Army of the Potomac, particularly those men who served in the initial stages of the war when every experience was a novelty.

The army that marched with Sherman to Savannah and through the Carolinas, however, was vastly different from the Army of the Potomac. Sherman's was an army of veterans, men who had learned the art of soldiering through several years of actual campaigning. Nearly all the troops had received their training in the West, where prolonged campaigns, lengthy marches, supply shortages, and success in battle were the rule, rather than the exception. And even their companions from the Eastern Twentieth Corps had warred in the West for over a year, long enough to erode their old habits and reshape them in the image of those of the westerners. At the expense of rigid discipline, precision drills, and tidy appearance, all trademarks of the Army of the Potomac, Sherman's command developed a sense of self-reliance and self-confidence based upon the lessons of several years of active campaigning. They had learned the best ways to perform certain duties and how to handle themselves in all sorts of situations.

It was this veteran character that utterly dominated Sherman's army, the same veteran character that made the March to the Sea and through the Carolinas possible. These two expeditions required company-level officers and enlisted men to bear a much greater burden and shoulder a much larger share of the responsibility for success than did men participating in more traditional campaigns. They demanded mastery of all aspects of soldiering, a criterion which Sherman's army alone could fulfill. Only special types of soldiers could traverse a hostile countryside in small parties every day in search of provender for themselves and their comrades and drive rapidly through the swamps and mud of South Carolina, wading streams, hauling wagons, constructing bridges, and corduroying roads as they went. They were, as the military historian B. H. Liddell Hart once wrote, "probably the finest army of military 'workmen' the modern world has seen. An army of individuals trained in the school of experience to look after their own food and health, to march far and fast with the least fatigue, to fight with the least exposure; above all, to act swiftly and to work thoroughly."[2]

Even the most famous aspect of the campaigns, the implementation of the concept of total warfare, was the product of this veteran character. The strategy to make southerners feel the iron hand of destruction derived from prolonged years of hardship and sacrifice and an unfaltering commitment to the cause of reunification. Sherman's veterans adopted the total-war concept as retaliation for the deaths and tragedies that their ranks had endured and also because they saw it as the most effective means of winning the war.

The best way to understand these veteran soldiers and their nature, I believe, is to study the Savannah and Carolinas campaigns from their own and particular perspective. It was my intention in writing this book to examine the campaigns from the level of the common soldier, both enlisted men and officers, to illuminate that veteran character. I have, therefore, tried to discuss the duties and actual hardships of the march, the boredom and frustration of camp life, and the utter confusion and pure chance of battle.

Yet studying experienced troops in camp and on the march alone will not fully develop the nature of Sherman's veteran army. Just as the process of becoming veterans altered the way soldiers performed their duties, so it affected the way they viewed their world. Veterans had undergone attitudinal changes that were just as profound as their behavioral changes. To understand the veteran character, then, it is essential to explore the attitudes of the men toward their comrades, blacks, Southern whites, the war, destruction, and reconstruction.

Against this background of the veteran character of Sherman's army, I have attempted to develop several peripheral themes. First, the plethora of campaign studies have, to a substantial degree, stripped away much of the reality of warfare. War as seen from a headquarters field tent, although important in understanding the campaign or battle, is very different from war from a soldier's perspective. By examining these campaigns from the level of the common soldier, I hope to restore much of that reality, at least from the viewpoint of the soldiers.

Second, the Civil War historian Frank E. Vandiver once said with tongue-in-cheek that communities from Texas to Virginia swear that Sherman's army marched through them. Beneath the lighthearted side to that statement, however, is a very powerful message. It clearly indicates the enormous effects of total war as implemented by Sherman's army, both in actual devastation and in the generation of fears. Scholars in military history have dealt little with the concept of total warfare from the perspective of the aggressors, and certainly no one has investigated total warfare from the perspective of Sherman's army. By examining the campaigns from the level of the Federal troops, and by relying upon the testimony of Confederate soldiers and Southern civilians who experienced the march, I hope to understand the underlying motivations of Sherman's men for adopting a policy of devastation and to shed some light on the total-war concept in military history.

Finally, another distinguished military historian, the late Louis Morton, reminds us that "Military forces in every age reflect the societies they are created to defend."[3] Civil War letters, diaries, and reminiscences are probably the single best source of mid-nineteenth-century attitudes. These soldiers came from civilian life to participate in the war, and when it was over, they returned. Their attitudes to-

ward blacks and Southern whites and their fears, aspirations, and motivations all provide an insight into those same beliefs and sentiments
throughout the North.

Ever since Sherman and his army embarked upon their march to
the coast of Georgia and, later, through the Carolinas, the two campaigns have earned the dubious distinction as the most controversial
of the Civil War and possibly in American military history. My objective, however, is neither to condemn nor to condone the behavior
of Sherman and his men. As I see it, my job is not to cast moral judg-
ments upon the conduct of others; rather, it is to ascertain exactly what
they did and understand why they did it. I only hope that I have abided
by that rule at all times. In this respect, any failures or errors in the
book are the responsibility of the author.

In this study I have quoted heavily from my sources. My contention here is that, in studying soldiers and their attitudes, the way they
expressed themselves was very much a part of their attitudes. To strip
the ideas from the manner in which an individual presented them would
be, in many cases, an injustice to both the soldier and the reader.

Acknowledgments

As is often the case, I have a long list of people who deserve thanks. Dr. Richard W. Smith of Ohio Wesleyan University rekindled a childhood passion for the Civil War with his brillant lectures. Dr. Marion McKenna of the University of Calgary, the aunt of a long-time friend of mine, has been a constant supporter and very helpful counselor. During my schooling at Rice University, Dr. Frank E. Vandiver and Dr. Sanford W. Higginbotham taught and encouraged me, and since then they have continued to help with advice and friendly support. Mike McManus, my officemate and friend, taught me a considerable amount of history over beers at the Village Tavern. Mike listened to my topic with interest and refined some of my coarse points. Pete Knupfer helped me hammer out many ideas, and Pete Lysy provided me with some stimulating conversation and long-distance research help. Dr. Richard H. Sewell, who is currently working on Sherman, provided excellent advice and vastly improved the manuscript with his superb editing skills. Dr. Thomas Archdeacon took time from his own work to show me some things on a computer, and Marilyn Archdeacon, a statistics expert, guided me in my sampling techniques. Dr. Stan Schultz has helped me in sundry ways. Along with those people previously mentioned, Dr. John Hollitz, Dr. Jim Krukones, Mary Lee Muller, Dr. Bob Otto, Judy Cochrane, and Marjorie Pettit aided me on various occasions and made time pass a little quicker. Lastly, my lunchtime colleagues—Hans van Dyk, Jeff Javid, Tom Satterthwaite, Ed Hughes, Mark Stover, and Marc Dion—deserve mention for opening my eyes to the value of social history.

Without the help of friends scattered across the country, I never could have researched this project. Sincere thanks go to Yvonne Franzen Hoban in Minneapolis; Mark Sommers in Chicago; Keith Cotton and Barbra Slater in San Marcos, Texas; Chris and John Moretta in Houston; Mike Havran in Atlanta; Steve and Ed Meinsen in Chapel Hill, North Carolina; Niels Holch in Washington, D.C.; Kitty, Ken, Susan, Tom, and Sonny David in Bethesda, Maryland; Tom Goodman and Dan Trerotola in New York; my parents in White Plains, New York; Bob McFarland in North Reading, Massachusetts; and Rob Richards in Chagrin Falls, Ohio. Everywhere I researched, archival staffs treated me like royalty. Two people in particular, however, I would like to single out for their great consideration and help: Dr. Richard Sommers of the United States Army Military History Institute and Daniel Brown, historian of Kennesaw Mountain National Park. At my home base, the State Historical Society of Wisconsin, Sharon Mulak; Jonathan Cooper; Jill Moriearty; and Lloyd Velicer, master of the Government Documents Collection, were extremely helpful. My friend Yvonne Franzen Hoban expertly prepared two maps for me and the North Carolina Division of Archive and History graciously granted permission for the use of the map of the battle of Bentonville.

Colette Powers helped me in all sorts of ways, and my parents and family supported me beyond anything that could be expected. Colin Jones, Director of New York University Press, and Dr. James Kirby Martin, series editor, have treated me wonderfully throughout the publication process.

Finally, I would like to thank my advisor and friend, Dr. Edward M. Coffman. In every sense of the word he is a true scholar, devoted to research, writing, and undergraduate and graduate education. He is also one of the most interesting and enjoyable people I have ever met. As his graduate student, he assisted me in every stage of my study, even during his one-year sabbatical to teach at the Air Force Academy. My admiration and affection for Dr. Coffman are such that words do not do him justice. The best I can do is wholeheartedly encourage anyone interested in the study of American military history to go work under him. You positively cannot do better.

I have dedicated this book to my grandmother, Mrs. Mary J. O'Sullivan, and to my friends, most of whom know little about this book and care even less, and for that I appreciate them all the more.

THE MARCH TO THE
SEA AND BEYOND

Introduction

By 1864 the Union and Confederate armies had for almost three years met each other in regular combat to decide whether the Southern states could secede from the United States and form an independent country. For President Abraham Lincoln and his reunion supporters the war was not going well. To be sure, there had been victories during that time. A West Point graduate with a reputation as a drunk, Ulysses S. Grant, had captured two Confederate armies and had helped secure control of the Mississippi River. New Orleans, the largest port in the South, had fallen to Adm. David Farragut and his fleet, and the Union had checked three different Confederate invasions into the North. But in the East the Confederates had stalemated the ponderous yet powerful Army of the Potomac while in the West the fighting had progressed only to the southern border of Tennessee. With the presidential election less than nine months away, Lincoln knew that, if the war did not swing substantially in his favor, he and the Union party might lose all chance of reuniting the two sections.

Since the war began Lincoln had searched high and low for an individual who could win victories for the Union. His commanding general at the outbreak of hostilities was Winfield Scott. In his heyday Scott was quite a soldier, but he had been a general in the U.S. Army since 1814, and his enfeebled body would no longer permit him to function in that capacity. After one hour his attention span ran thin, and no matter who he was with, even the president, he would slip off into a deep sleep. Scott's replacement was the youthful, dashing George Brinton McClellan. No doubt, McClellan had organizational expertise, but he also had, among many faults, what Lincoln called "the slows," the unwillingness to fight. In McClellan's place Lincoln selected a very promising officer from the West with an excellent reputation, Henry W. Halleck. Nicknamed "Old Brains" for his scholarly endeavors in the prewar army, Halleck disappointed Lincoln, just as McClellan had done, when he turned out to be a paper shuffler rather than a commander.

All along, though, Lincoln had had at least one eye on Ulysses Grant. Ever since he got his first command for combat, a mere 3,000 inexperienced troops at Cairo, Illinois, Grant had displayed initiative and a willingness to fight. His first major engagement was in northern Tennessee, when he captured Forts Henry and Donelson and took a small Confederate army prisoners. Five weeks later another Confederate army nearly swept his command into the Tennessee River, but Grant managed to rally his troops and, with the aid of heavy reinforcements, routed the Confederates on the following day. Although many people insisted that he was drunk at Shiloh and was thus unfit for command, Lincoln refused to listen. By early July the next year Grant had vindicated Lincoln's faith in him when he captured the Confederate bastion of Vicksburg, along with its entire army. Again in the early fall he helped rescue a Federal army trapped in Chattanooga, Tennessee and oversaw the rout of another Confederate army. This, then, was Lincoln's man, and in early March 1864 the president appointed Grant lieutenant general, the highest-ranking officer in the U.S. Army.

Several weeks later the new general in chief and his successor in the West, Maj. Gen. William Tecumseh Sherman, journeyed from Nashville to Cincinnati together to plan the spring offensives for that year. Their object was to utilize the vast Federal superiority in manpower and resources against the Confederates, to apply pressure on all fronts until the Rebel war effort collapsed. Sherman, the two decided, would remain in the West to head those veteran troops who had won the lion's share of the Union campaign victories. He would move in the direction of Atlanta, already then a rail and industrial center, against a major Confederate army with the object, as Grant later wrote his friend, "to break it up and to get into the interior of the enemy's country as far as you can, inflicting all the damage you can against their war resources." Grant, however, would return east and keep headquarters in the field with the Army of the Potomac. Lincoln had selected him as general in chief not only to formulate grand strategy but to oversee its execution, and because the Army of the Potomac had had such difficulties against its Confederate foe, he belonged with it. He proposed to go after Gen. Robert E. Lee's army and toward the Confederate capital of Richmond.[1]

In the East the Army of the Potomac first collided with Lee's army in a densely wooded area in northern Virginia known as the Wilderness, opening the most tragic series of engagements in the war. For one month the Federals crashed into the Confederate ranks, recoiled, tried to slip around Lee's right flank, and then battered them again. Eventually, as Federal casualties mounted on an unprecedented scale, Grant decided that it was necessary to adopt a new course of action. Instead of sidestepping Lee's army, he would swing the Army of the Potomac way around and advance toward Richmond from the south via Petersburg. This new plan baffled Lee for several days, yet the Federals could not exploit the maneuver. A combination of Confederate heroics, a temporary lapse in the Federal command system, and the psychological effects on the Union troops of the staggering losses in frontal assaults over the previous month enabled Lee to recover and check the Federal advance. From then, mid-June, until late March in the following year the Union and Confederate armies remained deadlocked in trench warfare around Petersburg.

Compared with the fighting in the East, the campaign on the Georgia front was much more mobile. Through the late spring and into midsummer Sherman maneuvered and battled his way toward the outskirts of Atlanta against a tough Confederate army under the leadership of a wily general, Joseph E. Johnston. Except for Kennesaw Mountain, where he attempted to take the Confederate works by storm and failed badly, Sherman managed to utilize his numerical superiority and to outflank strong Confederate defensive lines, yet Johnston always seemed to fall back to another strong position. As the Federals neared the city, though, Confederate President Jefferson Davis, dissatisfied with Johnston's constant retreats and doubtful that his army would hold Atlanta, intervened and replaced Johnston with a junior corps commander named John Bell Hood. Hood was young, impetuous, and aggressive, and he wasted no time in throwing his command into action. In eight days Hood responded by attacking the Federals

three times and lost all three battles. Four weeks later Sherman tricked
Hood into thinking that he had fallen back; actually, he had swung
below Atlanta and captured the last open railroad into the city, despite a desperate attempt by Lt. Gen. William J. Hardee's Corps to
protect the line. At this Hood's only recourse was to evacuate the city.

With Atlanta now in his hands, Sherman began to prepare for his
next campaign. The original plan called for Sherman to hold Atlanta
with a detachment and strike for the coast. En route his army was to
occupy key junctions on the two east–west railroads in Georgia, which
would effectively sever the Confederacy for the second time in the war.
Sherman, however, preferred to alter the plans, realizing that against
superior Confederate cavalry forces his command would not be able
to keep the supply line—a railroad from Nashville to Atlanta via
Chattanooga—open for long. He opted, instead, for a plan that involved the destruction of Atlanta and a subsequent march toward the
state capital, Milledgeville. This would force Hood to protect either
Augusta to the north or Macon to the south, both key industrial cities.
Sherman's army would then capture the city that was undefended and,
after its destruction, would advance on the other. Such a campaign
deep into Georgia would require the army to live off the land and move
rapidly, a difficult task in the face of a sizable enemy, yet the rewards
were great. It was, Sherman admitted, a gamble, but if Grant could
secure a base for him at Savannah, he would chance the campaign.[2]

Late in September, Hood simplified matters when he struck out for
Sherman's supply lines. Convinced now that the remainder of Hood's
army was not a serious threat—especially after the Confederate commander had opened the door to an unopposed invasion eastward—that
with the bulk of the army he could make the march through Georgia
and still provide Maj. Gen. George H. Thomas with enough troops
to check any invasion by Hood into Tennessee, Sherman submitted
his new proposal. Neither President Lincoln nor his chief of staff,
Henry W. Halleck, approved the plan and Grant was rather skeptical,
but Sherman provided his close friend Grant with more and more reasons why he should undertake the expedition. He described the weakness of Hood's army, the impossibility of capturing such a small mobile force, and the foolishness of a retrograde movement. Finally, on
October 11, Sherman struck a responsive chord when he wired Grant:
"Instead of being on the defensive, I would be on the offensive; instead

of guessing at what he means to do, he would have to guess at my plans. The difference in war is full 25 per cent." Over the course of the next three weeks Grant had his reservations about the march, but his trust in the judgment and abilities of Sherman outweighed them.[3]

Grant and Sherman had forged over the course of several years a strong friendship and a high-level working relationship that was probably unequaled in modern military history. It had begun in early 1862 when Grant had needed someone back at headquarters to forward all available troops and matériel for the campaign against Forts Henry and Donelson in northern Tennessee. A cooperative Sherman stepped in to perform the service. At the time, Sherman was Grant's senior in command, but that did not matter. Grant needed the manpower and supplies; it was Sherman's duty, as he saw it, to assist in any and every way possible, even to serve at the front under Grant's command. While other high-ranking officers would have squabbled over seniority, Sherman cheerfully did all he could, and it truly impressed Grant. Shortly after the forts fell, Grant received a promotion and a new subordinate, division commander William T. Sherman. One month later Sherman's gallant performance on the battlefield at Shiloh earned him Grant's complete respect and, eventually, a corps command in Grant's Army of the Tennessee. From that moment on, as Grant's star ascended, so too did Sherman's, directly behind him. Together they served in the Vicksburg campaign and at Chattanooga, and as Grant received promotions from commander of the Army of the Tennessee, to the head of the Military Division of the Mississippi, to commanding general of the U.S. Army, Sherman filled the vacancies.[4]

On first glance they seemed to have had a great deal in common. Both were born and raised in the Midwest, attended West Point, and served in the Regular Army, yet neither looked the part of a general. Grant was a small, meek-looking man, with brown hair and gray eyes. Only a private's jacket with general's stars on the shoulders gave him away. Sherman, on the other hand, was tall and lean, with piercing black eyes, reddish brown hair, and a face lined with wrinkles. He might have been more striking, except for the cigar stub in his mouth and his disheveled appearance. From the way they both dressed it was quite obvious that the pomp and ceremony of the military did not interest either of them. Foremost in their minds was that the purpose of the army was to wage war, not to parade.

Moreover, each man had a skeleton in his closet. During his days in the prewar army, Grant had had a serious drinking problem, and Sherman, in the first year of the war, had experienced a mental breakdown. Some people never forgave them and continued to challenge their competency, but Grant and Sherman used those unfortunate incidents to cement the bonds between themselves even more. As Sherman once said, "He stood by me when I was crazy and I stood by him when he was drunk; and now, sir, we stand by each other always."[5]

In reality, Grant and Sherman possessed many dissimilar qualities, yet they complemented one another very well. Grant was a quiet, unassuming individual whose best qualities shone in wartime. He did not have the sort of personality that enabled him to become the favorite of his men, as did Sherman or George B. McClellan, commander of the Army of the Potomac in 1861 and 1862. Instead, he was always calm and clear-headed, even in the most desperate moment of battle. He had the rare ability to recognize the key elements in a problem and to implement a solution. At the critical moment, Grant always seemed to be master of the situation.

While Grant fought with the calmness, confidence, and persistence of an assured winner, Sherman campaigned with the passion of a crusader. He was the intellectual of the two, a true master of detail whose knowledge of everything save politics seemed to have no bounds. Yet he was also much more emotional than his friend Grant. Impulsive, imaginative, and prone to incessant conversation, Sherman was a nervous sort who was lacking in self-confidence, particularly after his breakdown. In Grant he found a surety and support, something at the time he badly needed, which enabled him to blossom as a brilliant military strategist and a first-rate army commander.

From Sherman's viewpoint, this type of campaign from Atlanta to Savannah would offer success on two different levels. In one respect, Sherman intended the march to be a giant raid against the war resources of Georgia. He planned to destroy railroads, mills, and factories all the way along the route to Savannah. But Sherman also wanted to demonstrate to southerners the terribleness of war, so he wrote to Thomas in mid-October: "I propose to demonstrate the vulnerability of the South, and make its inhabitants feel that war and individual ruin are synonymous terms." Those who were not victims, who did not suffer from the march, had to realize that they were just as vulnerable to such destructive marches. As Sherman wired Grant in early November, "Even without a battle, the result operating upon the minds of sensible men would produce fruits more than compensating for expense, trouble, and risk."[6]

Thus it began November 12, when Sherman's army, over 60,000 strong, destroyed the tracks, repair shops, mills, and a number of homes along the railroad from sixty miles north of Atlanta way back to the city itself, and then began its march on Savannah. Sherman divided his command into a Left and a Right Wing. The Fourteenth and Twentieth Corps constituted the Left Wing, later renamed the Army of Georgia, under the irascible New Yorker and West Pointer, Maj. Gen. Henry W. Slocum. The Right Wing, which consisted of the Fifteenth and Seventeenth Corps, the Army of the Tennessee, was under the command of Maj. Gen. O. O. Howard, another West Point graduate who combined deep religious beliefs with aggressive combat leadership. The cavalry, under Brig. Gen. Judson Kilpatrick, reported directly to Sherman. Along with the men Sherman brought 1.2 million rations; the rest he intended to take from the inhabitants of Georgia.

Four days later, from a hill just east of Atlanta, Maj. Gen. William T. Sherman and his staff gazed around them. On the road to the southeast they could see the gleaming reflections from the rifle barrels of the men in the Army of the Tennessee. Before them, filing along the road to the east, were the members of the Fourteenth Corps. Beneath their feet was the battlefield of July 22, where the Confederates had nearly rolled back the Federal left flank and where Sherman's friend and protégé, Maj. Gen. James B. McPherson, had fallen. To the rear was the city of Atlanta, which had cost the Federals over 30,000 casualties to take, and now it lay in smoldering ruins. For the first time since the war began three and one-half years before, Sherman and his men sensed that final victory was within their grasp.[7]

At Decatur, not far from Atlanta, the Fourteenth and Twentieth Corps took separate roads. The Twentieth Corps pushed as far northeast as Madison and swung through Eatonton into Georgia's capital, Milledgeville, while the Fourteenth Corps followed a much more di-

A photograph of Sherman and his generals. They are, from left to right, Maj. Gen. O. O. Howard, Maj. Gen. John A. Logan, Maj. Gen. William B. Hazen, Maj. Gen. William T. Sherman, Maj. Gen. Jefferson C. Davis, Maj. Gen. Henry W. Slocum, Maj. Gen. Joseph Mower, and Maj. Gen. Francis P. Blair. (National Archives).

rect path to rendezvous at that city. From there the two corps continued on separate roads and passed through such towns as Sandersville, Louisville, and Millen and destroyed or confiscated anything of any military value—railroad tracks, machinery, cotton mills, horses, mules, and foodstuffs—and much more. Confederate resistance, primarily some Georgia Militia and Confederate cavalry under Maj. Gen. Joseph Wheeler, was practically nonexistent for the Left Wing until they approached Savannah, where they encountered coastal troops under command of Lt. Gen. William Hardee.

The Fifteenth and Seventeenth Corps, the Right Wing, marched along separate roads farther to the south toward Macon, via McDonough, Jackson, and Clinton. North of Macon at Griswoldville a reinforced brigade from the Fifteenth Corps repulsed an assault by Georgia militiamen and inflicted heavy losses; otherwise, the Right Wing too encountered little opposition until near Savannah. From the area

Map of the Savannah campaign.

north of Macon the Right Wing continued on various roads through Irwinton, Millen, and Statesborough to the outskirts of Savannah as it simply wrecked the Georgia Central Railroad from Macon to Savannah.

The cavalry, meanwhile, had covered the flanks of the Right Wing early in the campaign and shifted over to the Left Wing near Milledgeville. Throughout much of the campaign Kilpatrick's horsemen had a running skirmish with Wheeler's cavalry, although these fights never matched the intensity in which both commanders portrayed them in their official reports.

As the army approached Savannah, it encountered some 13,000 Confederates under Hardee strongly entrenched around the city. Sherman's first move was to secure communications and a supply line with the navy, which he accomplished when the Second Division, Fifteenth Corps, under the leadership of Brig. Gen. William B. Hazen stormed the Confederate Fort McAllister on the Ossabaw Sound to the south of the city. After the fall of Fort McAllister, however, the Union army commander indicated an initial reluctance to assault the main Confederate lines. He had received a letter from Grant on December 15 suggesting that Grant wanted Sherman to transport his army by sea immediately to reinforce the Federals at Petersburg. If that was the case, Sherman determined that the fall of Savannah was not worth the loss of lives in his veteran army. Yet several days earlier he had planted a seed in the mind of the chief of staff, Halleck—that an overland march to join Grant in Virginia would be much more profitable and no more time consuming than travel by sea. This suggestion, combined with Thomas's resounding victory over Hood's army at Nashville and the inability to accumulate enough transports to ship Sherman's army by sea for two months, convinced Grant that the overland route would be better. At that time, though, Sherman was unaware of Thomas's victory and of the logistical problems, and the more he thought about the march through the Carolinas, the more apparent it became that the fall of Savannah was a necessity for its approval.[8]

Nonetheless, the problem of taking Savannah was immense. In spite of Sherman's threats to the safety of the inhabitants and their property, Hardee refused to surrender, especially since he still had one road, the Union Causeway, open via a pontoon bridge over the Savannah River to South Carolina. To close this road, Slocum wanted to send the Twentieth Corps across the Savannah River. This Sherman refused to approve, in part because he could not ensure the security of the troops across the river, but far more importantly because he needed them in the event of an assault on the Confederate works. Most of Howard's Right Wing had a river, swamps, and other difficult terrain to traverse in an assault, so that they could expect little success in that area. With the Twentieth Corps on the opposite side of the river, that would place the burden of a successful assault on the Fourteenth Corps, already extended to occupy the portion of the line that the Twentieth Corps would have vacated. A better plan, Sherman believed, would be to get part of Maj. Gen. John Foster's command in the South Carolina coastal islands to block the causeway. But while Sherman traveled by sea to Hilton Head, South Carolina, to discuss the cooperative movement with Foster, Hardee skillfully abandoned the city and 25,000 bales of cotton to Sherman's army.[9]

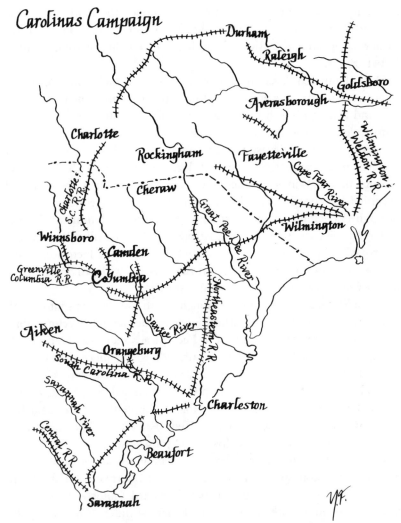

Map of the Carolinas campaign.

Three weeks after the fall of Savannah, Sherman sent the Seventeenth Corps and three divisions of the Fifteenth Corps by sea to Beaufort, South Carolina, to open the Carolinas campaign. The plan was for the Right Wing to advance inland and outflank the Confederates, who had flooded the fields and prepared fortifications to oppose the advance of the Fourteenth and Twentieth Corps. Unfortunately for the Federals, incessant rains so flooded the southern portion of South Carolina that the Left Wing had to wait ten days for the roads to dry, even after the Right Wing had cleared the invasion route of Rebel troops.

Once the march began in earnest, the front was highly mobile. Again Sherman had his four corps travel on separate roads whenever possible, and through South Carolina they again met little resistance. The army lived off the land, as they had done in Georgia, and implemented a policy of devastation that unquestionably surpassed that of the Savannah campaign. The Left Wing passed through Blackville, Lexington, and Winnsboro, across the border into North Carolina, and occupied Fayetteville. On the other flank, Howard's command drove through Pocotaligo; Orangeburg; the state capital, Columbia; Cheraw; and rendezvoused with Slocum's troops at Fayetteville. Both wings destroyed railroad tracks, stockpiles of ammunition, factories, mills, cotton, and the arsenal at Fayetteville, along with an incalculable number of private homes, barns, and stores.

While Sherman's army drove through South Carolina and into North Carolina, the Confederate authorities were desperately accumulating all available manpower to halt the Federal advance. Lt. Gen. Wade Hampton superseded Wheeler and brought along more Rebel horsemen. Remnants of Hood's shattered army augmented Hardee's infantry and artillery, as did some North Carolina coastal troops under Gen. Braxton Bragg. To command these forces, Confederate President Jefferson Davis, upon the advice of Gen. Robert E. Lee, appointed Sherman's old nemesis, Gen. Joseph E. Johnston.

With about 16,000 infantrymen and artillerymen and a cavalry force of 7,000 Johnston laid plans to crush one of Sherman's wings. From Fayetteville, Sherman's army marched toward Goldsboro, where it intended to unite with 40,000 more Federals under Maj. Gen. John M. Schofield. The two wings took different roads that, at one point, separated them by a full day's march. It was at this point that Johnston hoped to defeat Sherman's Left Wing.[10]

On March 16 Johnston had Hardee's Corps fight a delaying action near Averasborough, which Hardee did successfully despite the loss of over 800 casualties. This gave Johnston enough time to concentrate his command. Early on the afternoon of March 19 Confederate infantrymen crashed through segments of the Fourteenth and Twentieth Corps and routed an entire division of men, yet another division of bluecoats held firm even though Confederate ranks struck them from both the front and the rear. Reinforcements from the Twentieth Corps then rushed to the scene and secured the center and left flank of the Union line. Repeated Confederate assaults could not break the Federal position in the late afternoon as Johnston's army broke off the attack. By the following morning the Fifteenth and Seventeenth Corps reached the field of battle. In the face of overwhelming odds Johnston retained his position, but on March 21 a Federal reconnaissance-in-force nearly cut off his line of retreat. That night the Confederates fell back from the Bentonville battlefield, and three days later Sherman's army arrived in Goldsboro to rest and refit.[11]

After a respite of seventeen days, Sherman's army—which now consisted of Slocum's Left Wing, Schofield's two corps in the center, and the Army of the Tennessee under Howard on the right—took to the field in search of Johnston's army. Originally, Grant had wanted Sherman to push on into Virginia, but several days before the army left Goldsboro, Grant wired that Richmond had fallen and that Lee's army was on the run. Sherman's strategic objective was now Johnston's army. On April 10 the Federals broke camp, and two days later Raleigh, the capital of North Carolina, fell to Kilpatrick's horsemen. That same day Sherman received the joyous news from Grant that Lee had surrendered.[12]

When Johnston learned of the fate of Lee's army, he immediately proposed a truce for the purpose of negotiating a termination of hostilities. The Confederate cause, Johnston realized, was hopeless, and to prevent further bloodshed and a possible guerrilla war he offered to surrender all Confederate troops with the consent of Secretary of War John C. Breckinridge. Desirous of a quick peace, even more after he learned of the assassination of Lincoln, Sherman jumped at the offer, yet the basis for the agreement was completely unacceptable to the federal government. It exonerated all Confederates, seemed to recognize the existing state governments, restored the franchise and all other rights to Confederates under the U.S. Constitution, and allowed them to take their weapons home and surrender them at their state arsenals. The reaction of Washington officials was so vigorous that several insinuated Sherman was a traitor. The new president, Andrew Johnson, and his cabinet unanimously rejected the terms, and Grant volunteered to travel to North Carolina and straighten out the matter. On April 24, the commanding general arrived secretly at Sherman's headquarters and tactfully told his old friend that the government refused to accept the terms and that he must resume hostilities unless Johnston surrendered on the same terms as he had given Lee. Rather than prolong the inevitable, Johnston submitted on those terms. The Confederate Army surrendered on condition that the government would not disturb them as long as they abided by the laws. For Sherman's army, the Carolinas campaign and, more importantly, the war had come to an end.[13]

CHAPTER I

The Army

"There is nothing in this world like Sherman's Army."
—JOHN BROBST TO MARY, 2 APRIL 1865

Sherman realized from the start that in campaigns to Savannah and through the Carolinas the burdens were going to shift from headquarters to lower-grade officers and enlisted men. Once the march began, success would depend on the ability of company-level soldiers to perform critical tasks independent of high-level officer supervision. For this reason he had carefully amassed an army of veterans, experienced soldiers who knew what to do and how to care for themselves.

A reporter in Savannah in late 1864 quoted Sherman as saying that he commanded "the bravest and best army that ever trod American soil." His adversary, Joseph E. Johnston, perhaps paid the army its consummate compliment when several days after the war's end he told Twenty-third Army Corps commander Jacob Cox, in the presence of William J. Hardee: "there had been no such army since the days of Julius Caesar." This indeed was an incredible army, boasted one of its members, and "it is not likely that one equal to it will be seen again in this country in our day and generation."[1]

At its head was Maj. Gen. William T. Sherman, who helped establish and unquestionably reflected the tenor of the army. Like the bulk of his troops, Sherman was Midwest born and bred, with simple habits and tastes that Eastern-born soldiers could also appreciate. And with his army, Sherman shared a "don't care a damnativeness," as one correspondent phrased it, a distaste for anything smacking of pomp and ceremony. One young lieutenant recorded of Sherman: "His dress is as unassuming as the man. A field officer's coat without rank, low canvassed belt, hat with cord and none on his pants." He then concluded: "There's not a thing of the military in his appearance." Another soldier, barely literate, wrote home:

it is an honor to enney man to have ben on this last campain with Sherman you se him a riding a long you would think that he was somb oald plow jogger his head bent a little to one side with an oald stub of a sigar in his mouth.[2]

Sherman's nickname, "Uncle Billy," signified both familiarity and respect. He was a man who had no qualms about chatting on the march with a youthful private about the quality of Georgia soil or with a staff officer by a campfire on grand strategy. "His customary appearance," recalled a soldier, "was to walk along the roadside with his hands in his trousers' pockets . . . and talk good earnest common-sense with the person nearest him, regardless of rank. This was delightful for a subordinate, knowing his exalted position and yet feeling at ease."[3]

At the same time, Sherman was the premier veteran, a man who awed his troops with his vast knowledge of the terrain of Georgia and the Carolinas and all aspects of campaigning. Whether it was showing a soldier how to mend a harness, teaching several drummer boys how to light a fire in the pouring rain, or guiding his army through the swamps of Georgia and South Carolina without suffering heavy losses, Sherman always seemed to know exactly what to do and how to do it. The end result was an unfailing confidence in his generalship. "We all have great Confidence in Sherman," wrote an officer to his wife, "Although he was pronounced Crazy at one time, I wish all Generals were afflicted as he is." One soldier wrote his father, "Every man under Sherman has the greatest confidence in him, and make up their minds that where he strikes it is sure death to all rebs within his range"; another gloated, "It is wonderful what confidence this army has in Sherman. Every man seems to think the idea of these Rebels being able to do us any permanent harm is perfectly preposterous." Maybe the most expressive words came from a soldier who put his sentiments into verse:

Gen Sherman is the man,
He makes the Rebels waltz, sir!
And leads his men through all the South,
Just like a dose of salts, sir![4]

In his *Memoirs* Sherman wrote: "There is a soul to an army as well as to the individual man, and no general can accomplish the full work of his army unless he commands the soul of his men, as well as their bodies and legs." Sherman did just that, capturing the hearts and minds, or "souls," of his men. He was, as a member of his command put it, "a man perfectly worshipped by his Army." Only Sherman could impound money used in gambling on behalf of the soldiers' home at Chattanooga amid cheers from the gamblers or prompt troops to remove their hats and call out "Uncle Billy" in love and admiration for their commander as he rode past them. Pvt. George Shepherd probably expressed the feelings of the army for its leader best when he wrote his wife, "I am very tired of war But the Conterey Needs my help and I Never will turn my Back to it. I am a awful Cow hart you know But I Shall Die before I will Leave as true a Solger as Billie Sherman."[5]

His army had more actual campaign experience than any other Federal command. Constituting four infantry corps and one cavalry division, members of Sherman's army had fought on nearly every major battlefield during the first three years of the war. Moreover, three of the four corps in Sherman's army came from the Western theater, where campaigns demanded not only fierce fighting but long, arduous marches as well. Even the Twentieth Army Corps, orphaned from the Army of the Potomac late in 1863, experienced this additional burden in its trek from northern Virginia to southern Tennessee in the operations around Chattanooga and during the grueling campaign against Atlanta.

Members of the Army of the Tennessee, Sherman's Right Wing, fought at Paducah and Belmont in 1861. The following year many of the regiments participated in such battles as Pea Ridge, Forts Henry and Donelson, Shiloh, Corinth, and Iuka. Prior to the movement against Vicksburg in 1863, U. S. Grant organized these troops into the Fifteenth, Sixteenth, and Seventeenth Corps. This arrangement remained intact until September 1864, when O. O. Howard eliminated the Sixteenth Corps by merging its survivors from the Atlanta campaign with the Fifteenth and Seventeenth Corps. During the course of those eighteen months, however, regiments from the Army of the Tennessee added to their battleflags the names of Vicksburg, Meridian, Chattanooga, and numerous engagements while on the Atlanta campaign.*

The Fourteenth Army Corps of the Left Wing probably had the widest range of experiences before the March to the Sea. A handful of troops had fought in the East at such places as Bull Run, the coastal operations in North Carolina, and the Seven Days' Battles. Out west some men had received their baptism of fire in Missouri, and numerous regiments had engaged Confederate ranks at Mill Springs, Shiloh, Corinth, and Perryville. Assembled initially as part of the Army of the Cumberland in October 1862, the Fourteenth Corps underwent organizational adjustments that winter after severe losses at the battle of Stone's River. In September 1863 the Fourteenth Corps won the respect of blue and gray soldiers alike for its heroic stand on Horseshoe Ridge during the nearly disastrous rout of the Army of the Cumberland at Chickamauga. Two months later, the corps enhanced its reputation in a ferocious assault up Missionary Ridge that broke the Confederate siege of Chattanooga. It, too, participated in the Atlanta campaign and fought well on several occasions.

Serving alongside the Fourteenth Corps during the March to the Sea was the Twentieth Army Corps. Its soldiers had seen action in many of the greatest battles in the East: Stonewall Jackson's Valley campaign, Cedar Mountain, Antietam, Fredericksburg, Chancellorsville, and Gettysburg. In the fall of 1863 these troops, organized in the Eleventh and Twelfth Corps, left the Army of the Potomac to help rescue the Army of the Cumberland at Chattanooga and fought the "Battle above the Clouds" at Lookout Mountain. Destined never to see action again in the Virginia theater, the Eleventh and Twelfth Corps amalgamated in April 1864 to form the Twentieth Corps. They then partook in the Atlanta campaign during the spring and summer of that year.

*Portions of the Sixteenth Corps did not participate in the Atlanta campaign and retained the organizational name.

Even the cavalry that went through Georgia and the Carolinas was long on experience. It had members who had participated in nearly every major Western campaign in 1862 and 1863: Forts Henry and Donelson, Shiloh, Corinth, Perryville, Stone's River, Vicksburg, Morgan's Ohio Raid, Chickamauga, Knoxville, and Chattanooga. After service on the Atlanta campaign, Sherman reorganized the horsemen in the Military Division of the Mississippi, designating those he intended to take with him as the Third Division.[6]

Sherman's command would need all this experience to prepare them for the supreme test of the March to the Sea and through the Carolinas. They had to drive rapidly through a hostile country and, at the same time, live off the land and destroy all material useful for the Confederate war effort. For this task Sherman already had a magnificent army of veterans, but to make the campaigns work all participants had to contribute actively. Sherman had to rid the army of unnecessary men, to strip it to the bare essentials. He could take "only the best fighting material," soldiers accustomed to hardship and disease. All others had to remain behind.[7]

Beginning in the last two weeks of October, Sherman ordered his senior officers and medical staff to undertake what one soldier called "a rigorous weeding-out process." First, he restricted the number of wagons and artillery pieces each corps could take on the march and sent all others to Chattanooga, Tennessee. Any soldiers displaced by the cutbacks returned to their infantry regiments, and cavalrymen without good horses headed back to Tennessee for reorganization and remounting. Second, the Medical Department examined all soldiers with even slight health problems and sent those found unfit for arduous duty back to Tennessee. In examinations that were much more thorough than the ones the government gave to men at the time of their enlistment, the Medical Department weeded out over 1 percent of the army, "the greatest portion of whom," according to the acting medical director, "were recruits suffering from measles and diseases incident to newly enlisted men." The result, one officer boasted, was an army "composed of men whose bodies were so inured to hardship that disease could make no impression upon them."[8]

From a medical standpoint the results were astounding. During the Savannah campaign, Sherman's entire army averaged less than 2 percent of its men unfit for duty due to sickness on any given day, and on the much more demanding march through the Carolinas the average was a fraction over 2 percent. In comparison with all other Union troops, Sherman's army suffered 46 percent fewer illnesses per 1,000 men during the campaign months. No doubt, much of the credit for this good health must go to better food and sanitary conditions on the campaigns. But in an army that could not afford the burden of transporting and caring for large numbers of sick troops, rigorous screening certainly contributed to reducing illness.[9]

The weeding-out process also had an amazing effect on soldiers' morale. Those who participated in the campaigns, the best men from the best infantry corps and cavalry units in the West, considered themselves elite troops. Each veteran regiment had entered the war 1,000 strong, and after two or three years only a few hundred had survived the battles, withstood the hardships, and resisted the diseases. This in itself made them a very select group, but to undergo a second screening that eliminated all but the toughest physical specimens gave Sherman's men the feeling, as one veteran wrote, that "we had only picked men." Another soldier recalled how "The troops remaining with Sherman were veterans in the strictest sense of the word, and, owing to a rigorous weeding-out process, were of the best material." The army began to believe itself invincible, and with each day's march confidence in its own abilities grew. A veteran recorded in his journal: "We have weeded out all the sick, feeble ones and all the faint hearted ones and all the boys are ready for a meal or a fight and dont seem to care which it is." Another soldier, this one at Savannah, predicted: "Such vim and evidence of conscious strength and ability to conquer gives promise of splendid triumphs in our next campaign." Sherman, too, noticed the growing self-esteem. In a letter to Grant he wrote: "I do not like to boast, but believe this army has a confidence in itself that makes it almost invincible." The troops gloried in their strength and ability to overcome any obstacle and endure any hardship. Some soldiers proudly asserted that Sherman's army could best any army of comparable size in the world; others doubted if the whole Southern Confederacy could stop their march. For Sherman's army, as one private succinctly put it, "The present was ours; and, in our hearts, we were confident of the future."[10]

One key element in the success of Sherman's army was the astonishing amount of experience in the officer corps. Nearly all the officers had served for several years, many of them having worked their way up from the enlisted ranks. Just as two or three years of active service had culled the enlisted men, so had it rid the army of unfit officers and paved the way for competent young officers and men to achieve positions of authority. Sherman, Howard, and others also made a conscientious effort, first in the Army of the Tennessee and then in the Army of Georgia, to force into retirement certain officers who failed to perform their duties adequately, and to fill their places with "efficient, true, and hard-working men." Thus, proven ability now replaced popularity or political connections as a necessity for appointment to a responsible position in Sherman's army. In a random sample of twenty-five military units—twenty-two infantry regiments and battalions, two cavalry regiments, and one artillery battery, which totaled 8,743 men on a company level—all commanders and all company-level officers except three had joined the service in 1861 or 1862. Ninety-six percent of the regimental commanders had served previously in companies, with one in six coming from the enlisted ranks. More revealing are the statistics on company-grade officers, the men who dealt directly with the rank and file. Almost 50 percent of the captains and over 90 percent of the lieutenants served at one time as enlisted men. The result, then, was the formation of a body of ingenious young officers with a wealth of experience who, Sherman insisted, "accomplished many things far better than I could have ordered." [11]

An officer's life was not an easy one. It was his responsibility to get the most from his troops and still maintain a high morale, to fulfill the demands of superiors and provide for the needs of subordinates simultaneously, at times seemingly impossible tasks. Three years of experience had taught that promoting from within, particularly on the company and regimental levels, best served those interests. The unit obtained an officer with demonstrated ability who knew the troops personally and understood their problems, and such a promotion served as an example to other soldiers of the rewards for good service. [12]

Most of the soldiers who received promotions from within their units performed satisfactorily. Their familiarity with fellow officers and men around them usually ensured a smooth transition from one officer to another. But a few did get caught up in the trappings and added responsibility of officership and alienated the men. One young soldier from the 76th Ohio complained that the new regimental commander, Edward Briggs, lost the respect and friendship of the men through his harsh methods of dealing with the troops. Since his recent promotion, the soldier wrote home, "he is quite a different man," and "there is hardly a man that likes Briggs." The troops in the 109th Pennsylvania had to cope with a martinet in its regimental commander, Walter G. Dunn. A number of the men so despised Dunn that, when word of a freak boat accident that killed him reached the regiment, soldiers actually rejoiced. One soldier recorded in his diary:

he has been a tyrant to the men since he has been in command of the Regt [regiment], and had he lived and shewed himself after our boys got home, in all probability he would have been killed, for he was brutal almost beyond Endurance. at the least provocation he would catch a man by the throat and nearly choke him, the men not daring to Interfere.

It is little wonder that another soldier could become wary when his young division commander, John M. Corse, had just received a promotion to brevet major general: "For my part I think Uncle Sam is piling it onto him rather quick. He is a good officer but I fear the two stars will spoil him." [13]

At other times, officers received promotions beyond their ability, at least according to their troops. A corporal who witnessed Maj. Gen. Jefferson C. Davis curse out his lieutenant confided in his diary: "I do think our Government is hard up when such men are allowed to command." After three weeks of active campaigning in the Carolinas, Maj. Gen. Henry Slocum, commander of the Left Wing, suddenly became furious over the number of large, cumbersome wall tents the Commissary Department had brought on the march and restricted their use. A bright young lieutenant, unaffected by the directive, since he did not use the tents, nonetheless criticized Slocum for the way he handled the problem:

Had the order been issued when starting out on this campaign there might have been some reason in it. seems more like a petty act of malice. tis always the way however. These are the men placed in responsible positions with out the judgment to sustain themselves. orders to that Effect should have been issued at Savannah. Slocum is about played out. Prosperity has been too much for him.

The lieutenant concluded with a statement that the men liked Slocum as a division and corps commander but not as the head of an army.[14]

No doubt, an officer who stepped in to take command from outside the unit faced a far more difficult task. Since such a move often resulted in internal tensions, Sherman and other senior officers preferred to promote from within except for important field positions, and then only under unusual circumstances. O. O. Howard had a difficult assignment: to replace the commander of the Army of the Tennessee, the beloved James B. McPherson. Instead of promoting Fifteenth Corps commander Maj. Gen. John A. Logan, the acting army head who was "the idol of his soldiers," Sherman brought in the more experienced Howard, formerly from the Army of the Potomac and Army of the Cumberland. In such an awkward situation it took the quiet competence of Howard to win the hearts of this Western army. When William B. Hazen came over from the Army of the Cumberland to head Sherman's old division in the Fifteenth Corps, the men immediately put him to the test. After a brief struggle in which the troops came out second best, Hazen gained the respect and confidence of the men through his command skills. The promotion that may have caused the greatest stir of all went to Maj. Gen. Joseph Mower. Sherman wanted a more aggressive officer to command the Eastern Twentieth Corps for what seemed to be the final, decisive campaign of the war and appointed Mower, a westerner, to replace the popular and solid Brig. Gen. Alpheus S. Williams. This move aroused the ire of Eastern troops, as one young soldier indicated: "We have been *honored* with a new Corps Commander Maj. Gen. Mower, a pet of Shermans, . . . [who] was given this command to bring him before the world from the obscurity in which he has hitherto dwelt." Only the swift succession of events that ended the war avoided a very difficult situation for Mower.[15]

There was no set formula or guideline that determined who were the good officers and who were the bad ones. For the most part, it depended upon the judge. One soldier praised Howard as "the bravest

of the brave," while another considered Mower, a man no less coura-
geous, as reckless. A member of the Twentieth Corps could overlook
Slocum's temper tantrums; a second soldier held him fully accounta-
ble for such behavior. And a third enlisted man, this one from the
Fourteenth Corps, condemned his corps commander, Jefferson C.
Davis, for the same fault: "I think every man should show due respect
for his officers but when the General or any other officer descends
from his rank to curse and abuse the man below him he is not entitled
to any respect." One officer complained bitterly when his superior
treated blacks callously, yet another saw nothing wrong with arresting
soldiers for drinking and less than two weeks later getting drunk with
fellow officers, the regimental commander "leading the way."[16]

Most soldiers esteemed officers who cared for the lives of their men.
Veterans had learned long ago that death was an integral part of war,
but the squandering of troops in unnecessary operations and futile
frontal assaults appalled them. Sherman, who seldom did either, won
the love and admiration of his troops. After the fall of Atlanta, when
the Union Army had an opportunity to examine the Confederate defenses, it realized what an incredible feat Sherman had accomplished
by forcing the Confederates out of Atlanta with comparatively little
bloodshed. Sherman had proven, as one officer noted, "Truly the Spade
wins more Battles than the sword." Always careful of his men, Sherman never shied away from battle but did avoid unnecessary risks.
Thus, with only slight exaggeration, he boasted to his brother: "Not
a waiver, doubt, or hesitation when I order, and men march to certain
death without a murmur if I call on them, because they know I value
their lives as much as my own."[17]

An officer like Joseph Mower, commander of the Fourth Division,
Seventeenth Corps, never won the adoration of his men because they
believed that he took unnecessary chances with their lives. Mower, an
audacious soldier who once complimented a fellow officer by saying
"you are the only man I know who can ride as far into hell as I can,"
earned the nickname "Swamp Lizard" from his men for the way he
drove them through the nearly impassable swamps of South Carolina.
Whether it was standing conspicuously on the firing line or in a waist-
deep swamp in early February for twenty hours directing his troops,
no one in Sherman's army bore more hardships and greater danger

than Mower. Yet Mower was a little too careless with the lives of his men, and none in the Fourth Division shed tears when he got promoted to Twentieth Corps commander.[18]

The least popular officers were often the most severe disciplinarians. In the 127th Illinois a sergeant accused an officer of being "an old tyrant" and insisted: "The boys all hate him worse than a Reb." The most notorious disciplinarian in Sherman's army was Brig. Gen. John W. Geary, head of the Second Division, Twentieth Corps. Geary had an unfortunate habit of trying to impose his version of discipline on other commands that, needless to say, did not go over well with the men. As one young officer wrote to his sister, "Gen. G[eary] has such a reputation for severity that every poor soldier does not like to approach him." Yet Geary was a first-rate division commander, and this helped offset some of his poorer qualities in the eyes of the men.[19]

Soldiers who suffered abuses at the hands of officers could seek recourse within the military judicial system, but no one in Sherman's Army did so. There were better, more expedient ways of getting even. Shortly after Col. George Buell berated the 58th Indiana for its sloppy dress on a hot day when Buell himself had substituted a linen jacket for the standard wool issue, the men retaliated by performing pathetically on dress parade. One man even went through manual arms with his rifle upside down, though he reversed it before Buell could figure out who he was. Pvt. Robert Strong and a friend got revenge on the inspector general of the Twentieth Corps when he spoiled their breakfast and threatened to beat them with the blunt end of his sword. They dragged him out of the saddle, gave him a bloody nose and a pair of swollen eyes, and made a hasty escape back to their regiment. The pair then escaped punishment when the inspector general could not identify them shortly afterward. Nor did troops rule out the possibility of killing an officer, although no evidence indicates that they actually resorted to such an extreme measure.[20]

Nothing officers did could incur the wrath of troops, and Western men in particular, like abusive punishment. Whether it was bucking and gagging, hanging men up by their thumbs, or tying them to a spare artillery wheel for a day, most soldiers would agree with an enlisted man who confided in his diary: "It is brutish in my opinion to treete men that way." Another westerner thought that his company and regiment had a "splendid and kindly set of officers" but honestly believed that "if one of our officers had used his men that way, he would have been killed during the first battle thereafter." Whenever possible, soldiers tried to check such abuses by cutting loose prisoners covertly, but on one occasion an officer's behavior so incensed some Western troops that a small riot almost erupted. A member of the 33rd Massachusetts received an order to gather rails for a fire before he had finished setting up his tent. When the soldier continued to work on his tent, an officer had the man hung by his wrists from a tree limb. Troops from the neighboring 22nd Wisconsin, appalled by the officer's conduct, promptly cut down the man. The officer then responded by grabbing a key member of the rescue party and taking him away for punishment. Word of what happened spread quickly, and soon three armed regiments, two from Wisconsin and one from Indiana, demanded the release of their comrade. For a while it looked as if the mob of soldiers would settle for nothing less than the hanging of the Massachusetts officer. Only the timely intervention of the Western brigade commander, Daniel Dustin, and guarantees that no one would be punished, allayed the Western regiments.[21]

Despite these problems, officers and men in Sherman's army got along extremely well. If any single thing stood out in the relationship between officers and men, it was the way most officers created a comfortable working environment by downplaying distinctions in rank and performing their duties without any pomp. "The disipline of this army," wrote a sergeant to his mother, "is not so strict in matters of trifling importance as to cause hard feelings towards our superiors. Rank is not royalty in Sherman's army." Another witness, a northeasterner residing in Beaufort, South Carolina, who was knowledgeable only in the ways of Eastern regiments, found little which distinguished officers and men:

The officers and men are on terms of perfect equality social[ly]. Off duty they drink together, go arm in arm about the town, call each other by the first name, in a way that startles an Eastern man. A friend heard a private familiarly addressing a Brig. Gen., as "Jake." Miss Lee saw another General taking hold with his men to help move a lot of barrels on a wharf. He took off his coat and worked three hours, like a common porter. This seems strange to us, accustomed to the aristocratic system adopted in the Eastern regiments.[22]

There were several reasons for this closeness between officers and men. In part it was due to a volunteer army recruited locally, where officers and men frequently knew one another in peacetime. Sherman's nature was also partly responsible in tearing down the barrier between officers and men. At ease with everyone, Sherman might just as well chat on the march with a private as he would with his senior officers, and this created a relaxed atmosphere within the entire army. Most of all it was the product of prolonged field service. Spending day after day in a combat zone and depending upon one another for survival, sharing the physical and emotional burdens of campaign life, the differences between officers and men tended to break down. It was not unusual for a captain to carry the knapsack of a sick soldier or for a private to have a company commander who "would divide his last cracker or last water in his canteen with the boys." Nor was it beneath Brig. Gen. Alpheus S. Williams to carry rails to help corduroy a road or Maj. Gen. John A. Logan, covered with mud from head to toe, to work nearly all night pulling wagons through the quagmire. The fact that "Our Division Commander Brig Gen [Charles R.] Woods is a more common man than a Potomic Lieut[enant] in both dress and deportment" and fellow division commander James D. Morgan had adopted a "method of plain living in the army," sleeping under a fly tent on a lawn like his men while Morgan's staff spent the night in a fine house in town, could only have had a positive effect on the troops. Sgt. Burke Wylie probably expressed the sentiment best when he wrote:

You would hardly credit but I have seen on the last march men making roads in the mud working from Private to Brig General, all lending a helping hand. There is strength in unity and in this way I account for our universal success.[23]

Sherman's enlisted ranks were primarily veterans, men with several years of service behind them. Most soldiers had been together at least two years, and many had served for three years or longer by the time of the Savannah campaign. Approximately one of every two soldiers had reenlisted for a second three-year term, compared with one in fifteen in the Union armies, and nearly four in every five members of Sherman's army had enlisted by 1862. Even more impressive was that over 98 percent of the noncommissioned officers, the backbone of any military unit, entered the service in either 1861 or 1862. During the course of that time these men faced the enemy shoulder to shoulder on numerous occasions and marched over 1,000 miles alongside one another. They had borne danger, hardship, and privation; slept under the same blanket; trudged through the same mud; and drunk from the same coffee tin. Over time they had shared stories, jokes, dreams, and aspirations. The result, as one veteran wrote, was that "a comradeship had grown as only such conditions could form."[24]

The troops composing Sherman's army were citizen soldiers, men who came from a variety of occupations and brought to the army all sorts of skills. Primarily Western in origin, although a fair portion hailed from the East, they exhibited a degree of self-reliance that shocked and impressed observers. One officer thought his men were "bright, thoughtful, intelligent, and brainy, and do a lot of thinking and reasoning on their own account." Another officer, this one from an Eastern corps, informed a general: "Sherman's appears to be an army of independent commands, each individual being a 'command.' "[25]

It was experience that gave Sherman's army this sense of self-reliance. "The experience of twenty years of peaceful life," pondered one of Sherman's boys on the third anniversary of his first battle, "has been crowded into three years." After two or three years of campaign experience, one astute soldier commented, he and his comrades had "learned nearly all that was worth knowing, at least far more than their [our] generals knew three years before." They mastered their adopted trade during actual field service, learning through trial and error when to throw the book away and when to abide by it, which shortcuts were beneficial and which ones were detrimental. Sherman's troops, wrote one young officer, knew "just what to do and what not to do."[26]

Years of experience taught soldiers how to survive on long, tough marches. The veteran learned early to march light, to reduce his load to a few simple necessities. "You may distinguish him [the veteran] from his fellows in the column," noted a staff officer, "by his small, well-packed knapsack and blanket tightly rolled; his well-ordered musket and accoutrements." Experience also enabled the army to subsist, even in seemingly barren regions. One sergeant during the Carolinas campaign wrote in his diary: "I believe if we were as green as we were

Cpl. Fergus Elliott, Company G, 109th Pennsylvania Volunteer Infantry, posed for a photograph for the folks at home. Elliott was one of hundreds of soldiers who kept a diary during the Savannah and Carolinas campaigns. (U.S. Army Military History Institute, Carlisle Barracks, Pa).

when we first *came out*—(as the 'Vets' say) we would starve to death."
Yet Sherman's army lived well enough off the land for another veteran to describe his companions at Goldsboro, North Carolina, as
"ragged but fat and saucy and their experience has taught them to look
out for themselves."[27]

In combat, experience really paid dividends. Despite all the months
of marching and maneuvering, every soldier realized that there would
come that moment when, as an officer wrote, "the victory must be
won by the army that could outfight the other." Under the enormous
stress and confusion of battle veterans had learned to perform those
small yet critical tasks that often decided engagements, such as main-
taining a line of battle while passing through woods and over ravines
or selecting a good defensive position under fire and fortifying it with
dirt, logs, and whatever other material was available.[28]

Of course, assembling an army of veterans from different theaters,
as Sherman had done, did have its drawbacks. Training, morale, the
types of campaigns fought, and success in battle combined to mold
these corps in a particular fashion. The Fourteenth, Fifteenth, and
Seventeenth Corps, all from the West, had undergone similar experiences and had adopted what the soldiers called a Western style. The
Twentieth Corps, however, had come from the East, where the conditions that shaped troops were dissimilar. In addition, regional prejudices within American society emphasized the differences. Easterners often thought people from the West were uneducated, untamed,
and irreligious, products of the Western frontier; many from the West
stereotyped easterners as being either urban criminals or well-mean-
ing, reform-minded sophisticates, utterly devoid of practical sense, who
had never performed a day's physical labor in their lives. The result,
then, was a clash of styles, an East–West rivalry that permeated Sherman's army.[29]

The Twentieth Corps, at least initially, seemed out of place in
Sherman's army. Twenty-six of its regiments and three artillery batteries came from Eastern states; the other three infantry corps jointly
had only three Eastern regiments and no Eastern artillery batteries.
Despite a long history of unsuccessful Eastern campaigns, the corps
took pride in its field service with the Army of the Potomac. These
men realized that failure on the battlefield was due, not to the lack of

combativeness of the troops, but to political pressures and mediocre army leaders. While serving in the East the regiments of the Twentieth Corps were always in the public eye, subject to governmental and international scrutiny. Naturally, its commanding officers placed a great emphasis on discipline, drill, and appearance. The end product, then, was a sharp-looking, superbly disciplined body of troops, with excellent fighting skills and a high morale, in essence the prototype of a mid-nineteenth-century army, yet one without a winning tradition.[30]

Although regional prejudices never interfered with the combat efficiency of the troops, they were a divisive element within the Twentieth Corps. Nearly 45 percent of its regiments came from Western states. At first these westerners stood out among the small Eastern majority, but in time they shed many of their Western habits and, as one westerner commented, accepted the ways of the Army of the Potomac: "Our Ohio Brigade served so long in that Army that they [we] changed in looks in due time for the reason that we adopted their styles in many things and were drilled and disciplined in like manner." Yet in other ways they always remained "those Western troops." As a minority in the corps, they frequently took a razzing from Eastern men and never seemed to meet the disciplinary standards of Eastern officers. A number of Western troops complained of mistreatment by Eastern officers, and one sharp young lieutenant even argued that Eastern officers received a disproportionate share of promotions within the corps. Most, however, accepted these minor abuses as merely part of "the beauty of being a Western Division in a Corps of Eastern troops."[31]

The Fourteenth, Fifteenth, and Seventeenth Corps were, on the other hand, thoroughly Western. They, too, were first-rate combat troops, but unlike the Twentieth Corps these men, especially those in the Fifteenth and Seventeenth Corps, were very successful. In drill and appearance, however, the Western boys were no match for the Army of the Potomac. Instead of drilling on parade grounds, they did most of their marching on prolonged campaigns. The worn, disheveled look so characteristic of Sherman and his Western soldiers was the product of extended campaigns and inadequate supplies, a problem that plagued Western armies throughout the war. As for discipline, again the Western troops could not compare with the Twentieth Corps. Frequent campaigning undercut strong discipline by fostering a sense of independence and self-reliance. When the situation demanded it, they were obedient enough, but on a relaxed march or in camp they were, as several observers noted, a bunch of schoolboys. Troops in the Western corps thought nothing of teasing a corps commander as he rode past; hollering to officers for food when rations were late; playing pranks day and night; or prowling through the countryside in search of food or adventure, none of which reflected good military discipline.[32]

To the men of the Twentieth Corps this Western style came as quite a shock. The Western corps seemed more like an armed rabble than an army. Capt. Daniel Oakey of the 2nd Massachusetts remembered: "We observed in the Western troops an air of independence hardly consistent with the nicest discipline." Another Twentieth corpsman, Frederick Winkler from the Badger State, wrote his wife:

in raggedness and uncleanliness of apparel and looseness and negligence of appearance generally, the 20th Corps could not think of competing with the Army of the Tennessee or that of the Ohio. For those high soldierly qualities, those bodies are preeminently distinguished. Laxity of discipline and carelessness of personal appearances is the spirit of those corps. The Army of the Cumberland also has a tendency that way, but not so much as that of the Tennessee.

Some naively interpreted these deficiencies as an indication that westerners were not very good troops. A young soldier felt that "The 20th has surpassed the Western Army as much in its fighting quality as it does in appearance, drill and discipline. It seems men can make a neat appearance on dress parade & fight well too." Yet most members of the Twentieth Corps acknowledged the combat skills of Western boys. Oakey recalled how the "cool self-reliance" of westerners in battle "excited our admiration." Even Winkler, after his lengthy rebuke of Western army habits, admitted, "notwithstanding the Army of the Tennessee is a most efficient body of troops."[33]

Members of the Fourteenth Corps, because of their proximity on the march to the Twentieth Corps, bore the brunt of Eastern slanders and retaliated in kind for all three Western corps. Most times the westerners responded in a spirit of good-natured rivalry, but in two instances it became much more than that. By some quirk of fate the Twentieth Corps, because it entered a number of prominent towns first, had provost duty, that is, the privilege of governing the area. At Winnsboro, South Carolina, officers of the Twentieth Corps confiscated all property in the town, including forage brought in from the countryside by soldiers of the Fourteenth Corps. When word spread to the body of the Fourteenth Corps that the Twentieth Corps had stolen their food and fodder, the westerners swore revenge. Three weeks later the Fourteenth Corps entered Fayetteville, North Carolina, first, and this time it acted as provost guards. Scuffles quickly broke out between men in the two corps, resulting in the death of a soldier from a Pennsylvania regiment. Only the strenuous efforts of officers from both corps averted a donnybrook. Fortunately, the rigors of the final week of the campaign, which included two battles, helped ease tensions between the two corps, and the soldiers soon forgot the incidents.[34]

In actuality, after several campaigns together the differences between the Twentieth and the other three corps diminished. Prolonged campaigns, lengthy marches, and living off the land forced Twentieth Corps officers to relax discipline and its veterans to exhibit greater self-reliance. That spit-and-polish look, once the trademark of the Eastern corps, became a thing of the past shortly after Sherman cut the supply lines. Western campaign conditions had reshaped the Twentieth Corps so much that by the time Sherman's army reached Goldsboro, North Carolina, appearance and behavior were no longer a means of distinguishing between the Eastern and the Western corps. Men from both the East and the West had come to learn, as one Hoosier corporal conceded, that "when the time comes to stand up on the battle front there is no discount on either and one is anxious to have the other on hands." Equally important, veterans of the Twentieth Corps had begun to think of themselves as members of Sherman's army and took great pride in its accomplishments.[35]

Alongside the veterans were the recruits, men who entered the service in 1863 and 1864 and constituted approximately one-fifth of the enlisted men in Sherman's army. Nearly all had participated in the Atlanta campaign, a tough yet effective indoctrination into the war, and some had served as far back as the capture of Vicksburg and the battle of Gettysburg. Several hundred, however, had been with the army barely two weeks when the March to the Sea began.[36]

Most recuits were enlistees, soldiers who had joined the army voluntarily for a wide variety of reasons, ranging from patriotism to pecuniary rewards, a search for adventure, or simply to avoid the draft. A much smaller number were draftees and substitutes for drafted men. These soldiers, especially the substitutes, often had no worse motives for entering the service than enlistees, but in an army of veterans that equated enlistment with patriotism, status as a draftee or a substitute carried a stigma.[37]

Recruits, like veterans, came from various regions with different backgrounds. As with the men who enlisted in 1861 and 1862, some made first-rate soldiers and others did not, but most learned to perform their duties reasonably well. Company K of the 2nd Minnesota received five Chippewa Indians as enlistees. A lieutenant, after scrutinizing the new men, concluded: "They make splendid soldiers as far as they can understand." An enlistee in a Massachusetts regiment who had immigrated from Germany, a region even then notorious for its superb soldiers, while on picket service one day surrendered to a group of unarmed runaway slaves dressed in gray. (Picket service was duty whereby a group of soldiers took positions well beyond camp with the purpose of warning the other soldiers when the enemy approached.) He also had the misfortune to have an officer nearby observing the entire affair, which resulted in a general court-martial. Possibly the strangest case was a Quaker and a pacifist who served as a private in the 10th Iowa. Torn between his sense of patriotism and his religious beliefs, the man would neither enlist nor seek an exemption from the draft. Once selected for service in a local lottery, he refused to bear arms or work as a pioneer, but "for the relief of suffering humanity I could labor." After some consideration his regimental commander assigned him to the Ambulance Corps and later the Freedmen's Bureau where he performed admirably.[38]

At this stage of the war, it was rare for a man with little or no military training to enter the service as anything except a private. To promote an experienced noncommissioned officer to the rank of second lieutenant rather than experiment with an untried individual was much more practical. Occasionally, under very unusual circumstances, a few recruits made it to the officers' ranks, but those who did met with some hard times afterward. The governor of Minnesota, desperate to fill up his depleted ranks, awarded three lieutenancies to civilians who recruited thirty men to serve in the 4th Minnesota. In the 21st Michigan, Pvt. Charles S. Brown, who performed the work of a regimental staff officer, had the audacity to forge the signature of his commanding officer in a letter to the governor requesting a commission for himself, which the governor unwittingly issued. In both cases the appointments infuriated the veterans, who felt that they, not outsiders, deserved the promotions. Members of the 4th Minnesota "tried to make it lively for these new officers during their terms of service," whereas Brown found that "the spite in the Regt is so unpleasant" that he wanted to transfer.[39]

Earlier in the war, when the government needed more troops, it recruited entirely new regiments, from colonels down to privates. Since very few people had any real military training, inexperienced civilians had to fill many vacant officers' slots. Later in the war it made much more sense to place recruits in the ranks. By 1864, after three years of war, they simply took enlistees, draftees, and substitutes and plugged them into what Sherman called the "old and tried regiments with their experienced officers on hand." The purpose was to spread recruits evenly throughout the army so that, as one veteran officer asserted, these "new men would, by association with the veterans and under the instruction and care of veteran officers, have soon become efficient and reliable."[40]

In general the process was very effective. Most regiments received a handful of recruits who blended well into the veteran units. Once in a while a regiment or a company might get overloaded with recruits, such as the 47th Ohio, which received 189 draftees and substitutes, or Company I, 33rd Ohio, which was 61 percent draftees; but these were unusual circumstances, and even then the new soldiers served under experienced officers and noncommissioned officers. Recruits arrived in a condition that veterans referred to as either green or raw, without any real training, although some did have the privilege of putting a rusty old rifle back into service with several days' worth of elbow grease. There was no time for formal training. Recruits had the benefit of observing the seasoned troops but learned mainly on the job, during the march, the way the veterans had originally done it. Unused to the weight of the knapsack and often the victim of overpacking, recruits learned their lesson within a few days and discarded all but the essentials. With blistered feet and sore shoulders they cursed the military as they trudged through the rain in knee-deep mud, struggling to keep up with the rest of the unit. "It was with the greatest exertion I can keep up with the veterans," complained a recruit on his third day of marching in words that spoke for nearly all, but in several weeks the green troops would get accustomed to such conditions.[41]

All the while recruits were the butt of veterans' jokes and pranks. In part it was good plain fun, testing and getting acquainted with the new men, but it was also a means of getting even with recruits who received larger bounties and shorter terms of service for enlisting than had the more experienced troops. One veteran tried to convey this sentiment to a friend when he wrote how unfair it was that recruits

enlisted for one year, Ondly thay will get out afew days before I do and thay are agetting four times the money that I did I dont think that is hardly fair   thay for Coming in one year get enough for to buy afarm.

Some of the meaner veterans found satisfaction in stealing from recruits, as one sergeant noted:

Our boys don't play fair with them [recruits] they steal their knapsacks and guns and everything else. They [recruits] will find out how to watch their things closer after they soldier a year or two.

Thievery was such a problem that one recruit either "lost" or had stolen $51.50 worth of goods and equipment during his first year of service. Most veterans, though, preferred to give green troops misinformation about combat, army rations, and what it was like to be a soldier. One morning a lieutenant in the 50th Illinois got up and could not find his pants and boots, and shortly afterward he spotted a new recruit walking around camp wearing them. Some men grabbed the fledgling and brought him before the company commander for questioning. There the recruit told the officers some veterans had said that "unless a soldier could steal, he did not amount to much," and this recruit wanted to impress his comrades in a big way. He explained the tale with such innocent honesty that the officers decided not to punish the man beyond some extra duty.[42]

Despite all the gags and teasing, veterans knew that their survival depended in part on how well recruits performed on the campaign and did not take their tutoring chores lightly. They might let green troops learn how to pack a knapsack for themselves, but veterans not only instructed recruits carefully in the more critical aspects of campaigning; they also assigned them to duty with experienced soldiers. It was valuable to have a veteran explain how to do certain tasks; it was even better to have some perform the chores alongside recruits. With this sort of instruction recruits did not transform into veterans overnight or even in a few months. That took time. What it did was prepare recruits, as one officer commented, to "take care of themselves and do any duty of the soldier."[43]

This indeed was a very special body of troops Sherman commanded. At first glance, the men looked more like a mob than an army. They were an unkempt, boisterous, seemingly unruly lot, in no way resembling the stereotypical professional army of the mid-nineteenth century or even their counterpart at Petersburg. Yet they were an army, superbly skilled in both marching and fighting. While other Union commands took pride in their spit-and-polish dress and expertise in marching drills, Sherman's men cared little for that; instead, they took extra pride in their ability to endure all hardships and still achieve in battle and on the march. The sinewy frames, bronzed skin, scraggly beards, and dilapidated clothing were merely trophies from the last successful campaign. Upon their arrival in Beaufort, South Carolina, one member of Sherman's army overheard a black soldier in a shiny, new uniform comment, " 'they alls are about as black as we alls', which," he felt, "though not very complimentary told something how we did look and though dirty and ragged we were proud to belong to Sherman's army." Another witness in Beaufort, a transplanted Yankee accustomed only to the troops stationed in the vicinity, found Sherman's legions fascinating and refreshing:

Strange, rough-looking, unshaven, and badly dressed: they seem like a gang of coal-heavers, when compared with the trim and snug fellows here, who have nothing to do but guard-duty with white gloves. These western marauders came trooping through the streets, roaring out songs and jokes, making sharp comments on all the tidy civilians, and over-flowing with merriment and good-nature. Their clothes were patched like Scripture—Joseph's. Hats without rims, hats without crowns, some with no hats at all. . . . It was a treat, I assure you, to see some real soldiers, who had won battles.[44]

By the time Sherman's army reached Goldsboro, North Carolina, it was in all its glory. Hatless heads, frazzled pants, threadbare shirts, torn shoes or barefoot, faces blackened by Carolina pine smoke, they looked, as a member of Schofield's army noted, "very hard." "When Gen Terry's & Schofields troops joined us," wrote a young lieutenant in Sherman's ranks, "you could tell one of Shermans Soldiers in a moment, in a crowd of them. They were all well dressed & equiped having just started on a campaign. Our men were dirty, ragged & in many cases barefoot. They grumbled about living on 9 hard tack a day. Our men were Jolly on parched corn, cow beans or whatever they could find. They thought this marching 90 miles in ten days was dreadful. Our boys would think nothing of doing it in three days. It seemed to them they were getting a long way from anywhere. It seemed to us that at Goldsboro we were almost home."[45]

Sherman had an army of veterans, soldiers who knew what to do and how to take care of themselves. Instead of stifling their initiative by keeping tight rein or attempting to mold the army in a particular fashion, Sherman gave his officers and men enough freedom to put their experience to work, and they responded by attaining the goals he selected for them. And though his troops may have been a little lax on discipline, they succeeded where no other Union army could have, for as one soldier wrote with evident pride, "There is nothing in this world like Sherman's army."[46]

CHAPTER 2

The Army and the Cause

*"We can see nothing but a vigorous prosecution of
the war and a final Victory not far distant."*
—OSCAR [KIMBERLEY] TO PARENTS,
11 NOVEMBER 1864

In an army where nearly 50 percent of the company-level troops had
reenlisted and over 28 percent more had worked with them closely
since 1862, the men seem to have had a very clear understanding of
whom and for what they were fighting. They had enlisted originally
for many of the same reasons as recruits—patriotism, excitement, travel,
and money—yet for most men it was patriotism that kept them in the
service. Veterans had already seen too many battlefields and a lifetime's worth of the South, and with the shortage of manpower in civilian life people could make plenty of money without risking their
lives. Scarcely more than a dozen of the 1,800 soldiers in the random
sample who joined Sherman's army as recruits in 1863 and 1864 had
previous Civil War experience, which seems to indicate that troops
whose enlistments had expired and who decided to leave the service
found ample job opportunities in the civilian world. These were citizen soldiers who constituted Sherman's army. Long before, they had
made a commitment to restore the Union, or to destroy slavery, or
both, and they would remain in the blue uniform until they finished
the job.[1]

A primary reason why there was such wholesale support for a vigorous prosecution of the war was the single-mindedness of belief as to who was responsible for the war. "Tis the educated class of the South caused all this trouble," confided a young soldier in his diary. "The poor unlettered masses and they constitute almost all the population have been from time immemorial their dupes and instruments. . . . they cannot seem to understand they are in reality fighting for the negro and not for themselves." A Massachusetts officer also placed the blame with the upper class of the South, who "lived down here like so many lords and princes; each planter was at the head of a little aristocracy in which hardly a law touched him. This didn't content these people; they wanted 'their rights,' and now they are getting them."[2]

Variations came over the question of what soldiers hoped to attain by going to war. Some joined the army solely to put a stop to slavery. One semiliterate private shrugged off a bland Christmas dinner outside of Savannah by writing, "I can afoard to go hungry somb times if it will help to free the slaves." Another soldier in a more patriotic vein hoped that the folks at home "realize that the Sacrifice of our brave and noble comrades who have fallen in the Struggle are every *one* of them martyrs. Justice demands at our hands that they shall not have fallen in vain, but that Every vestige of the great National sin: (Slavery) Shall be washed ayway with their blood." Others, however, wanted nothing to do with the abolitionist cause. A German soldier on the march just east of Atlanta barked at a Southern woman: "Fight for the nigger! I'd see 'em in de bottom of a swamp before I'd fight for 'em." For another it was his military experience that sapped his antislavery fervor. He claimed to be "quite an abulitionist when I came in the army" until the hardships of army life turned him sour on the cause. A few even entered the war with no particular goal in mind. One officer joined Lincoln's legions, not because he agreed with Republican policy, but because he felt that "it is the duty of every good citizen to support the government as elected by the majority of the population, even though oneself might not be in agreement with all the laws which are passed."[3]

Foremost in the minds of most soldiers in Sherman's army was the restoration of the Union. "i Came out pure to do my Duty and to fight the rebes and poot Down rebelyon," wrote a Hoosier corporal to his wife, "i did not Come to get the Countrey bountey and then play of[f] as some has Done such is no gud solgers nor is not respected as solgers here in front." No more articulately, a New York corporal voiced similar sentiments when he wrote, "I never tirn my back to a reb has long has i have two armes to fight," and a scant three months later he elaborated on this theme:

And we now like true Soldier go determed not to yeal one inch rather than yeal. We will Stane this Suthrn Soil with our blood. And leave meney of our boddyes there in memory of the day that we Stood like a Stone wall and fight to the last to Conquer this Rebelien or Die.[4]

A handful of these men had a narrow interpretation of the Union's objective and vigorously opposed any interference with the institution of slavery. As the war progressed, however, most troops began to see emancipation as a powerful tool in crushing secession. They followed Lincoln's lead, first by seeking to restore the Union without freeing the slaves, then endorsing it as a necessary wartime measure. Some had abhorred slavery before the war, considering it, as one officer insisted, "incompatible with a free Republic," but had tolerated it in the interest of avoiding a civil war. Once Lincoln announced the Emancipation Proclamation, they immediately threw their support behind it. Others cared less about blacks and acknowledged the wisdom of Lincoln's policy strictly from a military viewpoint. "I am no more in favor of negro equality now than I was three years ago," wrote an Illinois soldier to his folks. "I am in favor of emancipation because Slavery stands in the way of putting down the rebellion."[5]

As Sherman's troops passed through Georgia and the Carolinas, opposition to slavery grew stronger and stronger. "We could not resist the conviction," wrote an Ohio officer, "that a civilization in which a score of lives are impoverished and embittered, are blasted and debased and damned, in order that one life may be made sweeter, is a system of wrong that no language can properly condemn." More important, soldiers began to realize that slavery was so intertwined in both Southern society and the cause of the war that the three issues were nearly inseparable. While struggling with this concept one private scribbled a note in a book at the court clerk's office for the people of Bennettsville, South Carolina:

General Sherman's army passed through this place. We will fight until every rebel in arms is slain unless they will lay down their arms and come back into the union under the old constitution. South Carolina was the root of secession. The South are to blame for this war and none others. Why did not the Southern States wait and see whether A. Lincoln would interfere with slavery before they seceded?

Thus, when a Wisconsin soldier claimed after the Carolinas campaign that the volunteer army was all abolitionists, he exaggerated only slightly. Campfire discussions no longer centered on whether or not slaves should be free. That was a willingly accepted fact. Instead, they revolved around what rights freedmen should have in peacetime.[6]

Of course, not everyone in Sherman's army took such a strong interest in fighting the Rebels. Some soldiers dodged front-line service; others formed elaborate plans to desert from the ranks. One substitute in the 39th Ohio hated the army so much that he unsuccessfully attempted to desert four times in his first three months of service. To keep him from escaping before the court-martial, guards had to tie him to a tree. A chaplain in the 10th Iowa reported "a copperhead substitute shot himself through the great toe, to get rid of the [Savannah] campaign"; according to another soldier, a recruit in the 29th Ohio "shot himself through the hand evidently with a pistol." Brooding over army service and a wife at home who was cheating on him, a draftee in the 33rd Indiana hanged himself, much to the shock of the rest of the men. Still another soldier, a Hoosier private, got fed up with army life and lashed out at several members of his company, calling them "abolitionist sons of biches." He went on to "damn Abe Lincoln and his hirelings" and "damn this Army to Hell," saying, "I wish the Southern army would scatter it to the four winds of the Earth." The outburst, a court-martial decided, merited a dishonorable discharge and one year of hard labor.[7]

Most soldiers who disliked the army or disapproved of the cause simply served out their term and grumbled much of the time, especially to the folks at home. These were men who constantly harped on the misbelief that the Union armies had made no progress in the war, that the Confederacy was no nearer defeat than it was one or two years earlier. They complained how the government mistreated its soldiers and how they could not wait to get out of the service. A Michigan recruit disgustedly wrote his wife that the war was "nothing but a speculation from beginning to end and the end is not yet . . .

it is the love of money that keeps this war alive, the soldiers are swindled out of thousands of dollars every day by these miserable government pimps." After telling his folks how much he was looking forward to spending next New Year's in Chicago at the expiration of his three-year enlistment, another soldier commented: "Then we will be man again and not slaves and even less slave liberators." A member of a New York regiment, a one-year enlistee, hated the service so much that he counted the days until his term expired: "I have five months & 8 days Longer to work for Old Abe & then I am done for him & he haint got money enough to hire me an other year in the sirvices."[8]

The poorly motivated troops had no monopoly on complaints. Enduring the hardships and sacrifices of several years of service, it was natural for even the best soldiers to experience moments of disconsolation too. As one Iowa sergeant wrote to his cousin, "We are all creatures of an impulse, at one time we are soaring on the wings of fancy and at others we are dragging through the Slough of Despondency. One extreme is sure to bring the other." Despite all the good times soldiers had, despite the camaraderie, joking and, in the case of Sherman's army, success, occasionally the hardships of prolonged campaign life became so unbearable and the personal sacrifices and tragedies seemed so severe that men could not help but feel momentary pangs of remorse. After nearly one week of marching in heavy rains on light rations, building roads and pulling wagons by hand through deep mud every inch of the way, an Ohio private admitted that this "Tires the patriotism, fortitude and patience of our boys severely." Another soldier who could no longer tolerate the cruelties of war unburdened himself to his wife by writing:

I am most heartily sick of this kind of life. Oh what a pleasant retreete from the repulsive. scenes of this man slaughtering life, would be the society of my family in some secluded spot, shut out from the calamities of war.[9]

Yet no matter what the hardships were, Sherman's men, outside of the grumblers, endorsed a policy of vigorously prosecuting the war. After the fall of Atlanta and the narrow escape of the remnants of Hood's once magnificent army, it was evident to Sherman's troops that final victory was not far away. "I don't go in for yielding one inch to the rebs," wrote a Connecticut private to his wife before the Savannah

campaign. "They are already licked and they, in my opinion, will begin to own licked before long." It would take months, possibly a year
of further sacrifices and hardships, but the troops were willing to make
the effort now and finish the job. "I wouldn't miss going on this expedition for 6 months pay," jotted an ecstatic officer in his diary before the march to Savannah, while a private informed his father, "I
shall not try to get a furlough because when I came out I said that I
would not enter Rockton [Illinois] again untill after the war is Settled."[10]

Just when it seemed to Sherman's troops that the final victory was
near, antiwar Democrats, commonly known as Copperheads, launched
a vigorous campaign to halt the bloodshed and grant the Confederacy
its independence. By the late summer and early fall, when the Copperheads got their movement into full swing, the Union armies seemed
no closer to winning the war than they were before the spring offensives. The fighting in the East, which had stalled outside Petersburg,
Virginia, several months earlier, had seen no appreciable changes, and
until the fall of Atlanta on September 2, an apparent stalemate existed
in the West as well. To obtain more manpower the government had
scheduled drafts, an extremely unpopular means of raising troops, for
September, followed barely two months later by the presidential election of 1864. The time was ripe for an antiwar crusade, and the Copperheads had no intention of letting this opportunity slip by them.

Believing that victory was close at hand, it is easy to see why Sherman's troops bitterly resented any attempts to impede the war effort
or terminate hostilities without a reunification of the states. They, along
with their fallen comrades, had made enormous sacrifices to get to this
stage of the war. They were not about to give up the cause after enduring all that hardship and suffering; nor were they willing to let the
efforts of hundreds of thousands of Union soldiers who had lost their
lives or health in the war go in vain. To Sherman's men it was a cut-
and-dried issue. All those who supported the war were loyal to the
cause and the Constitution, and everyone else was disloyal. "All loyal
men must take one side and all disloyal must take the other," penned
an acute young officer to his wife. "The disloyal ones should be outside our picket lines." Upon mistakenly hearing that a prominent
Copperhead died at the hands of a soldier, a private wrote, "I can't

help but say 'Good.' That should be the doom of all such traitors. It may be wicked but I can't see any difference between them and the Rebels in arms against us. They are all working for the destruction of this glorious Union." Later the same man wrote:

Oh!! those base copperheads. I would like to have them down here in front of our guns and then make them do allegiance to their government or die a traitor's death. Those are my true sentiments, and no doubt it looks hard to you, but to those that have been serving their country for the last three years in trying to crush the Rebels, and now to have those dastardly cowards crying for peace when we have got them so nearly used up. That is the feeling of three-fourths of the army.

Finally, an Ohio corporal wrote his sister, with an initial touch of sarcasm:

well now about that new beux of yours   I am Surprised that you have Slighted thoes brave patriotic young men that stile themselves butternuts and now take up with one of old Abe Linkens abolitions Soldiers that is fighting for nothing but the nigers I feel proud of your Selection and hope you will never be So foolish as to take up with a butternut or a home coward again when there are so many Soldiers in the army.[11]

Certainly one of the most eagerly awaited events for Sherman's army was the draft, which sparked hopes in many of the boys that the board would select all their Copperhead enemies for military service. One Indiana officer wittily recorded in his diary: "Our men are rejoicing in the fact that this is the day of the draft and hoping that some of their copperhead neighbors may draw their fortunes in uncle Sam's lottery, where all have a chance and don't have to pay anything for their tickets." Others hoped there would be draft riots as in previous years and that soldiers would get sent north to implement the program by force. A Wisconsin soldier wrote to his sweetheart: "I hope if they do have to take soldiers home to enforce the draft that I will be one that will have to go, for I could shoot one of them copperheads with a good heart as I could shoot a wolf. I could shoot my father if he was one, but thank God he is not." Fortunately, the draft came off with no real problems, and when the names of the chosen few reached Sherman's army the soldiers applauded. A handful of others, however, regretted the fact that so many Copperheads had escaped the selection process. As one soldier told his parents, "I hear Brodhead

[Wisconsin] is again clear from the Draft, too bad, I should liked to have seen some in town taken." [12]

The event that really aroused the ire of the soldiers, though, was the presidential election of 1864. A sizable number of men, particularly Democrats and members of the Eastern Twentieth Corps, rejoiced when they learned that George Brinton McClellan, former commander of the Army of the Potomac, had captured the Democratic presidential nomination but quickly soured when they heard that the Copperheads had gained control of the party and pushed through an antiwar platform. McClellan "would have stood a good show," thought an Illinois private, but "after the soldiers got to see the papers and to see where he stood they cussed him for all that was out." An intelligent Wisconsinite informed his parents: "The Chicago [antiwar] Platform has placed McClellan in obscurity; we would have voted for him had it not been for that. We can see nothing but a vigorous prosecution of the war and a final Victory not far distant." Even members of the Twentieth Corps turned against their old commander. Around the time of Antietam, in September 1862, a New Jersey lieutenant thought "a great deal of 'Little Mac,' " and believed "as a general he has his defenders still. But he has got into most terribly bad company; he is the Representative of a party whose principles no *Soldier* can uphold." An Illinois soldier, ineligible to vote because the state legislature had failed to pass a law granting soldiers in the field the franchise, wrote his folks: "I know if I was whare I could vote I would give old Abe a lift. I would just as soon vote for Jeff Davis at once as to vote for McClen runing on the platform he is, but I think thare is know doubt but what old Abe will get elected." [13]

Politically, these troops were no simpletons. On the main campaign issues they were extremely well informed. Soldiers regularly received newspapers and magazines while in camp, which kept them in touch with the current political situation, and during the two months prior to the election troops received political speeches in pamphlet form. They had easy access to political lectures, usually sponsored by the regimental or brigade chaplain, and at night around the campfire politics was "at a discount again." In fact, Sherman's men were so well versed in national politics that most had cut through the lengthy debates and extraneous positions and narrowed the November election down to a single issue, a referendum on the cause: Should the nation continue to fight for the restoration of the Union and the destruction of the slave system? "This Day will Deside weather the Union will be Saved or Distroyed," wrote a corporal in his diary on November 8. Another just hoped his regiment would be in camp that day "so as to fight treason with our votes as well as our guns."[14]

In the minds of the men the issue was crystal-clear. A Minnesotan wrote home two months before the election date: "There seems to be considerable speculation in the North in regard to the coming Presidential election and thinking that the peace party will come off victorious. But I think not. The majority of the army want peace but in a different way. They want it when every armed foe is subdued by the arm of our yet strong government." Another soldier, even more precisely, told his girlfriend what this election was all about: "If McClellan gets the reins he will have peace sooner than Abe, but by letting them have their slaves. Then we can fight them again in ten years. But let Old Abe settle it, and it is always settled."[15]

As in any large group of adult males, there were a few who expressed no interest in the election, and there were quite a few more who endorsed McClellan, but they were, as one soldier predicted, "about as scarce as Angels visits or Uncle Sam's green backs in the army." Most men supported the president in his bid for reelection simply because he would prosecute the war to the fullest extent. In the four states where complete election totals were available, Lincoln won a staggering 86 percent of the soldier vote in Sherman's army, and incomplete tabulations from three other states that permitted their troops in the field to cast ballots showed no appreciable change in the way the men voted. Only one regiment, the 17th Wisconsin, cast a majority of its votes for McClellan, and that unit had a heavy Democratic-Irish contingent, augmented by an unusually large number of draftees.[16]

Despite the one-sidedness of the election, there is no evidence of any sort of corruption, nor is there any justification for the belief that the officers told the men for whom to vote. In at least one case the troops went directly against the political preference of their division commander and voted for Lincoln, as one soldier attested: "It is said that the 113th [Ohio] cast a larger vote for McClellan [only 76, compared with 165 for Lincoln] than any other Ohio regiment in the division. That will make us the pets of the division commander." Lincoln's success derived from his ability to maintain the support of the Republicans and cut deeply into the traditional Democratic vote. Solidly Democratic units, such as the 26th Wisconsin, which "two years ago cast an almost unanimous democratic vote," swung over to Lincoln. With the Copperhead platform, Democrats in the ranks felt they had little alternative but to vote for the Republican Lincoln.[17]

As expected, veterans were thoroughly behind Lincoln's reelection bid. For them, especially those who had reenlisted, to disregard their two- or three-year effort to defeat the Confederates and vote to end the war was a nearly impossible task. It was very difficult for a veteran to argue with a soldier who posed the right question, as this one did:

Is it possible that a soldier, after serving in this victorious army for three years can cast his vote for men whose platform declares that we have fought and struggled in vain and just as we are about to realize the great reward of our labors and sacrifices, they cry for an "immediate cessation of hostilities[?]."

The result was that very few veterans, according to the testimony of the men, voted for McClellan, and most of those who did opt for the former army commander served in companies or regiments organized in Democratic strongholds.[18]

In general, the troops seem to have respected the right of their fellow soldiers to vote for whomever they preferred, but in at least one instance a veteran took a razzing shortly after the polls closed. A sergeant in the 29th Ohio recorded how the men in his regiment treated a veteran who cast his sacred ballot for McClellan: "There was one of our Veterans voted for Mack but he was alwais considered ignorant so not noticed much but the boys got on a train in the evening and brought him out of his tent and exhibited him as one of the long eared gentry. I am confident that he will, yes and has, repented more than once for what he has done."[19]

For recruits the situation was somewhat different. They were the group most likely to vote for McClellan, at least according to the men themselves, and it was here that veterans often tried to influence the voters. This pressure to vote for Lincoln, which was by no means universal in Sherman's army, varied in form and subtlety from one regiment or company to another. In some units pro-Lincoln men converted recruits through debate; in others, it was the pervasive sense of conformity that drove recruits to mimic the veterans and vote for the incumbent. "Copperheads are so very few among us," wrote a veteran in his diary, "that they do not come forward & vote the ticket which they are of course at perfect liberty to do so." With other units there was a stigma attached to recruits who were partial to McClellan. "A soldier who votes for McClellan," wrote a Wisconsinite on Election Day, "is looked upon by his comrades as an ignoramus or a coward & wants to get out of the service & so votes for Mac." Yet again, as with veterans, there is no evidence that indicates anyone inhibited the men from voting freely. Veterans simply shook their heads in disappointment and assumed that the recruits who voted for McClellan were conscripts or, as one soldier insisted, "illiterate, pro-slavery, swearers, drinkers and gamblers."[20]

Casting their votes for Lincoln was not the only way soldiers influenced the election, however. Probably a more important contribution was the letters Sherman's men sent home discussing the election. Whether they had the vote, were too young to vote, or had not received the right to vote in the field—which affected the Connecticut, Illinois, Indiana, Massachusetts, and New Jersey troops—soldiers made their preference known to friends and relatives in no uncertain terms. A Wisconsin private encouraged his brother to "Do your best for old Abe in the election. Every man who votes against him is a soldier's enemy, so vote for old Abe and Johnson." A member of the 50th Illinois, with brothers also in the service, coached his father on where to stand in the upcoming election: "Now, Father, do not, if you love your country, your God and your children, have anything to do with destroying this glorious Union, which your sons have, and are, periling their lives to protect. Shun all disloyal company and do not vote the copperhead ticket, no matter who may say it is right." Undoubtedly the bluntest statement of all, however, came from an Ohioan who told his sister, "Tell Ben if he votes for Mc[Clellan] I will never speak to him again."[21]

In a sense, the Lincoln victory at the polls, coupled with the fall of Atlanta, renewed the commitment of Sherman's troops to the cause.

Bursting with confidence in their own ability, the men regarded the election as the last major obstacle to the unification of the states, so one corporal attempted to explain to a friend: "Fore we go with our Hartes contented nowing that we have a President that will not declare peace on no other tirmes then an Uncondishnell Surrender. An we now that our Generls in the field are true to there cose."[22]

A fresh outlook on the war was just one change that resulted from the presidential election. Lincoln, too, had taken on a new image in the eyes of the troops. The man who had originally won the presidency with less than 40 percent of the popular vote and had retained it four years later with a 55 percent majority gradually became the symbol of that cause for which he and the troops had battled so very hard to attain. Through good times and bad, Lincoln had stood like a tower of strength, refusing to bend when it came to the cause. His contributions to the war were so important that Sherman's army, with very few exceptions, viewed his reelection as absolutely essential in the fight to restore the Union and abolish slavery. In the minds of the men, Lincoln had come to represent that struggle to preserve the Union.[23]

After the election, these men sensed that the end was in sight. With each step Sherman's army took, their devotion to see the cause through to its fruition grew. "I would like to see home as well as eney one," wrote a private to his wife during the siege of Savannah, "but I wish to see theas rebes cleand out nearly as bad." By the time they had taken Savannah, it was obvious to the men that the Confederacy could not stand "one or two more of Sherman's crazy spells." In mid-January a young officer revealed his eagerness for the upcoming Carolinas campaign when he confided in his diary: "We are ready to move whenever the word is given. I hope it wont be long for I am waiting with patience to move so we will be able to crush this cursed rebellion." Then, two weeks later, he joyously recorded: "We are on our way thank God once more to do something to crush this Rebellion out. I never was more anxious to meet them than now. I feel as though I would grow fat fighting them." The men, as Sgt. Rice Bull stated, had sacrificed and suffered enough in this war. All they wanted to do was to complete the work and return to their loved ones:

The prevailing feeling among the men was a desire to finish the job; they wanted to get back home. The mass of those in this Army were veterans, nearly all had served three years, many much longer, and all were tired of army life. They had faced the loss of home comforts and loss of business opportunity and endured privation and danger to maintain the integrity of their country. They were not in the service as soldiers of fortune, they were intelligent and could see that the Rebellion was nearing its end, so were willing and anxious to meet quickly any privation or danger that would bring a speedy end to the war.[24]

On March 4 an Illinois chaplain confided in his diary: "old honest Abe is inaugurated today—God bless him & spare his life to see the close of this war." Barely six weeks later, an assassin's bullet nullified that prayer. News of the tragic death utterly devastated Sherman's troops. A corporal wrote in his diary: "I have seen the bravest Soldiers today shedding tears over the President's Death." Another soldier, an Illinois captain, recalled that awful day: "Such a time I hope never to see again. Men who were habitually profane forgot to swear, tears ran down from eyes unused to weeping. Everywhere men were seen to weep who had never flinched in the white heat of battle." And a captain, thinking back several days to the moment the troops heard the disastrous news, and then reflecting on the cause and all the sacrifices they had endured, sadly commented: "I don't think we knew how much we did think of him until then." Fortunately, by late April, the cause was won.[25]

CHAPTER 3

The Army and Blacks

"It is claimed the negroes are so well contented with their slavery; if it ever was so, that day has ceased."
—FREDERICK WINKLER JOURNAL-LETTER,
23 NOVEMBER 1864

Before the Savannah campaign most members of Sherman's army had few experiences with blacks. Many had seen slaves at work in Mississippi, Kentucky, or Tennessee, and a few had known some free blacks during peacetime, yet during the course of the next six months the vast majority of Sherman's troops had to deal with black soldiers, black settlements, or black refugees for the first time on a daily basis. For some this was a welcome and rewarding experience, a chance to assist blacks in their struggle for freedom and equality. Others, however, found blacks a nuisance and vented their prejudices and wartime frustrations on the black race.

An Ohioan commented in his diary that blacks "exhibit commendable will & determination to extracate themselves from that low state of degradation & bondage for which a so called enlightened class of whites is responsible." Some two and one-half months later a soldier made a stump speech, declaring that this country was for white men only, and wished "to have the entire negro race on an immense platform and power sufficient to blow them all to atoms," amid the cheers of his comrades. A soldier thought a black regiment was "a fine looking lot of men" and noted: "The boys that have seen them under fire say that they stand up to it as well as the best whites, which is saying a good deal." Three months earlier an Iowa officer complained when he learned that black troops stationed at Beaufort, South Carolina, had failed to capture a nearby bridge: "that is as might be expected I dont go much on Nigger soldiers." One Wisconsin soldier considered the black refugees who followed the army to Savannah "a great hindrance, if not to say nuisance"; another wrote home: "it is anough to start the tears on a pretty hard looking fase to see wih what joy our troops are greeted with by the poor down trodden slaves." Finally, an Indiana sergeant wrote: "The Darkies come to us from evry direction. They are all looking for freedom but realy dont seem to know just what freedom means." About the same time a Minnesotan got a completely different impression of the refugees: "Men, women and children are willing to endure all the hardships of a long march to secure their liberty, yet the slave owners say that the slaves are contented and do not wish to be free."[1]

These quotations exemplify the wide range of racial attitudes maintained by the men of Sherman's army. At one end, constituting a fairly sizable porportion of the troops, were soldiers who advocated social and political equality. Many of these men had entered the war with the hope of freeing the slaves and securing for them their rights as full and equal citizens. Others, through their wartime experiences with blacks, were able to overcome prewar prejudices and adopt the cause of black equality. These men, impressed with the wartime contributions of blacks and their almost fanatical desire to gain freedom and equality, felt that blacks had proven that they merited the same rights as whites. One Ohio captain maintained: "Sooner would I lose my right arm than do aught to disappoint their expectations." At the other end there were those who were absolutely intolerant of blacks. Constituting a small segment of the army, these men despised all blacks and harassed them whenever the opportunity presented itself. The clear majority of the army, however, fit somewhere between those two groups. They possessed some degree of racial prejudice, varying from individual to individual, yet most treated blacks reasonably well.[2]

But racial attitudes alone did not determine how soldiers in Sherman's army treated blacks. There were other factors at work that affected the behavior of the troops toward blacks, in particular the tensions, stresses, hardships, and other experiences of army life.

One influence was the enormous number of blacks and their proximity to the army. An estimated 10,000 slaves followed the army to Savannah, and in the Carolinas another 7,000 reached safety at Fayetteville, North Carolina. Everywhere soldiers went, crowds of ecstatic blacks came out to see and encourage them, whether on the march, foraging, or in camp. With blacks milling about camp constantly, problems were inevitable. A private of the 54th Illinois lashed out at a black who kept insisting that a member of his company had stolen his frying pan by throwing a bayonet at the freedman and yelling, "Leave here you Black Son of a Bitch or I will kill you." This threat and the ensuing fight the private had with his superior officer won him six months at hard labor. In a more tragic instance, Cpl. Robert Rabbitt narrowly escaped a death sentence or life imprisonment when his rifle accidentally discharged, a fairly common occurrence, and killed a youthful black bystander. Only the testimony of witnesses who saw Rabbitt sobbing after the incident and heard him say that it was the "most careless and meanest trick [thing] he had ever done" convinced a court-martial board that the incident was purely unintentional.[3]

A second factor that influenced the way Sherman's men behaved toward blacks was the frustration they experienced during those campaigns. By 1864 practically everyone in Sherman's army had realized that slavery was at the root of the rebellion, and although almost no one supported or would even tolerate the enslavement of blacks in the South, many soldiers felt resentment toward Southern blacks. Several years of absence from loved ones, the death of family and friends, and the hardships borne by the men all came to a head and focused on the blacks. Soldiers reasoned that, were it not for the blacks, they would not have had to make all the sacrifices and suffer all the casualties. Regardless of how strong the commitment of Sherman's men was to the cause, an occasional sense of bitterness during moments of despondency was unavoidable. Most men vented their anger by complaining that blacks should not ride in army wagons or ambulances when troops had to walk or that the army should not permit blacks to ride horses and mules when sick soldiers had to walk, but occasionally a soldier reacted violently. In one instance, a Wisconsin captain witnessed an angry soldier murder a black because the freedman was sleeping by the road while the soldier, sleepy and worn out, had to continue to march. As he shot the innocent black man the soldier shouted, "Take that you d——d Niger and see if you'll sleep again when I have to march."[4]

Still another element that affected soldiers' treatment of blacks was their belief that the government pampered blacks at the expense of the troops in the field. This was especially evident to the members of the Fifteenth and Seventeenth Corps, who passed through Beaufort, South Carolina, although similar complaints came from soldiers in the other corps as well. Beaufort was a coastal island town involved in the Port Royal Experiment, a federal government pilot project to establish a fully functional black community, with emphasis on agriculture, education, and religion. Those soldiers in Sherman's army who passed through Beaufort and endorsed the experiment admitted that it was "a very nice place" or that they had never seen Southern blacks "look so neat and tidy and cheerful." Others thought that it was unfair that the federal government had provided so bountifully for the blacks when it failed to meet the needs of its armies in the field. One soldier wrote of Beaufort to his mother: "there is a great many niggers here, niggers Regiments, nigger schools and churches, the eternal nigger is everywhere and the only place that I care about seeing him is with a musket in his hand." Even a Northern white volunteer working with the blacks in Beaufort sensed how irritated Sherman's troops were over the preferential treatment received by the residents: "Sherman and his men are impatient of the darkies, and annoyed to see them pampered, petted, and spoiled, as they have been here. They hustled them out of the way, and the blacks were rather afraid of them." Nor was it solely the troops who had passed through Beaufort who complained about preferential treatment for blacks. A New Yorker in the Twentieth Corps told his wife after the Carolinas campaign: "I was quite an abulitionist when I came in the army but I have got over it now, for it is first a nigar then mual & then a soldier & the soldier is used worse than any of them."[5]

Without a doubt, though, the mistreatment of blacks stemmed mainly from racial prejudice. As one Ohio captain stated: "The silly prejudice of color is as deeply rooted among northern as among southern men.

Very many of our soldiers have as yet no idea of treating the op-
pressed race with justice." Racial prejudice varied in degrees throughout Sherman's army, from individuals who simply accepted some
Southern stereotypes of blacks, whether for cultural and sociological
or physiological and evolutionary reasons, to those who possessed severe racial biases. Racial comments ranged from absurd yet inane remarks to vicious slurs that insinuated that blacks bordered upon being
a subhuman species. One soldier innocuously contended that alligators "do not like colored people. They will pass by a white man to
catch a colored man—something very strange." Another brutally la-
beled lowland slaves "unmixed descendants of a breed as low in intelligence as can be found." Still a third soldier described a group of blacks
outside Savannah in accordance with the "Great Chain of Human
Color," where whites were at the top of the scale and blacks at the
bottom:

Every shade, every caste, every size; all varieties of form and physiognomy
were there represented—the handsome octoroon, the natural negro, and the
uncouth, animal looking blacks who seem scarcely one removed from the our-
angoutang.

For the most part, prejudiced troops treated blacks reasonably well,
but when one or all of the other three factors—the constant proximity
of blacks, preferential treatment of blacks by the government, or campaign frustrations—began to affect the men and interacted with severe
prejudice, the result was often cases of bitter discrimination and violence.[6]

In some instances these cases of mistreatment were petty, albeit humiliating, such as when a Pennsylvania private found his company
commander's servant asleep next to the fire and "took a hand ful of
flour and rubbed in it his face." At other times extreme prejudice took
the form of legal discrimination. In North Carolina a black man named
John Allen, beaten and bleeding from the head, rushed into camp
begging for help. An officer heard the row and came out of his tent
to investigate the matter. He heard the frantic Allen explain that a
soldier had beaten him and his wife and was attempting to rape his
wife. The officer immediately dispatched some horsemen to the vicinity. A short distance from Allen's home the troops arrested an Illinois

corporal whom Allen recognized as the culprit. At the trial the prosecution could only place the subject in the vicinity of the crime and
needed the testimony of Allen for a conviction. When he introduced
Allen as his next witness, the judge advocate objected, claiming as many
Southern attorneys had done before him that "the witness had not
sufficient intelligence to comprehend the nature of the oath." The panel
of judges concurred without questioning Allen, and the court dismissed all charges against the corporal.[7]

All too often, as in the John Allen case, the mistreatment of blacks
took the form of physical violence as well. Some members of Sherman's army, like Sherman himself, had great difficulty accepting the
concept of blacks in the military. One Hoosier sergeant remarked: "the
Negro Regiments . . . make pretty good looking soldiers but our boys
dont think much of them. They still say this is a white man's war."
Another soldier, an Ohio corporal, recorded in his diary how his comrades reacted to blacks in the service:

some of the boys would make some cute remarks at seeing the negro Ser-
geants & Corporals with their stripes on, one would say look at that darned
nigger he is higher than I am. another Tom salute your superior & c & c.

In Sherman's entire field command there was only one black regiment, the 110th U.S. Colored Infantry, which joined the Army of the
Tennessee at Savannah. But instead of being assigned to a brigade as
general infantrymen, members of this black outfit served inconspi-
cuously as pioneers with picks and axes, hospital guards, and team-
sters, probably to avoid any racial problems that could detract from
the military efficiency of the army. Most racists could tolerate this
limited sort of integration, but when Sherman's army encountered black
citizens and troops at Beaufort who, as a result of their personal
achievements, possessed a sense of accomplishment and a degree of
self-pride beyond that of most freedmen, trouble was inevitable. The
ensuing altercations, "in which the darkeys have always got the worst
of it," according to the testimony of white troops, left two or three
blacks killed and several more blacks wounded. Harassment of blacks
by Sherman's men was so common that officers eventually had to keep
the two groups separated, but not until the black troops "were taught
to know their places & behave civilly," so an Ohioan wrote.[8]

Since black troops had in general very little contact with Sherman's army, they endured only a small percentage of the abuse; instead, it was the black refugees who bore the brunt of the physical violence, often with little provocation. Near Savannah an Indiana sergeant participated in a foraging party that passed through a black community. There several soldiers and blacks had a misunderstanding, and when the expedition left town two blacks lay dead and two others were wounded. On the march in the Carolinas an Illinois private tried to force a black refugee to carry his rifle. After the black man refused, a scuffle erupted as the two wrestled for the weapon. When the private won control of the rifle, he took aim and fired an errant shot at the fleeing freedman.[9]

In several instances soldiers assailed innocent bystanders without any provocation. An Illinois officer reported that one night while he and others stood around campfires, "some scoundrel went up to a negro not 75 yards from us, and with one whack of a bowie knife," killed the man. In Georgia a drunken Irishman from an Ohio regiment while on a foraging expedition got off his horse and deliberately fired into a crowd of black children and seriously wounded one of them, so a fellow soldier testified. The court found him guilty and sentenced him to death, which General Howard commuted to life imprisonment because there was no evidence that the child had died, but the Judge Advocate General's Office released the prisoner and returned him to duty on a technicality. Another soldier, for no apparent reason, simply blasted into a crowd of black women out to greet Sherman's army, the ball passing directly through the chest of one of them. A court then acquitted the man of manslaughter charges, since no one could testify that the woman had died.[10]

Yet these instances of senseless violence directed at blacks were in no way reflective of the general conduct of the troops toward freedmen. The bulk of the men in Sherman's army who bore some sort of prejudice against blacks at the very least tolerated the freedmen and frequently befriended them. Often these were the soldiers who made a snide racial comment one day and the next praised the admirable qualities that individual blacks possessed, without ever having come to grips with the incongruity of their racial arguments. In mid-February an Indiana sergeant commented on lowland slaves by writing:

"The slaves here are more monkey than human. I can't understand half they say." Three weeks earlier blacks had impressed the same sergeant with their tireless efforts to learn to read: "I have noticed that nearly every darky with the army has some kind of a book and put in their leisure hours trying to read." Another soldier who recorded instances that portrayed blacks in an enlightened, charitable manner also made some prejudicial remarks about blacks, such as, "His crude soul was trying to praise God for a joy that he did not know how to express" or "In their deep and childlike gratitude these humble people were proud to offer any service to the soldiers." On the very same page he wrote that slaves left their masters because "their human souls were responding with a higher devotion to the gift of the dearest right of life—a man's right to himself." Both these soldiers, along with many others, had befriended several blacks on the march and had immense respect for blacks who had endured the ordeal of slavery, but neither of them could shake their prewar prejudices.[11]

Other soldiers who seemed to possess some shade of prejudice, however, began to wonder whether the inferiority of blacks was not the product of culture and society, or of opportunity, rather than of evolution. A New Jersey lieutenant, despite his belief that Southern free blacks were not impressive people, compared them favorably with poor Southern whites, while an Illinois soldier compared the differences between Northern and Southern blacks with those of a cultivated gentleman and a circus clown. Thus, at least some soldiers were beginning to allow their experiences, not their predetermined beliefs, guide them in formulating opinions about the black race and were beginning to recognize the critical role of culture and society, as well as of opportunity, in the development of a race.[12]

The soldiers who had only a slight prejudice against blacks, along with the contingent who advocated social and political equality, constituted the vast majority of the army. These were the troops who endorsed the enlistment of blacks and considered them, when properly officered, the equal of any white regiment. "They look like men in any action," commented an officer on the black troops in Beaufort, and an artilleryman at Goldsboro thought blacks in the Tenth Corps "presented a very good appearance." Of course, not all these soldiers would volunteer to serve alongside black troops, but they would comply with such assignments. Some, such as a Wisconsinite who found the black troops at Beaufort impressive, would officer in black units: "if I get a chance to get a commission by going in a Black Regt I am a going."[13]

These were also the men who watched in amazement as thousands of blacks flocked to see and encourage Sherman's army and then joined in the march to freedom despite the threats of their masters and the enormous hardships and sacrifices they endured. Their conduct and their unrelenting desire for freedom were an inspiration for Sherman's troops. A private wrote to his wife, "the poor creturs will stand amoust enney thing for liberty"; and an officer who spoke the sentiments of many others jotted in his journal: "It is claimed the negroes are so well contented with their slavery; if it ever was so, that day has ceased."[14]

In clusters of ten to thirty the slaves gathered roadside to greet the army of salvation. "Oh Lordy Lordy we knowd youuns was coming," cried one woman upon viewing row after row of blue-clad troops, while an antiquated slave urged them: "go on brudders—fight de good fight— we know de Lord am wid you—bress you all." Still another, a young woman, "so white that only the experienced eye could detect the African blood," seized a colonel by the arm and shouted, "Yesterday I was a slave, to day I am free   We are all white now." They followed Sherman's command to freedom, a small army unto themselves. Women packed bundles of clothing on their backs and carried infants in their arms as small children clung to their skirts. Those who had a mule or an ox sewed pouches on a blanket that they threw over the animal's back and loaded with toddlers. Others were fortunate enough to have wagons or plush carriages that they had taken from their masters to transport the young and aged and some essentials. Like the army they pursued, the freedmen quickly learned how to survive on long marches. After a few days blacks had discarded all nonessential items and, as one soldier described, "come down to light marching order, with a few blankets and some cooking utensils." To subsist, black refugees had to forage as the army did, but they almost always got what the soldiers had left behind. "Not with standing," noted an Illinois soldier, "they Keep up as *well as we do*," and that left a marked impression on the minds of Sherman's men.[15]

At times troops witnessed some of the most touching moments of

An extremely rare photograph of black refugees, reportedly in Georgia. (Library of Congress).

their lives. One soldier recalled that some men cried while others laughed to hide the tears when they witnessed a black woman reunite with her lost daughter, who had been sold away ten years earlier. Much more typical was the "sad parting scene" an Illinois private recorded—four women crying on the roadside as a black man named Matt left with the Union Army. In Madison, Georgia, a hardened veteran observed an old black couple departing from a kindly master. Despite urgings by the troops and the owner to remain on the plantation, the elderly pair insisted upon leaving: "We must go, freedom is as sweet to us as it is to you." Finally, in North Carolina a surgeon spoke to an old black man on a horse with two young children who told him they were his grandchildren and all that was left to him and that "he did not mean that they should be slaves all their lives." Such experiences had a profound effect on many soldiers.[16]

At other times the atmosphere along the march, especially in Georgia, resembled a celebration. The utter jubilation with which blacks greeted Sherman's command; the ragtag assemblage of people, animals, and vehicles; and the humorous exchanges between troops and blacks put smiles on the faces of even the most stoic soldiers. In Georgia one large slave woman grabbed a drummer boy and gave him a big hug, howling, "We'uns done heered dis wuz an army ob debils fum hell, but praise de Lawd, praise de Lawd, it's de Lawd's own babes an sucklin's!" All the while the youngster struggled to free himself from her grip as the veterans roared with laughter. In another instance, when members of the 70th Indiana urged a black woman to drop everything and follow them, she rushed into the ranks, teasing them, "Yes Ise gwine but some of you-uns must marry me," to the amusement of the troops.[17]

In camp during the march Sherman's troops found blacks "a new source of almost constant fun," recalled a sergeant, while another soldier noted that "we find them no bad fellows to have a loung [long]." Several attended black church meetings and found them thoroughly refreshing. Other soldiers enjoyed talking to freedmen and hearing of their experiences as slaves. When one private asked a black what he thought of the Confederates, the freedman replied, "Oh, boss, dont you get me a' talkin 'bout dese yere rebels or you will not git to leave heah dis day." The freedman then proceeded to enter into a monologue on the iniquities of slavery. Another soldier recalled the laughs both the troops and blacks had when someone read a Rebel newspaper account of how the Confederates intended to stop Sherman's army and then listened to the blacks describe the hasty evacuation of white families. Still others enjoyed listening to slave music and "hearing some of the most melodious singing that was ever listened to in our land."[18]

Unquestionably the favorite evening pastime for Sherman's men was the plantation dance. For Northern white troops who had never seen a slave dance, it was an awesome spectacle: "It is worth more to see them than all your theatres or circuses, or prayer meetings in the whole North." Interest was so keen in these dances that the 104th Illinois troops built a platform and provided some blacks with a fiddle. That regiment boasted "one old fellow dancing on his head, and keeping time to the music," but a Minnesotan insisted that his brigade had the "Tates Boys that can Beat anything in the Plantation dance."[19]

As to sexual relations between soldiers and black women, there is very little evidence to suggest much contact between them. One soldier indicated that married members of his company had flirted with some black women and hinted that there was some sexual intimacy between them. On the other hand, a reliable diarist bluntly stated: "I here record my opinion that few of our soldiers had connection [sexual intercourse] with blacks, very few."[20]

For the most part, any personalized relationship between soldiers and blacks were with males. Usually soldiers hired black men to perform mess duties or to act as servants, mostly for officers, and during the course of the campaign they became good friends. Often these friendships resembled an older brother–younger brother or teacher-student relationship in which soldiers spent considerable time preparing the blacks for their new lives as freedmen by teaching them how to read and other essentials, such as "the value of money." At least one officer felt such deep affection for his young black servant that, when he resigned his commission and returned home, he brought the lad with him.[21]

No doubt, everyone except the most close-minded soldiers who participated in the Savannah and Carolinas campaigns returned home with an enhanced opinion of Southern blacks. Escaped prisoners of war who had reached Sherman's army told anyone who would listen how blacks risked their lives to protect and assist the men. One former prisoner insisted: "The slaves universally were the prisoners' friends"; another confided to an Ohio chaplain that "though formerly prejudiced against the African, [he] is now enthusiastic in his praises of the down-trodden, but soon to be emancipated slave." Not one soldier, argued an officer, ever claimed that a black hesitated to risk his life for a Union escapee. Foraging parties, too, obtained the assistance of blacks. Freedmen directed soldiers to hidden sources of food, provided directions, helped protect parties stranded overnight, and warned them of Confederate troops nearby. One old black man went so far as to give his shoes to a barefoot forager, telling him, "Soldier, honey, doan't you know dat I'se glad to go barefooted to help you fight de battle of freedom?" Even the psychological impact that blacks had on Southern whites when they abandoned their homes and work and followed Sherman's army by the thousands was a substantial contribution to the war effort.[22]

On sundry occasions the troops defended their sentiments with actions as well as with words. In courts-martial the army never had a problem eliciting testimony from the troops for cases that involved the mistreatment of blacks. Nor did they tolerate some segregationist policies. When the captain of a vessel transporting the 25th Wisconsin to Beaufort ordered a black family to the lower deck, the troops immediately brought them up top again. The captain protested, but as one soldier stated, "the boys told him it was not right and that they were running that boat and so it did the Captain no good to remonstrate."[23]

The sense of outrage was overwhelming when Fourteenth Corps commander Jefferson C. Davis committed the single greatest abuse of blacks during the campaign. On the march between Augusta and Savannah the Fourteenth Corps had to lay down a pontoon to cross Ebenezer Creek. Once the soldiers had crossed the waterway but before the black followers could use it, Davis ordered the pontoon bridge up and simply abandoned hundreds of blacks to Wheeler's cavalry, who were in hot pursuit of the Federals. Unknown numbers of terror-stricken blacks, rather than suffer at the hands of Wheeler's men, tried to swim across the swift stream and drowned. Others, according to Union soldiers, died at the hands of Confederate guerrillas. Of the blacks who reached the opposite bank, some made it on hastily constructed rafts; others swam to safety; and many more crossed on the logs felled by Sherman's troops. Davis later claimed that he needed the pontoon bridge immediately, but his troops knew otherwise. "Let the 'iron pen of history' write the comment on this action of a Union General," wrote an unidentified Illinois officer. Another officer thought that it was "a burning shame and a disgrace, and inhuman to leave them to struggle in thirty feet of water for their lives; for they prefer sinking in the water to returning to slavery." And a Minnesota private wondered: "Where can you find in all the annals of plantation cruelty anything more completely inhuman and fiendish than this?"[24]

Sherman's troops had come a long way in their views on blacks. Soldiers had sampled their culture, primarily music and dance, and their institutions, particularly their churches, and had come away impressed. They had seen blacks performing all sorts of services for the army and had heard others tell how blacks had risked their lives to help them. As one officer argued, "What they have done for the army entitles them to their freedom, or whatever they may desire." They had also found the dedication of blacks to the cause of freedom nothing less than inspiring. By the end of the Carolinas campaign, even though a majority of the troops in Sherman's army still bore some sort of racial prejudice, most soldiers would agree with an officer who wrote: "the more we become acquainted with the negro character, both as men and Christians, the more we are compelled to respect them."[25]

CHAPTER 4

The Army and Southern Whites

"I feel revengeful sometimes as I could be at home enjoying peace and happiness but for the war."
—WILLIAM B. MILLER DIARY,
5 DECEMBER 1864

Just as Sherman's men had to deal with blacks on two levels, on a personal level and on a more general one in which stereotypes and prejudices against the black race played a dominant role, so it was with Southern whites. Members of the invading army had good and bad relationships with individual southerners, but they also saw the Southern people as the sole cause of the war and bitterly resented them for it.

While blacks flocked to Sherman's command in such numbers that they nearly inundated the army, the troops had surprisingly infrequent contact with Southern whites on the march. Virtually all the males of military age were in the service, and many of the people left—the elderly, women, and children—fled before Sherman's army. Thus it was not unusual, particularly in South Carolina where thousands throughout the state evacuated to "safer" areas, for some troops to go several days without seeing any white inhabitants. Only in the larger towns and cities of Georgia and the Carolinas did Sherman's men find

Southern whites in sizable numbers. Yet it did not require much contact with Southern whites for Sherman's troops to recognize the vast divergence in the distribution of wealth and the clear stratification within Southern society. Unlike the North, where people seemed to be neither wealthy nor poor, Sherman's men saw around them a region of economic extremes.[1]

On one hand, there were the so-called aristocrats, apparently both opulent and cultured. Their mansions, acreage, and other possessions impressed the Federals so much that a Connecticut captain commented in his diary: "These old planters were kings in a way, and no wonder they fight well for their institution of slavery." Yet most soldiers who met upper-class southerners disparaged them. One soldier complained that "these so-called South Carolina ladies used worse language and more obscene words . . . than the roughest and most brutal soldier." When a Minnesota private saw wealthy women in Savannah attend church in their silks and finery, it left him with the conviction that "they came out, more to Show them Selves than for the good of there Never dieing Souls. Which Should of been the main object of attending Divine Servis." Probably the most favorable comment on coastal elites came from an Iowan who found "the Ladies (I speak of them becaus we do not see hardly any boddy else but Women in this country) of North & South Carolinies much better educated and more enlightened than they wer in Ala & Georgia, they do not use quite so much tobacco, & c."[2]

Even more distasteful to Sherman's troops were the by-products of this stratified society that the wealthy had developed. The enslavement of anyone was bad enough, but some slaves were as white as most members of the Union Army. This fact, along with the notion that slaves were subject to the sexual whims of their masters, shocked many soldiers and infuriated one sergeant: "It makes one's blood fairly boil to see the different shades on the streets of this city [Savannah]." Soldiers also found the imposed segregation, especially among whites, most irritating. A Wisconsin corporal noticed a sign in the vestibule of a Georgia " 'Patrician' Church" that stated: "Officers are requested to occupy the Middle and front seats. All other persons are invited as cordially to attend and occupy the remaining seats." Although this policy offended officers as well as men, the corporal seems to have gotten the best of the incident when he continued in his diary: "We will accept this as evidence that Soldiers can behave themselves without having officers among them, or, that we shall not be defiled by mixing with them." Very closely associated with segregated institutions such as the church was the prevalent belief in a sort of white slavery in the South, in which the rich prospered both financially and politically at the expense of the poor. "Talk about negro slavery!" howled a member of Sherman's staff, "—if we haven't seen white slaves from Atlanta to Goldsboro, I don't know what the word means." Outside the major towns and cities, Sherman's army found very few families who resembled the middle class in the North and saw even fewer opportunities for economic mobility, particularly through education, for the poor. The extremely lopsided distribution of wealth, the dearth of schools for the poor, and the rigid stratification within Southern society indicated to some of Sherman's men that a handful of wealthy southerners were subjugating the vast majority of the population.[3]

On the other hand, there were the poor, or piney woods folk, of Georgia and the Carolinas. One soldier likened them to the soil in the region, insisting, "The soil is very poor and the inhabitants, if possible, are poorer than the soil." Although they seemed more intelligent than the poor people in other Southern states, Sherman's men nonetheless found them shockingly ignorant. An Illinois officer met a woman in Bentonville, North Carolina, whom he thought was "as intelligent as a door post." A Wisconsinite also agreed that North Carolinians were "very ignorant." When he told some of them he was from Wisconsin, they asked in what state was it: "Sometimes we would tell them Illinois or Iowa, and they would Know no difference." In Georgia a sergeant noted some spellings on the headstones of graves in a rural cemetery, such as "bornd," "dide," and "hoo," and in South Carolina a soldier wrote in his diary with equally poor grammar and spelling, "if one were to talk the english Language they would no more comprehend wat you were saying there if you were talking Latin." Some troops thought the poor whites were no more intelligent than slaves, whereas others believed the slaves had it all over them.[4]

What really puzzled Sherman's men about the poor whites was why they fought in the war. Some soldiers thought the poor cared very little about the war, particularly since they had little at stake, but most men realized that the poor constituted the bulk of the Confederate ranks and "though poor," an Illinois captain wrote, "are all bitter rebels." Since the poor had no real political power and certainly had no financial investments in slavery, the Yankees believed that wealthy southerners had manipulated the poor folk into adopting a cause that was not really their concern. What the Federals failed to understand was that, whether rich or poor, these people were still southerners and possessed many of the same cultural traits as the wealthy class, especially their attitudes toward blacks. The same process that coalesced opinion in the North for the war, a perceived threat to their rights under the Constitution, also took place in the South.[5]

From printed statements made by prominent southerners and articles gleaned in the Southern press, it appeared that the Georgia populace was rising up in defense of its home state and would crush Sherman's army. A Georgia senator announced to his constituents: "You have now the best opportunity ever yet presented to destroy the enemy." Gen. P. G. T. Beauregard called on the people of Georgia to "Arise for the defense of your native soil!" and encouraged them to obstruct all roads and "his [Sherman's] army will soon starve in your midst!" The *Savannah Daily Morning News* told its readers: "We have reason to believe they will be seriously bushwacked, and, we trust, cut to pieces." Other periodicals claimed that Sherman's Army was "scattered and starving" or that Sherman would be lucky to escape Georgia with a corporal's guard—two men. By the time the bluecoats reached South Carolina, the newspapers had toned down their predictions, but the public addresses bore the same excessive optimism.[6]

The Union troops thought that these pronouncements were simply preposterous. At Goldsboro a private wrote his brother, "We used to get rebel papers, and they furnished plenty of laughing material so we did not get the blues." A surgeon outside Savannah penned with a touch of sarcasm: "What bragarts. And if they were not too honorable and chivalrist, I would think they indulged a little in lying." The army instead found a Southern people who admitted, upon seeing the blue columns of Sherman's command, that the Union had whipped the Confederacy. Before the November presidential election a Missouri officer, after extensive conversations with residents of Georgia and northern Alabama, grouped Confederate morale into three categories: (1) those who hoped a Democratic victory at the polls might shift the momentum of the war to the Confederacy's favor; (2) those who saw absolutely no hope of victory and were both sick and disgusted with the war; and, by far the largest group, (3) those who were gloomy about the prospects of a victory, particularly with the exhaustion of many key Confederate resources, yet retained a faint glimmer of hope. Once southerners learned of Lincoln's victory and Sherman began his march, Southern morale degenerated rapidly. With each step Sherman's troops took, Confederate supporters along the course of the march and beyond the reach of the Union invaders lost their enthusiasm for the war. At Covington, a town just east of Atlanta, a Southern physician told a Union officer that the South would surrender if it could obtain terms that would not be humiliating, such as compensated emancipation. By the time Sherman's army arrived at the gates of Savannah, a lieutenant believed that in one respect many Georgians welcomed the Union troops because "they think our coming will end the war." In South Carolina an Ohio private recorded in his diary: "Citizens through here appear very much demoralized and admit they are whipped; say that the 'Yanks' can go where they please, and all their soldiers can do is boast of what they are going to do, etc." Defeat was so imminent that a Wisconsin private even heard some little boys remark, "our men cant whip you-ones."[7]

A handful of citizens, such as the pro-Union residents of Lexington, South Carolina, greeted Sherman's army joyously, but Sherman's men found most inhabitants to be in a state of terror. Rumors of mistreatment by Sherman's troops, whether or not they had any basis, had spread throughout Georgia and the Carolinas and left the people frantic. Soldier after soldier recognized a look of alarm on the faces of southerners in Georgia. "Nearly all of them had the greatest horror of the Yankees," wrote an Iowan to his wife, while a Minnesotan described the citizens as "scared out of their wits by the Yanks." In Savannah a woman told a New Yorker she had heard that Yankees cut off fingers to steal rings and simply tore earrings off women. Other Georgians supposed that Sherman's demons would burn all their homes and commit all sorts of personal outrages.[8]

South Carolinians were particularly susceptible to such tales, for they had good reason to fear Sherman's army, especially after they learned of the fate of Columbia and other towns. One soldier recorded in his diary that South Carolinians "are told such terrible tales of our Brutal deeds they expect to find us devils incarnate." Another soldier discovered a large portion of the townsfolk of Bennettsville, South Carolina, concealed in a swamp to avoid contact with Sherman's fiends. Even the citizens of Beaufort, under Federal occupation since 1861, dreaded the arrival of Sherman's troops.[9]

A handful of Union soldiers actually went out of their way to propagate the myths by telling South Carolina women stories intended to terrorize them. At Barnswell two soldiers told some women that there were no gentlemen in Sherman's army, as convicts released solely to subjugate the South constituted the entire enlisted population. When a woman replied that at least the officers would treat ladies properly, one of the men quickly rebuffed her: "You will find the officers worse than the men." In Columbia a guard informed a group of women that Sherman intended to burn the city to the ground, take all the food, and then unleash his troops on them. This statement "frightened them out of their senses," but one composed woman checked with a senior officer and learned that the story was completely false.[10]

Of course, not all Southern women cowered in the face of Sherman's hordes. Some defiantly displayed their anti-Union sentiments at every opportunity and, at times, without regard to the consequences. In Georgia several women insulted a division commander and his staff officer, apparently without provocation, in "language which no well bred ladies use." Near Winnsboro, South Carolina, a group of women gave their guards such a tongue-lashing for the conduct of their fellow troops that the men left, claiming that the women talked too "damn strong" and did not deserve protection.[11]

Some women even got violent with Federal troops. In Milledgeville, Georgia a woman hurled a large stone out of a second-story window at some troops below. Several days later a woman dressed in silk walked up to the Union columns and spit on a soldier, and the troops retaliated by burning down her house. A South Carolina woman tried to drive away some foragers by throwing scalding water in their faces but instead got a dunking in a barrel of molasses to sweeten her temper.[12]

Many of these women possessed a bitter hatred of Union soldiers that could compare with the sentiments of any male fire-eater. While the Confederate troops shed their prewar contempt for the Yankees on the battlefield, these women had no such opportunity. On the contrary, wartime propaganda at home intensified their burning hatred for the Union Army. One Savannah family found the mere presence of Union troops so intolerable that they could not eat, or even speak to them. A woman in that same city confessed that a Union officer had treated her courteously, yet she described his exit from the house by writing in her diary: "he walked out like a well bred dog." Finally, a North Carolina woman told a soldier that she would not give a cup of water to a dying Yankee. Later, after becoming better acquainted with the man, she admitted, "I would give you a cup of water to soothe your dying agonies, and, as you are a yankee *I wish I had the opportunity to do so.*"[13]

Sherman's troops understood that under similar circumstances some Northern women would act no differently and, therefore, exhibited a surprising degree of tolerance. Most of the time, when a Southern woman berated or threatened them, the men just laughed. As one soldier contended, "had we believed these members of the 'tender sex' it was folly to advance." Sometimes, another soldier wrote, "The boys would stir up the female Rebels, just to hear them talk, like the boys at the menagerie stir up the lions to hear them roar." But, for the most part, the "bitter Secesh" women often conversed quite freely, albeit with shocking candidness, with their hated foe. Possibly this was the reason why a New Jersey lieutenant paid tribute to these Southern women when he wrote: "There is not a particle of the Craven fear in them—determined and resolute no giving in."[14]

In general, Sherman's army treated Southern civilians well. The fact that three prominent Confederates—Lt. Gen. William J. Hardee, Maj. Gen. Gustavus W. Smith, and Col. Edward C. Anderson—left their wives to the care of Sherman's occupation forces in Savannah indicated that the soldiers opposing the march had no reason to doubt that Sherman's men would treat civilians properly. But, just as members of Sherman's army had perpetrated violent crimes against fellow soldiers and blacks, so were there similar offenses committed against Southern whites. In several instances members of Sherman's command hanged southerners to the point of death in an attempt to find where the citizens had hidden their valuables. A Bennettsville, South Carolina, youth fell victim to a soldier's minié ball when he hesitated to show where he had concealed the family's horses and mules. Still another tragedy involved a very recent recruit who, in May 1865, got drunk and attempted to rob a citizen. When the civilian refused to surrender his money, the soldier shot him. A court-martial convicted the cavalryman and sentenced him to execution by firing squad.[15]

As with all other criminal offenses, no one will ever know the actual number of rapes committed by Sherman's troops. The two instances in which the army prosecuted soldiers for assaulting Southern women highlight the power of the pardon and the peculiar sense of justice dispensed by Union courts-martial rather than the behavior of troops. A court convicted a sixteen-year-old Illinois private, John Bass, of attempted rape when he and another soldier had a row with a Georgia woman. At the trial, held shortly after the incident occurred, the woman could not identify Bass and admitted that she had instigated the confrontation when she called him a "Nigger Stealer." She also testified that Bass had never laid a hand on her or even threatened her. The headquarters of Maj. Gen. O. O. Howard rushed the case through trial so quickly that Bass's companion not only failed to testify but did not learn of the trial until afterward. In a sworn affidavit prepared after the trial the eyewitness denied that Bass had drawn a revolver, as the woman asserted. Finally, when Bass's regimental commander, John W. Ingersoll, complained to Howard about the procedures, the general replied, according to Ingersoll's sworn affidavit, "he must make an example of some one and just as well a 48th [Illinois] man as anyone else." The sixteen-year-old Bass had his head shaved and received a dishonorable discharge. In the other case an Ohio sergeant, Arthur McCarty, raped a teenage woman near Bennettsville, South Carolina, at least according to three eyewitnesses from the 10th Illinois. The three Illinois men testified that they witnessed part of the act and saw the victim and her parents frightened and crying. McCarty contended, with the testimony of a friend, that he and his companion had not raped her but had paid the woman for sexual favors. The court found McCarty guilty of rape and sentenced him to a dishonorable discharge and two years in a state prison. The corps commander, Maj.

Gen. Frank P. Blair, then remitted the jail term, and President Andrew Johnson dismissed the entire sentence and restored McCarty to his previous rank and regiment when he received petitions from officers and men attesting to McCarty's soldierly qualities, a letter from a soldier impugning the character of a witness, and a letter from McCarty that substantially contradicted his testimony at the trial.[16]

These sorts of criminal acts, however, were so rare that nearly all the troops who wrote on the unjustified abuse of southerners assumed that it occurred but also confessed that they had never seen such acts. Again, as with mistreatment of blacks, most officers and men alike abhorred this sort of conduct and showed a remarkable willingness to testify against fellow soldiers or prosecute them in a military court. Some officers even issued standing orders to shoot on the spot any soldier found abusing citizens.[17]

Time after time, members of Sherman's army performed acts of kindness for southerners, especially the poor. On numerous occasions soldiers shared their rations with hungry adults and children. In North Carolina, "the Boys [in the 33rd Indiana] give their hard tacks freely" to a poor family begging for food, "so that they soon had a large bundle of bread." Near Atlanta an officer protected an old woman's dairy cow, her only source of food, by hiding the animal in her kitchen and driving away hungry soldiers. The most fantastic incident occurred on Christmas Day when a captain and ninety men loaded several wagons with foodstuffs and carted it outside Savannah to a region that Union and Confederate troops had stripped bare of edibles. The men tied tree branches to the heads of the mules, converted them to "reindeer," and distributed the food to the needy.[18]

Nor were these kindly deeds restricted to the sharing of food. After a Christmas Mass a church held a special collection for the local orphan asylum, and both Union troops and citizens contributed freely, which prompted a soldier to remark, "It did not seem as though we were enemies." On the march to Savannah members of the 21st Michigan found two grimy little girls, abandoned and nearly starved to death. The men fed them, cleaned them up (someone even stole new clothes for them), and when no one could locate the children's parents, the soldiers took turns carrying the girls to Savannah. At the coast a wounded lieutenant took the regiment's sweethearts home to Michigan and adopted them. In North Carolina a little girl rushed out of her house and screamed to members of the 31st Ohio that her home was on fire. Within seconds several companies charged to the dwelling and, after ten minutes of frantic effort, managed to extinguish the blaze.[19]

Although Sherman's men and southerners were enemies in war, that did not stop them from forming intimate relationships with one another. Many of Sherman's troops were eligible bachelors, and since there were very few Southern men outside the Confederate Army, they found in Georgia and the Carolinas a considerable number of unattended and unspoken-for women. Soldiers of every rank commented on the attractiveness of Southern women with such statements as: "some verey nice looking ladies here"; "real smart looking pieces"; and, to the more poetical, "They were a feast to the eyes and refreshing to the soul." Most relationships between "enemies" took time to cultivate, and so quite understandably they developed while the army was in camp. Once both parties got over their initial hesitancy, all sorts of relationships blossomed, from lifelong friendships to marriages. A private wrote his mother about the women in Rome, Georgia: "when we first came they said they wouldent have anything to do with the union soldiers. they have got to liking the yank to well to see them leave." He then went on to say that the ladies thought he was sending the songs they taught him to a girlfriend at home and were very jealous. Another soldier recalled how "Many of the boys were loth to leave Savannah. Some of them had found acquaintances among the Fair sex and some that were not so fair." Even a few married men established intimate relationships with Southern women during camp life. In a classic letter, easily one of the best written by a member of Sherman's army, a semiliterate private named Farnum let his secret slip to his wife:

you sed in one of your last letters to me that I could not write to menny letters but if you knew how I am cutting round a rebe girle I recon you would not want meney more of my letters but I shant say a worde a boute it so you will think I am all rite   Well never minde we are going to leave heare in a few days so I will forget my rebe girle and be as good as ever.[20]

On the march the relationships were much more difficult to nurture, but that did not stop some Federal troops from trying anyway.

Outside Atlanta an Ohio captain met a Miss Glenn, whom he described as "well dressed polite and agreeable . . . Pretty foot and ankle, beautiful complexion." Later that day, he met two daughters of a man named Thomas, "one talkative, rebellious but sensible in every other way, both good looking and one finely developed bust, lucious." He found all three women very impressive, but "I almost lost my heart to Miss Glenn," he confided in his diary. Another soldier met two women in Blackville, South Carolina, who sang and played the piano so well that he penned, "If I had set out with the intention of falling in love with a Southern Lady I think I should have been smitten there." Probably the most startling affair was between an Iowa sergeant and a Miss Mollie Hook of Columbia, South Carolina. Wrote the sergeant to his parents, "I almost fell in love with her and she declared she would marry a Hawk Eye or never marry." He thought Mollie was "a perfect beauty" and considered her an accomplished pianist. He then concluded his discussion of the burgeoning romance between Mollie and him by stating, "If you could of seen us bidding them [the women of the household] farewell. Oh, gosh, but we did have a heavy time. I kissed Mollie over the gate and away I went."[21]

Soldiers may have developed personal relationships with individual southerners, but Sherman's troops also viewed the Southern people in another way, on an abstract level. Sherman's men stripped away the component characteristics of each individual southerner, ignored all positive qualities, and concentrated on one overriding feature—that southerners, at least from a Federal perspective, had caused this war and were fully culpable for all the sacrifices and sufferings Union soldiers had endured throughout the war. The result was that soldiers could feel genuine affection for individual southerners, yet possess such a deep-seated hostility for the Southern people that they could seek vengeance through the destruction of military and nonmilitary property on an unprecedented scale.

Part of the reason for this bitter hatred of the Southern people and the adoption of a policy of destruction by Sherman's troops was that nearly 80 percent of Sherman's army were veterans. During several years of service they had borne physical hardships and witnessed the tragic deaths of thousands of their comrades, sacrificed employment opportunities, and suffered the absence of loved ones as well. It pained them to think that their children had seen their fathers only once during his furlough in the last three years or that their mothers or fathers had breathed their last breath while their son was hundreds of miles away. All these things Sherman's troops endured to preserve the Union against Southern aggressors, but it made them angry nonetheless, as an Indiana sergeant indicated: "I feel revengeful sometimes as I could be at home enjoying peace and happiness but for the war."[22]

Recruits initially had a great deal of difficulty reconciling themselves to such a policy of devastation. They had not endured the endless hardships of army life or the prolonged absence from loved ones as had veterans. But, as the march progressed, as recruits rubbed elbows with the veterans and began to understand the motives of their more experienced comrades, many of them too found ample justification for the destruction.[23]

Also contributing to the bitterness felt by Sherman's army was the horror of the Confederate prison camps they uncovered on the march and the physical condition of exchanged and escaped Union prisoners of war who joined the army before or during the campaign. At Camp Lawton in Millen, Georgia, and Camp Sorghum outside Columbia, South Carolina, substantial portions of the army had an opportunity to examine the burrows that soldiers had dug for shelter, the deadlines beyond which guards shot all prisoners who passed, and the graves that marked the resting place of fallen comrades. Those who saw these camps felt an almost unbridled sense of outrage over the deplorable conditions. "Everyone who visited this place," wrote an officer about the Millen prison, "came away with a feeling of hardness toward the Southern Confederacy he had never felt before," while an Iowan noticed similar sentiments about Camp Sorghum: "The threats of the men as they beheld this scene of suffering cruelty and murder were not loud but deep." Those Union prisoners who joined Sherman's army as exchanged soldiers or escapees were filthy, ragged, and emaciated. They told stories of how prisoners practically starved on meager food rations, when Sherman's men knew all too well that the state of Georgia alone had enormous food supplies. Moreover, former prisoners told of the sufferings they had endured and of the insults and indignities they had borne from the Southern people that, one soldier revealed,

The interior of Millen prison, as sketched by an artist with Sherman's army. The deplorable conditions prompted one soldier to write: "Everyone who visited this place came away with a feeling of hardness toward the Southern Confederacy he had never felt before." The sketch was in the January 7, 1865 issue of *Harper's Weekly*. (Reproduced by permission of the Illinois State Historical Library).

"instilled a hatred into the minds of the soldiers against these old rebels they had never felt before."[24]

For the Southern people Sherman's troops had no sympathy. Their hatred for southerners was so intense and their desire to end the war was so powerful that almost to a man the army felt completely justified in their course of action. "The wealthy people of the South were the very ones to plunge the country into secession—," recorded a chaplain, "now let them suffer." Any compassion these men had felt for southerners had expired by the end of the Atlanta campaign. An Illinois soldier believed that Atlanta "and every other southern city deserve nothing better than general destruction from Yankees" for "Buying and selling their betters." A Massachusetts officer wrote his family on the verge of the Carolina invasion: "Pity for these inhabitants, I have none. In the first place, they are rebels, and I am almost prepared to agree with Sherman that a rebel has no rights, not even the right to live except by our permission." Still another officer, this one from Ohio, felt no remorse about taking women's food and destroying their cotton crops, since it was their "wild enthusiasm" that sent many Confederate men to arms.[25]

Soldiers in Sherman's army firmly believed that a policy of devastation was the best means of terminating the war. "Anything and Everything, if it will help us and weaken them, is my motto," wrote a man from the Badger State to his parents. Just prior to the Savannah campaign a Minnesotan declared in his journal: "Let the Confederates be assured that they must either whip our armies, or be themselves annihilated unless they give up the contest, and many of them will lay down their arms." And another Wisconsinite, a corporal, proposed: "Let them howl and get down on their Bended Knees and Beg Pardon from father Abraham for their past sins."[26]

The army then kept its word and embarked on a policy of destruction more devastating than anyone could have imagined. The Georgians and North Carolinians suffered badly, but nothing like the residents of South Carolina. More than any other southerners, Sherman's troops despised South Carolinians, the people who instigated the secession movement and fired the first shots of this war, and for them the Federals vented full venom. "South Carolina cried out the first for war," an Iowan wrote at Savannah, "and she shall have it to her hearts content. She sowed the Wind. She will soon reap the Whirlwind." An Illinois cavalryman warned his friends at home of the treatment South Carolinians would receive: "One thing certain S Carolina is about to feel the 'Iron Hand of War' placed on her and it will be no gentle manner, all Soldiers know that it was the birth place of Dark Treason and we will make it the death place of some Traitors." Soldiers opposed to wanton destruction now encouraged it wholeheartedly. "I have never burnt a house down yet," a corporal confessed to his sister, "but if we go into South Carolina I will burn som down if I can get the chance"; another soldier bluntly stated: "nearly every man in Shermans army Say they are in for disstroying every thing thing in South Carolina." From privates to generals, Sherman's army wanted revenge on the people of South Carolina. Maj. Gen. Henry Slocum, commander of the Left Wing, opposed the widespread devastation but had to admit: "It would have been a sin to have had the war brought a close without bringing upon the original aggressor some of its pains." A chaplain was even more explicit in his condemnations of the South Carolinians and his satisfaction with the course of action taken by Sherman's men: "The thousands of homes she has filled with mourn-

ing, the unnumbered hearts she has wrung with anguish, are all witnesses of the justice of her punishment. Let her drink the cup she has
brewed, and lie on the bed she has made." Sherman's army knew, as
an Ohio lieutenant indicated, that history might deal with them harshly
for adopting such a policy, but they believed that their motives and
methods were sound.

I suppose; in fact, I know, that the course of this army in South Carolina will
be severely condemned by many in the North. If you hear any condemning
us for what we have done, tell them for me and for Sherman's Army, that
"we found here the authors of all the calamities that have befallen this nation
& the men & women whose hands are red with all the innocent blood that
has been shed in this war, and that their punishment is light when compared
with what justice demanded." [27]

CHAPTER 5

Camp Life

"You can hardly imagine how good it seems
to get back and rest once more."
—F. H. PUTNEY TO FATHER,
14 SEPTEMBER 1864

Both scholars and participants who have written about the Civil War have concentrated their efforts on discussing campaigns, much to the neglect of camp life. In fact, most Civil War soldiers spent considerably more time in camp than fighting their opponents. Even an army such as Sherman's, extremely active in comparison with other Federal commands, remained in camp for five and one-half months during 1864, and the following year two of its corps spent as much time in camp as on the march.

As the troops entered camp after a lengthy campaign, they looked forward to some rest and relaxation. Most soldiers shared good moments campaigning, particularly on the march to Savannah and through the Carolinas, but such active operations took their toll on the men both mentally and physically. Prolonged marches, dragging wagons and animals through deep mud, building bridges across swamps and rivers, and constructing fortifications wore the men out, as did coping with the loss of comrades and the fear of falling victim to a Rebel bullet or shell. The overnight transition from this tense, hectic existence to the sedateness of camp life left quite a mark on the troops. A young Wisconsin lieutenant wrote his father:

You can hardly imagine *how good* it seems to get back and *rest* once more, where we no longer hear the shrill whistle of the "minnie" or the screaming of the "Parrott Shells," to feel when you lie down at night, that you can rest *all night*, . . . in fact to feel that your life no longer hangs by a *thread*.

Men accustomed to the ever present sounds of battle had problems adjusting to the night-long silence of camp life. One soldier outside Savannah insisted that the men got so used to the noise of heavy shelling that "we can hardly sleep if it is still." Another man on guard duty in Atlanta wrote his parents:

around me Everything is quiet and I can hardly think, or collect my thoughts Enough to write a decent letter owing to the Stilness: I do not wish you to think that I prefer confusion to quietness, by any means. No! but it is so novel, and I have been accustomed to confusion for so long a time. I feel the most at home, where there is the most noise, about me.[1]

The first few days of camp life were very enjoyable for the men. The army was in the process of shifting from campaign duties to the routine of camp life, and the demands upon the men were light. Aside from settling a new campsite, fortifying the area, and an occasional stint of guard duty, the troops had ample time to pursue their own interests. Some soldiers spent their free time writing letters home; others utilized their spare moments in a less productive yet no less rewarding fashion, catching up on some sleep.[2]

One of the soldiers' most popular activities was "skirmishing," or ridding themselves and their clothes of infectious lice. These pests plagued everyone from privates to generals, afflicting clean and filthy alike. Even those who adopted a conscientious program of frequent bathing and washing of all their clothes often wound up with lice. As one soldier sadly admitted, "I find some on me in spite of all I can do." During the march troops tried their best to keep free from lice, more commonly called graybacks by the men, but without adequate time to bathe and clean clothing it was a losing battle. Nor was it an easy task to eliminate "those 'friends' which stick closer than a brother" in camp. One private recorded in his journal that "To devise ways and means for his extermination has exhausted the inventive skill of the greatest genius the army has ever produced." For several years soldiers had tried to kill lice by boiling their clothing while they bathed, yet some graybacks managed to survive. By late 1864 veterans had adopted what one soldier called "our most improved method for securing this relief," holding clothes and blankets directly over a hot fire. This gave the fabrics a smoky odor and, especially in the Carolinas where they burned pine, a sooty color, but it seemed to do the trick, at least for a while.[3]

Another elective chore for the men was the construction of living quarters, more familiarly known as shebangs, which were shanties built by an entire mess, usually a group of four soldiers who cooked and ate their meals together, for their personal use. The men erected shebangs with whatever material was available, mostly wood and nails that they stripped from nearby fences and barns. One soldier, however, boasted to his sister that his mess carried boards about a mile and "tore down houses to get them"; another helped dismantle a church to obtain the necessary material, recording in his journal without remorse: "Rank treason had been preached from the pulpit in that church." The shebangs were of simple construction, with heavy wooden posts serving as the frame and lighter wooden boards as the walls. Waterproof shelter tents buttoned together usually provided the roof, although some of the more industrious troops built their roofs out of timber. Naturally, the quality of these shanties depended upon the skills of each mess and the type of material that was accessible. A Connecticut officer had the good fortune of having a carpenter in his company who gladly built him a fine shack to get out of drill duties. Other shebangs certainly were not of that caliber, but soldiers did take considerable pride in their construction.[4]

Troops furnished their shebangs only with the bare essentials. During the warm weather, when these shanties served mainly to shelter the men from rain and the hot afternoon sun, soldiers had little more than a couple of bunks, often made of railroad ties, leaves, straw, and cotton; some stools; and a small table. A summertime luxury might include hooks to hang up rifles and knapsacks. In the wintertime, however, shebangs were slightly different. Since troops spent considerably more time indoors, they built their shebangs with a little more care and designed them for a little more comfort. The major accession

A photograph of a company of troops from the 21st Michigan Infantry in camp. Notice the construction of the shebangs. (National Archives).

in wintertime was a fireplace, which the men constructed from clay and sod or, if available, brick. Once in awhile, some soldiers did even better than that. At Savannah a captain in a New York regiment learned of some box stoves that the Confederates had abandoned and that were under guard. While he occupied the guard in conversation, two of his messmates sneaked up from the rear and carried a stove off to their shebang.[5]

Considering the time and material available to the men, these shanties were a product of remarkable ingenuity. In one day four men with a single small ax could build a shebang that could compare with almost anyplace "where the niggers had lived in days when Old massa was here," so argued an Iowan. Where people at home "would not discover material fit for the meanest hovel," wrote a corporal, "we find that from which we erect shelters which we esteem more than palaces."[6]

Once the army got settled at the new camp, it was back to the old camp life routine. For officers there was plenty of paperwork to occupy them for some time. Campaign reports, muster rolls, payrolls, and a number of other forms and reports demanded immediate attention; and when they finished those chores officers had to supervise drills more vigilantly and, occasionally, attend brigade officers' instruction classes.[7]

Those troops whose division had entered the city first had the privilege of acting as the provost guard. Their duties consisted primarily of patrolling the city; seizing contraband such as cotton, tobacco, and property smuggled into town; examining passes and leaves of absence; and arresting criminals. Beyond the obvious advantage of running the town, these troops had easy access to such coveted items as tobacco and civilian-made cakes and pies, as well as a viable excuse to avoid drilling.[8]

The bulk of the army, however, had no excuses. Sherman's command, especially the Western corps, was notorious for its laxity when it came to drills and dress parades, but the influx of raw recruits at Atlanta necessitated training exercises. In October they received a temporary respite to chase Hood's army through northern Georgia and Alabama and resumed it only sporadically until the army reached Savannah, when it was back to the old routine of squad and company drill in the morning and company drill and parade in the afternoon, often six days per week. Veterans knew how important it was to perform these different maneuvers in battle, and how it fostered unit cohesiveness, but after two or three years in the service drill was a nuisance. A Missouri sergeant spoke for the bulk of the army when he complained that the army's march had halted "and as usual takes up her Old tricks for as soon as the men Stop traveling and marching drills dress parade inspection and reviews must Be going on in dependent of the feelings of the men." Another soldier thought foolery was a proper description of a review, while an Illinois man sarcastically commented in his diary after two consecutive days of inspection: "it seems that we were so attractive that they had to take the second view of us." Occasionally the troops got motivated for a dress parade, such as the time the secretary of war reviewed Sherman's army in Savannah or when a division commander offered to reward the best regiment in each brigade with a thirty-day exemption from another odious chore, picket duty, but these moments were exceedingly rare. Soldiers found such labors so distasteful that one surgeon contended that many of the soldiers who answered to the surgeon's call shammed simply to avoid tedious campground duties.[9]

The respite from campaign duties also enabled the army to assemble courts-martial for offenses allegedly committed on the march. A panel of eight officers, predominantly company commanders appointed by a division commander, heard cases that varied in seriousness from gambling to rape to murder. As in civilian courts, the panel presumed that all defendants were innocent until proven guilty, and all witnesses swore an oath to tell the truth. Another officer, called the judge advocate, served as the prosecutor, and the defendant had the right to an officer or enlisted man as counsel, although nearly all soldiers in Sherman's army defended themselves.[10]

Despite the lack of official military training for the judges, and more than likely the lack of any legal training unless they had held civilian occupations as judges or attorneys, the panels generally seem to have evaluated the evidence justly. The big discrepancies arose when judges meted out sentences. While most soldiers on the march never even went to trial for entering a home, courts usually imposed a sentence of loss of one month's pay upon conviction, but one Ohio private lost four months' pay and had to wear a ball and chain for twenty days. One court sentenced two pillagers to spend the duration of their term of service in the military prison at Dry Tortugas in Florida; several months later a different court sentenced a pillager to a public reprimand and deduction of pay for four months.[11]

To protect the defendant against greater inequities in sentences, the corps and army commander, as well as the president, had the right to remit sentences. In practice, however, this only increased the problem. A court convicted an Illinois private of murdering his friend while intoxicated and sentenced him to life imprisonment. After the private served five months in confinement with the army, Seventeenth Corps commander Frank Blair remitted the sentence and restored him to rank because of the length of time he had been under arrest and his previous good character. Not long before a court had sentenced another Illinois private, a reenlisted veteran, to five years in prison for leaving the picket line on the day of a battle and remaining absent from the unit for one month. In his defense the soldier produced a note from a division hospital surgeon who maintained that the soldier had been in the hospital the entire time. Possibly the soldier had a poor reputation or had forged the note, but no one introduced testimony at the trial to indicate it. The court ordered a five-year prison sentence, and Blair endorsed the penalty.[12]

The least popular duty during camp life was the direct result of a court-martial, that of attending the execution of a soldier convicted of a capital offense. Fortunately, it was an infrequent one. At Goldsboro troops from three divisions of Sherman's army watched as a firing squad executed a member of Schofield's command convicted of raping a middle-aged woman near Kingston, North Carolina. One soldier recorded in his journal that quite a few men sought any excuse to avoid seeing the horrid affair, and others simply failed to respond when the drum beat assembly. Some men deeply resented senior officers who forced them to witness such events, but as one lieutenant admitted that day in his diary, viewing the execution "certainly would have a great tendency towards deterring others from committing a similar crime."[13]

Despite all the grumbling, drills and other camp life duties did not occupy all the troops' time. There was plenty of leisure, and one good way to pass an afternoon or evening was to write letters. Always someone at home merited a letter, and soldiers realized that if they wanted to receive mail they would have to respond at least occasionally. With the minor exception of Fayetteville, North Carolina, where every soldier had an opportunity to send one letter, Sherman's army could neither receive nor send letters while on the march. It was not until the army reestablished communications at Savannah and Goldsboro that the mail routes opened to the Northern states. Thus, if a soldier wanted to write a letter, he had to do it, with a few exceptions, during his days in camp.

Stylistically, the letters the troops wrote varied greatly, yet there was remarkable similarity in their contents. Often a soldier began his letter with some reference to the fact that he was still healthy or "in the land of the living." After queries about various folks at home and possibly about the farm or business, he usually embarked upon a discussion of military affairs and/or some political event about which the army had just heard. Sometimes a soldier had to answer questions that ranged from very sensible to incredibly absurd, yet none could compare to the question posed by the wife of Emory Sweetland, who asked her husband after the Atlanta campaign if she should purchase a cemetery plot! Understandably disconcerted, Sweetland told his wife that he knew nothing of the matter and recommended that she rely on her own judgment. Then, if the soldier was writing to his wife or girlfriend, and sometimes even to family members, he might have to explain again that he wanted to come home to see everyone but that the army would not grant him a furlough or a leave of absence. An Indiana captain probably outlined the government's policy best when he wrote: "A man has to be 9/10 dead himself and then certify all his friends, family & acquaintences are about to breath their last, before a leave is granted him—." Near the end of the letter troops often left room for some teasing or a touch of sarcasm. One soldier, after explaining Sherman's strategy during the Savannah campaign, told his brother, "With all your smartness Alex you are not quite able yet to instruct Genl Sherman in Military Strategy." Another soldier lectured his father in the conclusion of a letter by saying, "when you write again, please write so I can read it. it would take a philadelphia lawyer to read the last one." [14]

Letters written at the end of a campaign differed noticeably from those penned just before the army undertook a new campaign. After a campaign the letters tended to be longer and more informative. Soldiers thoroughly enjoyed discussing details of their military exploits and the march itself, as well as providing the reader with a commentary on the people and places they saw en route. Those letters written before a new campaign were, quite naturally, more speculative, but also more sensitive and reassuring. Soldiers first discussed possible military objectives and campaign preparations; then, after reminding the folks at home that the army planned to rupture communications with the North, the men tried to reassure their loved ones that, in spite of the bad news they might hear, the army would turn up safe and sound. One soldier warned:

You will hear Sherman is cut off; that his army is cut to pieces, demoralized—captured; and many other such tales, started by rebel sympathizers, but wait patiently & see the stait of it, in a letter, dated at Mobile Ala or Savanna Ga Dec ____ 1864. [15]

With the knowledge that Sherman intended to sever communications indefinitely, troops also preferred to tie up any loose ends in their personal lives before they began the march. Edd Weller, a lieutenant in the 107th New York, had always thought it was better not to involve himself with a woman at home while he was in the army, "in case I was killed or crippled for life." But with a prolonged campaign approaching, he decided to take his final opportunity to propose to his girlfriend, Nett: "if you are willing to risk your destiny, fortune, happiness and lifes cares and troubles with me—it shall be my aim through life as always to make our lives ones of happiness and pleassure." About the same time that Weller proposed to Nett, a Wisconsin soldier broke off his engagement. She "delights to go with others" and "has an awful temper," explained Oscar Kimberley to his parents. He then concluded by writing indignantly, "a woman cannot Boss me around."[16]

The real reward in writing letters, however, was receiving mail in return. Without doubt, mail call was the most popular moment of the day, sparking interest in even the most lethargic soldiers. "The eagerness with which men in the field watch for mails from home is quite pathetic," one officer wrote. Another soldier jotted down his feelings in anticipation of some mail: "Expect mail today and then oh! then, we will have a jollification." Yet there was always a sense of suspense, a subtle feeling of apprehension that some great tragedy had befallen their loved ones, as a soldier in a disconsolate mood revealed: "How are you all getting along at home? I am almost afraid to open the next letter for fear that it will contain some sad news. How do I know that you are all now living?"[17]

For most men, mail from home, whether it was a letter or a package or just a note, carried them through the difficult times and made the worst hardships seem a little more tolerable. "Letters are the only links a soldier has to bind him to civilization," an Illinois officer recorded, "and no one but a soldier knows how highly he prizes them." An Indiana corporal thought that "Nothing will make the heart of a soldier glader than to receive some little token from home no difference how small."[18]

Just as receiving mail from home did wonders to restore soldiers' morale, so failing to hear from home had a devastating effect on the men. A resilient, self-assured Michigan officer handled the problem quite well. He simply took out a sheet of paper and penned in a sarcastic vein: "tell me which or when all my correspondents died." Much more representative of soldiers with this problem was a Wisconsin man who experienced a sense of abandonment. After sending several missives over the course of two months and receiving no response, he wrote his father in dismay: "I am in hopes that letters may arrive before we leave this post. They are the connecting link between the Army and civilization; the 'golden chain' which binds us to home. Do not let it be broken!"[19]

When mail did arrive, particularly the first mail call since the army embarked on its most recent campaign, Sherman's entire command rejoiced. A Minnesotan announced to his company: "I can live a month now without eating; I have got five letters from my dear wife"; a Wisconsin officer thought mail was the best antidote for his company on light rations: "the boys all feel as well if not better than if they had got there Hard Tack." Mail was such a precious commodity that when a rumor spread through camp that some Confederate cavalry under Maj. Gen. Joseph Wheeler burned the incoming mail cars, Sherman's entire army unleashed such anger and abuse that one soldier claimed: "if the one hundredth part of the maledictions invoked upon him [Wheeler] should come to pass, he would be the worst afflicted mortal upon the face of the globe or under it." That night, much to the delight of the bluecoats, the mail trains reached Atlanta safely.[20]

Another popular activity for the men was taking a sightseeing tour of the nearby city. Most of Sherman's men came from agrarian or small-town backgrounds, particularly from the Old Northwest, and found it a real treat to visit a city, especially one in the South. The fact that only a small percentage of the army entered places such as Atlanta, Savannah, and Raleigh as occupation forces while the vast majority of the Union troops camped in areas designated by corps and division commanders outside the city only whetted their desire to explore the new surroundings. But once the provost marshal accumulated all the munitions and contraband and organized the provost guards, then soldiers could obtain passes to visit the city and satisfy their curiosity.

Soldiers flocked into the city, perusing with a critical eye the buildings, parks, monuments, cemeteries, and homes and reporting to the folks up north everything they saw. Raleigh, the capital of North Carolina, was a disappointment, partly because the troops concerned themselves more with the peace negotiations and partly because of the city itself. The most interesting thing about Raleigh was a lunatic asylum, which featured an inmate who claimed to be a New Yorker whose pro-Southern father committed him for trying to enlist in the Union Army. His plight soon became a cause célèbre with the Federals and eventually led to his release, although one soldier disapproved: "he had that wild look in the eye that is so common among some kinds of crazy people."[21]

Atlanta, in spite of the scars of a two-month siege, was considerably more popular then Raleigh. By 1864 it was a major industrial and rail center and one of the most enterprising cities in the South. When Sherman's army occupied Atlanta in September, it was in shambles, with shell marks riddling brick and stone walls and giant gopherholes used as bombproofs outside nearly every home. Yet Sherman's men gazed admiringly beyond the destruction to what the city had been like several months before. The handsome brick houses and buildings and the attractive countryside were alluring even to Yankees, as one admitted: "If I ever return to the South after the war I will pitch my tent in Atlanta."[22]

Unquestionably the most impressive of all cities was Savannah. To the east was the Atlantic Ocean, providing many of the Western troops with their first glimpse of the sea. Some Western boys spent an entire day sitting on the docks in wonderment observing the waves and oceangoing vessels. Others found the swamps that surrounded Savannah on the other sides intriguing, with their peculiar animals and tree bows draped with Spanish moss.[23]

Savannah was an old, established city with a heritage all its own. As in European cities, there were expansive parks and narrow, paved streets. "The residences," noted an officer, "are more like those of New York than are the houses anywhere else I have seen south." And for an army infatuated with the American Revolution, there were remnants of the earthworks from the siege of 1779 and statues to commemorate the deeds of two of America's great military men: Count Casimir Pulaski, who gave his life in the Savannah siege, and Nathanael Greene, the hero of the war in the South. Savannah, then, was large enough to satisfy the demands of the most avid sightseer yet the sort of city where a soldier could walk alone and lose himself for a few hours.[24]

Savannah offered Sherman's men still another advantage over Atlanta and Raleigh—the ability to supplement their diet of rations with spices, cakes, and other edibles. While on the march troops generally ate well, taking "the best that the country affords," but in camp, as one soldier complained, "we have to use dry rations which don't agree with me." At inland cities such as Atlanta and Raleigh the Union troops had difficulty obtaining butter, spices, and cakes to offset the blandness of everyday rations. In Savannah, however, the situation was considerably different. Despite the blockade, ships carrying spices and other foodstuffs still managed to provide for the people in Savannah, and once the city fell to Sherman's command Federal merchant vessels began to service the area. Prices were exorbitant, but for Union soldiers with money in their pockets these potables were irresistible.[25]

In addition, the Georgia coast provided Sherman's troops with a saltwater delicacy, oysters. Soon after arriving at the coast, easterners and westerners alike feasted on "Oyster stew Oyster pie Oyster Soupe and Oyster's fried." For many of Sherman's men, particularly the westerners, this was their first opportunity to sample these delightful little shellfish. A Missourian who tasted oysters for the first time pronounced them "firstrate," yet many Western boys seem to have had experiences comparable with one of Nelson Stauffer's, a veteran private of the 63rd Illinois. In late December, Stauffer found himself quartered in a house with nothing to eat except raw oysters and so decided to give them a try. After opening his first shellfish and looking at it awhile, a feeling of reluctance overcame him and he threw it away. Later in the day, however, when hunger pangs grew intolerable, Stauffer shelled a second oyster and again hesitated, but this time his messmates began to tease him over his cowardice. Mustering all his courage, Stauffer closed his eyes and popped one into his mouth, until suddenly "A strange feeling came up in my throat and pushed it out." The oyster itself, however, did not taste badly, and in a few moments Stauffer gave another one a try. This time the oyster went down, although "it was some time before I was right sure it was going to stay." Within an hour Stauffer had eaten his fill of oysters and felt fine—"But I always took them with closed eyes," he confessed.[26]

Camping around cities exposed the men to an interesting dichotomy of vices and virtues. Not only did it provide the troops with easy access to alcohol and prostitution as well as to churches and spiritual meetings, but it made the contrast between the best and worst habits, between religion and immorality, clearly visible.

Listening to the moralists, it would appear that their fellow soldiers were on the verge of reverting to heathenism and barbarianism. A recruit found gambling so rampant that he wrote his wife: "the more wee see the more wee are convinced that this war is the most damnable curse that ever was brung upon the human family." An Iowa sergeant felt that the drinking habits of younger soldiers were "too disgraceful for a native Hottentot" and found the general behavior of the men so bad that he grumbled: "I see enough every day to almost make one curse the race to which he belongs." Finally, a hospital steward lectured his wife on the sexual conduct of both southerners and his Northern comrades:

The lower class (both black & white in the south) seem to be totally ignorant of the meaning of the word "Virtue" & both officers & men appear to have cast off all the restraints of home & indulge their passions to the fullest extent.

Then, after discussing the use of alcohol and tobacco by the men, he concluded by saying, "it is sad to think of some many fine brave young men being ruined for life."[27]

Yet this was the same army that packed church houses of nearly every denomination and organized prayer meetings and Christian associations to which masses of soldiers flocked. An Iowan attended a Baptist service in Savannah and estimated there were 1,000 other attentive soldiers present. At Atlanta a chaplain in the 69th Ohio held nightly services for seven consecutive weeks, attended predominantly by soldiers, which prompted a churchgoer to remark, "there has been decided religious interest manifested." Members of the 4th Minnesota joined together to form the 4th Regiment Christian Association and held regular prayer sessions, and the First Brigade, Third Division, Twentieth Corps, held protracted meetings at Goldsboro and Raleigh in the old campground spirit under the guidance of three chaplains.[28]

The most impressive of all organizations was the Christian Association of the Second Brigade, Third Division, Twentieth Corps. It began at Purysburg, South Carolina, in late January when the 33rd Indiana reestablished its Christian society and invited individuals from other regiments in the brigade to participate. During the march through the Carolinas the group held meetings whenever it could, but it was not until the army arrived at Goldsboro that the religious organization and movement caught fire. Over the course of three weeks the association expanded from 50 original members to 321, plus several hundred nonmembers in attendance nightly. Despite the construction of a large, outdoor meeting place with log benches, a pulpit, and an altar, hundreds had to stand in the rear to attend the nondenominational sessions. Here dozens converted to Christianity, and hundreds more renewed their religious commitment as the spirit soon caught hold in other units throughout Sherman's army. By the first week of April a member of the association told his brother, "this great work is not only Confined to our Brig alone, but it is in every brig, Division, and Corps."[29]

With religious fervor on the rise in Sherman's army, those incidents of moral lapses seem to have grown out of proportion. A member of the 8th Indiana Cavalry may have been correct when he complained that married members of his company had "undue communication with negro wenches down here" in Savannah, but the only statistics that shed any light on the sexual promiscuity of the men, the frequency of venereal disease, indicate a surprisingly restrained command. During the months from November 1864 to April 1865, Sherman's army averaged only 15 cases of venereal disease per 10,000 men monthly, while during the same period the Army of the Potomac reported twice as many cases per 10,000 men and the entire Union Army, excluding Sherman's troops, had proportionally four times as many sufferers. Part of the credit belongs with the senior officers, who placed sentinels at the doors of prostitution houses "to keep them Straight," yet most of the success rests with the troops themselves. As a Michigan private wrote to his wife, he considered himself "as great a lover of the fair sex as most men," but because "I left a virtuous wife at home, I have tride to respect that virtue." He then concluded by stating: "I should not want to look my wife in the face" if he had cheated and "she had lived as she ought."[30]

Gambling and alcohol consumption were much more common in Sherman's army, but in an occupation where there is such a peculiar blend of high risk and unrelenting tedium and where money can buy very little except alcoholic beverages, such vices will almost inevitably

flourish. Those who gambled knew it was illegal and, if caught, usually forfeited one month's pay and performed some extra duty. On
one occasion a provost marshal broke up a dice game called chuck-a-
luck and mailed the money with an explanatory letter to the arrested
soldiers' fathers. As one officer commented, "This was deemed a sufficient punishment and would indeed be severe to a man with self-
respect." Most incidents of drunkenness, and most complaints by other
soldiers, tended to be on holidays such as Christmas and New Year's.
One sergeant disapproved of the whiskey rations on Christmas, stating: "I think this is worse than useless for there are too many of the
soldiers get to like it and drink too much whenevery they can get hold
of it." Another soldier, a private in the Fifteenth Corps, wrote his
mother on the third of January: "new years was a high day with the
20*th* Corps. they tore up the old buildings & had lots of whiskeys and
wines I guess by the aperances of the men they havent got sobered of
yet." The result of these drunken episodes was the assumption by tee-
totalers that "The popularity of drinking is I fear, on the increase in
the army." In actuality, there is no evidence to justify such statements. The policy in Sherman's army toward those who drank while
off duty seems to have been fairly lenient, but for those such as a
Pennsylvania officer who overimbibed and went on a brawling ram-
page through the streets of Savannah, punishment was swift and severe.[31]

As for tobacco, while some zealots may have criticized others for
smoking or chewing the weed, its usage was widespread in the army,
from its commander down to the privates. Many had tried tobacco
before the war, and certainly others adopted it simply because tobacco
was a standard issue whenever available. For others, tobacco helped
them relax or cope with everyday life in the army, as an Illinois soldier candidly explained to his sister: "The way I comensed using it, I
use to get lonesom that I did not know what to do with myself. I took
up chewing." Its popularity was so great and the army's dependency
on it so strong that a Wisconsinite once remarked: "The average soldier can bear cold, heat, hunger, thirst, forced marches and loss of
sleep with comparative cheerfulness; but when he is out of tobacco he
is as 'cross as a bear.' "[32]

If there was one vice in Sherman's army that was more prevalent than all others, it was swearing. An Ohio recruit complained in his diary: "Around me is the gibber of reckless men & I am compelled to Listen day and night to their profanity, filthy talk and vulgar songs. I have some conception how Lot felt in Sodom when he had to listen to and be cursed by the filthy conversation of the wicked." Another soldier near Atlanta told his girlfriend: "Thair is somb pretty wicked boys in our Regerment   I just hurd one swaring anaugh to make ones hart ache   I wish that they could see the folley of it." Profanity reached such proportions in the Carolinas that Maj. Gen. O. O. Howard issued a general field order to call to the attention of officers and soldiers "the gross and criminal practice of profane swearing which prevails and is increasing amongst us", and the *Veteran Banner*, newspaper of the 20th Ohio, had a three-page editorial at Goldsboro on the subject. Nor was this a problem solely of the enlisted men. Many soldiers found swearing by officers, particularly generals, extremely distasteful, both because of the language itself and because of the example it set for others.[33]

A soldier's girlfriend once asked him how he got along spiritually. The man responded by writing to her: "I must say that I doe not live faithful as I ought to. . . . You can not Imagine the temptations that beset a Soldier on every hand." By removing men from their family and friends and placing them in an environment where they had to endure tragedy and intense pressure on one hand and boredom and homesickness on the other, it was inevitable that everyone would falter at times, some more than others. Judson Bishop, a perceptive lieutenant colonel of the 2nd Minnesota, recognized the hazards of soldiering and refused to hire a Methodist minister as regimental chaplain until the man had spent three months performing all the same duties as the troops and had observed at first hand the motivations and temptations that affected the men. Then, if "his christian character suffers no damage," Bishop intended to hire him.[34]

Most men, however, seem to have handled the pressures and temptations quite well. A soldier might grumble that "while preeching is going on some of the boys is pleighing cards some talking and laughing," yet he ignored the fact that many others attended the mid-January outdoor service. Another soldier might complain of his companions, "there is the least religion among them than any Reg't I know of" and in the same paragraph admit to his parents, "the Boys are good, honest, intelligent sett of men, some exceptions of course; full of fun & frolic; will share their last biscuit." Sherman's command was no more nor less amoral than a similarly selected group of young adult males. Like society in general, the army had its share of thieves, rogues, and even murderers, as well as men who would do credit to any community in the land. The vast majority of the men were good, decent people before, during, and after the war, citizens who made mistakes but lived for the most part within the bounds of the law and society's code of morality.[35]

Despite the offerings of such places as Atlanta, Savannah, and Raleigh, recreational activities did not revolve solely around the cities. Quite the contrary, once soldiers had seen the sights they spent far more of their free time participating in various sporting events or simply amusing themselves around camp.

Water activities, particularly around Savannah but also at Goldsboro, were a popular pastime with the men. Although the ocean and the sound were too cold for swimming, saltwater enthusiasts could take up sailing or oyster fishing near Savannah. Unfortunately, a number of Union troops learned the hard way that the ocean could be extremely dangerous. Two members of the 100th Indiana lost their lives and others narrowly escaped when the tide came in and capsized their small boats, which were loaded with oysters. A Minnesota sergeant and some friends also tried their luck at oyster fishing and got stranded in the mud and reeds when the tide went out to sea. Undaunted, they arose the next day at 2:00 A.M. to try their hand again, and this time caught thirty bushels of oysters, but when their boat nearly capsized the men concluded: "we had enough of Oyster fishing." Others took to the fresh water, mainly hunting alligators and snakes. A member of the 75th Indiana reported wild times in his regiment when "Some of the boys caught an alligator and brought him into camp." Another Hoosier boasted of shooting a seven-foot alligator, which earned him laurels from the local citizenry as a crack shot. Still a third man in blue, after informing his wife that he had seen just one rattlesnake and a baby alligator, summarized his experiences in the Georgia swamps by stating emphatically: "Those are all the varmints I have seen here except Secesh."[36]

For landlubbers and soldiers with an aversion to bogs, there were sundry activities open to them too. Horseracing was a premier sport for participants and spectators alike, at times attracting over 1,000 soldiers. No less competitive, yet somewhat less thrilling, was pitching quoits, or horseshoes, a very popular game around camp. To occupy their time, a sergeant wrote to his sister, members of the 1st Minnesota Light Battery at Atlanta made rings from old shells, "drew a little, tell stories a little, [and] visit with the 20th Corps fellows a little (very little though for we cant stand their continual bragging about the Army of the Potomac to which they used to belong)." And, for the more studious types, there were newspapers, magazines, and books available in camp to wile away the hours.[37]

Even at night there were usually a few different activities for Sherman's men. The more athletically inclined might participate in an occasional dance or ball; culturally or intellectually oriented troops could see plays performed by fellow soldiers, sit around and listen to a regimental band, or attend lyceums that offered such topics of debate as "is capital punishment right" and "excellency of human character depends more on natural ability than on Education."[38]

When everything else failed to amuse a soldier, there was always something going on around a campfire. Soldiers, especially in the wintertime, loved to crowd around the campfire and to tell tall tales or poke fun at one another. It was here that soldiers held lively political discussions and pondered the upcoming campaign, roughhoused, and conspired to play tricks on some friend. And it was also here that the men talked about their families and friends and their future plans when the war ended.[39]

Some troops enjoyed camp life and hoped that they could sit out the rest of the war in a cozy place such as Atlanta or the Savannah area. There was ample free time to pursue personal interests, and the work, although tedious, was not very demanding and was certainly less hazardous than campaigning. Yet many others found camp life, after two or three weeks, monotonous at best. One soldier recalled that nothing pleased a soldier more than "change spiced with adventure." "Give me campaigning," wrote another soldier in his diary, "where there is something new and exciting all the time; fighting, marching, and building breastworks, is preferable to this." More important, troops at this stage of the war had begun to realize that "staying in camp will never bring us home again so the quicker we are on the move again the better."[40]

CHAPTER 6

The March

"Mother, you will soon begin to think we Shermanites are a migratory race of people, as we are almost continually on the move."
—BURKE WYLIE TO MOTHER, 14 JANUARY 1865

Sherman's Savannah and Carolinas campaigns were very different from any other campaign in the war. For one thing, success did not depend upon victory in combat; for another, the enemy was not just the Confederate Army. Sherman's objective was to demonstrate to the Southern people that the Confederate armies were no longer capable of protecting its citizens and that life outside the Union was much worse than life within the Union. The march itself, then, determined the success of the campaign, and its primary enemies were the mud and hunger rather than the Confederate troops.

Several days after Sherman had manuevered Hood out of Atlanta, a Union soldier wrote his wife, "I will tell you it is sometimes much easier to fight with the legs and feet than with muskets & cannon." Little did he know that in two months Sherman's army would embark upon the first of two campaigns in which successful operations depended even more on marching than during the bloody struggle for Atlanta.[1]

By late October it was evident to the troops that a major campaign was upon them. Sherman had sent his men into northern Georgia and Alabama to drive Hood's army off the railroad from Chattanooga to

Atlanta earlier that month, although a number of Federals felt at the time it was a halfhearted effort, and the Federal commander was now slowly drawing a large portion of his great Army of the West back toward Atlanta. Trains loaded with sick and wounded, along with much of the army's artillery, headed north while carloads of ammunition, hardtack, coffee, sugar, and pork came back in return. Soldiers with orders to strip down to campaign condition boxed all their extra clothing for storage at Chattanooga and received any winter clothing they might have. Men on horseback galloped here and there, night and day, as mules jerked wagons in every direction, which convinced an observer that all this was "such mad confusion." At Savannah, three months later, when the army prepared to march there was much less fanfare, but it was nonetheless hectic. An officer in the Fifteenth Corps recorded in his diary: "at 4 this P.M. we got orders to march at 8 in the morning. Consequently all the camp is excitement. So we are again about starting another great campaign. All is bustle and confusion— Troops going & coming little aware of what awaits them on the campaign." Many of the troops regretted leaving Savannah, but at least they knew that the next campaign would take them through South Carolina, the state that founded secession. Back in November soldiers had felt little remorse over leaving Atlanta; their main problem was trying to figure out where "Uncle Billy" was leading them. As a Minnesotan wrote on the ides of November, "This march is a conundrum for the boys and more guessing and betting going on than we ever had before."[2]

In an effort to ensure a rapid march, Sherman imposed rigid restrictions on the size of the wagon trains and the items the army could take with it. He ordered four teams of horses to each piece of field artillery instead of the standard three, which meant that artillery privates had to carry their own packs, as did the infantry. He prohibited everyone from taking along wall tents except brigade, division, corps, and army commanders, who had to perform essential paperwork, and punishment was swift and severe for all violators. Even as the march progressed, Sherman did not hesitate to order Maj. Gen. Jefferson Davis to double up his horses and burn part of his corps' wagon train to speed up Davis's column.[3]

The items that soldiers took with them on the march varied, depending upon how much each soldier was willing to carry. Since the object was to bring along only necessary items, the more experienced campaigners were at an obvious advantage. They knew exactly what to take and what to leave behind, whereas the recruits tended to over-pack and unnecessarily burden themselves. Each infantryman carried a musket and a bayonet and eighty rounds of ammunition, forty in their cartridge boxes and forty in their pockets; whatever else they carried was personal. Most veterans shouldered a haversack that held food; a canteen; a tin cup or can and a mess knife; a rubber blanket that served as a poncho; and either a canvas fly tent or a woolen blanket. Sometimes they might bring an extra pair of socks or a spare shirt, especially if they had a knapsack, but many soldiers had discarded their knapsacks and extra undergarments long ago. For the most part, only recruits brought overcoats along, and in the warm November days in Georgia many quickly unloaded them. Nearly all soldiers kept some paper and a pencil or pen and ink, and many also had a deck of cards on their person.[4]

Occasionally a mess had to carry a frying pan, which one member affixed to the middle of his musket, although usually each company had a mule to haul the pots, pans, and coffee pots. As troops began to capture a large number of mules, a mess might have its own mule and hire a freedman to cook and take care of the animal. Unfortunately, the quartermasters confiscated extra mules and horses at selected river crossings, which meant that the mess would either have to abandon some nonessentials it had accumulated on the march, since the company mule toted only mess kits, or get another mule immediately.[5]

The amount of food troops kept in their haversacks also varied. Because the men found such a superabundance of food during the first three weeks of the Savannah campaign, they carried little more than some coffee, sugar, a few hardtacks, and some salt. The rest they could obtain easily from the roadside. In the Carolinas, however, forage was more difficult to find, and troops might have to carry as much as seven days' rations at one time, about eight pounds more weight.[6]

The day began with reveille that, depending upon the order of march within the corps, sounded anywhere between 4:00 A.M. and 6:00 A.M. This gave the troops enough time to make some coffee, gobble down a quick breakfast, and gather everything together before assembly call. At assembly the adjutant read marching instructions and any other orders to the troops. They then had a few minutes to get in line for the day's march.[7]

Marching order varied every day, with regiments rotating positions in the brigade, brigades rotating in divisions, and divisions rotating within the corps. The lead brigade in each corps sent out flankers on its wings to touch with the next corps, usually marching on a parallel road, or to protect the exposed flank of the corps. To avoid one enormous line of wagons that were cumbersome and difficult to protect, Sherman ordered each division to care for its own train, but it was usually the brigade level that handled supply, ambulance, and ammunition wagons.[8]

For the troops the march was very systematic. They frequently walked four abreast, sometimes on the road and sometimes alongside it, with the troops selecting the length of the step and on which shoulder they preferred to carry their rifle. The standard pattern was to march for fifty minutes, then rest ten minutes. At noon the column halted for forty minutes to an hour to enable the men to cook dinner. Each messmate had a specific job (e.g., start the fire, fetch some water, cook the meal, clean the mess kit afterward), so that in no time the men had a meal of coffee, meat, and potatoes or bread ready. After dinner there was usually enough time for a leisurely smoke or a wash before the afternoon march.[9]

Troops much preferred to march at the head of the column than at the rear. Units in the front might get stuck with skirmish-line work or picket and guard duty at night, but they had the best opportunity to keep their haversacks filled and to settle into camp before anyone else. The worst position was the rear, mainly because they got stuck with train-guard duty that, as a captain described it, was the "Abomination of abominations." Brigade, division, and corps commanders located their wagons three-fourths of the way back in the unit, which placed an enormous burden on the troops in the rear. All day long they marched in "jerks," as wagons broke down or got stuck in the mud. Meanwhile, the column gradually extended, sometimes to as much as fifteen miles between a corps' skirmishers and the rear guard. The end result was not only that train guards had to protect the wagons and pull them through the mud but that they found the roadsides stripped of forage by the soldiers farther up on the line and frequently went into camp at 10:00 P.M. or 11:00 P.M. and occasionally after midnight.[10]

Once in camp for the evening, messes divided chores, as they had done at noontime. One man would cut the tent poles; another would start the fire and cook supper; a third would locate water and bring a bucketful back, a particularly difficult chore after dark; and the fourth member of the mess would gather straw for bedding. Meals, even on the march to Savannah, were plain. Coffee was the universal beverage that, an Ohioan claimed, was "almost a necessity to campaigning." The men simply dropped some beans in water and brought it to a boil. It was a common practice to reuse the coffee beans until constant usage had sapped them of all flavor. When coffee ran out, soldiers made a substitute from wheat that, according to a cavalryman, "answered very well." Probably the single greatest advantage the march offered to Sherman's men was the opportunity to eat a variety of fresh meats. Beef, pork, chicken, and, less frequently, turkey were available to the men, which they cooked either on the end of a stick or in a frying pan. Served alongside some fresh roasted sweet potatoes or ears of corn and either flour pancakes or cornmeal hoecakes, this plate was a culinary delight for the troops.[11]

Of course, there was not always a variety or abundance of food. In the areas around Savannah and in the northern portion of South Carolina and southern North Carolina foragers brought very little back to camp. Around Savannah a few regiments occupied positions in the line near the sea and were fortunate enough to supplement their diet with shellfish, but most lived almost solely on rice or parched corn. Despite an occasional complaint, most soldiers seemed to accept the rations cutback rather well, as evidenced by an Iowan who wrote to his cousin:

To day they issued 3 ears of Corn a piece. I am getting to look quite mulish, my ears ar getting very long; packing us & feeding us on Mule rations fetches them out wonderfully. I think in a few days I can put to shame (in the way of ears) any thing of the mule kind.

In South Carolina an Illinois man recorded some sarcastic comments in his diary on the meager rations he received: "Nothing for the stomach except meat and coffee. think in a few days we can do without the meat. then gradually we hope to weaken the coffee down to clear water. then if we can live, we shall have learned the art of cheap living."[12]

After supper there was always time for a smoke and a little recreation. Games of chance, such as chuck-a-luck or cards, were popular. In the Twentieth Corps the craze was cockfighting. The troops pitted roosters taken on the march that day against one another. The victorious cocks earned nicknames such as "Billy Sherman," "Johnny Logan," or "Pap Williams," and losers went into the cook's fire. If some troops felt energetic they might hold a dance, often called a shindig, while those who preferred a more quiet evening could read or update their diaries, as long as the rich black smoke from the Carolina pine knots did not drive them away from the campfire light. When nothing else interested a soldier, there was always something lively going on around a campfire. Here men gabbed about the day's adventures, politics, the future, and life back home until they retired.[13]

The common practice was for soldiers to bed in pairs. Both men had a six-foot-square canvas fly tent that they buttoned together for shelter from rain, frost, or snow. On the ground they piled straw or pine needles and placed their rubber blanket on top to form a mattress. When it rained, troops substituted wood about six inches thick for the straw; though less comfortable, it was much drier. If the soldier had a woolen blanket, he naturally used that as a cover, and those with knapsacks converted them to pillows, but many troops had neither. At one end of the fly tent soldiers maintained a campfire, and at the other they draped a cloth to keep out mosquitoes and other insects. In case of an emergency most men slept with all their clothes on, and if they had tramped through swamps or creeks that day they also wore their shoes to prevent them from shrinking overnight.[14]

Most members of Sherman's army would have agreed with an Illinois lieutenant who described the march to Savannah as a "pleasure trip" in comparison with the grueling Carolinas campaign, but there were some difficult moments near the coast during the Savannah campaign, just as there were thoroughly enjoyable times in the Carolinas. In reality, both marches were a peculiar blend of excitement and fun with hardships and hazards, as a Michigan officer at Goldsboro tried to explain to his mother: "There are some pleasant things connected with the hardships of a campaign like that from Savannah, a soldiers life being as changeable as the weather in April."[15]

Certainly one aspect of the march that lifted the spirits of the troops and helped them forget, at least momentarily, the arduous duties of campaigning was the opportunity to see some sights. As a corporal wrote home from the outskirts of Savannah, "father I have seen some country that Places Illinois in *Oblivion* as far as Beauty is concerned." It thrilled the troops to think that the army "passed through a country never poluted by the foot of a 'yankee,' " a region that had never felt the effects of war. They saw the wild grasses east of Atlanta, which reminded Midwestern boys of home, and the beautiful towns of Madison and Covington. Milledgeville, the capital of Georgia, was a complete bust. Probably the nicest comment about the city came from a Michigan sergeant who called it "a sort of one horse town." To the east of the capital, sandy soil and tall pine trees replaced the red Georgia clay. As the army neared Savannah, pine forests gave way to pine swamps, suitable for growing rice and "nothing else unless to raise Aligators." One cavalryman who tried to describe the region to his wife wrote: "If you want an Idea of the face of this country just think of the swampiest country you ever seen, and then imagine one a hundred times swampier, and you have it." Nonetheless, Sherman's troops appreciated the haunting beauty of the Georgia–South Carolina cypress swamplands. In the Carolinas they found themselves either wading through "Frog Heaven," a nickname soldiers coined for bogs, or tramping over highlands of dense pine, passing through some impoverished towns and attractive cities like Columbia en route.[16]

The excursion through Georgia and the Carolinas also enabled Sherman's troops to examine enough of Southern agriculture to provide some expert criticism of their methods and equipment. A Minnesotan declared that "Cotton and slavery have ruined the soil as they are now trying to ruining the country." An Illinois soldier took none other than the eminent Georgian Howell Cobb to task for the ill-shaped fields, inadequate fences and poor planning on his plantation. The huge, antiquated hoes that South Carolina slaves used, solely because they were difficult to break, convinced a New Jersey lieutenant that northerners were far more efficient farmers. Only a few grudgingly acknowledged the impressive output of rice by coastal planters and sweet potatoes, molasses, and hogs by Georgia farmers.[17]

Frequently it was little things, such as pranks, games, or wisecracks, that took the minds of the men away from the ordeal of the march and provided for the lighter side of campaigning. In the pine forests a group of soldiers sometimes livened a monotonous march by instigating a sham battle with pine cones. One side would suddenly attack the other and drive them back with a shower of cones until the aggressors exhausted their "ammunition," which opened the door for an effective countercharge. The 17th Ohio got a good laugh when some drunk soldiers shaved the tail of their commander's favorite gray stallion. The lieutenant colonel, livid with rage, offered a $500 reward, but mysteriously no one seemed to know who had done it. On an island in the Congaree River across from Columbia, South Carolina, a demented prankster set fire to some grass at the far end of the island and drove a hoard of rattlesnakes down into the camp. Commented one soldier: "We had quite a lively time for a while but no one was bitten." In the North Carolina pine country a favorite trick was to set on fire a bucket that collected pitch from a tree while a soldier napped at the base. The heat drew more pitch from the tree, which oozed to the bottom and glued the sleeper to the tree. Troops loved to watch the soldier's frantic efforts to escape when he awoke to find the tree ablaze. Such games and pranks, despite the inherent danger in some of them, seemed to work wonders for the morale of the men.[18]

Others preferred to ease the tension and improve the spirits of the men with more harmless gags and jokes. At Sandersville, Georgia, a Michigan private somehow managed to find a "mumy" that he left "standing on the side walk leaned up against the fence grinning at the passers by," the rest of his corps. Of course, the universal favorite was teasing. When a cavalryman with big, expensive top boots walked by, he often heard shouts from the line: "Come out of them boots—Come out!—too soon to go into winter quarters I know you are thar see your arms sticking out." A soldier with a big hat might take a razzing in a similar way: "Come down out of that hat. *Come down* taint no use to say that you aint up there. I see your legs hanging out." Nor would the troops let a staff officer, a favorite target, with a handlebar mus-

tache get away without hearing, "take them mice out of your mouth—
take 'em out—no use to say they aint thar—see their tails hanging
out."[19]

For the most part, however, campaigns were arduous at best and
frequently very dangerous. As Sherman's army marched to Savannah
and through the Carolinas it had to deal with an increasingly larger
and highly mobile Confederate force. Moreover, it had to conquer
Mother Nature and the topography of Georgia and the Carolinas, both
of which seemed at times insurmountable.

The Confederates had little success delaying Sherman's army with
gunfire, but they did slow the march somewhat through the use of
other tactics. One practice was to fell trees across the road that, despite one soldier's claim that it was "always a sign of the enemies
weakness," still demanded the attention of the pioneers, whose job it
was to clear such obstructions from the path of the army. Another
tool that the Confederates employed to check Sherman's advance was
land mines, known to the Federals as torpedoes. These subterranean
explosives, used exclusively around Savannah and southern South
Carolina, had a crippling, sometimes fatal effect on their unsuspecting
victims, prompting Sherman, strangely enough, to declare them a vi-
olation of civilized warfare. Initially Sherman had Confederate prisoners of war remove the mines, but after awhile Union troops could
generally locate and disarm them, as an Ohio sergeant wrote: "It re-
quires the greatest of caution in remooving these Torpedoes. We were
very lucky today indeed, no one getting hurt by them horrable horned
hobjects." Confederates also lit barrels of turpentine or pine trees to
delay the Union march. These fires blocked off the roads and scared
the horses and mules as the "air filled with pitch pine smoke made it
almost unbearable to breathe."[20]

Undoubtedly a major problem that the army had to endure, since
it was impossible to overcome, was the weather. During the Savannah
campaign it rained only twice, but from January into early March the
weather was simply awful. From January 27 to March 10, the dates
during which the Twentieth Corps marched through South Carolina,
it rained, frequently in downpours, over 50 percent of the days. At
one point, in late February and early March, it rained nine out of ten
consecutive days. Combined with occasional low temperatures of a

Georgia or South Carolina winter, the rainfall produced a rawness in the air that chilled Sherman's army to the bone. One Wisconsinite commented in his diary that it "Rained all of last night and still raining cold and disagreeable and the boys have concluded not to enlist again," and a Connecticut private complained to his wife, "The snot runs and I am shivering like a dog you know what over a briar."[21]

Aside from the discomfort of the damp coldness, rains greatly increased the load each infantryman had to carry, as a Minnesota private with a remarkable sense of humor indicated in his journal:

It rained steadily all night and as the water persisted in running under our beds all night we found ourselves this morning a trifle the worse for wear. Our blankets, tents and overcoats were saturated with mud and water which made our loads exceedingly heavy. I estimated mine as follows, wool blanket twenty-five hundred pounds. Overcoat one ton, shelter tents fifteen hundred pounds. other traps a trifle.

More important, though, was the fact that the heavy rain converted the roads into deep mud, which became the greatest bugbear of Sherman's army during the Carolinas campaign.[22]

Mud had always been one of the most dreaded campaign conditions for troops. A Minnesotan in Georgia commented on the attitudes of his comrades while tramping through the mud: "we floundered through it in as cheerful frame of mind as a squad of bounty jumpers going to execution." Another soldier, one from Illinois, recorded the reaction of his reconnaissance patrol when they ran into some knee-deep mud: "If there were any *rebes* within 2 miles they must have heard the shouting, for so much noise, by an equal number of men, is seldom made." In Georgia, Sherman's men had only two or three muddy marches, but in South Carolina the army encountered mud the depths of which they had never seen before. Said one Connecticut sergeant: "The bottom seems to be out so as soon as the top breaks through the wagon goes down almost out of sight." At the start of the campaign the mud immobilized the Fourteenth and Twentieth Corps for ten days, yet the problem continued to plague the entire army for the next two months. Throughout the march soldiers traveled over roads so muddy that "even profane [wagon] drivers find themselves unable to do justice to the subject," or that troops literally lost their shoes and had to plunge their arms in deep mud to search for them.[23]

Sherman had a knack, so wrote an Illinois musician, of making "good roads bad & bad roads good." Excessive use, particularly by the animals and wagons, cut deeply into the roadbed and transformed a decent road into a quagmire in no time. Once the horses and mules got stuck in the mud, they immediately became nervous and refused to pull the wagons. When that happened, so a New York sergeant described, the men were in for a rough day:

In many cases the mules had to be taken from the wagons, logs had to be brought and placed across the road, the wheels pried up with long levers, ropes hitched to the wagons, and then a hundred men pulling and pushing, yelling and swearing would after a while get the wagon out of the mire and on higher ground.

Sometimes the mud was so deep that soldiers had to lift up wagons and carry them to firmer ground. Even worse, troops often had to perform these labors throughout the night, cook some breakfast, and return directly to the mud.[24]

Standard practice for the troops was to corduroy the roads, meaning to cut and lay trees, limbs, and rails over the road to provide support for the wagons and animals. Sherman's chief engineer, O. M. Poe, reported that his engineers and mechanics alone corduroyed 400 miles of road during the Carolinas campaign, and according to the information that corps commanders provided, the entire army reworked nearly 800 miles of road. There were, however, several significant problems with corduroying the roads. First, it took time to cut enough trees and limbs to support a road. Second, under the weight of the wagons and animals the logs sank into the ground, so that the troops had to lay down new corduroy. Finally, even when soldiers corduroyed the roads, animals still sank in the mud, and there were some serious accidents when animals got their hooves caught between rails or logs. Thus, the entire process of hauling wagons through the mud and corduroying roads was exhausting and exasperating, as a Connecticut soldier indicated after several difficult days in northern South Carolina: "On the whole it is the roughest nastiest muddiest & worst time I've had in this Department. Every one is about used up."[25]

Rivers and streams, in general, were not much of a problem for Sherman's army. Each wing had a pontoon train that could provide a

This is a sketch by an eyewitness of the Fourteenth Corps crossing the Catawba River at Rock Hill, South Carolina in the rain over a pontoon bridge. The drawing was in *Harper's Weekly*, April 1, 1865. (Reproduced by permission of the Illinois State Historical Library).

900-foot bridge, and a crew of pontooneers, the mechanics and engineers who assembled the bridges, performed their duties with such skill that one soldier recorded in his diary: "The 'Johnnies' say Sherman's men just put their tents under their wagons and make a bridge quicker than we can burn one." A pontoon bridge consisted of a number of prefitted light wooden frames with canvas tarpaulin stretched over them. The pontooneers launched these "boats" and anchored them along a line about 12 feet apart. They then laid light wooden timbers called stringers from one boat to another and placed wooden planks on top for the floor. Once they fastened everything securely, the bridge was complete. When they took apart the pontoon bridge, each pontoon boat, with its anchor, clamps, stringers, and floorboard, conveniently fit into one wagon. From start to finish, it would take Sherman's pontooneers approximately ninety minutes to lay a 200-foot bridge, and if troops salvaged part of an existing bridge it took much less time.[26]

In the Carolinas, however, Sherman's army had some difficulties crossing streams and rivers. The heavy rains had so flooded the waterways in South Carolina that they were too wide to bridge and too deep to ford. The army had to wait until the flood level subsided, and even then crossings were dangerous. Sometimes the currents were swift and flotsam threatened to break apart the bridge. At other times, powerful currents pulled pontoon boats below the surface of the water despite the chains and ropes that secured them. One Illinois private fell off the pontoon bridge across the Great Pedee River in northern South Carolina, and the current and weight of his accouterments pulled him underwater before a rescue boat could save him. "It seems as though any moment it [the pontoon bridge] would succumb to what almost seemed to be the inevitable, and be swept away in the 'twinkling of an eye,' in spite of everything," an Ohio private confessed in his diary. "The relief we felt upon approaching the other shore, can better be imagined than described."[27]

Unfortunately for the troops, the army could not use its pontoon bridge in the swamps. In Georgia, Sherman's command traversed several deep, dark swamps, which prompted one soldier to speculate: "Had it rained it would have been impossible for us to get through these swamps." A member of the Twentieth Corps informed his father that several bogs were so dark that the troops had to light pine knots to guide them. A member of the Seventeenth Corps recorded a somewhat different experience with his comrades: "it was so dark that we couldn't see our hands but it soon lighted up with cussing and swearing that came out of every soldier's mouth as they tramped through the swamp up to the ears."[28]

Yet these swamps were nothing compared with those in South Carolina. The heavy rains, accompanied by the ensuing floods when the Confederate troops cut the water gates to the ricefields, overflowed swamps and made them nearly impassable. A New Jersey lieutenant remarked that "SC is proving herself very inhospitable, welcoming us to watery, muddy graves," and an Ohio sergeant half-jokingly quipped, "In Ky [Kentucky] we marched until we came to water before camping but here we had to reach dry land before camping." Just across

This is a sketch by William Waud of Weaver's Brigade, Third Division, Fifteenth Corps, charging across the Little Salkahatchie River in South Carolina in February 1865. The sketch was in *Harper's Weekly*, April 8, 1865. (Library of Congress).

the Georgia–South Carolina border soldiers in the Fourteenth and Twentieth Corps had to cross an immense bog called Black Swamp, which a private described as "about ¾ of a mile in width, and mostly under water and filled with a dense growth of bushes and vines." (The Fifteenth and Seventeenth Corps advanced from Beaufort, South Carolina, and had their own swamps to traverse.) Approximately thirty-five miles north, after marching through several more swamps, the entire army had to wade through two or three feet of icy water in the Salkehatchie Swamp. Unquestionably the worst of all, though, was the Edisto Swamp. Depending upon where in the swamp and on what day they crossed, soldiers had to march through icy cold water from knee deep to shoulder height and from one-quarter to three-fourths of a mile in length. The first line of troops had to fight their way across, but the bulk of the army had the privilege of removing their shoes, socks, and pants and tying them to their rifles. A Massachusetts sergeant told his sister: "We shouldn't have minded if it had been warm but it was cold, ice on the water, when I got across my feet, and legs were so numb I could hardly step"; a Wisconsin man wrote: "It did seem to us as if we would never get to land as our legs got so benumbed that we could hardly walk." It was so cold that some men cramped and required their friends to carry them out as others felt so numb and discouraged that they climbed on top of tree stumps and refused to go any farther. Only ridicule by friends got them back into the water. Most men, however, shouted curses, hollered, or sang songs at the top of their lungs as they waded through the swamp. Officers had the supreme advantage of riding on their horses across the swamp and avoiding the water, so that when a horse fell into a hole or slipped on a cypress root and dumped its rider, the men cheered lustily.[29]

Probably the most terrible marching experience for the troops resulted when a wagon got stuck in one of these swamps. As many as seventy-five men had to plunge back into the frigid water and either unhitch the team and lead it to shore or carry its cargo to the opposite bank. Then they had to return to the wagon and pull it out of the swamp by hand.[30]

A Massachusetts lieutenant wrote a friend at home that initially "this new mode of warfare was very exciting and interesting, but the long tramp from Savannah to Goldsboro lasting over fifty-six days and over a track of nearly five hundred miles became very tiresome." Distance, road and weather conditions, and topography all took their toll on Sherman's men, but so did the demands Sherman placed upon them. At times troops had to march twenty-five miles and destroy railroad track in one day or march all day and perform some other service, such as corduroying roads, through most of the night. On one occasion during the Savannah campaign part of the army had to march all day and throughout the night. One soldier was so tired that he fell asleep and awoke to find himself still marching in his proper place.[31]

Moreover, Sherman's men accomplished these tasks and endured all the hardships despite the handicap of inadequate clothing. By the time Savannah fell, a surprising number of troops were poorly clad, and by the end of the Carolinas campaign the army was in tatters. The day Sherman's troops entered Goldsboro a Wisconsin corporal described himself in his diary: "Arrived in camp out of rations & out of clothing. The soles on my Shoes were gone . . . Had no socks, only one shirt which Had not been washed in 5 weeks . . . Trousers were all in rags . . . coat was the same & I was as black as any Nigger with dirt." He then concluded: "But Thank God I was far ahead of the general run in my general appearence." An Ohio chaplain elicited a chuckle from the officers at brigade inspection when he showed up wearing a pair of gray-and-plaid dress pants because his regulation issue gave out on the march. Still another soldier reported to his mother that "we have a little sawed-off Irishman in our company who is wearing a long linen coat and a high plug hat. It is as good as a circus to see him." [32]

Shoes were the biggest clothing problem in Sherman's army. The shoe shortage first appeared during the Savannah campaign, and the army did get a supply at the coast, but those who received them found that the soles fell off after brief usage and there were not enough for everyone in need, as a New York private indicated to his father before he embarked upon the Carolinas campaign:

I am in a bad way for covering my feet, and if you can spare the money. I would like a pair of boots. . . . Alonzo Rice took the measure of my right foot this morning; it is on the paper that I enclose; take it to Cowan in the village, he will know by the marks on the paper; tell him to make them a little loose as this paper is the exact measurement.

By the time the army reached Goldsboro, there were nearly 4,000 men barefoot in the Seventeenth Corps alone. "I am barefoot and my feet are extremely sore," recorded Minnesota Sgt. John Risedorph in his diary, "when I step on them the blood oozes from the bottoms in such profusion that if I was on the snow I could be easily tracked I have thought I could not go another step but some irresistable influence urges me along." Some shoeless men tied gunnysacks or rawhide strips around their feet to protect them from the cold; others merely took advantage of the lenient policy toward barefoot soldiers and rode on captured horses and mules or in wagons and ambulances. [33]

Even those with shoes were not always well off. Frequently the feet of these men were wet for weeks at a time, resulting in all sorts of foot problems. An Iowa sergeant filed a formal complaint in his diary: "My

Sgt. John E. Risedorph, 4th Minnesota Veteran Volunteer Infantry, recorded in his diary during the Carolinas campaign: "I am barefoot and my feet are extremely sore   when I step on them the blood oozes from the bottoms in such profusion that if I was on the snow I could be easily tracked I have thought I could not go another step but some irresistable influence urges me along." His diary and photograph are from the Minnesota Historical Society.

shoes are whole yet, but owing to so much sand, and wading through water, my feet are sore. My right foot is worn through on the bottom, and my toes are wet with blood every day." And those troops who had gone some time without shoes had difficulty readjusting to new ones, as Minnesota sergeant John Risedorph did:

This morning I realized a new pair of boots and I was anxious in the morning to start so I could experience the pleasure which I anticipated but my hopes and anticipations were cast asunder when I had traveled about five miles for they raised about a dozen blisters on my feet.[34]

An Illinois private thought, "If a man was not used to the privations of war it would kill him right off." Another soldier, from a Michigan regiment, claimed he still enjoyed soldiering "well enough," although he admitted to his friend Charlie: "This ruffing it is d——d hard work if you make the best of it" and suggested the artillery or cavalry as a more preferable branch of service. Yet Sherman's veteran army withstood the hardships of the campaigns amazingly well. An Iowa private outside Savannah told his parents: "*you* have heard more *coughing* in the Synngrove Meeting house than I have heard in the whole army." From Fayetteville, North Carolina, an Illinois surgeon wrote: "there has not been half the deaths by battle accidents & sickness that there would have been if we had remained in *camp* in Savannah or *any other place*." Not only was there a very small percentage of soldiers ill during the campaigns, but many soldiers, in spite of the rigors of the march, actually improved in health and put on weight, while the bulk of the troops maintained their good physical condition throughout the campaigns, as did an Ohio private who announced: "This old chick continues to enjoy good health; is able to chaw his own terbacker without friendly assistance & is sometimes able to help others get rid of the obnoxious weed." Moreover, marching overland, despite poor conditions, was infinitely more preferable than traveling by sea, at least according to the men of the Fifteenth and Seventeenth Corps who steamed from Savannah to Beaufort, South Carolina. "I had rather go the distance a foot than to be Sea Sick," penned a corporal to his father, "the Sea was very ruff & so we have up Jonah a good deal."[35]

Notwithstanding all the hardships of the march, the army looked back from Goldsboro upon the two marches fondly. Part of the reason was the novelty of the campaigns, and part, as a Wisconsin lieutenant wrote, was human nature: "The soldier is ever forgetful and when times of plenty and ease come soon forgets the time when he was so weary almost heart sick and wholly hungry, all this is forgotten and he gives himself up to enjoying the good things his Uncle Samuel provides." A major part, though, was the ability of Sherman's army to march enormous distances and withstand such hardships. An Iowa youth wrote home from Savannah: "Mother, you will soon begin to think we Shermanites are a migratory race of people, as we are almost continually on the move." Another soldier, just prior to the invasion of South Carolina, speculated that "by the time we reach home our legs would be worn clear up to the knees." Finally, an Ohioan stated with evident pride: "the Army of the West, Slowly transformed itself into the Army of the East."[36]

CHAPTER 7

Foraging

*"I am practising them in the art of foraging
and they take to it like ducks to water."*
—W. T. SHERMAN TO ELLEN,
21 OCTOBER 1864

On the march to Savannah and through the Carolinas, together a distance of over 800 miles, the Union Army could neither maintain a supply line nor carry enough foodstuffs to feed over 60,000 mouths. Instead, Sherman had to adopt a policy of foraging, or living off the land, and its success was critical in the outcome of the campaign.

A New Yorker at the gates of Savannah wrote his mother that Sherman's army gobbled up so much food in Georgia that "The privates in the ranks have lived like princes every day." In South Carolina the troops stripped a 50-mile-wide area so bare of edibles that a Rebel prisoner claimed "a crow could not fly across it without carrying a haversack." In reality, the Federals did not live like princes throughout the entire Savannah campaign, and although they may have eaten every bit of available food along the march through South Carolina, it sometimes was not enough. Much more representative of the soldiers' understanding of the task of foraging and their lifestyle on the march was a statement that an Illinois private made: "We were told in no uncertain terms that henceforth we must live off the country or go hungry. We did both."[1]

Sherman was certainly not the first army commander in the war to forage for subsistence. Some eighteen months earlier, as a corps commander under U. S. Grant, he had witnessed the potential of marching light and living off the land in the Vicksburg campaign. His primary adversary on the March to the Sea and through the Carolinas, Maj. Gen. Joseph Wheeler and his cavalry, did not receive a government ration from July 1864 until the very end of the war. They simply took whatever they needed from the Confederate civilians, and this policy sparked considerable animosity. Moreover, both Union and Confederate troops were notorious for pilfering food wherever their armies went, despite orders to the contrary. As one New York sergeant confessed during the Atlanta campaign, foraging was technically illegal, but most officers looked the other way, especially since they too were susceptible to the temptation of fresh pork, beef, or chicken after weeks of army rations. When Sherman legalized foraging, a Michigan man stated that the recent order merely legitimized a widespread practice: "The fiction of respecting property rights of citizens in food was no longer maintained." What made foraging by Sherman's army during the Savannah and Carolinas campaigns unique was that no army of that size during the war had lived off the land for such a prolonged period of time.[2]

In the month prior to the Savannah campaign, Sherman had tried his troops at the art of foraging, and by late October he proudly announced the verdict to his wife: "they take to it like ducks to water." The troops responded ecstatically to the opportunity to supplement their diet with whatever the region could afford. The portion of the army that chased Hood's command from northern Georgia feasted on chickens, hogs, geese, sweet potatoes, corn bread, and some fruits. An Iowan announced to his folks that he was glad "to helpe them to market with their produce," and a Hoosier officer thought that "it is but right that these people should feel some of the hardships of war, they will better appreciate peace when it does come, and be not so ready to rush wildly into the same vortex again." The artillerymen and Twentieth Corps stationed in Atlanta had no choice except to live off the land, once Hood's army cut the railroad from Chattanooga. Maj. Gen. Henry Slocum, upon the recommendation of Sherman, sent out four separate foraging expeditions of 650 wagons each and filled them with almost 2 million pounds of corn and 140,000 pounds of fodder, plus livestock, sweet potatoes, and syrup in sufficient enough quantities to prompt a New York private to report home: "you better believe we lived bully." A member of the 1st Alabama (Union) Cavalry explained the procedure to his father:

We take out the whole regt with our wagons, stop at a corn field dismount in a few minutes the boys have the wagons filled with corn. On the way home they have to defend themselves as well as they can against the attacks of Hogs, Fowl & Etc & c.

Thus, by the time Sherman's army marched east from Atlanta, they had received sufficient schooling in the practice of organized foraging to provide for themselves adequately.[3]

In the order that established foraging parties for the Savannah campaign, Sherman specified that his men "forage liberally on the country during the march." Each brigade commander was to organize a foraging party under "one or more discreet officers" to gather food and fodder, "aiming at all times to keep in the wagons at least ten days' provisions for the command and three days' forage." Sherman specifically prohibited soldiers from entering homes and left the destruction of public and private property to the corps commanders alone.[4]

Initially, Sherman hoped to organize foragers for each brigade, but that soon proved unsatisfactory, since too many division commanders sent out only fifty men per brigade, not enough to provide for all the troops. As the brigade organization began to break down, many commanders decentralized the system even more and had each regimental commander assign foraging duties to one or two companies. The forage they gathered no longer went to the brigade commissary; it went directly to the men in each regiment.[5]

Sherman, it seems, also intended that foragers leave camp on foot and return with food and horses and mules. Once competition for forage grew keen, however, parties had to penetrate deeper into the countryside, traveling up to thirty miles per day and returning loaded with supplies, which necessitated a mount of some type for all foragers.[6]

Virtually every man in Sherman's army, at one time or another, participated in a foraging expedition. Brig. Gen. Mortimer D. Leggett, a division commander in the Seventeenth Corps, specified that foragers should be "men who were distinguished for their physical ability for marching, their personal bravery, and for strict obedience of orders." In practice, Leggett's instructions notwithstanding, almost anyone who volunteered for foraging duty could participate on the expedition. Foraging, like almost every special duty in the army, had its advantages and disadvantages. It was, on the one hand, difficult and sometimes dangerous work. On the other hand, foraging had its charms, particularly its opportunity to escape from the discipline of the march. That sort of situation appealed to most men on occasion, but the individuals it attracted on a regular basis were a different class of soldier. These men suffocated on army routine, whether in camp or on the march, and yearned for a chance to function more independently. They willingly accepted the higher risks and endured the hardships for some excitement. It was this type of man who formed the core of foraging parties, and during the Carolinas campaign regimental commanders designated them as regular foragers. Other troops could still participate in foraging expeditions, either as replacements for regulars or as additional personnel, but day after day these men performed the bulk of the foraging duties for Sherman's army.[7]

The term "bummer" mostly applied to the regular or everyday foragers. Members of the Twentieth Corps, particularly easterners, tended to use the term to refer to self-appointed or unauthorized foragers, but most troops in Sherman's army considered a bummer anyone who foraged on a regular basis, with or without authority. The word "bummer," as used before the March to the Sea, referred to a soldier who took it easy and shunned what he considered unnecessary demands and discipline, yet executed to the best of his ability in times of crisis. This, then, was the forager in Sherman's army—a man who, when properly motivated, performed superbly but had scant interest in disciplined routine. According to an artilleryman's description, a bummer was a peculiar-looking sort:

a man dressed in a nondescript suit part blue, part homespin grey or Butternut, with a white hat and tremendous rents in his Breeches, and perhaps barefooted, with his Belt & cartridge box on (for we always go well armed) his trusty carbine by his side, and a revolver stuck in his belt.

Shabby in dress, Sherman's bummers were also imperturbable in crises. A member of the Twenty-third Corps at Goldsboro described bummers as "a rough looking set of soldiers and care for nothing" and a newspaperman who accompanied the army said, "They appear to be possessed with a spirit of 'pure cussedness.' " They had an uncanny ability to locate hidden food and animals and the ingenuity to bring them back to camp. One Georgia black attested to their unusual skills when he told a brigadier general:

Dese Yankee soldiers have noses like hounds. Massa hid all his horses way out dar in de swamp. Some soldiers come along. All at once dey held up dere noses and sniffed and sniffed, and stopped still and sniffed, and turned into de swamp and held up dere noses and sniffed, and, Lord'a Massy, went right straight to where de horses was tied in de swamp.

Moreover, these men were a daring, reckless bunch who, possessing firepower and mobility, performed the service of a mounted infantry superbly. They were almost always in advance of the army and, as a Missouri colonel insisted, "were really more valuable than cavalry in protecting our front and flanks." Bummers were notorious for seizing key towns or railroad junctions and holding them stoutly until reinforcements arrived or for picking up important information from locals on Confederate plans or whereabouts and riding through hostile territory to report the news at headquarters.[8]

Foragers usually left camp before anyone else, immediately after they learned of the prescribed route and length of march of the main column. To reduce the distance they had to transport their forage, expeditions pushed ahead of the army to the left or right of the main road, yet it was quite common for parties to travel much of the day in search of provender. In the area east of Atlanta some plantations had more forage than several parties could carry, but throughout eastern Georgia and the Carolinas the distance between one plantation and the next was considerable, and the amount of food on each plantation was not enough for even one party, so that foragers had to break up into smaller groups. The result of so many foraging expeditions was a competition or race against one another to locate a well-stocked plantation reasonably near the line of march. Those fortunate enough to find a conveniently located plantation could gather the food and then waste away several hours before returning to the column; less fortunate foragers had to penetrate deeper into the countryside to gather food, which increased their travel time as well as the possibility of an encounter with Confederates and guerrillas. Thus, when two foraging parties found that they were on the same road, a mad race ensued to beat one another to the first plantation.[9]

Once a party located a plantation, it immediately searched the grounds for Confederates and, if it had enough men, established pickets. After the soldiers gathered enough food for themselves and put a black woman or two to work as their cooks, they got down to the business of foraging for their comrades on the march. Several men hitched any horses or mules they could find to the plantation wagons and buggies and began to fill them with barrels of flour and cornmeal and any cured meats available. Corn could be difficult to load, but foragers shrewdly developed a method that was quick and easy. Someone drove an empty wagon up close to the side of the crib and raised the wagon cover on that side. The men then knocked the boards off the side of the crib and, lying on their backs, pulled their feet up and shoveled the corn into the wagon. Honey was such a highly coveted commodity that foragers frequently eschewed the risks to acquire this precious nectar. Some fleet-footed bummers simply drove their bayonets into hives and ran as fast as they could—faster, they hoped, than the bees could fly. Such was not always the case, though, as an Illinois private suggested after a honey raid: "We had a sweet time and some swelled eyes besides." Cattle they could attach with a rope to the rear of a wagon or a mule's tail and lead to camp, but hogs and fowl were a different matter. In an effort to preserve ammunition and to ensure the secrecy and security of foragers, commanding officers enjoined bummers from firing at animals, which frequently made for some wild antics as the troops tried to tackle hogs, chickens, geese, and turkeys. These animals foragers partially butchered on the spot and tied on the mules or loaded in wagons.[10]

On a few occasions Yankee foragers actually helped Southern women hide their forage, in return for all the food they could carry. An Illinois sergeant and several other soldiers took two meals' worth of food and hid the remainder for a woman in the loft and under the pantry floor. After a Minnesota sergeant and a companion concealed a year's supply of food for a woman, they took everything else they could handle in payment. One forager, according to a Winnsboro, South Carolina, woman, even gave her some meat to hide for her family after Union soldiers had taken practically everything from them. Yet for the most part foragers dealt with southerners harshly, which was neither better nor worse than the way the vast majority of Sherman's army treated them. As one officer noted, foraging had a demoralizing effect on some of the troops and created "a morbid appetite to take things" that made it "impossible to restrain some from carrying the thing to an extreme." "The most stringent orders have been issued with regard to foraging," the inspector general of the Seventeenth Corps recorded in his journal, "and we do all we can to check these excesses." Unfortunately, once foraging parties split up into details to gather food at different plantations, officers could no longer supervise the work and scrutinize troop behavior. Senior officers tried to change the composition of foraging parties in the hope that these new men would act more responsibly and leave the inhabitants at least a little food, and Maj. Gen. O. O. Howard even went so far as to dismount all foragers, although he immediately had to rescind the order when a senior division commander presented statistics showing that without mounts the foragers could not feed the army. In the end, as Sherman indicated in his official report, concerned officers and men had to accept the good with the bad: "A little loose in foraging, they 'did some things they ought not to have done,' yet, on the whole, they have supplied the wants of the army with as little violence as could be expected."[11]

Sometimes foraging parties came across plantations with almost no food, which immediately cast suspicion upon the residents. They usually claimed that the Yankee or Rebel troops had cleaned them out one or two days earlier, and this occasionally was true; but when foragers failed to find tracks for a sizable group of men, it was clear that the residents had concealed their food somewhere. A Wisconsin man once found eight sacks of ham and bacon tied up on tree limbs in a forest. Others located foodstuffs hidden in houses or cellars, sometimes beneath the floorboards. The most common hiding place, however, was the ground. Southerners concealed such a wide variety of items in the earth with such skill that a Union officer once insisted: "Surely the people of the south must have some Yankee blood in them

to do this." Unfortunately for southerners, Sherman's bummers had an even greater talent for "prospecting," or finding buried treasure. So skillful, in fact, were bummers that a Federal private claimed that some civilians "think that the yankeys have somb kinde of an instrement to find things." Foragers carefully scanned the landscape for anything unusual, especially patches of freshly churned soil. The men then prodded the ground with bayonets and ramrods until they hit something. "Needless to say," a lieutenant wrote, "whatever was unearthed, whether food or family jewels, was confiscated, for all buried treasure whatever its nature, was regarded as fair spoils of war." Some soldiers dug up a coffin and found it loaded with foodstuffs; another time, troops found a corpse inside, which they quickly reinterred. An Ohioan discovered $600 in silver coin buried in the ground, enough for a decent-sized farm in the North, and an Illinois sergeant uncovered a valise with $16,300 in Confederate money. Several times Union troops unearthed Confederates who were hiding from the Yankees, and in one instance four Indiana men dug up a wooden box that exploded when they tried to open it. The bomb blinded all four and seriously mangled two of them.[12]

Other times foragers refused to play games and used threats to force whites and blacks to reveal where they had hidden the food and animals. A New Jersey man recorded a classic bummer's ploy to obtain the information: "[Q:] Where is your bacon [A:] Did not raise any [Q:] Where is the corn meal? [A:] got none [Q:] Where's your horses and mules? [A:] runoff or confiscated [Q:] Got nothing? [A:] no Whereupon the Bummer tells them, as they have nothing—they cannot live here any longer," and he began preparations to burn down the house, which immediately convinced the family to surrender everything they had. An even more common and more ruthless practice was to place a revolver to the head of a slave and threaten to shoot him unless he disclosed the whereabouts of the goods. If the family had anything the black would speak, and if the slave still insisted that the family had nothing, the foragers believed him and walked away.[13]

Any attempts to destroy food to keep it out of the hands of Sherman's foragers resulted in worse problems. Sherman announced a policy to his army and the Southern people that, if civilians destroyed food and forage, he would order the complete devastation of the entire area, and he lived by that decree religiously. A few southerners burned crops and quickly found themselves victims of authorized firebugs, which convinced others not to resist Sherman's army. The Confederate troops could destroy the food and fodder, and at times they did, but they also learned that doing this caused more problems both for themselves and for Southern inhabitants. Civilians bitterly resented their army for destroying the crops, and the army always had to leave enough food behind for the inhabitants to subsist, which Sherman's foragers promptly stripped from them and still fired many of their homes and barns.[14]

When the meal was ready, the foragers dropped whatever they were doing and came in for a feast, the best that the plantation could afford. This was one of the benefits of foraging duty, and the men took complete advantage of it. One soldier, a Hoosier sergeant, on a foraging mission outside Savannah recorded that he ate so much ham and sweet potatoes that "I thought I was hollow clear to my toes." After dinner the boys usually lounged and chatted with the blacks or convinced some to entertain them with stories or music. In South Carolina an Ohio private on picket duty for a foraging party returned to find his comrades in a slave cabin: "A young black fellow was pounding on an old tin can, and the boys were dancing with some fat old wenches, and having a royal good time." If there was more work to do, the foragers would have to cut their noontime break short after an hour or so, but if they had finished the job of foraging, they might laze away the better part of an afternoon.[15]

Of course, foraging duty was not always so easy. Sherman's foragers spent practically every daylight hour in an extremely hazardous situation, traveling through a hostile land in relatively small numbers well beyond supporting distance from the main column. Confederate troops and guerrillas dominated the surrounding countryside, and for that reason foragers left camp in groups of at least thirty or more. As they foraged, however, these groups divided into very small parties and spread throughout the area. Those men who gathered enough forage returned to camp while others continued to collect foodstuffs. It was in this exposed condition that Confederates and guerrillas attacked foragers. Sherman's bummers were for the most part a tough set, and if the Confederates or guerrillas engaged them with anything remotely near equal numbers the attackers had their hands full, but in many instances the southerners mustered three to five times as many men. Even worse, some Confederates and guerrillas took foragers as prisoners and executed them at the first opportunity. In Georgia, Sherman's army recovered at least 64 bodies of Union soldiers, and in the Carolinas a minimum of 109 more, either hanged, shot in the head from very close range, or with their throats slit; in a few cases, someone had actually butchered them. Many times the culprits placed the bodies alongside a main road for all Union troops to see and pinned signs on them such as "Death to all foragers" or "Hear Hangs Hams." The result was that foragers desperately tried to fight their way to safety whenever there was the slightest chance of success and sacrificed many lives in the process, "For they knew," wrote an Illinois soldier to his parents, "if they did not cut their way out that they would not be among the living."[16]

Since it was exceedingly dangerous to travel through a hostile land filled with Confederates and guerrillas, particularly at night, foragers always tried to leave with ample time to reach the main column during the daylight hours. With blacks serving as guides and, if necessary, packhorses, this peculiar caravan of rough-looking soldiers and freedmen; wagons; buggies and plush coaches; and mules, horses, and cattle—all loaded with bundles and barrels of meat, vegetables, and fruit—rolled over country roads in search of its brigade or regiment. Early in the Savannah campaign the foragers brought their appropriations to the roadside and loaded the brigade commissary wagons as they passed, but once the brigade foraging system broke down, parties simply waited for their regiment to pass and distributed the food directly to the men. Usually the regimental commissary sergeant and the foragers cut the beef or pork into ten- to twenty-pound portions, and as the men passed by they stabbed a chunk with their bayonets. Other foragers doled out as fairly as possible sweet potatoes, cornmeal and flour, and anything else they had confiscated.[17]

Foraging details brought back to camp much food, yet seldom was it enough to feed the entire army. An authorized party of fifty foragers per brigade meant that each forager had to return to the column with enough food for thirty men, three meals a day, every day. In the lush farmland east of Atlanta this might have been possible, but around Savannah and in the Carolinas, where the soil was poorer and the plantations smaller, it was extremely doubtful that they could provide sufficiently for the men. Nor were foraging expeditions as regular as officers and men hoped. Despite the efforts of details to return before nightfall, sometimes they ran into trouble with Confederates or guerrillas, got lost, or met with some unanticipated delays that forced them to spend the night in the countryside and the regiment to go without supper, and possibly without breakfast. Even if the foragers found the army by nightfall, there was certainly no guarantee that they could locate the regiment before the next morning; for the men in the regimental ranks that meant no evening meal other than a few crackers they carried in their haversacks.[18]

To provide better for the men in the columns, senior officers let details leave the line of march with wagons and fill them with food from farms adjacent to the road. Still, this was not enough, and as often happened in an army of veterans such as Sherman had, the troops themselves took on the responsibility of obtaining the necessary food. Any chance the men had, whether it was the ten-minute rest per hour along the march or during some special duty, a few individuals from each company would slip away to gather a little extra food for the rest of the boys and return as quickly as possible. Most officers either looked the other way or realized that the strict orders against unauthorized foraging were inapplicable and tolerated these abuses as long as the men acted discreetly. In those few instances when officers from other units upheld both the spirit and the letter of the orders, the worst punishment soldiers received for unauthorized foraging, or "foraging on the hook" as the men called it, was temporary arrest and confiscation of their forage. During the Savannah and Carolinas campaigns, no one in Sherman's army was ever brought to trial for unauthorized foraging.[19]

With so many illegal bummers on the prowl and confiscation of forage as a standard punishment, a number of officers who met foragers from other units tried to use the advantage of rank to ensure that they and their mess had several good meals. Even in the case of legitimate foraging, by the time the arresting officer received confirmation from the foragers' regiment, at least part of the food had somehow managed to disappear. This was not much of a problem in the Army of the

Tennessee, in which the men of the Fifteenth and Seventeenth Corps got along splendidly and never tried to pull such stunts on one another. Whenever an officer outside those corps accosted them, foragers usually announced that they were working for some notoriously ill tempered general in their corps and continued on their way, or if cavalry stopped them, the Western corpsmen simply sneered and disregarded the attempted arrest.[20]

The real problem was between members of the Fourteenth and Twentieth Corps. It began, according to a lieutenant in the Fourteenth Corps, in Barnwell, South Carolina, when bummers from that corps had first entered the city and loaded their forage into a house, with the intention of waiting for their column to pass. Instead, the main column of the Twentieth Corps entered the city first, and an officer ordered the foragers to clear out immediately and leave their provender behind. This was too much for the Fourteenth corpsmen to tolerate, and a fight erupted that attracted the attention of Brig. Gen. Alpheus S. Williams, commander of the Twentieth Corps. Williams then ordered the foragers out of the house, and again the men refused to leave. Fortunately, when the situation seemed critical, Fourteenth Corps commander Jefferson C. Davis rode up and, since he outranked Williams, decided in favor of his own corps. After that incident, members of both corps tried their best to confiscate one another's forage, and in the end several soldiers lost their lives during these squabbles.[21]

Altogether, Sherman's foragers took from the country a staggering amount of food, fodder, and animals. From Georgia alone they confiscated 6,871 mules and horses, 13,294 head of cattle, 10.4 million pounds of grain, and 10.7 million pounds of fodder as Georgia farmers unwillingly contributed almost 6 million rations of beef, bread, coffee, and sugar to the Union infantry and artillery. Statistics from the Carolinas campaign are much less complete, yet they do indicate that foragers stripped the countryside of at least 7 million pounds of foodstuffs, 11.6 million pounds of corn, 8.3 million pounds of fodder, and 11,825 horses and mules.[22]

Despite this enormous quantity of food and fodder, the army had problems feeding itself at times. Wagons could hold only so much, and bummers did not return to camp with a steady stream of provender. Instead, the army passed through some areas that were fertile and others that could not support even one corps of infantry, let alone four corps plus cavalry. Just east of Atlanta the army feasted on an amazing variety and quantity of meat, vegetables, and fruits. One week outside that city an Ohio private noted in his diary:

An epidemic of good appetites seems to have struck us all; and the only remedy the surgeons have to prescribe is plenty of chickens, sweet potatoes, fresh pork, etc. and it is not given or taken in homeopathic doses, but in "quantum sufficit."

A Connecticut corporal jotted down in his diary the comment that:

It makes one sometimes laugh to think of the northern people's idea at the commencement of the war of starving out the southern army. There is enough raised in the south at the present time to supply the whole southern confederacy if it was not taken from them by our army.

From eastern Georgia a Minnesotan wrote his wife: "this State alone could Subsist the Army of Virginia Before the Raid was made for One Year with the crops that She had gathered But she cannot do it now." At other times, particularly in the vicinity of Savannah and in northern South Carolina, either not enough food was raised in the surrounding countryside to feed Sherman's army or too many troops had to live off the same region for too long. One soldier complained in his diary of the skimpy meal he ate one day: "We had a piece of cracker and a cup of coffee for supper. We were never so hungary since a soldier. The boys were out of eatables." When his regiment ran out of food outside Savannah, a colonel could only advise his troops "to draw in your belt one more hole each day." For Sherman's army, then, it was either feast or famine. In times of plenty soldiers wasted shocking amounts of food, as a private confessed to his wife: "it is a nough to say we lived on the top shelf and destroide all we could not eat or cary with ous," and in moments of paucity they moaned about their meager diet, as did a Minnesotan who "lived 5 ds [days] on Nigger Peas or Beans as the Boys call them."[23]

Despite the seriousness of the foraging business, there was something comical about its duties and the men who performed it. Whether it was a gangling bummer in the most ridiculous array of civilian and army clothing astride a haggard mule, a sinewy crew of foragers chasing pigs and chickens in a pen, or a scraggly looking bummer in a plush carriage seated atop piles of foodstuffs, foraging was an amusing spectacle. More than that, though, Sherman's men found humor in the whole idea of legalized stealing, as evidenced by a facetious order written by a private in the 113th Ohio that parodied the one General Sherman had issued before the start of the Carolinas campaign:

HEADQUARTERS MILITARY DIVISION OF THE MISSISSIPPI, ⎫
IN THE FIELD, SISTERS FERRY, S. C., Feb. 5, 1865. ⎭

GENERAL ORDER ⎫
   No. 10. ⎭

The army during the ensuing campaign will subsist chiefly by foraging off the country through which it passes, and foraging parties will be governed by the following rules:

I. Each regimental commander will detail a foraging party each day while upon the march.

II. No detail shall be made to exceed the whole effective force, including negroes.

III. Not more than one thousand pack-mules will be allowed to a regiment.

IV. No soldier will be allowed to take any horses or mules that cannot walk.

V. No soldier will be allowed to take anything from a plantation which he cannot carry, unless provided with a wagon or pack-mule.

VI. No person shall carry more than two hundred pounds unless he is a negro impressed for the purpose.

VII. No soldier shall carry off a grindstone weighing more than five hundred pounds, as a greater weight would injure the knapsacks.

VIII. No soldier will be allowed more than three negroes as private servants; the surplus, if any, will be sent to these headquarters, if females.

IX. Burning of property is strictly prohibited, unless accidental; and any soldier caught attempting to fire any incombustible material will be arrested.

X. Foraging will be conducted with as little shooting as possible, and no soldier will be allowed to shoot anything already dead. Division and brigade commanders will see that these orders are strictly enforced. Any soldier violating the above orders will be deprived of the privilege of participating in any engagement during the present campaign, and will be summarily dismissed from the service immediately upon the expiration of his enlistment.

      By order of   MAJOR GENERAL W. T. SHERMAN.
        OFFICIAL,
(Signed) No—T. WISEMAN,   OFFICIAL,
(Signed) L. M. DAYTON,

                                   A. A. A. G.[24]

Yet underlying the whole concept of foraging, never lost in the humor, was a belief that it was an effective weapon against southerners. A handful of soldiers, mainly recent recruits who had not endured hardships and sacrifices for several years, detested the foraging system, as a Wisconsin private complained to his wife:

On the march we have live pretty much entirely off of the country; there is not enough left in the country to support the women and children. This is a wicked, damnable, accursed war; if you could see and hear the poor women and innocent children crying and begging that they leave them a little meal or something to eat; yet the last morsal would be taken and they left to suffer.

These individuals, however, were few and far between. Some men in Sherman's army justified foraging on the ground that the army's needs outweighed those of southerners, as did a Michigan private who defended the practice in a letter to his sister: "You seem to think that our *foraging* 'filching you call it' does not speak well for our *morals*. I think if *your stomyach* was crying for *bread*, you would not think of morals or names." The bulk of the men supported this contention, but they also saw foraging as an effective means of breaking the Southern will to fight and as a weapon to punish southerners. During the Carolinas campaign a sergeant, clearly showing the effects of more than three years of service, commented in his diary that "many a time I have let my consious [conscience] over rule my appetite—but that is played out." About the same time an Ohio corporal expressed the sentiments of many other bummers when he recorded an incident in his diary: "The Old lady beged me to leave her just enough corn to live on. Oh I told her they brought it on themselves. So they would have to be satisfied with what we choosed to leave them." Even more blunt, though, was a statement a private in Georgia made to his wife: "I dont know what the wemon and children is going to do for something to eat but I dont know as I care if they nevver see eny more to eat."[25]

CHAPTER 8

Destruction and Pillaging

"It seems hard for the women and children, but this
rebellion must be put down and we are doing it."
—ALONZO MILLER TO SISTER, 14 MARCH 1865

"True it is, as General [Sherman] said to me the other day, 'Pierce the shell of the C.S.A. and it's all hollow inside,'" recorded Henry Hitchcock, assistant adjutant general on Sherman's staff, in his diary less than ten days into the Savannah campaign. "Yet such a march as this," Hitchcock continued, "the mere fact of it, is bound to have a powerful influence of itself: it shows the real hopelessness of their 'cause' first to those who suffer, and to the people of 'The South,' and then to all the world." In a sense, Hitchcock was right, but his views on the campaign were very different from that of the bulk of Sherman's army. Hitchcock was an army neophyte, on his first campaign, and so thought of the march in very traditional terms. Rather than envisioning the campaign as one of destruction and pillaging, Hitchcock believed that Southern inhabitants along the course of the march would suffer from the mere presence of a Federal army. Most of Sherman's veterans, however, saw this as a golden opportunity to teach the people of Georgia and the Carolinas the hardships and terrors of war.[1]

In October 1864 a New York lieutenant wrote his father: "The power of the Confederacy is in their Armies. If we can destroy or capture these Armies, the confederacy, of course, no longer has an existence."

Three months later, from South Carolina soil, a sergeant discussed strategy with his brother: "We may capture every city of importance in the South but as long as the Rebbels have an organized Army the war will and is bound to continue. when we once subdue their Armies then the war will close and not till then." Lincoln, too, endorsed this strategy, although it was not until 1864 that he got competent people in command positions to implement it. What these two soldiers from Sherman's army and Lincoln were slow to realize, and what Sherman and many of his veterans had come to understand, was that this was a revolution, that the Union armies not only had to defeat the Confederate armies in the field but also had to break the will of the Southern people to resist Federal authority. As Sherman wrote to Chief of Staff Henry W. Halleck from Savannah, "We are not only fighting hostile armies, but a hostile people, and must make old and young, rich and poor, feel the hard hand of war, as well as their organized armies."[2]

For the bulk of Sherman's army, so amazingly in tune with its commander, the Savannah and Carolinas campaigns were the best opportunities to employ a different type of strategy. Motivated in part by revenge for several years of hardships and sacrifices endured during what they considered an unnecessary war, and by an overriding passion to crush the rebellion, the veterans wanted more than anything else to make the South feel the awfulness of war, to convince them that war against the Union was much, much worse, even to the point of unbearableness, than life within the Union. From Acworth, a rail town on the line between Chattanooga and Atlanta, an Illinois officer recorded in his diary in mid-November:

It is evident our soldiers are determined to burn, plunder and destroy everything in their way on this march. Well, that shows that they are not afraid of the South at any rate, and that each individual soldier is determined to strike with all his might against the rebellion, whether we ever get through or not.

An Illinois sergeant noticed on the march: "The men worked with a will, seeming to take savage delight in destroying everything that could by any possibility be made use of by their enemies." From the gates of Savannah a Connecticut officer wrote: "They have just begun to find out what war is in Georgia but have never Known it before"; in

South Carolina near Orangeburg an Ohioan announced: "General devastation surpasses my nearly 4 years experience soldiering." Finally, from North Carolina, a Wisconsinite renewed his commitment to end the war when he declared: "Old Sherman's Smokehouse Rangers will destroy the whole Southern Confederacy if it don't stop before another year."[3]

No doubt, these were harsh policies that Sherman's men implemented. An Iowan told his wife, "It is truly a terrible thing to have a hostile army pass through a country," and a Michigan man wrote his brother, "You can have but a faint idea of the effect of an army passing through a country like this when there is no good feeling toward the inhabitants and when it becomes necessary to live upon the substance of these people." Yet Sherman's men imposed just such a program of devastation because they believed it was the best means available to put down the rebellion. From South Carolina an Ohio sergeant commented in Shermanlike terms in his diary: "Every house, barn, fence and cotton gin gets an application of the torch. That prospect is revolting, but war is an uncivil game and cant be civilized." Another soldier, this one a private, wrote his sister in expectation of the burning of Fayetteville, North Carolina: "It seems hard for the women and children, but this rebellion must be put down and we are doing it."[4]

Sherman concentrated much of his army's destructive strength against what he loosely defined as military targets and contraband of war. As one soldier bluntly recorded, "everything useful to the rebels is being burnt." In Atlanta, so documented a Confederate official, "The [train] car shed, the depots, machine shops, foundries, rolling mills, merchant mills, arsenals, laboratory, armory, etc., were all burned," and "every species of machinery that was not destroyed by fire was most ingeniously broken and made worthless in its original form." Any other machine shops or factories along the march, such as the arsenal at Fayetteville or the giant cloth factory, Ocmulgee Mills, in Georgia, the army destroyed and then burned. At Columbia and Cheraw, South Carolina, Sherman's men found large supplies of ordnance, which they destroyed, although carelessness at both places caused explosions that took 12 lives and wounded 53 more men. On the two campaigns the army burned over 90,000 bales of cotton, valued at $36 million, along with thousands of cotton gins, presses, sawmills, and gristmills. The army killed dogs, which southerners used to track escaped Union prisoners, and also worn-out horses and mules, because if they turned them loose a few weeks' rest would restore most of them for use by the Confederates. Even whipping posts, slave pens, and auction blocks, all symbols of the power of the Southern aristocracy and the worst evils to Sherman's men, received the torch.[5]

Railroads, more than anything else, were the key military targets on the two campaigns. During the march through Georgia, from late October to December 1864, Sherman's army destroyed 317 miles of track, and in the Carolinas they wrecked another 126 miles. Damage to the two key east–west railroads in Georgia—the Central Railroad from Macon to Augusta or Savannah and the Georgia Railroad from Atlanta to Augusta and continued to Charleston, South Carolina—was so extensive that the earliest date when Confederate authorities optimistically hoped to have one line repaired was mid-February 1865, and only then if southerners took rails from another line and "impressed all the labor that can be had." In South Carolina, Sherman's men wrecked four separate lines: the Charleston & Savannah Railroad; the South Carolina Railroad (called the Georgia Railroad in that state) that ran from Augusta to Charleston; the Charlotte & South Carolina Railroad from Charlotte, North Carolina, to Columbia and extended on into the South Carolina Railroad at Branchville; and the Greenville & Columbia Railroad from Greenville, South Carolina, to Columbia. In addition, they damaged two more lines in North Carolina. So much damage, in fact, did Sherman's command inflict on Southern railways that one soldier told his cronies that he thought it would be a good idea for Sherman to buy a coal mine in Pennsylvania and spend his postwar years smoking cigars and rebuilding the railroads he had wrecked during the war.[6]

No command on either side, North or South, had the knack for destroying railroads like Sherman's army. An entire regiment or more lined up along one side of a railroad track and picked up the wooden ties at one end. Upon command, the men flipped the ties over, which jarred them loose from the iron rails on impact with the ground. Troops then broke off the ties and gathered them and telegraph poles and started fires, upon which they laid the rails. When the middle of the rails became red hot, the men destroyed them by picking up both ends and

A photograph of the destruction of railroad tracks by Sherman's army near Atlanta, Georgia. (Library of Congress).

twisting them around trees or poles or with a device that Sherman's chief engineer, O. M. Poe, invented called a cant hook, a giant wrench that soldiers affixed to the ends of the rails and turned in opposite directions, which again twisted the rails. Sherman stressed to his men the importance of twisting the rails because the Confederates could easily hammer bent rails straight, whereas Confederates had to reheat and reroll twisted rails at rolling mills, something exceedingly scarce in the South. Oftentimes, to remind civilians along the route who had wrecked the line, Sherman's men shaped rails into giant letters U.S. and placed them in conspicuous locations.[7]

A substantial portion of the total devastation, however, was to private property. Part of this was the destruction of fences and barns for firewood, although such damage was fairly common throughout the war. What constituted the bulk of this type of destructiveness, aside from the loss of crops and livestock, and what made these two campaigns so unusual, was the enormous destruction of private homes.[8]

This seemingly unbridled devastation of private homes began as the army prepared to abandon the railroad from Chattanooga to Atlanta and march east to Savannah. From the Etowah River nearly 50 miles south to Atlanta, Sherman's troops destroyed the railroad, but equally premonitory of future events was the burning to the ground of most of Kingston, Acworth, Big Shanty, and Marietta. According to an officer at Acworth, the troops were so intent upon destroying the town that, while he watched one house, some soldier set another on fire until almost the entire town was in flames.[9]

Both proportionally and in total numbers, the devastation in Atlanta was greater than that in any other large city in the two campaigns. Sherman had cautioned his chief engineer to use fire only "toward the last moment," and Poe acted responsibly, yet firebugs lit homes ablaze in various locations around the city so that a Minnesotan one and one-half miles away commented in his diary: "We could see to read newspapers at midnight at our camp from the light of burning buildings." Despite orders to troops performing provost duty to "shoot on the spot all incendiaries," fires that eventually consumed an estimated 4,000 to 5,000 homes and buildings continued to break out in various sections of the city. In a letter to his father, one soldier, a sergeant in the 1st Michigan Engineers & Mechanics, charged with the duty of destroying anything of use to the Confederates, exuded the passion with which troops torched the city, although he personally could not bring himself to fire a home before the eyes of its youthful resident:

Most of the people left their houses without Saying a word for they heard the cry of *Chambersburg* [Pennsylvania] and they knew it would be useless to contend with the soldiers. but as I was about to fire one place a little girl about ten years old came to me and said, Mr Soldier you would not burn our house would you. if you do where are we going to live and She looked into my face with such a pleading look that I could not have the heart to fire the place So I dropped the torch and walked away. but *Chambersburg* is dearly paid for.

Undoubtedly the only thing that prevented complete tragedy in the burning of Atlanta was that seven weeks earlier Sherman had evicted nearly all the residents.[10]

Along the march, senior officers of both the Left Wing and the Right

Wing spotted homes ablaze during the first few days, but crackdowns soon tapered off the devastation. Nine miles west of Sandersville, about halfway to Savannah, a citizen burned a bridge to impede the march of the army and, in turn, had his property fired. At Louisville, Union soldiers burned more homes because Confederates had shot at them from inside houses and destroyed a bridge that delayed the march. In late November, Confederate cavalry leader Joseph Wheeler reported that some retreating Federals had fired a few homes, which the Confederates quickly extinguished, and also burned part of Waynesborough one week later. Otherwise, if Georgians did not bushwack or impede the march or attempt to conceal cotton inside, Sherman's troops did not set fire to their homes, except in the case of prominent Confederates, whose homes universally received the torch.[11]

South Carolina, however, was an entirely different matter in the eyes of Sherman's men. As members of the Fourteenth Corps crossed over a bridge into South Carolina, a soldier at the head of the column turned around and shouted, "Boys, this is old South Carolina, lets give her hell," to which the troops responded with cheers. A Wisconsin officer in the Seventeenth Corps commented in his diary in late January: "Today commences the destruction of S.C. and we gave her a good initiation." This was not only the hotbed of secession but also the state that fired the first shots and, as an Ohioan intimated, "our army did not feel bound by the ordinary restraints of human warfare." Officers quickly found out that, although the troops performed all their duties, they would not be denied their "right," earned through three or four years of service, to teach South Carolina a lesson. Twentieth Corps commander A. S. Williams wrote home that "The soldiers quietly took the matter into their own hands"; a New Jersey lieutenant commented:

It seems almost as though there was a Secret organization among the men to burn Every thing in the State for thus far, in spite of orders, & the utmost efforts of officers, houses, in Some way, get on fire & nearly all we have passed thus far are I think in ashes.

From the enlisted ranks it was obvious that the exact sentiment that the two officers had suggested prevailed. A Minnesota sergeant wrote in his diary: "The man that does the most jay hawking [destruction and looting] is considered the most loyal for them he is putting down the rebellion." An Ohio musician recorded in his diary: "The houses are mostly burnt by stragglers, & is against orders, but the men say that not a house shall be left standing in South Carolina, & they are doing their best to carry out their threat." Finally, a resident of Beaufort, South Carolina, sensed the intent of the members of the Army of the Tennessee when he penned to a friend: "They are a hard set of fellows, and woe be to S. C. when they enter that state. They are determined to destroy to their utmost power." [12]

An Ohio private told his sister with considerable exaggeration that "I do not beleave there is a man in the army but has set fire to one or more buildings," but he nonetheless got across his point. Despite the greatest vigilance on the part of officers, when troops wanted to fire a home they did it. Eventually the guards and officers designated to protect houses had to leave, and some soldiers or foragers who lingered in the area would set them ablaze. In one instance Brig. Gen. William T. Ward, a division commander in the Twentieth Corps, personally tried to protect a house, but somehow troops fired it "2 or 3 times in his very presence" until flames engulfed the building. The result, then, was that Sherman's army burned whatever homes it desired, which amounted to many of the houses it passed in South Carolina. [13]

In the countryside very little along the route of Sherman's march survived the destruction. Some soldiers discriminated between the rich and poor, but many did not, so that a large number of poor people felt the same "Iron Hand of War" as did the wealthy. Others declared that they would burn only abandoned homes, and they kept to their word, yet very few South Carolinians had enough courage or foolishness to remain in the path of the Federals, particularly once word of their devastation spread. One foraging party went into the best room of an "unowned" plantation, broke up the furniture for firewood, and cooked their meal right there. None of the men mentioned whether they extinguished their "campfire" after dinner. An Illinois lieutenant near Orangeburg entered an abandoned home, and while he played some tunes on a beautiful piano someone else entered the house and started a fire in the adjoining room. The flames quickly chased the young officer away. In an occupied home, while a New York bugler

A sketch by William Waud of the burning of McPhersonville, South Carolina on February 1, 1865. (Library of Congress).

told a family that Union soldiers did not ravage and burn inhabited dwellings, another soldier came into the room loaded with plunder. Then, as the bugler strolled out the front door and down the path, he noticed that the back section of the house was on fire.[14]

Yet the countryside by no means endured all the destructiveness. Towns and cities also suffered atrociously at the hands of Federal firebugs. Within the first three weeks of the invasion of South Carolina, portions or most of the following towns received the torch: Gillisonville, Grahamville, Hardeeville, McPhersonville, Springfield, Robertsville, Lawtonville, Barnwell, Blackville, Midway, Orangeburg, and Lexington. Only at Orangeburg was there any suggestion that someone other than the Union Army had begun the fire, and even then soldiers admitted that their comrades had plundered the town nonetheless. Of this initial segment of the campaign, an Illinois sergeant recalled that there was so much smoke in the air from burning railroad ties and buildings that the soldiers almost suffocated. By February 10, an Ohio major remarked, "The country behind us is left a howling wilderness, an utter desolation," with schoolhouses and churches as the only survivors, though not always. Again, officers tried to save these South Carolina communities, but they, like the houses

William Waud's eyewitness sketch of the burning of Columbia, South Carolina on February 17, 1865, as published in *Harper's Weekly*, April 8, 1865. (Reproduced by permission of the Illinois State Historical Library).

in the countryside, fell victim to Sherman's men, as a cavalryman unaffectedly described in his diary: "Heavy patrols sent out to prevent the men from setting fire to the buildings" in Barnwell, but the "Town [was] all burned before the troops left." [15]

Just as Sherman's troops burned a dozen towns en route to Columbia, so they torched the capital of South Carolina. Some individuals including Sherman claimed, no doubt sincerely, that bales of cotton set afire by retreating Confederate cavalrymen rekindled in high winds during the night and spread through a large part of the city. A handful of others argued that prisoners released by Sherman's army fired the city in revenge for mistreatment by locals. Still others, such as an Ohio lieutenant, insisted that *"whisky done it* and *not the* soldiers,"* as hundreds of members of the Fifteenth and Seventeenth Corps got drunk on alcohol that blacks and whites provided for them in bottles, barrels, and pails once they marched into Columbia. The vast majority of the men, though, admitted that if Sherman's troops entered Co-

A photograph taken by George N. Barnard from the new State Capitol Building in Columbia, South Carolina after the fire of February 17, 1865. (National Archives).

lumbia, they would burn it, as they had other South Carolina towns. An Ohioan wrote home that "Our men had such a spite against the place they swore they would burn the city, if they should enter it, and they did." A Minnesota private in affirmation commented: "The Boys had long desiered to See the City burned to ashes which we all had the pleasure of seeing that Night." Harrowing stories from escaped prisoners of war, the sight of Camp Sorghum, the Confederate prison camp on the outskirts of the city, and heavy consumption of alcohol certainly exacerbated the situation, but Union troops would have burned Columbia regardless, as they had other South Carolina towns. Even if the high winds did revive the fire in the cotton bales, Sherman's men unquestionably facilitated the spread of the flames throughout the city. Despite specific orders that patrol details received to "preserve order, to protect the people in their homes and places of business, [and] prevent all rowdyism and destruction of private property," as well as the tireless efforts of certain officers and a few en-

Another photograph taken by Barnard of the ruins of Columbia, South Carolina after the February 17, 1865 holocaust. (National Archives).

listed men, drunk and sober soldiers managed to set the town ablaze in various locations. Once the fire spread in the high winds, one soldier noted, "the men were so excited, that discipline was at an end, & very little attention was paid to orders," as troops rushed into the city. A Wisconsin man informed his parents that "fire and soldiery had full swing, or sweep if you like that better, and vied with each other in mischief. Never in *modern* times did soldiers have such fun." Some men entered the city to help extinguish the blaze; others plundered shops and homes or started new fires. A captain recorded in his diary: "we got all the fire Engines in town out to work but it was no use for there was as many men setting fires as there was trying to put them out." Some soldiers actually cut the hoses, according to a Minnesota sergeant, and turned them on the firemen. By the early morning hours, after the winds had died down and a fresh brigade of infantry had entered the city and arrested some 3,500 soldiers and civilians, the fire fighters finally got the blaze under control, but not until the flames had consumed nearly 460 homes and buildings, one-third of the city.

The next day an Iowan announced: "The Capital, where treason was cradled and reared a mighty raving monster, is a blackened ruin." A Missourian without an ounce of regret declared: "Columbia is nothing but a pile of ruins, a warning to future generations to beware of treason."[16]

Nor was the destruction of Columbia enough to satiate Sherman's army. Portions of Camden, Winnsboro, Lancaster, Chesterfield, and Cheraw also suffered the effects of devastation at the hands of the troops. By the time they left the Palmetto State, the army felt satisfied that its policy of devastation had been a success. "We have left our mark through South Carolina," a Pennsylvanian wrote home, "one which will take years to repair & the sufferings of the people will never be forgotten." Another soldier predicted: "I don't think it will ever want to seceed again," and an Illinois officer jotted down his concluding thoughts on the destruction of South Carolina: "I think she has her 'rights' now. I don't hate her any more."[17]

As if the army had undergone a massive transformation overnight, North Carolinians received treatment similar to that of Georgians. Senior commanders issued orders to remind the soldiers that they were in North Carolina, the last state to secede and one with a sizable pro-Union minority, and that "a marked difference should be made in the manner in which we treat the people and the manner in which those of South Carolina were treated." No doubt the orders and arguments had a good effect, as an Ohioan admitted: "Our troops are not plundering near so much as they did in South Carolina, there being many loyal people in this state." A handful of men continued their depredations, mostly stragglers who burned some isolated houses and several blocks of Fayetteville, but for the most part Sherman's men ceased their policy of destruction.[18]

Despite the overwhelming support of the rank and file of Sherman's army for the policy of devastation, not everyone supported it. Two days' march east of Atlanta an Ohio major pondered: "In what way will the destruction of so much property aid us in restoring peace, harmony and union to our distracted country?" In South Carolina an Ohio sergeant urged that house burners "should be hung on the nearest tree." Finally, an Indiana captain was so upset over the conduct of the army in the Carolinas that he lost all interest in reuniting the country: "I would rejoice to hear of peace being made on some kind of terms and I must confess with regret that I care but little what those terms are for I have abandoned all hope of having again such a government as we once had." The army tried a number of methods to protect private property during the two campaigns, including swift and harsh punishment of violators and officers who failed to control their men. Only at Winnsboro, where Brig. Gen. John Geary made a deal with the Confederate cavalry in which he would leave a detail to guard the city after its evacuation until Confederate authorities reestablished control, in return for safe passage for the Union men, did a Federal officer find an effective means of protecting a town. At that point in the war, though, such arrangements were very difficult to maintain, particularly with the number of guerrillas in the area and the animosity of many Confederate troops. The crux of the problem was that the campaign depended heavily upon the ability of Sherman's troops to function independently or semiindependently and that the troops themselves, motivated by a spirit of revenge and a desire to crush the Southern will to continue the war, adopted Sherman's policy, at times overenthusiastically. Vigorous control, the only solution to the problem of destruction, would have stifled the independence of the troops and detracted from the overall effectiveness of the campaign, and possibly would even have endangered its success.[19]

Like the policy of devastation that the troops had adopted, plundering too was an outgrowth of the relaxation of discipline on the two campaigns, but here Georgians and North Carolinians felt a considerably larger share of the burden. Initially, most troops agreed with an Illinois sergeant who scribbled in his diary:

Tis true we are in an enemy's country, and that the enemy is responsible, to a great extent, for all the calamities and devastation incident to civil war, yet I cannot find an excuse for unlicensed marauding and vandalism.

Others, however, felt completely justified in their actions. Members of the 1st Alabama (Union) Cavalry, notorious in Sherman's army for their plundering antics, felt that they had a right to retaliate for the way pro-Confederate southerners had pillaged their family homes, imprisoned family members, and drove them from their communities.

Still other troops, according to an Ohio private, "felt a kind of freedom to take anything they wanted and could lay their hands on that
could be utilized for our comfort."[20]

Once the army entered South Carolina, the number of pillagers and
the amount of plundering increased to an even greater level. In part
this was due to the clothing needs of Sherman's troops. A large segment of the army had worn away their shoes, pants, and shirts and
tried to replace them as best they could from Carolina homes. Most
soldiers, however, did more than just take clothing. As a Massachusetts sergeant penned his sister, "I believe in taking food, clothing and
all necessary articles, that we cannot obtain otherwise, but overhaul-
ing everything even ripping open beds, and emptying them in search
of money & plate looks a little too much like plundering to me." Motivated by a spirit of revenge and a desire to strike a serious blow at
the South's will to resist, many troops came to the conclusion that
ravaging homes was as effective as burning them to the ground. An
Ohio cavalryman argued: "Previous to this I had been opposed to entering houses when foraging but now that we were in South Carolina,
the leading State in bringing on this war, I felt like the people were
entitled to share its hardships." Another soldier, a Michigan private,
disapproved of the way his comrades in arms ransacked Carolina homes,
but he earnestly believed that "it is one of the best weppons of ware-
fare for they dont want we should visit them the second time."[21]

In most cases of plundering, troops wrecked everything of financial
or sentimental value within the home. "You never can imagine a pillaged house, never—," a young Michigan lieutenant wrote with obvious distress, whereas an Ohio officer described the dismal scene of
a plundered home much less emotionally. The men, he wrote, had
broken all the dishes and jars, ruined all the furniture, shredded all
the mattresses, and drove the woman and children away with a threat
to burn them along with the home. In another instance a sergeant in
the Fourteenth Corps recorded more wanton destruction: "Some of our
soldiers are very reckless and smash everything that comes in their way.
One fellow played on the piano while his comrades danced a jog on
the top of the instrument and then he drove an axe through it, a fine
piano, today." Some men, it seems, plundered for the sheer thrill of
massive destruction and to teach the South a lesson, but many were

intent upon finding gold, silver, or jewelry. A Minnesotan confessed to his wife that a number of troops entered private houses in Louisville, Georgia, and "got Silver Pitchers & Plate of considerable value." At Columbia an Ohio private admitted he and several others pounded the door off a safe with sledgehammers and found practically nothing, while "Some members of our company, however, found rich booty during our occupation of Columbia, in the way of gold and silver ware, which they contrived to smuggle home." A member of the 1st Alabama (Union) Cavalry got caught with a loaded pistol pointed at a Georgian's head, trying to rob him of all his valuables. Other soldiers simply dropped the facade of ransacking homes and robbed civilians of their watches, jewelry, and money and left. These lawless individuals, so argued a Minnesota sergeant, were "a set of thieves who are fit candidates for Sing Sing."[22]

A large part of the pilfered goods, such as bed quilts or chinaware, soldiers used for the night and abandoned the next day at the campsite. Stolen goods that they hoped to take along with them had to be small enough to be concealed in knapsacks, blankets, or pockets. Moreover, many valuable articles, such as gold and silver items, were very heavy, and as the men tired on the march they discarded such prized possessions along the roadside. An Illinois captain noted in his journal that "Articles of siverware, that have been carried along, are thrown into the road, where the heavy wagons crushed out all semblance of anything useful, and the tired and thirsty soldier, relieved of his burden, passes on." A Wisconsin corporal regretfully told his brother: "I got a lot of nice books but I had to give them away for I could not carry them," and an Illinois soldier who found a bag of silver coins in an outhouse, because the silver was too heavy to carry, had to make a deal with a soldier who could conceal it on a baggage wagon, in spite of the good possibility that a provost guard would spot it. With sound logic Brig. Gen. Manning F. Force, a brigade and later a division commander, also wrote that "soldiers who were so exact about their burden that they cut off and threw away every unnecessary inch of blanket in order to save weight, would not encumber themselves with plunder." He then substantiated his statement with the results of a surprise search of the Seventeenth Corps conducted by the provost marshals in the Carolinas, which turned up a small amount of tobacco

and a little clothing. Only items that were light and readily conceal-
able, such as watches and jewelry, did pilferers take with them.[23]

The Union authorities responded swiftly to acts of plunder committed by the troops. Senior officers issued orders that strictly prohibited men from entering houses and specified that punishment for ar-
son or plunder would be execution by firing squad. No one was actually
executed for pillaging, but punishments were nonetheless severe, such
as a dishonorable discharge for stealing a watch; death commuted to
imprisonment for the duration of the individual's term in the service
at Dry Tortugas, a miserable military prison, for desertion and pil-
lage; and two and one-half years in jail for breaking into a home and
stealing a trunk of women's clothing and attempting to steal chloro-
form from a hospital. Officers responsible for men who plundered also
received stiff punishments. A New York major was placed under arrest and had his sword broken for permitting his foragers to plunder
houses. Maj. Gen. Frank Blair, commander of the Seventeenth Corps,
notified Col. George Spencer, commander of the 1st Alabama (Union)
Cavalry, that "the outrages committed by your command during the
march are becoming so common, and are of such an aggravated nature, that they call for some severe and instant mode of correction."
Blair then told him bluntly that if the plundering did not cease immediately he would place every officer in the regiment under arrest
and recommend to Maj. Gen. O. O. Howard that they all receive a
dishonorable dismissal from the service. To keep officers and men
honest, regimental, brigade, division, and corps commanders held frequent inspections, including knapsacks and blankets, although one officer noticed some men burying stolen items before an inspection.
Provost marshals examined all the wagons, as frequently as once every
two or three days in the Carolinas, and confiscated all unauthorized
items. General Howard, livid over the conduct of his men in South
Carolina through the fall and burning of Columbia, went so far as to
organize a detective force under the charge of his chief signal officer
"for the purpose of discovering the authors of numerous outrages that
have been committed by persons of this command" and to concentrate
on "those who have taken or may take such articles as watches, jewelry, money, & c., from persons or houses of citizens." And in case

troops attempted to mail stolen articles home, the provost marshal in-spected all packages and confiscated stolen goods.[24]

Despite the genuine attempts by Howard, Blair, and many others to check unlicensed marauding, the problem was an amazingly com-plex one. For one thing, as a New Jersey lieutenant recognized, it was hypocrisy to issue and read orders against pillaging to the rank and file when his entire train command had witnessed "a leading General" let some officers take a melodeon from a church and place it on a ship the day before and for "another leading General" to donate a magnif-icent chair to the same group of officers. For another, most soldiers firmly believed that in a hostile country they had every right to take whatever they needed from the people, in particular food and cloth-ing. Still another reason was that in the war it was not unusual for soldiers to strip their prisoners of watches, rings, and other items, but during the march to Savannah and the Carolinas the practice became widespread. Confederates robbed Sherman's men of jewelry, watches, money, boots, and sometimes entire uniforms, and Sherman's troops felt the need to retaliate in kind. Lastly, as the war wound down and Confederate control collapsed, plundering became rampant through-out the South. From Louisiana east to Georgia and through the Car-olinas senior Confederate officers, politicians, and citizens complained of marauding bands of soldiers and civilians who plundered homes and towns. In Georgia and the Carolinas, where plunderers overran the region, Sherman's pillagers competed with Southern whites, blacks, guerrillas, and Confederate troops. Testimony from Union and Con-federate soldiers as well as from civilians conceded that as Federal troops entered the major cities on the march—Atlanta, Savannah, Columbia, Fayetteville, and Raleigh—Confederate soldiers and local blacks and whites had already looted or were in the process of looting stores.[25]

According to many southerners, Wheeler's cavalrymen were worse plunderers than Sherman's troops, although in part this reputation was undeserved. Since mid-1864 these Confederate horsemen had received no government rations and, therefore, had to live off the land. They also had the unenviable task of destroying food, forage, cotton, and mills before they fell into the hands of Sherman's men. Neither of these practices endeared them to the inhabitants of Georgia and the Carolinas. Yet there was no doubt that some of Wheeler's troops, as well as mounted Confederate deserters who claimed to be in Wheeler's command, wantonly stole from and abused the inhabitants of those states. After the fall of Atlanta a Confederate cavalryman noted: "Our soldiers have become lawless to an alarming extent, steal and plunder indiscriminately regardless of age or sex. It is this which in a great measure alienates the people and makes them ready for reconstruction upon almost any terms." From the area around Savannah a signal corpsman wrote, "Wheeler is in command & is there with his cavalry, & the people say it is a question of which they should prefer, Wheeler's cavalry or the Yanks." Another soldier, an Alabama cavalryman, insisted: "The citizens of Georgia have more animosity towards Wheeler's Cavalry than they have against the Yankees." One Alabama lieutenant sent home a "silver basket a silk basque a fine piece of Leather and a pair of large scissors and a small pair" and also "a nice silk shawl" that "I captured," whereas some Texans held the town of Rome, Georgia, hostage until they received a ransom. When the remnants of Hood's army arrived, they proved little better than Wheeler's men. Another soldier, a Texan in Granbury's brigade, declared they were the best fighting unit in the army

and a set of thieves other wise Our Brig behaved shamefully all the way around from Tupelo Miss to Raleigh, N.C. The Boys had not been paid off for (10) ten months they would not issure [issue] Tobacco and that made the Boys angry They would break open stores, get the Tobacco and Lichorz. I was not in the game. I never seen men go do as our Brigade done.[26]

Despite the state of confusion in Georgia and the Carolinas, many Confederate soldiers responded to the plundering and devastation, as did guerrillas, by blaming Sherman's army and executing any troops they captured. This was in part a reaction to what they considered the mistreatment of southerners by Sherman's men, but it was also a response to their frustration, bitterness, and desperation as the bottom fell out of the Confederate war effort. In Georgia when a woman asked a Confederate soldier what happened to prisoners, he admitted:

Sometimes, when they [Confederates] was in a hurry, the guns would go off an' shoot 'em, in spite of all that our folks could do, But most giner'ly they took the grapevine road in the fust patch of woods they come to, an' soon as ever they got sight of a tree with a grape vine on it, it's cur'ous how skeered their hosses git. You couldn't keep 'em from runnin' away, no matter what you done, an' they never run fur before their heads was caught in a grape vine and they would stand thar, dancin' on nothin' till they died.

Near Savannah another soldier, a Texan, boasted to his family that flaming buildings and women's tears were stronger than the prayers of Yankee prisoners, even when on their knees begging for their lives. In the Carolinas a Georgia lieutenant told his brother: "We have captured many marauding Yankees but the men are so indignant that they generally shoot them immediately without bringing them to Gen Iverson." A Texas cavalryman told his family: "Old Sherman cuts up a great deal about finding his men murdered which he allows to insult women and plunder houses, retribution meets them in due time." Unfortunately, these Confederates rarely caught soldiers in the act of firing or pillaging homes. Instead, they erroneously assumed that all Union troops had performed these deeds at one time or another or blamed all men for the actions of some and executed them regardless of evidence, innocent and guilty alike.[27]

In response to the attacks and executions committed by bushwackers and Confederate soldiers, Sherman sought retribution, but not necessarily parity. Any bushwackers his men caught he ordered held for trial, although a handful of soldiers once executed six guerrillas on the spot and others nearly stormed a guardhouse in an unsuccessful attempt to hang several notorious murderers. Sherman also directed his men to burn any buildings from which the bushwackers had fired on them. In two instances, when Confederate Army members murdered prisoners in the sight of Union troops, Sherman retaliated by authorizing the execution of an equal number of Rebel soldiers, an order that his troops found regrettable but necessary. Otherwise, when his army discovered the body of a Union soldier either hanged, with a slit throat, or with powder burns around the fatal wound, he had his men burn all buildings within a certain distance of the body. Strangely enough, in an effort to put a halt to the destruction, some Confederates and guerrillas executed Union prisoners for burning and plundering homes and buildings, yet each body the Union Army recovered led to more devastation.[28]

As to the effectiveness of the policy of devastation, there can be no doubt. A handful of civilians, particularly those who had suffered badly at the hands of Sherman's men and had little more to lose, felt a renewed commitment to the cause of Southern independence. A seventeen-year-old Columbia woman recorded in her diary less than a week after Sherman's troops had sacked and burned that city: "Somehow I am still as confident as I ever was. If only our people will be steadfast. The more we suffer the more we should be willing to undergo rather than submit. Somehow I cannot feel we can be conquered." A North Carolina woman who nearly had her home burnt to the ground by Union troops three times exhibited a similar sense of dedication when Johnston surrendered: "Can we ever live in peace with the desecrators of our homes & the murderers of our Fathers, Brothers & Sons— *Never*—We are bound to rise again." Most civilians, however, recognized the march of Sherman's army as the death knell of the Confederacy. After watching the Union troops pour into Winnsboro, a woman recalled: "The Confederacy seemed suddenly to have changed, a glory had passed from it, and, without acknowledging it, we felt the end was near." Another woman, at the time of her letter several hundred miles removed from the march, did not need to see the blue rows and the devastation to spot the coming of the end: "I feel very blue, sometimes utterly hopeless about C.S.A. The army has walked through Georgia, destroying cities and laying waste the country. Sherman threatens S.C. terribly . . . we have not the men to meet him or check him."[29]

For the Confederate troops in the field, far away from home, the experience was a nightmare. "When the men learned of the suffering of their women at home," a South Carolina private wrote, "many of them not unnaturally deserted, and went to their aid." After letters from home reached the 4th Georgia Cavalry, the troops were so upset over the condition of their families caused by Sherman's army and, even more, by Wheeler's cavalry, that their command had to send a detachment from Alabama to correct the abuses. When Col. Charles H. Olmstead's brigade passed through Georgia to reinforce Gen. Joe Johnston in the Carolinas in late February and early March 1865, hundreds of men left the ranks "to look after their families, and who can blame them for doing so?" their commander wrote. Eventually

Olmstead had to return for them, and by the time they reached North Carolina, Johnston was asking for terms of surrender. Nor did the effect of Sherman's campaigns spare Robert E. Lee's army. In late February Lee wrote North Carolina Governor Zebulon B. Vance:

The state of despondency that now prevails among our people is producing a bad effect upon the troops. Desertions are becoming very frequent and there is good reason to believe that they are occasioned to a considerable extent by letters written to the soldiers by their friends at home.

In the two previous weeks several hundred men had deserted from A. P. Hill's Corps alone, composed mainly of North Carolinians.[30]

CHAPTER 9

Battle

". . . somewhere in all the months of weary marching,
maneuvering and campaigning, there was to come an
hour of actual battle, when the victory must be won
by the army that could outfight the other."
—JUDSON W. BISHOP, REMINISCENCE

Success in the Savannah and Carolinas campaigns depended less on achievement in the field of battle than did other major Federal land operations. It was the march itself and the massive consumption and destruction of Confederate property that contributed to the Union war effort. Yet this in no way diminished the importance of combat. For the individual soldier in Sherman's army, survival still demanded that he perform adequately in battle.

In campaigns such as those to Savannah and through the Carolinas, in which soldiers had to function much more independently than in other operations, possessing experienced troops who could take care of themselves in difficult situations was crucial. Despite the over-all Union numerical superiority, time after time the Confederates were able to bring an equal or larger number of men to bear on groups of Federals, yet usually Sherman's veterans managed to extricate themselves or beat back the attackers. Even without the guidance of officers, these troops knew how to position themselves, outflank a Confederate party, or conduct an organized retreat in the face of overwhelming opposition. Without officer supervision they took the initiative to rush to the sound of combat and join in a fight or to seize and hold a key town or railroad junction until reinforcements arrived.[1]

Of course, there were some recruits whose baptism under fire dated only as far back as the Atlanta campaign and a handful of others who had no combat experience whatsoever. One of the first days out of Atlanta, the 9th Ohio Cavalry had a skirmish with Wheeler's cavalry. One youth, according to a veteran private, got so excited in the firefight that he forgot that, to load a carbine, he had to press a spring that dropped down the barrel. The raw recruit tried twisting it and breaking the lock over his knee and was about to smash it on a tree stump when another soldier stopped him.[2]

Fortunately, soldiers in Sherman's army who could not handle themselves in battle were rare indeed. During actual campaign experience troops had learned to disregard much of Hardee's *Infantry Tactics*, the standard army manual, such as marching in step elbow to elbow, a physical impossibility in the heavily wooded South. Instead, these men understood the importance of the underlying principles that troops act as a coherent unit and remain manageable under all circumstances. They recognized the importance of pure firepower, for thousands of soldiers spent $48 of their own money to buy repeating rifles. One Hoosier sergeant wrote: "I think the Johnnys [Confederates] are getting rattled; they are afraid of our repeating rifles. They say we are not fair, that we have guns that we load up on Sunday and shoot all the rest of the week." In the hands of recruits these weapons were often an enormous waste of ammunition and a resulting burden on army logistics, but with veterans who knew the importance of ammunition conservation on campaigns such as those to Savannah and through the Carolinas, it was an extremely useful firearm, especially in critical situations.[3]

Experience had taught Sherman's men the foolhardiness of frontal assaults, particularly against earthworks held by nearly equal numbers. As a Missouri captain noted, frontal assaults "were generally costly mistakes." Flanking maneuvers, they found, conserved lives and were much more successful. Equally important, these battlefield lessons also conveyed to Sherman's men the advantages of fortified positions. An Illinois corporal recorded during the Carolinas campaign:

Old soldiers know the value of protection even a little protection is much better than no protection. we commence to dig as soon as we come in front of the enemy—often we use fence rails or timber—anything that will stop balls. A little protection Saves many lives and often wins a Battle.

Whenever the troops had time, they adopted the "head log" system. At the very top of the fortification the troops placed a thick, strong piece of timber and left several inches of space between it and the top of the other material so that troops could fire their weapons without exposing their heads. Frequently, though, the troops did not have enough time to prepare such a system, yet in a matter of a few minutes they created substantial works nonetheless. This ability impressed a Wisconsin doctor who, at the battle of Bentonville, saw his first battle from a superbly situated hill in the rear:

It was surprising to see the rapidity with which men will intrench themselves under fire—a few rails piled up in a twinkling, then dirt thrown upon them with numberless tools, bayonets, frying pans, bits of board, bare hands, anything to move dirt and it is not long before a protecting mound rises sufficiently to cover men lying behind it and as the digging proceeds, the ditch deepens as fast as the mound rises until in an almost incredible space of time an intrenchment has been thrown up sufficient to protect from cannon shot as well as rifle balls.

Even Sherman's chief engineer, O. M. Poe, a perfectionist stingy with his compliments, admired the facility with which the men constructed fortifications and their skill in the selection of the positions:

The constant practice of our troops had made them tolerably good judges of what constitutes a good defensive line, and lightened the labors of the engineer staff very materially. I was frequently surprised by the admirable location of rifle trenches and the ingenious means adopted to put themselves under cover.[4]

These were all things that came naturally to veterans that they, in turn, taught to recruits. Yet the veterans could not teach others the psychological component of experience, the incredible confidence Sherman's veterans had in themselves and their officers. This was something cultivated slowly through hard work and excellent performance on nearly every major battlefield through 1863 and in the Atlanta campaign of 1864. During several years of service the veterans had proven to their officers and themselves their ability to cope with, and perform successfully under, the enormous stress of combat in a wide variety of circumstances. Likewise, officers in Sherman's army had risen through the ranks and had won the trust and confidence of the men with their demonstrated ability on various levels within the service. It was this self-confidence and mutual confidence that was the heart and soul of Sherman's army, the key to its continuous success.[5]

The main force in opposition to Sherman's army was Wheeler's cavalry, augmented in South Carolina by Wade Hampton's cavalry. The Union infantrymen and artillerymen thought very little of their mounted enemy, whom they derogatorily nicknamed the "chivalry." After some infantry drove off an attack by Wheeler's horsemen in Georgia, an Illinois soldier recorded, "Our leaden spurs possess more genuine virtue in sending the Johnnie's horses into a double quick than the best brass or steel ever worn on rebel heels." From Fayetteville a member of Sherman's staff penned his wife, "of all the mean humbugs, 'South Carolina's chivalry' is the meanest," and seventeen days later at Goldsboro a Wisconsinite commented: "The campaign just ended has been the hardest the army has seen, not on acct [account] of the rebes, for the 'chivalry of S.C.' depended too much on their heels for their safety to make it any dangerous for *us*."[6]

Then again, Sherman's infantrymen and artillerymen had little faith in the fighting capacity of any cavalry, save possibly that of the brilliant Confederate, Nathan Bedford Forrest. An Illinois infantry officer, after witnessing a fight between Wheeler's troops and Union cavalry under Brig. Gen. Judson Kilpatrick, declared: "a cavalry fight is just about as much fun as a fox hunt; but, of course, in the midst of the fun somebody is getting hurt all the time. But it is by no means the serious work that infantry fighting is." From senior officers down to the enlisted ranks, members of Sherman's infantry and artillery belittled their own cavalry. Division commander Absalom Baird told Maj. Gen. Jefferson C. Davis that "the cavalry will not move one inch toward the enemy in advance of my column, and I have to go with it in order to accomplish what is necessary to be done." Another officer, of considerably lower rank, filed the same complaint about his army's mounted comrades: "These cavalry men are a positive nuisance; they won't fight, and whenever they are around they are always in the way of those who will fight." Even a member of their own ranks, an enlisted man in the 92nd Illinois Mounted Infantry, admitted to a friend at home: "To tell the truth cavalry are not worth much and espechaly the Ohio. The 92nd can whip more rebs than the 1st 9th & 10th all together."[7]

As reported by Kilpatrick and Wheeler, the intensity of the fights between the Union and Confederate cavalry on the march was in the same class as the battles of Shiloh, Antietam, Gettysburg, and Chickamauga. Both official reports were replete with remarks such as "completely routed" or "flee in uncontrollable confusion." In late November, in a fight near Waynesborough, Georgia, Wheeler asserted that his troops completely stampeded Kilpatrick's cavalry and nearly destroyed his command, but Kilpatrick insisted that the engagement was "one of immense disaster" to the Confederates in casualties. Wheeler claimed to have inflicted more casualties in killed and wounded in this single fight than Kilpatrick's command actually suffered during the campaign; Kilpatrick, not to be outdone, reported that 600 Confederates, nearly 20 percent of Wheeler's entire command, fell victim to Yankee lead there. One week later, near the same Georgia town, the Union and Confederate horsemen met in combat again. According to Kilpatrick, two Union cavalry assaults shattered the Confederate center and forced them to abandon the town and retreat precipitously for 8 miles. Wheeler fled in such haste that he left 200 Rebels in Union hands "wounded by the saber alone." To the contrary, Wheeler contended that his men thwarted four cavalry assaults and had to fall back when Union infantry outflanked his men on both sides. Then, warmly pressed, his column withdrew from the town, but again they killed or wounded 200 Federal mounted men, more than Kilpatrick's cavalry lost in the entire Savannah campaign. Maybe the only statements made by the two cavalry commanders that even approached the truth were when Kilpatrick termed his opponents "Wheeler's irregular, lawless cavalry" and when Wheeler maintained that the Union cavalry was "too much demoralized to again meet our cavalry" without infantry support nearby.[8]

Aside from the "chivalry," Sherman's army encountered little opposition through most of the two campaigns. There was the Georgia militia, which, according to a Missouri colonel, "once in a while got in our front, and pretended to fight 'just a little,' " but they were no real obstacle. Only once, at the battle of Griswoldville, Georgia, near Macon, did the militia attempt to check the advance of a portion of Sherman's army in the open, and the episode was a miserable failure. Here three militia brigades plus some artillery assaulted a brigade of veteran infantry from the Fifteenth Corps, many armed with repeating rifles and augmented by four pieces of artillery and, later, by a very small Indiana regiment to elongate a flank. In this debacle the Georgia Militia suffered nearly ten times as many casualties as it inflicted, and most of its losses were "Old grey-haired and weakly-looking men and little boys not over 15 years old." As an Illinois captain sadly commented, "I hope we will never have to shoot at such men again." Other attempts by Confederate authorities to supplement their cavalry in opposition to Sherman's army were equally fruitless, such as their reliance on land torpedoes and "galvanized" Yankees, units of Federal prisoners who spent more time trying to desert than fighting their fellow Yankees. Resistance, in fact, was so weak except around Savannah and in North Carolina that some men did not fire their weapons during the Savannah campaign, and one regiment in the Twentieth Corps reported that it did not suffer a battlefield fatality from late July 1864 through the occupation of Fayetteville, North Carolina.[9]

During the early days of the Savannah campaign the Confederates were powerless to do anything except "skedaddle" or take "leg bail," as Sherman's troops called it, in the face of the blue columns. As the Union Army neared Savannah, Wheeler's cavalry and the Georgia State Militia also gained the services of Confederate troops stationed in the coastal areas of Georgia, South Carolina, and Florida, and on the march through the Carolinas segments of Hood's shattered army arrived to help stiffen resistance. Nevertheless, until the Federals invaded North Carolina, the Confederates were still too weak to hope to halt Sherman's advance. Instead, they attempted to harass the Union wagon trains and foragers and to delay them in skirmishes while they concentrated more men beyond Sherman's reach. In every instance Sherman's veterans brushed aside any Confederate opposition, even strong positions in swamplands or across rivers. Near Savannah, at a place called Turkey Swamp, members of the Twentieth Corps outflanked a strong Confederate position by wading through a bog and easily drove them off. As a Wisconsin captain boasted, "we had a most magnificent view of their coat tails standing out at right angles to a pair of legs that was doing their best to take their owners to a place of safety." In one day in South Carolina, at the cost of six casualties, a division captured a superbly fortified position at Pocotaligo, which had defied the Federals stationed at Beaufort for two years. The Confederates had the Union troops pinned down throughout the day and inexplicably evacuated during the night. In one week the men in the Army of the Tennessee crossed four difficult rivers, each one surrounded by dense swamps, yet the Confederates "hardly give us a chance to look at them before they are off," an astonished Minnesotan wrote.[10]

Needless to say, there was a great deal of speculation within Sherman's army about why the Confederates resisted the Federal advances so feebly. From 1861 through the fall of Atlanta 41 months later, the Confederates had always fought doggedly, but by November 1864, "The Confederates," as a perceptive New York sergeant noted, "seemed to have lost their old vigor." Many soldiers correctly attributed the Confederate weakness to a manpower shortage. From Savannah a Minnesotan wrote: "Grant told the truth when he said that they had every available man in the field and were robbing the cradle and the grave to fill their thinned ranks." To others, the facility with which Sherman's troops captured their opponents indicated a speedy decline of Confederate morale. In November an unarmed Hoosier private talked two Rebel soldiers into a careless mistake and stole a rifle from them and "finely by puarsuading and got them to Come with me to Camp." One month later a Wisconsin corporal simulated a revolver by placing his hand in his pocket and captured an armed Confederate. During and after the battle of Bentonville, Confederates surrendered in substantial numbers and under the least threatening circumstances. An Iowan captured four soldiers with only a revolver, and a captured Illinois private tricked five Confederates and took them prisoner. The old-timer of the 123rd New York, "Uncle" Joe Young, took two Rebels prisoner single-handed. When someone asked how he did it, Uncle Joe quipped, "Why I surrounded them." The most incredible feat, though, occurred when a lieutenant and two orderlies captured seventy-three Confederate cavalrymen.[11]

No matter what the reasons were, it was obvious that the war was drawing to a close. A New York private told his brother: "We think here the rebs are about whiped for they wont wait to give Sherman battle any more." A more articulate Wisconsinite penned: "The troops are perfectly joyous at the discomfiture of the rebels who can only make a show of strength at most." On a march deep into hostile territory, the inability of the Confederates to muster a decent-sized force to strike the invaders was, for Sherman's veterans, a clear signal of Confederate weakness. As a Minnesota corporal asserted after he and his comrades had destroyed five miles of a Southern railroad without any resistance from the Confederates, "In my opinion the thing is fast dwindling away."[12]

Despite these predictions, Sherman's veterans had confronted the Confederates too many times on the battlefield to assume that they would surrender before the cause was utterly hopeless. "They are a Gritty set," a Wisconsin corporal in South Carolina insisted, "and so may hold out a good while yet." Moreover, combat was still a very serious business with Sherman's veterans. It was a place where men lost their lives, and a Georgia militiaman's minié ball could prove just as fatal as one from the best marksman in Hood's army. After four years of war, an Illinois captain related, "We don't hear so many young men spoiling for a fight as we did early in the war. The edge has worn off. The boys have got over it. They are different now. They have had a taste of it."[13]

Just prior to a battle was the tensest moment for soldiers. Some men got sick to their stomachs; others handled the prefight jitters better by nervously fidgeting. Occasionally some lighthearted soldier broke the tension with a joke or a peculiar statement, as did a hungry member of the 17th Ohio who, in the midst of an assault, interrupted the colonel's instructions with a request: "Colonel, I want to charge by way of that turnip patch." Most men, it seems, experienced the same sensations and fears as did a veteran Ohio private who wrote:

Many a time, if not every time while we were waiting and expecting to be pushed into an engagement, would I have given almost anything to be out of it, back at the rear in some safe place. But despite such sensations, I always had enough strength of will and valued my reputation too much, to shirk—so was enabled to collar myself and compel myself to face the danger.

They remained at their post and performed in combat, not because they lacked fear, but because of discipline and an enormous sense of obligation. One captain in the Seventeenth Corps, after reflecting upon why they stood up to the Confederate bullets, concluded that it was a "species of moral cowardice. We wanted to 'go home' but did not dare to." [14]

As these men involved themselves in the battle, as they began to perform the assigned tasks, their fear took a secondary position. An Ohio veteran noticed that "in instances where we found ourselves suddenly, without time or forethought, under fire, or when once in the turmoil and excitement of battle, I declare I was not conscious of fear." The bitter taste of gunpowder; the choking clouds of exploded powder; the awesome spectacle of battle, with its peculiar assortment of beauty, destructiveness, and incomparable chaos; the deafening roar of artillery and musketry fire, interspersed occasionally by a violent string of curses or orders barked out by some officer; and the searing heat of a musketry rifle after prolonged use so preoccupied the senses of the troops that none really stuck out in their minds. They simply performed their duty, almost as if they were automatons. As a Wisconsin private wrote home, "I did not think of the bullets that was whizing around me, about all I thought of was just what I was doing my self but I thought about home." [15]

One thing that was strikingly evident to veterans was the pure chance of battle. Nearly everyone had had some close calls during the war, and for thinking soldiers there was no clear reason why they had survived in all the battles while some of their comrades had lost their lives. As a member of the 32nd Wisconsin bent down, a shell shredded his knapsack and drove him into the ground, yet he received not a scratch. Had he remained erect, the shell would have killed him. A rifle ball passed through the clothes of an Indiana sergeant and just nicked him. Had he stood two inches over, the wound could easily have proved fatal. Instead, he sustained only a scratch and a sick stomach after the close call. At the battle of Averasborough a Wisconsin corporal took his knapsack into battle, something unusual. That night his diary entry read: "Had a bullit put into my knapsack, The knap. saving my life."[16]

To counteract the randomness of combat, some troops relied on instinct or intuition. An Ohio private told his sister that invisible friends protected him in battle, and others confessed that some peculiar premonition saved their lives. A Minnesota sergeant, directing artillery fire outside Savannah, gobbled down a hardtack and began to walk over to his haversack that hung on the pole of his tarpaulin to get another one. "But when half way to it, *something told me not to go.* A moment after, and a ten pound shot bounced over the low parapet on our left . . . & plunged right through my tarpaulin." A member of the 100th Indiana recorded a similar yet tragic incident in South Carolina. A sergeant became sick "as he always was when we have to wait in line expecting a fight," although the troops considered him "brave enough after he is in battle." When the colonel found out the sergeant had left the ranks, he berated the man for his conduct until the sergeant said, "I will go, Colonel, since you insist, but I am sure if I go up there I shall be killed." Ten minutes later, the last shell the Confederates fired struck and killed the sergeant. Nor were such presentiments always true. Before the battle of Bentonville a veteran sergeant believed that he would die and gave a letter addressed to his family to a lieutenant and asked him to mail it in case of his death. The lieutenant promised to mail it but insisted that the sergeant would survive nonetheless. In peculiar twist of fate, the next day the lieutenant lost his life and the sergeant came through the battle unscathed. Yet, whether men attributed their survival to invisible friends, premonitions, or just plain luck, the tenuousness of life in combat was always apparent.[17]

From both a physical and a psychological standpoint, the most difficult type of battle to fight was the frontal assault. With the deadly effects of case shot from field artillery and a rifled musket as the standard infantry weapon, firing accurately at 400 yards, most senior officers expected to suffer heavy casualties and believed that for a frontal assault to succeed the attackers needed at least three times as many troops as the defenders. From the soldiers' viewpoint, the mental aspects of a frontal assault were almost equally as devastating. An Illinois sergeant wrote:

A sketch by Theodore R. Davis, an eyewitness, of the storming of Fort McAllister by Brig. Gen. William B. Hazen's Second Division, Fifteenth Corps on December 13, 1864. The sketch was in *Harper's Weekly*, January 14, 1865. (Reproduced by permission of the Illinois State Historical Library).

It is the most trying moment in the experience of a soldier, when a charging column is preparing for the final dash against the enemy's works. The pressure on the brain and nerve is intense, and under the strain some become panic stricken, while others perform the most valorous deeds.

In the victorious assault at Fort McAllister near Savannah, which Sherman needed to establish a supply line with the U.S. Navy vessels, Brig. Gen. William Hazen handled the situation masterfully. His troops did not learn of the attack until late that very afternoon when staff officers told the officers and men exactly what to do. To reduce casualties, Hazen sent sharpshooters to within 200 yards of the fort to fire on the artillery gunners and deployed his men in one line as thin as possible. Then, as an officer who participated in the assault wrote to his wife, "The attention was sounded advance—charge—when the men went with one tremendous yell and in 13 minutes from the time we charged we had possession of the fort with all the booty." In the assault Hazen lost 24 men killed and 110 wounded, most of them from a line of torpedoes around the fort, and inflicted 250 casualties on the defenders.[18]

Around Savannah, the troops grew understandably reluctant to assault the Confederate works after they had spent several days in the trenches. Their original enthusiasm had dissipated, and the roads over which many of the troops would have to attack were only sixty feet wide and were well protected by Confederate artillery. Those assigned to attack off the roads would have to wade through swamps and creeks to reach the Confederate entrenchments. There was no doubt in the minds of the officers and men in Sherman's army that an assault would succeed, yet many of them feared the cost of victory. Thus, they regretted that the Confederates escaped but preferred to fight on better ground. As a Michigan private commented to a friend, "I am glad they took the hint and left for we would had a very bad swamp to charged through and perhaps our loss would ben very heavy."[19]

The two largest battles during the Savannah and Carolinas campaigns occurred in North Carolina over a six-day period. The first one, fought on March 16 and called Averasborough, was an engagement between Kilpatrick's cavalry and two divisions of the Twentieth Corps and a small corps of Confederates under Lt. Gen. William J. Hardee. Hardee had hoped to delay the advance of Sherman's Left Wing in order to gain time for Gen. Joseph E. Johnston, who was trying to concentrate enough men to attack either of Sherman's wings. On March 15 Hardee had halted the Union cavalry, and the following morning he not only resisted stubbornly again but actually seized the initiative until the arrival of one entire infantry division and part of another from the Twentieth Corps. In person, Sherman directed Col. Henry Case's infantry brigade to swing around the Confederates' right flank and strike their fortifications from the rear, which completely routed the Confederates. An Illinois private who participated in the flank attack wrote his parents:

As soon as we got in behind them we started with a yell on the double quick and I tell you I was never so pleased in my life as I was to see the rebs get up and try to get out of the way, but I tell you what thare was a good many of them bit the dust. I never saw the dead so thick on the field before.

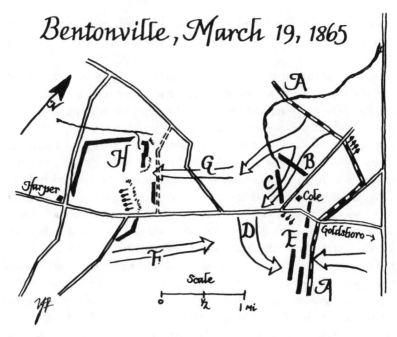

Map of Bentonville

This sketch is drawn from aerial photographs, with troop dispositions being placed according to reports in the *Official Records*. With the exception of one road, here represented by dotted lines, the location of the roads is essentially the same today as it was in 1865.

Preliminary movements. As Carlin's Union division approaches the Cole House it is exposed to artillery fire from guns located across the fields to the east. Scrambling into a wooded ravine in front and to the left of the Cole House, the Union troops throw up hasty breatworks (B). Morgan's division (E) and Robinson's brigade (C) arrive and also dig in. A probing attack against the main Confederate line (A–A) fails.

First Phase. About 3:00 p.m. the Confederates attack, outflanking and smashing through Carlin's division (B) and Robinson's brigade (C), which fall back upon the 20th corps (II) in disorder.

Second Phase: The Confederates next attempt to pinch off Morgan's division (E), which is exposed by the retreat of Carlin's troops. Three brigades from Hill's corps break through (D) and assault the Union line from the rear while Hoke makes a simultaneous attack from the front. The timely arrival of Cogswell's brigade (F) forces Hill's troops (D) to retire. This is the decisive maneuver of the battle.

Another private counted thirty-three Confederate bodies within a few dozen yards of one another. One Ohioan claimed that the attack was so sudden that the Confederates abandoned knapsacks, guns, and swords to the Federals, and Confederate testimony corroborated the panic along the line. Somehow the Confederates managed to reorganize these troops at a second line, which the Federals again threatened to outflank, and they retreated to a third, stronger line, held by another division. From here they resisted several Union attacks throughout the late afternoon and fell back at nightfall. At the battle of Averasborough, Sherman suffered 682 casualties and inflicted an estimated 865 casualties on the Confederates, or over 11 percent of Hardee's command.[20]

Three days later at Bentonville, by far the largest battle of the two campaigns, the Confederates failed in a last, desperate attempt to crush one of Sherman's wings. Gen. Joe Johnston, upon the advice of his cavalry commander, Lt. Gen. Wade Hampton, had skillfully deployed his troops concealed from the Federals' view in thick woods. Portions of the Fourteenth and Twentieth Corps, completely unaware of Johnston's position owing to poor reconnaissance by the Union cavalry, stumbled directly into his trap. Assuming that the force before them was relatively weak, Union brigade and division commanders selected their positions carelessly, and senior officers such as Sherman, Slocum, and Davis paid little attention to the Confederate resistance. On the extreme left were two brigades from Brig. Gen. William P. Carlin's division of the Fourteenth Corps, followed by two-thirds of a brigade from the Twentieth Corps. Unwittingly, they had selected positions within the Confederate right flank and were, therefore, extremely vulnerable to an attack. Several hundred yards over

---

Third Phase. About 5:00 p.m. the Confederates move against the 20th corps (H), trying to drive a wedge into an unoccupied portion of the Union line. Five desperate attacks (G) fail, and the Confederates fall back to the original line occupied by them in the morning. This ends the fighting on the first day of the battle.

Source: The map has been redrawn based on Jay Luvaas, "Bentonville—Johnston's Last Stand," North Carolina Historical Review, XXXIII, No. 3 (July, 1956), pp. 338 and 339. (By permission from the North Carolina Division of Archives and History).

was the third brigade in Carlin's division, and the division of Brig. Gen. James D. Morgan, also of the Fourteenth Corps, deployed on the right flank. Morgan placed two brigades along the front line and kept one in reserve and directed his troops to fortify their positions. After some skirmishers attempted to dislodge the Confederates, Johnston's troops unleashed an assault that crushed the left side of the Union line. These Federals from the Fourteenth and Twentieth Corps, many of whom were veterans, fought valiantly, but when the Confederate on-slaught became too much to handle and Rebel troops began to pene-trate their rear, a spark of panic shot through the blue ranks and many soldiers turned and fled. A Michigan lieutenant wrote to his sister that his regiment fought hard and held their position as long as they could, "& when that was no longer a possibility run like the duce." Others, however, retreated in good order and reassembled behind a line of men from the Twentieth Corps as they arrived on the field.[21]

The panic was, in a sense, a momentary case of mass hysteria. When the men suddenly realized that the Confederates were moving around their flank and behind them, the Union troops, according to a New York private, "lost the bonds of discipline and the power to reason" and raced to the rear, as a Wisconsin corporal described, "like a flock of sheep." Once safely within Union lines, these veterans quickly re-gained their composure and tried as best they could to reorganize and take a solid defensive position, yet "Every one who had been con-cerned in it looked ashamed."[22]

The troops under Morgan also had Confederates penetrate deep into their rear, but they remained at their posts and fought magnificently. As an Illinois lieutenant wrote his father, "all agree in saying it was the hottest place we were ever in. The rebels had us completely sur-rounded and nothing but the most obstinate resistance saved the en-tire division from capture." After the Confederates had routed the left portion of the Federal line, they rolled over the third brigade from Carlin's division and swung around toward the rear of Morgan's di-vision while other Rebel troops simultaneously assaulted from the front. Maj. Gen. Jefferson C. Davis, commander of the Fourteenth Corps, sent Morgan's reserve brigade under Bvt. Brig. Gen. Benjamin Fear-ing over to block the flanking maneuver, which, despite confusion caused by Confederates wearing Union uniforms, Fearing's men successfully accomplished until overwhelming numbers drove them back several hundred yards and exposed Morgan's rear.[23]

Meanwhile, Morgan's other two brigades had their hands full with a vigorous frontal assualt. Members of the 14th Michigan held their fire until the attackers came within 30 yards of their line before they "rose steadily as one man and poured into the enemy the most terrific fire I ever listened to," wrote its regimental commander. After several volleys the Michigan troops rushed over their barricades and launched a counterattack that took 160 prisoners. Soldiers in the other brigade formed in two lines: the men in the front fired the weapons while their counterparts in the rear loaded a second set of rifles. According to the testimony of an Ohio sergeant, the Confederate assault was so vicious that the two rifles he and his partner used got almost too hot to fire.[24]

Into the gap created when the Confederate right drove back Fearing's brigade came the Confederate hordes. Fortunately for Morgan's men, relief in the form of a brigade from the Twentieth Corps under Bvt. Brig. Gen. William Cogswell arrived to plug this breach between Fearing's brigade and Morgan's other two brigades, as they struck the Confederates in the flank and drove many of them back. Other Rebel troops, though, struck Morgan's men in the rear. The dusty, faded, threadbare uniforms of the Confederates, intermixed with other Rebel soldiers in Union uniforms, greatly resembled the Federal ranks and almost resulted in a disaster for the Fourteenth corpsmen. At first they hesitated to fire, assuming that these were Federal reinforcements arriving from the rear, but a reconnaissance party soon ascertained that these were Confederates in their rear. Some troops rushed the attackers and fought them hand to hand while most men simply jumped to the opposite side of their barricade and greeted the Confederates with a shower of lead. This deadly fire decimated the Confederate ranks, and a countercharge swept the rear clear of Rebels.[25]

Except for some scattered gunfire, fighting around Morgan's division ended for the day, yet heavy fighting on the left side continued until sunset. There the shattered remnants of Carlin's division rallied behind brigades from the Twentieth Corps as they arrived on the scene. Before them was an open field cluttered with unoccupied Federal hospital tents, assembled much earlier in the day and hastily evacuated in the rout, and beyond that were woods. Across that field the Confederate columns, hoping to follow up their initial success, launched assault after assault—seven in all—on the Union lines. Each time the Federals met them with a galling infantry and artillery fire and inflicted heavy losses on the attackers. Finally, at nightfall, victory having eluded them, the Confederates retired to their original position.[26]

That night and during the following morning the Army of the Tennessee, after an all-night march, reached the battlefield. The Fifteenth Corps took up a position to the right of Morgan's division; the Seventeenth Corps, to the right of that. With nearly three times as many troops on the field, the initiative now shifted to Sherman. That day there was some sporadic firing, and the next day an unsupported reconnaissance-in-force under Maj. Gen. Joseph Mower, a division commander in the Seventeenth Corps, penetrated deep into Johnston's rear and almost cut off the Confederates' escape route until some gray cavalry and infantry drove them back. Otherwise, Sherman elected to allow Johnston to retreat uncontested and rendezvoused with Maj. Gen. John Schofield's command at Goldsboro, rather than slug it out at Bentonville. On the night of March 21 the Confederates withdrew from Bentonville, and three days later Sherman's army entered Goldsboro. Johnston's army lost 2,606 men, Sherman's 1,527.[27]

The wounded victims of these and other battles and skirmishes suffered all sorts of injuries, from minor nicks that were more scary than harmful to wounds that were permanently debilitating or eventually fatal. Near Savannah a ball fired either from an excessive range or with poor-quality gunpowder struck a Wisconsin private in the back of the neck:

it maide a hole a bout one inch and a half deep   it fetched me down   it did not hurt mutch   it made me numb all over   I thought that somb thing struck me on the top of my head   it maid my head ring like a bell   I stuck to my pipe un till the docktor be gan to dig out the ball   then I wanted to drink.

An Ohio sergeant who stepped on a torpedo in the assault on Fort McAllister had a very different experience, both in the type of injury and in the amount of pain:

On recovering from the effects of the shock I found that the shoe of my left foot was blown entirely off and the foot badly burned. My left knee was slightly cut, the small finger and the one next to it on my left hand also cut, and the hand burned. My face and one ear considerably cut and burned. My eyes swelled shut in a short time. The sufferings of that night were terrible.

Despite this awful ordeal, at least the Ohio sergeant had his arms and legs intact. Others were not so fortunate. Grisly tales of field hospital tents with piles of limbs in a corner were true.[28]

Many wounded soldiers, some with very serious injuries, somehow managed to recover. In mid-April a Michigan private wrote his friend back home:

I hope you will pardon me for nor wrighting before but a hole through my leg caused by a minney has caused me some inconvenience as it has kept me from doing enny verry big running around. the ball went in a little above my knee and came out just under my a–s so it made a pretty big hole.

One month later he wrote his friend that he was moving well on crutches and felt he would recover completely. Those who underwent amputation, despite the tragic loss of a limb, had an impressive survival rate. During the Carolinas campaign the chief surgeon of the Fourteenth Corps reported that sixty-five of sixty-six amputations were successful and that the treatment of all nine cases of postoperative gangrene by "removing all unsound flesh and then applying nitric acid," was completely effective, though unbearably painful.[29]

Moreover, many amputees and others who sustained serious injuries were happy just to be alive. They had seen the randomness of battle and so many comrades who were even less fortunate than themselves. They also found deep within themselves some consolation that their loss was for a just cause and that some good would stem from it. A member of the 1st Alabama (Union) Cavalry wrote his parents: "When within 7 miles of Savannah on the 9th of Dec I met with an accident that made me a cripple for life." While examining an exploded torpedo, his right foot touched the cap of an undetected one, and the explosion shattered his leg so badly that the doctor had to amputate it above the knee. He then concluded: "The most wonderful part of the whole thing is that I wasn't instantly killed as my clothes were literally torn in rags." A major in an Ohio regiment who lost an index finger in the assault at Fort McAllister dictated a letter to his wife that stated: "I shall not attempt a description of my wound. suffice it to say that I esteem it a proud souvenir of the storming of Fort

MacAllister." Finally, a Connecticut private, wounded in the leg at Bentonville, told his children three days after his amputation: "I am thankful to God that I am so well as I am. I would have you be good children till I see you again which I hope won't be long. May God in his mercy spare us all to meet again once more in the flesh." Five days later he died.[30]

For those who could not pull through, there was at least religion to comfort them. While dying in a hospital around Savannah, an Ohio private dictated some final words to his mother: "I are a trying to Live a better life for time to come and I shal try to hold out faith full untill they End." For those who survived there were difficult moments, yet they lived in a world where death played a greater role in everyday life and fought a war in which death was commonplace. As a Michigan officer commented on the battle of Bentonville one month later, "by jove it looked hard to see intimate friends blown to pieces before your eyes but such is life." They shed tears for individual friends, especially men they had known from home or had served alongside for several years. A Hoosier sergeant, a hardened veteran, described the difficult time he had attempting to write a friend's wife of her husband's death: "when it come to telling about the way he died and how we buried him I could hardly write. I had to get away of by my self, and I am affraid she will have hard work to read it for I could not help blotting the paper some." For the survivors there was, nevertheless, some consolation, according to an Illinois sergeant: "It pained us to leave them buried in a strang land but we knew that they fell in a glorious cause and though their graves are far away they still live in the memory and always wil as long as we are permited to live."[31]

An Illinois surgeon near Savannah argued with considerable accuracy that "There is no God in war. It is merciless, cruel, vindictive, un-christian, savage, relentless. It is all that devils could wish for." Yet another Illinois officer, scanning row after row of graves without epitaphs as his command marched east from Atlanta, declared: "There was no time for sentiment, and death's work had no novelty here," and he was right too. After three or four years of fighting, Sherman's veterans hated to lose more lives, but they were unwilling to back down from their original goal, reunification, both for themselves and for their comrades who gave their lives for this goal.[32]

CHAPTER 10

The War's End

"tell mother to have a strawberry shortcake
for me to eat when I get there."
—JOHN LANGHANS TO BROTHER,
28 MAY 1865

As soon as Sherman's army entered Goldsboro, they began preparations for a new campaign. Nearly everyone in the army needed a new
outfit of clothing, yet supplies trickled in so slowly that many of the
men got only a pair of shoes or pants. The animals, too, required rest
and refitting. On the next campaign their load would be even greater,
since Sherman intended to bring his supplies with him and no longer
live off the land. Moreover, at Goldsboro, Sherman's army linked with
two corps of nearly 40,000 men, the Tenth and the Twenty-third, both
under the command of a familiar officer, Maj. Gen. John M. Schofield, who had participated in the Atlanta campaign, so that the army
now needed enough supplies for 100,000 men. The destination of this
giant command was, as the troops surmised, Richmond via Petersburg. "It is the talk with the Boys now that our next moove will be
in the direction of Richmond," wrote an Iowa sergeant, "but they say
it is hard to tell which way Crazy Bill (Sherman) will go for he goes
where ever he wants to and the rebs cant help themselves." This would
be the final showdown, the campaign to win the war, and possibly the
most difficult of the entire war. As another Iowa sergeant indicated:

You are aware in this that we have got through with our great expedition and are now fitting out for a new one some place else   I do not know where but I think in the direction of *Richmond* and then comes the tug of *war*   then comes war in reality   war that will make this nation tremble   let it come   let us have it in any shape that will satisfy Mr. *Jonnie Reb* that they must be good citizens as soon as this is done the War is over and piace and plenty will again abound.[1]

Then, in the course of less than one week, Sherman's army received some wonderful news from their comrades in arms around Petersburg. First, Grant had broken Lee's hold on Petersburg and Richmond and had taken both cities. As word spread the army erupted in celebration. Troops fired rockets, drank toasts, and wildly cheered the accomplishment of the Army of the Potomac. One captain recorded three days later that "For the three nights past the men have been so jubilant over the recent achievements of our armies that it has been difficult to restrain their enthusiasm." By the morning of April 11, Sherman set his command in motion, not to unite with Grant in Virginia as originally planned, but to crush Johnston's army. Then, the following day, as the army approached Raleigh, word arrived that Lee had surrendered his army to Grant. A Minnesotan wrote: "I never heard such cheering in my life. It was one continuous roar for three hours." Another soldier told his wife the boys gave "shout after shout . . . hats went up . . . the band struck up good, old, national 'Yankee Doodle,' even the roosters sitting on packmules that some facetious darkey or some other genius had brot along seemed to participate in the joys." He eventually concluded, "even Major Lisben could smile." With little hope of success, Johnston realized that further fighting would mean an unnecessary loss of lives, and on April 14, after Kilpatrick's cavalry had entered Chapel Hill and the infantry was not far behind around Durham, the Confederate commander arranged a cease-fire and undertook negotiations with Sherman.[2]

Here Sherman's army learned of the tragic assassination of their president and leader, Abraham Lincoln. Not even in South Carolina had the men felt such a desire for vengeance. A mob of some 2,000 soldiers marched on Raleigh that night with the intention of destroying the city, and only the timely intervention of Fifteenth Corps commander, Maj. Gen. John Logan, supported by field artillery, averted a second disaster. Fortunately for the people of North Carolina, Sherman and Johnston reached terms of surrender before the army began another march. Had Sherman's troops undertaken another campaign, as an Ohio artillery private wrote home, the devastation might have been worse than that in South Carolina:

if this army had gone on another campaign I should pitty the rebels that we met and the country through which we passed. For every man would take it upon himself to do every thing he could to avenge the death of old Abe, and dearly he would have been avenged for the boys would have shown no mercy.

For several days officers had to keep camps surrounded by trustworthy guards to ensure the safety of southerners and their property until the fury eased somewhat. Yet as quickly as the crisis came, so it passed. Progress in the peace negotiations turned the attention of Sherman's men away from the assassination and toward the end of the war and going home.[3]

With Johnston's surrender and the termination of hostilities near at hand, Sherman's troops had more and more peaceful contacts with the Confederates, which clearly reflected an attitude of understanding and a hope for a rapid and relatively painless reconciliation and reunification. Undoubtedly, a handful of Federals still felt bitter toward southerners for this war. A Michigan officer, wounded in the Carolinas campaign and a cripple for life, wrote a friend: "It may be fault or neglect of my early training, but for myself I *never* can forgive and forget those who plotted and labored for the overthrow of the Republic." The overwhelming majority in Sherman's army, however, "show to us a more liberal disposition than the most sanguine expected," a Georgia lieutenant recorded in his diary. For some, these kindly feelings toward the Confederates stemmed from the fact that four years earlier they were brothers under the same flag, and as long as the Rebels "are willing to admit that we have whipped them . . . that is all we want of them." Another soldier, an Indiana sergeant, jotted in his diary that Confederate troops earned considerate treatment on the part of the victors for their performance in the war: "Although I have met them on the battlefields and helped lay waste their country my heart goes out to them in sympathy for them. They have shown themselves to be worthy of Americans and brave men." While Sherman and

Johnston negotiated, Confederates and Yankees intermingled along the picket line, and paroled members of Lee's army visited the Federal camps en route home and received warm greetings, some food, and good conversation. Like their commander, Sherman's men believed that as long as the Confederates resisted they would conduct a war of devastation, but once the war ended they would treat the Rebels as fellow countrymen. An Illinois enlisted man noticed that "At the prospect of restoration all feelings of animosity are dispelled from the true soldier's breast & a warm feeling of fraternal brotherhood springs up." A Wisconsin captain declared: "I believe that we have been so completely victorious that we can afford to be merciful, and that a general amnesty will do more to cement the Union than the most rigorous punishment." That nearly all Confederates deprecated the assassination of Lincoln, at least in the presence of Federals, and announced that they too had now lost a truly compassionate leader, helped to reinforce feelings of magnanimity in Sherman's army. Yet despite these kindly sentiments, an Iowan prophetically wrote to a friend of the reconstruction of the nation: "Probably justice will be meted out a little more stern than it otherwise would have been, for Abe's heart was most too large."[4]

Blacks, too, had won the respect and sympathy of the vast majority of Sherman's army, but even the most optimistic soldiers were pessimistic about their chances of attaining true freedom and equality. A sergeant thought that the Western armies had recognized blacks as "true and loyal friends of the Union soldier" and had treated them with kindness and generosity around the camps, "but not many had learned to meet them on terms of equality in all the public and social conditions of life." In Georgia a Wisconsin officer intimated, "I hope they may gain what they so ardently desire—their freedom, but I fear they will in thousands of cases, find their freedom in death." Finally, an unidentified member of the 70th Indiana wrote home, "It is depressing to see their joy, when one thinks of the impossibility of their attaining their ideal of freedom." He then concluded with the statement: "We laugh now at their wild antics, and marvellous expectations, but cannot shut out the thought that the comedy may soon darken into tragedy."[5]

After Johnston's surrender, which the commanders finally accomplished with little fanfare, the army began its march for the nation's capital and the final muster. With Sherman temporarily absent in South Carolina, the march became one of the hardest the army made. The corps commanders placed bets on whose men could march the fastest to Richmond and drove their men twenty-five to thirty miles per day in the May heat and humidity of North Carolina and Virginia. Thousands of men straggled; hundreds became ill; and dozens who had survived the war died of heat prostration. Needless to say, the troops were enraged. A lieutenant in the Army of the Tennessee complained: "This brutality should be investigated." A sergeant in the Army of Georgia insisted: "We have never made a much harder march and some of our Generals deserve to have their necks broke for such 'Tom foolery' after the war."[6]

As the army reached the vicinity of Richmond it came into contact with more and more Eastern troops, resurrecting the old East–West bitterness. At Goldsboro some members of Sherman's army did not have much faith in the ability of the Army of the Potomac to defeat Lee without their help, and when the easterners did, the men in Sherman's army rejoiced mainly because it brought the war much closer to the end. A handful of other soldiers, such as an Illinois officer, saw an additional benefit in this victory for the Army of the Potomac, an avoidance of increased tensions between Eastern and Western armies:

We had all hoped we would be sharer's in the glory of the fall of the Rebel Capital & Strong hold but it is much better as it is for the western army can boast of enough *victories* without this one and the bitter feeling among eastern troops against western ones would have been increased if we had been participants in *their* glory of taking Richmond.

Unfortunately, the problems between the Eastern and Western troops grew worse the closer Sherman's army came to Washington. For one thing, as Sherman's troops marched over famous battlefields and across the prominent rivers of the Eastern campaigns, their impression of their Eastern counterparts diminished. A Minnesotan, no doubt tainted by the experiences and accomplishments of Sherman's army, told his sister: "The more I see of this Army (Potomac) the more I am disgusted with their operations for the last years. If there had been an army worth anything here, Richmond would have fallen three years ago." Somewhat less biased, an Illinois soldier around Richmond recorded: "The works about the city wear a formidable aspect but considering nature, Sherman penetrated many as strong positions in Georgia. Our estimates of the Eastern Army's merits grows less daily." For another, Eastern officers tried to prohibit Sherman's men from visiting cities and towns, even though Eastern troops had access to those very same places. This annoyed members of the Seventeenth Corps so much that they got in a brawl with soldiers from the Twenty-fourth Corps in Manchester, Virginia, and drove the easterners away with a barrage of stones and fists. Lastly, Sherman's troops were celebrities at the nation's capital. The people had seen the Army of the Potomac for four years, but Sherman's men were novelties. Everyone wanted to speak with one of Sherman's bummers and learn all about those mysterious campaigns through the South. The soldiers of the Army of the Potomac, a little jealous over the reception Sherman's army received, began to belittle them everywhere, calling them "Sherman's Greasers," "Slouch Hats," "Swamp Angels," and "Thieves." Sherman's men defended their appearance by arguing that "if they had marched as much as we have and could not draw any more soap or clothes than we did they would not look much better" and retaliated by calling the Eastern troops "paper collars, soft bread, featherbeds, white gloves &c."[7]

On May 23 the Army of the Potomac paraded through the streets of Washington before the president and his cabinet, Generals Grant and Sherman, and tens of thousands of folks. The enlisted men had new uniforms, polished brass on their accouterments, gleaming rifles, and white gloves; and their noncommissioned officers as well as officers wore sabers. The next day Sherman's army was to march. As usual, a number of men grumbled about reviews, as did a Minnesotan: "On the 24th our grand foolery came off (for which is the proper name for a review). It is too much like the Potomac to suit our army." The bulk of the army, however, realized that it was their last one and decided to cooperate a little and cleaned themselves up. The government had forced many of the troops to use their clothing allowance to purchase various items under the ruse of further campaigning or the parade, although actually to deplete the government stockpiles and avoid paying the men cash for the portion of the allotment they did not use.

Maj. Gen. Henry W. Slocum leading the Army of Georgia down Pennsylvania Avenue, Washington, D.C., in the Grand Review of 24 May 1865. (Library of Congress).

Nevertheless, most troops refused to wear the new issue and insisted that if their clothing was good enough for campaigning all the way to Washington, it was good enough for a review. Several days later, a Wisconsin private described the scene of the parade to his parents:

That day we all fell in, and it seemed the minute the order was given, our boys took on an apperance of glory and holiness, and they *marched, oh* how they marched, never before did they stride like that. Just imagine the scene, Mother and Father, if you can! Men marching in their old worn-out uniforms, some with new pants that stood out like sore thumbs, scuffed shoes, the guns seeming to speak out "we have seen better days", our flags tattered and torn, and all along the way, crowds upon crowds of people, cheering so loudly they deafened our ears. . . . How proud we were. The color bearers carried the flags that told of our conflicts with the enemy. As we passed the reviewing stand, all eyes went right, and the boys did right shoulder arms in perfect timing. President Johnson with his Government Officials, some Foreign Officers and General Grant stood up and cheered as we passed. I thought we would all lose some more buttons for our chests swelled up and our hearts throbbed.

An officer considered that review "the proudest day of my life," and a sprightly Iowa sergeant declared: "For once Sherman and his Boys were out-flanked, not by enemies, No! But by an enthusiastic multitude of fair ladies, men and children, old and young."[8]

For Sherman and his men, it was a big day for another reason. During the past month Sherman had been the center of controversy for his first version of the terms of surrender with Johnston. In an attempt to treat the Confederates leniently and to prevent the outbreak of a large-scale guerrilla war and help southerners put a halt to the marauding in the South, Sherman had clearly offered terms that were beyond his authority, but the reaction of a few key individuals in Washington had created an unnecessary stir. Secretary of War Edwin M. Stanton, livid with rage, suggested in a letter released to the press that Sherman might be a traitor, and Chief of Staff Henry W. Halleck maneuvered to recoup his combat record by seizing the opportunity and directing officers in Sherman's military division to disregard any of his orders and attempting to capture Johnston's army while the Confederate general negotiated with Sherman under a flag of truce. At the time there was great public outcry against Sherman, but his army stuck by his side almost to a man. Now, as the public acclaimed him and his army for their valiant service over the years, all seemed to be forgotten.[9]

Once the hoopla in Washington ended, it was time for Sherman's army to head home. Thoughts homeward had been foremost in the minds of the troops since they entered the service. The young soldiers had left home for some excitement and quickly found they were homesick. Back in October a private had written to his parents, "For my part I do not know how the word home sounded untill I came into

Pvt. John Langhans, Company H, 154th New York State Volunteer Infantry, asked his mother to "have a strawberry shortcake ready for me to eat when I get there." (US Army Military History Institute).

the army, but to hear the word spoken of or to think of it strikes a tender spot." One month later a seventeen-year-old Ohioan had penned: "Mother, a person does not know the value of home and parents, until he is away some time from them." For the older men, usually married and with children, thoughts homeward had helped them through the difficult days, as an Illinois officer recorded in his diary:

Were it not that one's mind has power to turn from scenes like these to contemplate the quiet and peace of home, with its endearments, its friendships and security, with a hope that they will some day be restored to us by a kind Providence, to live thus would be the sum of misery.

There was excitement everywhere as the troops prepared for home, this time for good. After all they had endured, it was hard to believe that the war really was over, but it was also hard to believe that so many comrades never made it. "Soldiers are happy at the thought of returning home," an Ohio captain commented. "But still our Joy is mixed with sorrow—sorrow for the many brave boys that have fallen in war to satisfy a few ambitious scheming statesmen."[10]

Most troops had big plans about their occupations and lives when they got home. Many of the men had saved part of their bounty money and had ample capital to purchase a farm farther west or to undertake some sort of business venture. Others, though, had had enough excitement for a lifetime and preferred to return home to their old way of life or to adopt a more peaceful vocation than they had in the prewar days. One thing was certain, however: nearly all had their fill of army life, as an Irishman in the 21st Wisconsin joked to his buddies. He told them after the war he intended to marry, settle down on a farm, and hire a fifer and drummer. "I will have them come to me door every morning to play reveille, just for the satisfaction of rolling over in bed and saying, 'To h——l with your reveille.'"[11]

Many, especially the unwed men, were uneasy about the transition from soldiering back to civilian life. Some worried that there were no single women left to marry when they returned home. As an Indiana soldier complained to his sister, "It is enough to make a fellow contemplate suicide, having all the girls facing on him, and marrying young men afraid of war." Others suspected that the war had so changed them that they could not fit back into their old way of life. A Massachusetts sergeant worried that after several years of almost constant noise and excitement "wheather this feeling would not have an influence over me duering the rest of my life—whether or no I should not want to seek some buiseness Exciting, or more active then I had before I became a soldier." Another soldier, a corporal, was certain that the war had changed him too: "I shall never be contented to remain in a town like Rockton [Illinois] after the war is done." Others were afraid that they had adopted some unsavory habits in the service and would not fit back into society. A soldier jokingly remarked in the Carolinas that it "would not do for Shermans army to go home now for they would be sure to tear up every road they come to without thinking what they were doing," yet the fear was very real for many soldiers. As an Illinois captain wrote, "we were getting pretty tuff but it soon wore off and we got back to a semblance of morality and decency and have kept out of the calaboose and the clutches of the law." [12]

In his farewell address, Sherman recapped the exploits of his army and hoped that, as they were good soldiers in war, so they would be good citizens in peace. Nearly all the men were volunteers in the fullest sense of the word. They came from civilian life at the call of their government, had completed their job, and now returned to civilian life. From East and West they had come to serve their country and would scatter throughout it again. A Minnesota sergeant appropriately said, "it seemed like breaking up a family to separate." They had faced the enemy on numerous occasions side by side and had endured the hardships and privations together, and "So," a New York sergeant wrote, "it was hard to separate and say goodbye, one with the other; but we shook hands all around, and laughed and seemed to make merry, while our hearts were heavy and our eyes ready to shed tears." [13]

Yet Sherman's men took back home with them a great sense of achievement. Originally, each veteran had assembled with 1,000 others to form a regiment; now, at the final muster, barely 300 remained, the rest victims of death, disability, capture, or a fading desire to see the war through to its fruition. For three or four years these veterans had voluntarily labored under all sorts of adversity to restore a system of government that they deemed sacred, and they returned home with the immense satisfaction of having contributed substantially to the final victory.

For them, the march to Savannah and through the Carolinas was the pinnacle of their military careers. They were, in a sense, members of a chosen army, one with a chemistry and mission all its own. They firmly believed that only a veteran army with several years of active campaign experience—only Sherman's army—could have marched swiftly through swamps and mud, foraged successfully in a countryside infested with a desperate enemy, destroyed railroads and public and private property facilely, and performed superbly in small skirmishes and large-scale battles. There were no apologies now, nor would there ever be, for what they had done in the heat of war to the people of Georgia and the Carolinas. There was only immense pride in being part of a very special body of men.

Appendix I

Percent of men who enlisted in 1861 and 1861–62 from Sherman's army:

1861	48.53%
1861 and 1862	78.32%

Breakdown of enlistments into U.S. Army and the percents, taken from *Executive Documents of the House of Representatives,* 39th Congress, 1st Session, 1865–66. (Washington, D.C.: Government Printing Office, 1866), p. 160.

	With Militia			*Without Militia*	
1861	766,843	28.9%	1861	673,517	27.6%
1862	534,553	20.2%	1862	519,553	21.3%
1863–64	374,807	14.1%	1863–64	358,446	14.7%
1864	768,916	29.0%	1864	685,264	28.1%
1864–65	204,568	7.7%	1864–65	204,568	8.6%
	2,649,687			2,441,348	

Only 6.5% of the soldiers in the Union Army (without militia) reenlisted for another three years, whereas nearly one in every two soldiers (48.53%) in Sherman's army did. Over 98% of the noncommissioned officers and over 99% of the company-level officers joined the service in 1861 or 1862.

Original rank of company-level officers in the sample of Sherman's army:

	Capt.	*Lt.*	*Sgt.*	*Cpl.*	*Pvt.*
captain	5	51	33	8	21
lieutenant	—	20	82	23	43

Original rank of regimental or battery commanders in the sample of Sherman's army:

Majors	*Captains*	*Lieutenants*	*Sergeants*
1	12	8	2

	Corporals	*Privates*	
	0	2	

The Sample and Computations

This was an attempt to determine the amount of Civil War military experience that the company-level officers and men in Sherman's army had at the time of the Savannah campaign. The availability and type of source material shaped my process of sample selection. First, since there was no list of names of the men who participated in the campaigns, I had to use muster rolls for October through December 1864; when this was not available, as in a few cases, I used the January through March 1865 ones (this was not much of a problem because information such as deaths, resignations, discharges, leaves of absence, or returns to duty usually carried over for several muster rolls). Packets of muster rolls are grouped by company and then by regiment or battery. I decided to work on a regimental and battery basis simply because it was easy to determine which regiments participated in the campaigns, whereas it was difficult to determine which companies in the regiments marched east to Savannah. Second, without regimental manpower totals for the campaign, I had to rely upon the total strength of the army in each specialized branch—infantry, cavalry, and artillery—for the proportions of the sample. I adopted a large sample, 25 units, to include representation of all three branches. To ensure breadth of representation from across the country, I relied upon proportional representation in the army by states.

According to the returns of 10 November 1864, OR I, XLIV,

p. 15, 88.7% of the army were infantrymen, 8.3% were cavalrymen, and 3% were artillerymen. Out of a total sample of 25 units, 22 would be infantry regiments, 2 would be cavalry regiments, and 1 would be an artillery battery. I then broke down the percent of troops from each state by field of service and assigned units in the sample to those states. In cases of artillery, cavalry, and the lesser-represented states that did not merit at least one unit alone, I grouped them together by branch of service.

Infantry: CT—1%, IL—23.3%, IN—13.2%, IA—8.2%, KY—.5%, MA—1%, MI—3.8%, MO—4.8%, MN—1%, NJ—1.6%, NY—7.1%, OH—23.8%, PA—4.4%, WI—6%.

Artillery: IL—19%, IN—6%, MI—12.5%, MN—6%, MO—6%, NY—12.5%, OH—12.5%, PA—6%, WI—19%.

Cavalry: IL—17.1%, AL—6.9%, IN—13.9%, KY—20.8%, MI—6.9%, OH—27.2%, PA—6.9%.

A computer then randomly selected the units included in the sample.

Inf.: IL—41st, 55th, 66th, 78th, 82nd
       IN—33rd, 74th, 100th
       IA—9th and 13th

MI—19th
NY—102nd and 134th
OH—21st, 33rd, 57th, 73rd, 74th
PA—109th
WI—3rd
CT, KY, MA, MN, NJ—4th MN
MO—18th

Artillery: Battery C, 1st Ohio Light Artillery

Cavalry: 3rd KY, 9th IL Mounted Infantry

I then went through the muster rolls and tabulated the year of enlistment of all company-level officers and men. I did not include the field
and staff in the sample because I wanted statistics on the fighting portion of the army, the men who performed the labors. Any soldiers on
temporary duty with the army I included, but those on detached service away from the army I did not consider. The two left columns
indicate units/years (brigade—division—corps):

	Pvts.	Cpls.	Sgts.	Lts.	Capts.	Total	%
100th IN(2–1–15)							
1862	276	55	41	10	8	390	98.0
1864	8					8	2.0
						398	
9th IA(3–1–15)							
1861	166	45	41	7	8	267	74.0
1862	3					3	0.8
1863	3					3	0.8
1864	88					88	24.4
						361	
13th IA(3–4–17)							
1861	141	33	31	6	4	215	79.0
1862	6	1				7	2.6
1863	2					2	0.7
1864	48					48	17.6
						272	
21st OH(3–1–14)							
1861	174	26	19	8	2	229	72.0
1862	18					18	5.7
1863	9					9	2.8
1864	62					62	19.5
						318	
19th MI(2–3–20)							
1861	2					2	0.4
1862	280	56	33	8	6	383	85.7

	Pvts.	Cpls.	Sgts.	Lts.	Capts.	Total	%
1863	28					28	6.3
1864	34					34	7.6
						447	

102nd NY(3–2–20)

	Pvts.	Cpls.	Sgts.	Lts.	Capts.	Total	%
1861	240	39	34	7	7	327	74.3
1862	46					46	10.5
1863	1	1				2	0.5
1864	65					65	14.8
						440	

134th NY(2–2–20)

	Pvts.	Cpls.	Sgts.	Lts.	Capts.	Total	%
1862	142	19	23	5	3	192	95.5
1863	4					4	2.0
1864	5					5	2.5
						201	

18th   MO(1–1–17)

	Pvts.	Cpls.	Sgts.	Lts.	Capts.	Total	%
1861	152	51	39	12	4	258	60.8
1862	45					45	10.6
1863	59					59	13.9
1864	62					62	14.6
						424	

4th   MN(1–3–15)

	Pvts.	Cpls.	Sgts.	Lts.	Capts.	Total	%
1861	179	61	53	16	9	318	52.9
1862	17	4				21	3.5
1864	259			3		262	43.6
						607	

33rd   IN(2–3–20)

	Pvts.	Cpls.	Sgts.	Lts.	Capts.	Total	%
1861	164	46	31	8	5	254	64.8
1862	62	8	3			73	18.6
1863	26	2				28	7.1
1864	37					37	9.4
						392	

	Pvts.	Cpls.	Sgts.	Lts.	Capts.	Total	%
3rd KY CAV							
1861	319	61	61	12	2	455	89.4
1862	12					12	2.4
1863	4					4	0.8
1864	38					38	7.5
						509	
41st IL(1–4–17)							
1861	154	19	12	4	1	190	91.3
1862	5					5	2.4
1864	13					13	6.3
						208	
78th IL(2–2–14)							
1862	268	41	31	9	5	354	96.2
1863	6					6	1.6
1864	8					8	2.2
						368	
74th OH(3–1–14)							
1861	155	38	35	9	3	240	72.5
1862	22					22	6.6
1863	1					1	0.3
1864	68					68	20.5
						331	
73rd OH(3–3–20)							
1861	131	22	27	7	7	194	58.8
1862	34	11	5			48	14.5
1863	2					2	0.6
1864	83	2	1			86	26.1
						330	
3rd WI(2–1–20)							
1861	112	42	35	8	8	205	40.2
1862	1					1	0.2
1863	13					13	2.5
1864	289	1	1			291	57.1
						510	

	Pvts.	Cpls.	Sgts.	Lts.	Capts.	Total	%
Battery C, 1st OH Light Artillery							
1861	38	10	7	4	1	60	47.6
1862	12	1				13	10.3
1863	26					26	20.6
1864	27					27	21.4
						126	
9th IL Mounted Infantry							
1861	60	13	9	8	3	93	27.0
1862	180	25	16			221	64.2
1863	4	1				5	1.5
1864	25					25	7.3
						344	
82nd IL(3–1–20)							
1861	1					1	0.7
1862	100	14	14	2	2	133	94.3
1864	7					7	5.0
						141	
57th OH(1–2–15)							
1861	96	35	34	4	2	171	62.9
1862	11					11	4.0
1863	5					5	1.8
1864	84	1				85	31.6
						272	
66th IL(2–4–15)							
1861	143	51	24	7	4	229	44.0
1862	90	12	5	2		109	20.9
1863	3					3	0.6
1864	180					180	34.5
						521	
33rd OH(1–1–14) loaded with draftees							
1861	140	31	36	6	4	217	46.7
1862	25	5	2			32	6.9
1863	2					2	0.4
1864	207	3	4			214	46.0
						465	

	Pvts.	Cpls.	Sgts.	Lts.	Capts.	Total	%
55th IL(1–2–15)							
1861	102	28	32	8	6	176	91.7
1862	4					4	2.1
1863	3					3	1.6
1864	8	1				9	4.7
						192	
109th PA(2–2–20)							
1861	74	15	16	4	4	113	55.1
1862	38	4	1			43	21.0
1863	20		1			21	10.2
1864	26	2				28	13.7
						205	
74th IN(3–3–14)							
1861	3					3	0.8
1862	197	32	29	9	6	273	73.6
1863	13					13	3.5
1864	82					82	22.1
						371	

Mean of a stratified sample for enlistees, 1861–62:

$$\bar{y} = \Sigma W_h \bar{y}_h$$

where $\bar{y}$ = mean, W_h = weights, and $\bar{y}_h$ = mean of group of units

W = artillery .04; W = cavalry .08; W = infantry .88

$\bar{y} = (.04)(.58) + (.08)(.915) + (.88)(.7805) = 78.32\%$

78.32% of the sample enlisted in either 1861 or 1862

$$\text{Variance} = \Sigma W_h{}^2 (1 - f_h) \left(\frac{P_h (1 - P_h)}{n_h - 1} \right)$$

where f_h = sampling fraction

P_h = proportion of the veterans (soldiers who enlisted in 1861 or 1862)

n_h = number in sample

$$V = 0 + (.08)^2 (.88247) \left(\frac{(.915)(.085)}{1} \right) +$$
$$(.88)^2 (.88247) \left(\frac{(.7805)(.2195)}{21} \right)$$

$= 0 + .00043 + .00556$

$= .00599$

Standard error of the mean $= \sqrt{V}$

$\qquad\qquad\qquad = \sqrt{.00594}$

$\qquad\qquad\qquad = \quad .07746$

Confidence level of 90%: 1.96 (.07746) = 15.18%

$\qquad\qquad$ 63.14%—78.32%—93.50%

$\qquad\qquad\qquad f = 212.7\overline{)25}$

$\qquad\qquad\qquad\quad = .11753$

Mean of stratified sample for soldiers who enlisted in 1861:

$$\bar{y} = (.04)\,(.476) + (.08)\,(.582) + (.88)\,(.4769)$$
$$= .01904 + .04656 + .419672$$
$$= 48.527\%$$

48.53% of the sample enlisted in 1861 and had reenlisted for a second three-year term, since Sherman would not take along nonveterans whose terms of enlistment expired in late November or December 1864, except in rare instances.

$$V = 0 + (.08)^2\,(.88247)\,(.24327) + (.88)^2\,(.88247)\,(.01187)$$
$$= 0 + .00136 + .00811$$
$$= .00947$$

Standard error of mean $= \sqrt{.00947}$

$\qquad\qquad\qquad\quad = .097314$

Confidence level of 90%: 1.96 (.097314) = 18.89%

$\qquad\qquad$ 29.64%—48.53%—67.42%

Mean of stratified sample for noncommissioned officers who enlisted in 1861 and 1862:

$$\bar{y} = .04 + .0794 + .8626$$
$$= 98.2\%$$

Mean of stratified sample for officers (company level) who enlisted or received commissions in 1861 and 1862:

$$\bar{y} = .04 + .08 + .87056$$
$$= 99.1\%$$

Sample statistic $\bar{y}$ is the unbiased estimator of the poplation parameter $\bar{Y}$.

Appendix II

Following are medical statistics compiled and calculated from *The Medical and Surgical History of the War of the Rebellion* (Washington, D.C.: Government Printing Office, 1870–88).

$$\frac{\text{Illnesses}}{\text{Mean strength of army}} = \% \text{ of ill soldiers}$$

$$\frac{\text{Deaths (excluding gunshot wounds)}}{\text{Mean strength of army}} = \% \text{ of soldiers who died of illness}$$

$$\frac{\text{Deaths}}{\text{Illnesses}} = \% \text{ of deaths per illness}$$

Sherman's Army

May 1864	*June 1864*	*July 1864*
$\dfrac{21,682}{142,206} = 15.0\%$	$\dfrac{27,170}{141,749} = 19.0\%$	$\dfrac{27,354}{137,176} = 19.9\%$
$\dfrac{51}{142,206} = .036\%$	$\dfrac{71}{141,749} = .05\%$	$\dfrac{274}{137,176} = .2\%$
$\dfrac{51}{21,682} = .24\%$	$\dfrac{71}{27,170} = .26\%$	$\dfrac{274}{27,354} = 1.0\%$

Aug. 1864	*Sept. 1864*	*Oct. 1864*
$\dfrac{27,375}{132,296} = 20.1\%$	$\dfrac{22,274}{129,405} = 17.2\%$	$\dfrac{14,967}{118,800} = 12.6\%$

Aug. 1864	*Sept. 1864*	*Oct. 1864*
$\dfrac{294}{132,296} = .2\%$	$\dfrac{300}{129,405} = .23\%$	$\dfrac{305}{118,800} = .26\%$
$\dfrac{294}{27,375} = 1.1\%$	$\dfrac{300}{22,274} = 1.3\%$	$\dfrac{305}{14,967} = 2.0\%$

Nov. 1864	*Dec. 1864*	*Jan. 1865*
$\dfrac{8,315}{78,927} = 10.5\%$	$\dfrac{7,682}{77,585} = 9.9\%$	$\dfrac{10,912}{75.851} = 14.4\%$
$\dfrac{49}{78,927} = .06\%$	$\dfrac{144}{77,585} = .18\%$	$\dfrac{161}{75,851} = .21\%$
$\dfrac{49}{8,315} = .6\%$	$\dfrac{144}{7,682} = 1.9\%$	$\dfrac{161}{10,912} = 1.5\%$

Feb. 1865	*Mar. 1865*	*Apr. 1865*
$\dfrac{5,986}{70,707} = 8.5\%$	$\dfrac{7,021}{69,818} = 10.0\%$	$\dfrac{10,116}{75,184} = 13.5\%$
$\dfrac{169}{70,707} = .24\%$	$\dfrac{162}{69,818} = .23\%$	$\dfrac{111}{75.184} = .15\%$
$\dfrac{169}{5,986} = 2.8\%$	$\dfrac{162}{7,021} = 2.3\%$	$\dfrac{111}{10,116} = 1.1\%$

All U.S. Troops Except Sherman's Army
(calculated by subtracting Sherman's men from all U.S. troops):

May 1864	*June 1864*	*July 1864*
$\dfrac{93,956}{499,170} = 18.8\%$	$\dfrac{110,641}{473,509} = 23.4\%$	$\dfrac{123,562}{430,670} = 28.7\%$
$\dfrac{2,347}{499,170} = .47\%$	$\dfrac{2,736}{473,509} = .58\%$	$\dfrac{3,914}{430,670} = .91\%$
$\dfrac{2,347}{93,956} = 2.5\%$	$\dfrac{2,736}{110,641} = 2.5\%$	$\dfrac{3,914}{123,562} = 3.2\%$

Aug. 1864	*Sept. 1864*	*Oct. 1864*
$\dfrac{123,280}{423,710} = 29.1\%$	$\dfrac{104,904}{411,173} = 25.5\%$	$\dfrac{100,832}{441,861} = 22.8\%$
$\dfrac{3,866}{423,710} = .91\%$	$\dfrac{3,234}{411,173} = .79\%$	$\dfrac{3,245}{411,861} = .73\%$
$\dfrac{3,866}{123,280} = 3.1\%$	$\dfrac{3,234}{104,904} = 3.1\%$	$\dfrac{3,245}{100,832} = 3.2\%$

All U.S. Troops Except Sherman's Army (*Continued*)

Nov. 1864	*Dec. 1864*	*Jan. 1865*
$\dfrac{90,771}{477,609} = 19.0\%$	$\dfrac{94,318}{492,006} = 19.2\%$	$\dfrac{89,579}{517,624} = 17.3\%$
$\dfrac{2,487}{477,609} = \quad .52\%$	$\dfrac{2,890}{492,006} = \quad .59\%$	$\dfrac{2,829}{517,624} = \quad .55\%$
$\dfrac{2,487}{90,771} = 2.7\%$	$\dfrac{2,890}{94,318} = 3.1\%$	$\dfrac{2,829}{89,579} = 3.2\%$

Feb. 1865	*Mar. 1865*	*Apr. 1865*
$\dfrac{82,384}{517,744} = 15.9\%$	$\dfrac{94,476}{533,019} = 17.7\%$	$\dfrac{93,149}{556,818} = 16.7\%$
$\dfrac{2,586}{517,744} = \quad .50\%$	$\dfrac{3,360}{533,019} = \quad .63\%$	$\dfrac{2,916}{556,818} = \quad .52\%$
$\dfrac{2,586}{82,384} = 3.1\%$	$\dfrac{3,360}{94,476} = 3.6\%$	$\dfrac{2,916}{93,149} = 3.1\%$

Statistics on Venereal Disease

Number of cases of syphilis
    Percent of cases of syphilis per command (cases/number of men in command)
    Number of cases of gonorrhea
    Percent of cases of gonorrhea per command (cases/number of men in command)
    Combined percent of cases of syphilis and gonorrhea per command

Sherman's Army

July 1864	*Aug. 1864*	*Sept. 1864*	*Oct. 1864*	*Nov. 1864*
S 161	S 127	S 126	S 83	S 58
.12%	.1%	.1%	.07%	.07%
G 220	G 165	G 173	G 125	G 74
.16%	.12%	.13%	.11%	.09%
T .28%	T .22%	T .23%	T .18%	T .16%

Dec. 1864	*Jan. 1865*	*Feb. 1865*	*Mar. 1865*	*Apr. 1865*
S 48	S 79	S 26	S 32	S 53
.06%	.10%	.03%	.05%	.07%
G 40	G 90	G 40	G 40	G 59
.05%	.12%	.06%	.06%	.08%
T .11%	T .22%	T .09%	T .11%	T .15%

Army of the Potomac

July 1864	*Aug. 1864*	*Sept. 1864*	*Oct. 1864*	*Nov. 1864*
S 176	S 118	S 152	S 206	S 161
.24%	.21%	.22%	.28%	.22%
G 124	G 76	G 189	G 202	G 123
.17%	.14%	.27%	.28%	.16%
T 41%	T 35%	T 49%	T 56%	T 38%

Dec. 1864	*Jan. 1865*	*Feb. 1865*	*Mar. 1865*	*Apr. 1865*
S 160	S 104	S 180	S 199	S 149
.16%	.16%	.17%	.18%	.15%
G 131	G 102	G 138	G 189	G 169
.13%	.10%	.13%	.17%	.14%
T .29	T .26%	T 30%	T .35%	T .29%

All Union Troops Except Sherman's Army

July 1864	*Aug. 1864*	*Sept. 1864*	*Oct. 1864*	*Nov. 1864*
S 1426	S 1542	S 1486	S 1518	S 1537
.33%	.36%	.36%	.34%	.32%
G 1853	G 1781	G 1771	G 1819	G 1833
.43%	.42%	.43%	.41%	.38%
T .73%	T .78%	T .79%	T .75%	T .70%

Dec. 1864	*Jan. 1865*	*Feb. 1865*	*Mar. 1865*	*Apr. 1865*
S 1754	S 1495	S 1419	S 1663	S 1729
.36%	.29%	.27%	.31%	.31%
G 1885	G 1634	G 1612	G 1945	G 1974
.38%	.32%	.31%	.35%	.35%
T .74%	T .61%	T .58%	T .66%	T .66%

All raw material on venereal disease is taken from *The Medical and Surgical History of the War of the Rebellion* (Washington, D.C.: Government Printing Office, 1870–88).

Appendix III

This is a collection of voting statistics in the 1864 presidential election for Sherman's army, compiled from information in letters, diaries, regimental histories, and official election statistics from various states. Some states, such as Connecticut, Illinois, Indiana, Massachusetts, and New Jersey, did not permit their soldiers in the field to vote. Authorities in Minnesota disallowed its soldiers' votes because they arrived too late, and there is no record of those tallies. New Yorkers sent their votes home individually for someone else in their district to cast, and so there is no record of how they voted either. Members of the 1st Alabama (Union) Cavalry, of course, could not vote. For the sources of this appendix, see note 16, chapter 2 ("The Army and the Cause").

State	Unit	Lincoln	McClellan
Iowa	4th IA	262	13
	6th IA	212	3
	7th IA	271	15
	11th IA	315	42
	13th IA	216	4
	15th IA	263	33
	16th IA	244	41
	25th IA	323	25
	26th IA	159	20
	30th IA	239	36
	31st IA	229	31
	Totals:	2,733	263

Lincoln received 91.2% of the vote.)

State	Unit	Lincoln	McClellan
Kentucky	18th KY	165	45

(Lincoln received 78.6% of the vote.)

	Unit	Lincoln	McClellan
Michigan	13th MI	401	220
	15MI	57	83
	19th MI	290	14
	21st MI	334	74
	1st MI E&M	689	164
	B, 1st MI LT ART	73	16
	C, 1st MI LT ART	49	17
	Totals:	1,893	642

Lincoln received 74.7% of the vote.)

	Unit	Lincoln	McClellan
Missouri	6th MO	76	10
	27th MO	60	0

Portions or all of the 6th MO, 8th MO, 18th MO, 26th MO, 29th MO, 31st MO, 32nd MO, and 1st MO E&M

		Lincoln	McClellan
		1,548	3
	Totals:	1,684	13

(Lincoln received 99.2% of the vote.)

	Unit	Lincoln	McClellan
Ohio	14th OH	173	35
	17th OH	303	26
	21st OH	206	44
	24th OH	200	17
	29th OH	344	40
	31st OH	205	16
	32nd OH	224	33
	33rd OH	214	111
	38th OH	250	8
	69th OH	123	66
	74th OH	143	6
	89th OH	157	35
	113th OH	165	45
	1st OH LT ART	85	1
Total votes for all other units that exist		311	107
	Totals:	3,413	635

(Lincoln received 84.3% of the vote.)

State	Unit	Lincoln	McClellan
Pennsylvania	46th PA	243	131
	111th PA	216	21
	Battery E, PA LT ART	95	18
	9th PA CAV	303	136
Total vote for all other units		416	83
	Totals:	1,273	389

(Lincoln received 76.6% of the vote.)

Wisconsin	3rd WI	305	21
	12th WI	338	57
	16th WI	223	98
	17th WI	52	206
	18th WI	103	33
	21st WI	253	68
	22nd WI	332	10
	25th WI	315	6
	26th WI	110	88
	31st WI	356	44
	32nd WI	498	73
	5th WI LT ART	65	0
	10th WI LT ART	60	22
	12th WI LT ART	64	26
	Totals:	3,074	752

(Lincoln received 80.3% of the vote.)
Unofficial counts from regiments not permitted to vote were as follows:

Alabama	1st AL CAV	383	24

(Lincoln received 94.1% of the straw poll vote.)

Illinois	34th IL	241	11
	55th IL	121	15
	Totals:	362	26

(Lincoln received 93.3% of the straw poll vote.)

Indiana	48th IN	51	1
	75th IN	310	7
	85th IN	309	15
	Totals:	670	23

(Lincoln received 96.7% of the straw poll vote.)

Abbreviations for Repositories

AAS	American Antiquarian Society, Worcester, MA
AL Dept. of A & H	Alabama Department of Archives and History, Montgomery, AL
Atlanta HS	Atlanta Historical Society
Chicago HS	Chicago Historical Society
Chicago PL	Chicago Public Library
CTST Lib	Connecticut State Library
Duke U.	Perkins Library, Duke University, Durham, NC
Emory U.	Woodruff Library, Emory University, Atlanta, GA
GA Dept. of A & H	Georgia Department of Archives and History, Atlanta, GA
GAHS	Georgia Historical Society, Savannah, GA
IASHMA	Iowa State Historical Museum and Archives, Des Moines, IA
IASHS	Iowa State Historical Society, Iowa City, IA
ILSHS	Illinois State Historical Society, Springfield, IL
INHS	Indiana Historical Society, Indianapolis, IN
Indiana U	Lilly Library, Indiana University, Bloomington, IN

INST Library	Indiana State Library, Indianapolis, IN
KMNP	Kennesaw Mountain National Park, Marietta, GA
LC	Library of Congress
LSU	Department of Archives and Manuscripts, Louisiana State University, Baton Rouge, LA
MAHS	Massachusetts Historical Society, Boston, MA
MISTU	University of Archives, Michigan State University, East Lansing, MI
MNHS	Minnesota Historical Society, St. Paul, MN
MS Dept. of A & H	Mississippi Department of Archives and History, Jackson, MS
NA	National Archives
NJHS	New Jersey Historical Society, Newark, NJ
NYHS	New-York Historical Society, New York, NY
OHS	Ohio Historical Society, Columbus, OH
SHC, UNC	Southern Historical Collection, University of North Carolina, Chapel Hill, NC
SHSW	State Historical Society of Wisconsin, Madison, WI
TNST Lib & A	Tennessee State Library and Archives, Nashville, TN
U. of Alabama	William Stanley Hoole Special Collection Library, University of Alabama, University, AL
Bentley Library, UMI	Bentley Historical Library, University of Michigan, Ann Arbor, MI
Clements Library, UMI	William L. Clements Library, University of Michigan, Ann Arbor, MI
U. of Georgia	University of Georgia, Athens, GA
U. of Iowa	University of Iowa, Iowa City, IA
U. of South Carolina	University of South Carolina, Columbia, SC
USMHI	United States Army Military History Institute, Carlisle Barracks, PA

WHC-SHSMO	Western Historical Collection, University of Missouri, and State Historical Society of Missouri, Columbia, MO
WMIU	Western Michigan University, Kalamazoo, MI
WRHS	Western Reserve Historical Society, Cleveland, OH

Abbreviations for Periodicals

CWH	Civil War History
CWTI	Civil War Times Illustrated
GHQ	Georgia Historical Quarterly
IJH	Iowa Journal of History
INMH	Indiana Magazine of History
JSH	Journal of Southern History
MH	Michigan History
MOLLUS	Military Order of the Loyal Legion of the United States
NCHR	North Carolina Historical Review
NDHQ	North Dakota Historical Quarterly
OHQ	Ohio Historical Quarterly
SCHM	South Carolina Historical Magazine
SHSP	Southern Historical Society Papers

Notes

PREFACE

1. Bell I. Wiley, *The Life of Johnny Reb* (Indianapolis: The Bobbs-Merrill Company, 1943), p. 13. Also see Bell I. Wiley, *The Life of Billy Yank* (Indianapolis: The Bobbs-Merrill Company, 1952).

2. B. H. Liddell Hart, *Sherman: Soldier, Realist, American* (New York: Frederick A. Praeger, Publishers, 1958), p. 331

3. Louis Morton, "The Military and Society," *Reviews in American History*, I, No. 1 (March, 1973), p. 53.

INTRODUCTION

1. Grant to Sherman, 4 Apr. 1865, *The War of the Rebellion: A Compilation of the Official Records of the Union and Confederate Armies* (Washington, D.C.: Government Printing Office, 1893), I, XXXII, Pt. 3, pp. 245–46. Also see OR I, XXXVIII, Pt. 1, pp. 1–2 and 61.

2. See OR I, XXXVII, Pt. 1, p. 28; Grant to Sherman, 10 Sep. 1864, Sherman to Grant, 10 Sep. 1864, Sherman to Grant, 12 Sep. 1864, and Sherman to Grant, 20 Sep. 1864, OR I, XXXVIII, Pt. 2, pp. 355, 356, 364, and 412.

3. Sherman to Grant, 11 Oct. 1864, OR I, XXXIX, Pt. 3, p. 202. Also see Sherman to Howard, 24 Sep. 1864, OR I, XXXIX, Pt. 2, p. 463; Sherman to Halleck, 25 Sep. 1864, OR I, XXXIX, Pt. 2, p. 464; Sherman to Grant, 1 Oct. 1864, OR I, XXXIX, Pt. 3, p. 3; Sherman to Thomas, 10 Oct. 1864, OR I, XXXIX, Pt. 3, p. 13; Halleck to Grant, 2 Oct. 1864, OR I, XXXIX, Pt. 3, pp. 25–26; Sherman to Grant, 9 Oct. 1864, OR I, XXXIX, Pt. 3, p. 162; Grant to Sherman, 11 Oct. 1864, and Grant to Sherman, 12 Oct. 1864, OR I, XXXIX, Pt. 3, pp. 202 and 222; Grant to Sherman, 18 Dec. 1864, OR I, XLIV, p. 740; Sherman to Grant, 16 Oct. 1864, OR I, XXXIX, Pt. 3, p. 305; Sherman to Schofield, 16 Oct. 1864, OR I, XXXIX, Pt. 3, p. 311; Thomas to Sherman, 17 Oct. 1864, OR I, XXXIX, Pt. 3, p. 334; Grant to Sherman, 1 Nov. 1864 and 2 Nov. 1864, and Sherman to Grant, 1 Nov. 1864 and 2 Nov. 1864, OR I, XXXIX, Pt. 3, pp. 576–67 and 594–95.

4. U. S. Grant, *Personal Memoirs* (New York: Charles L. Webster & Company, 1885), I. p. 315.

5. T. Harry Williams, *McClellan, Sherman and Grant* (Westport, CT: Greenwood Press, 1976), p. 46. Conversations with Dr. Richard H. Sewell, who is currently working on Sherman, has helped clarify my views on him considerably.

6. Sherman to Thomas, 20 Oct. 1864, OR I, XXXIX, Pt. 3, pp. 377–78; Sherman to Grant, 6 Nov. 1864, OR I, XXXIX, Pt. 3, pp. 659–60.

7. See W. T. Sherman, *Memoirs of W. T. Sherman By Himself,* (New York: Charles L. Webster & Co., 1891), II, pp. 178–79.

8. See Grant to Sherman, 6 Dec. 1864, OR I, XLIV, p. 636; Sherman to Halleck, 13 Dec. 1864, OR I, XLVI, p. 702; Grant to Sherman, 18 Dec. 1864, OR I, XLIV, pp. 740–41; Sherman to Grant, 16 Dec. 1864, OR I, XLIV, pp. 727–28.

9. See Slocum to Sherman, 15 Dec. 1864, and Hitchcock to Slocum, 15 Dec. 1864, OR I, XLIV, pp. 719–20 and 721; Sherman to Grant, 18 Dec. 1864, OR I, XLIV, pp. 742–43; Sherman, *Memoirs,* II, p. 216; Sherman to Grant, 22 Dec. 1864, OR I, XLIV, pp. 6–7; OR I, XLIV, pp. 11–12; OR I, XLIV, p. 280.

10. See Johnston to Lee, 11 Mar. 1865, and Johnston to Lee, 18 Mar. 1865, OR I, XLVII, Pt. 1, pp. 1053 and 1054; OR I, XLVII, Pt. 1, p. 1058.

11. See Johnson to Lee, 23 Mar. 1865, OR I, XLVII, Pt. 1, p. 1055.

12. See Grant to Sherman, 3 Apr. 1865, OR I, XLVII, Pt. 3, pp. 89–90; Sherman to Grant, 6 Apr. 1865, OR I, XLVII, Pt. 3, p. 109; Sherman to Kilpatrick, Schofield, Slocum, and Howard, 7 Apr. 1865, OR I, XLVII, Pt. 3, pp. 119–23; Sherman to Grant, 8 Apr. 1865, OR I, XLVII, Pt. 3, pp. 128–29, Special Field Order, No. 48, Mil. Div. of the Miss., 5 Apr. 1865; Sherman, *Memoirs,* II, pp. 341–43.

13. See Sherman, *Memoirs,* II, pp. 356–57 and 363, for the agreements.

CHAPTER 1

1. George Drake to parents, 31 Dec. 1864, Julia A. Drake, ed., *The Mail Goes Through or the Civil War Letters of George Drake (1846–1918)* (San Angelo, TX: Anchor Publishing Co., 1964), p. 125; Jacob D. Cox, "The Surrender of Johnston's Army and the Closing Scenes of the War in North Carolina," *MOLLUS–OH,* II, p. 256; William E. Strong, "Reminiscences of the March to the Sea," William E. Strong Papers, ILSHS.

2. Unknown diarist, 24 May 1865, D. R. Lucas, *History of the 99th Indiana Infantry* (Lafayette, IN: Rosser & Spring, 1865), p. 81; William Pittenger diary, 3 Dec. 1864, William Pittenger Papers, OHS: Jas. Sawyer to Nancy, 6 Jan. 1865, James T. Sawyer Papers, SHSW.

3. William Hemstreet, "Little Things About Big Generals," *MOLLUS–NY,* III, pp. 160–61. Also see Thomas Christie diary, 29 Nov. 1864, Christie Papers, MNHS; Henry Hitchcock diary, 28 Nov. 1864, M. A. De Wolfe Howe, ed., *Marching With Sherman: Passages From the Letters and Campaign Diaries of Henry Hitchcock, Major and Assistant Adjutant General of Volunteers, November, 1864–May, 1865* (New Haven: Yale University Press, 1927), pp. 110–13.

4. Robert to Wife, 10 Sep. 1864, Robert F. Bence Papers, INHS; John Cutter to Father, 18 Dec. 1864, Cutter Papers, MNHS; Charles E. Wills diary, 7 Oct. 1864, Charles E. Wills, *Army Life of an Illinois Soldier: Letters and Diary of the Late Charles W. Wills* (Washington, D.C.: Mary E. Kellogg, 1906), p. 307; Unknown poet in Edwin D. Levings, "Recollections of the Great March," Edwin D. Levings Papers, SHSW. Also see Hemstreet, *MOLLUS–NY,* III, pp. 160–61; O. D. Hormel, ed., *With Sherman to the Sea: A Drummer's Story of the Civil War as Related by Corydon Edward Foote* (New York:

The John Day Company, 1960), pp. 209–10; J. C. Taylor, *Lights and Shadows in the Recollections of a Youthful Volunteer in the Civil War* (Ionia, MI: Sentinel Standard, n.d.), p. 22; Sherman to Dearest Ellen, 16 Dec. 1864 and 15 Jan. 1865, Sherman Papers, University of Notre Dame, on microfilm, SHSW; Divine to J. H. Everett, 29 Jan. 1865, J. H. Everett Papers, GAHS; Julian W. Hinkley, *Service With the Third Wisconsin Infantry* (Madison: Wisconsin History Commission, 1912), p. 164; Edwin Hutchinson to Father, 29 Sep. 1864, Edwin Hutchinson Papers, LSU; R. S. Finley to MAC, 8 Sep. 1864, R. S. Finley Papers, SHC, UNC.

5. William T. Sherman, *Memoirs of W. T. Sherman Written By Himself* (New York: Charles L. Webster & Co., 1891), II, p. 387; Oscar [Kimberley] to Parents, 29 Jan. 1865. E. O. Kimberley Papers, SHSW; G. F. Shepherd to dear wife, 24 Dec. 1864, George F. Shepherd Papers, SHSW. Also see John Henry Otto, "War Memories, 1864," John Henry Otto Papers, SHSW; F. H. Putney to Father, 8 May 1865, Frank H. Putney Papers, SHSW.

6. For previous combat experience, check rosters published by various state adjutants general or see specific regimental histories, if available. Helpful in tracing the career of a specific corps is Mark M. Boatner III, *The Civil War Dictionary* (New York: David McKay Company, Inc., 1959).

7. Sherman to Grant, 22 Oct. 1864, OR I, XXXIX, Pt. 3, p. 395. Also see Sherman, *Memoirs*, II, p. 172.

8. George K. Collins, *Memoirs of the 149th Regiment New York Volunteer Infantry* (Syracuse: Published by the Author, 1891), p. 287; OR I, XLIV, Pt. 1, p. 79; William E. Strong, "Reminiscences," p. 4, William E. Strong Papers, ILSHS. Also see Special Field Orders, No. 93, Headquarters, Mil. Div. of the Miss., 17 Oct. 1864, OR I, XXXIX, Pt. 3, pp. 324–25; K. Jack Bauer, ed., *Soldiering: The Civil War Diary of Rice C. Bull, 123rd New York Volunteer Infantry* (San Rafael, CA: Presidio Press, 1977), p. 171; Wiley, *Billy Yank*, p. 23; Special Field Orders, No. 103, Headquarters, Mil. Div. of the Miss., 24 Oct. 1864; Special Field Orders, No. 115, Headquarters, Mil. Div. of the Miss., 4 Nov. 1864, OR I, XXXIX, Pt. 3, pp. 418–19 and 619; Special Field Orders, No. 23, Fourth Division, 15 AC, 31 Dec. 1864; Special Field Order Book, Fourth Division, 15 AC, RG 393. NA.

9. See Appendix II. Also see *The Medical and Surgical History of the War of the Rebellion*, I, Pt. 1, pp. 452–61 and 542–47; *Medical and Surgical History*, I, Pt. 1, Appendix, p. 322; OR I, XLIV, pp. 79, 189–90, 221, 237, and 333; OR I, XLVII, Pt. 1, p. 441; Judson W. Bishop to Sister, 6 Jan. 1865 and 29 Mar. 1865, Bishop Papers, MNHS; Monthly Report of Sick and Wounded, Twenty-first Wisconsin, January to June, 1865, James T. Reeve Papers, SHSW; Sam to Maggie, 18 Jan. 1865, Samuel K. Harryman Papers, INST Library; Henry D. Farr diary, 16 Dec. 1864, Henry D. Farr Papers, IASHS; Orville to Friends, 23 Jan. 1865, Joseph and Orville Chamberlain Papers, INHS; George Drake to Parents, 30 Dec. 1864, Drake, ed., *The Mail Goes Through*, p. 120.

10. Bauer, ed., *Soldiering*, p. 176; Collins, *149th NY*, p. 287; Oscar Osburn Winther, ed., *With Sherman to the Sea: The Civil War Letters, Diaries and Reminiscences of Theodore F. Upson* (Bloomington: Indiana University Press, 1958), p. 134; Unknown journalist, probably George Baird journal, 1 Jan. 1865, Alonzo L. Brown, *History of the Fourth Regiment of Minnesota Infantry Volunteers* (St. Paul: The Pioneer Press Company, 1892), pp. 356–57; Sherman to Grant, 24 Dec. 1864, OR I, XLIV, p. 798, and Sherman, *Memoirs*, II, p. 226; John C. Arbuckle, *Civil War Experiences of a Foot-Soldier Who Marched*

With Sherman (Columbus, OH: n.p., 1930), p. 105. Also see William H. Bartlett, "From Atlanta to Milledgeville," in S. G. Cook and C. E. Benton, eds., *The "Dutchess County Regiment" in the Civil War: Its Story as Told by its Members* (Danbury, CT: The Danbury Medical Printing Co., Inc., 1907), pp. 135–36; Benjamin F. Sweet, "War Record," Benjamin F. Sweet Papers, WHS–SHSMO; F. Y. Hedley, *Marching Through Georgia: Pen-Pictures of Everyday Life* (Chicago: Donohue, Henneberry & Co., 1890), p. 259; Henry J. Aten, *History of the 85th Illinois Volunteers* (Hiawatha, KA: Regimental Association, 1901), p. 243; M. Dresbach, "Reminiscences of Sherman's Campaign through Georgia and the Carolinas," p. 16, Dresbach Papers, MNHS: W. S. Fultz, "Reminiscences of Army Life," Fultz Papers, IASHS; OR I, XLVII, Pt. 1, p. 28; affectionate son to Mother, 11 Jan. 1865, Ebenezer Wescott Papers, SHSW; Richard Reeves diary, 13 Feb. 1865, Reeves Papers, MNHS; C. C. Carpenter to Emmett Carpenter, 25 Dec. 1864, Mildred Throne, ed., "A Commissary in the Union Army: Letters of C. C. Carpenter," *IJH*, LIII, No. 1 (January, 1955), p. 87; Hinkley, *Service With the 3rd WI*, p. 164; H. Hitchcock diary, 28 Nov. 1864, Henry Hitchcock, *Marching With Sherman*, pp. 108–9; Chas. M. Smith to Father, 7 Jan. 1865, Charles M. Smith Papers, SHSW; W. T. Sherman to Dearest Ellen, 16 Dec. 1864, Sherman Family Papers, University of Notre Dame, on microfilm at SHSW; William Miller diary, 13 Mar. 1865, William B. Miller Papers, INHS; Howe, ed., *Home Letters of General Sherman* (New York: Charles Scribner's Sons, 1909), p. 339.

11. Howard to Sherman, 17 Jan. 1865, OR I, XLVII, Pt. 2, p. 70; Sherman *Memoirs*, II, p. 184. See Appendix I taken from Muster Rolls for the twenty-five units, RG 94, NA. Also see Taylor, *Lights and Shadows*, p. 20; William B. Hazen, *A Narrative of Military Service* (Boston: Ticknor and Company, 1885), p. 299; James Congleton journal, 26 Mar. 1865, James A. Congleton Papers, LC; James A. Connolly diary, 5 Nov. 1864, Paul M. Angle, ed., *Three Years in the Army of the Cumberland: The Letters and Diary of Major James A. Connolly* (Bloomington: Indiana University Press, 1959), p. 289; Special Field Orders, No. 2. Hdqrs., Mil. Div. of the Miss., 3 Jan. 1865; Special Field Orders Book, Military Division of the Mississippi, RG 393, NA.

12. See Hazen, *Narrative*, p. 299; Garret S. Byrne diary 9 Feb. 1865, Garret S. Byrne Papers, Rutgers U; OR I, XLIV, p. 338. For an interesting contrast on attitudes about officers and promotions, see George Bargus diary, 27 Oct. 1864, and Fergus Elliott diary, 4 Jan. 1865, Civil War Times Illustrated Collection, USMHI.

13. Willie G. Baugh to Parents, 25 Dec. 1864, William G. Baugh Papers, Emory U; Fergus Elliott diary, 23 Jan. 1865, Civil War Times Illustrated Collection, USMHI; Frank Malcom to Wife, 18 Jan. 1865, James J. Robertson, Jr., ed., "Such Is War: The Letters of an Orderly in the 7th Iowa Infantry," *IJH*, LVIII, No. 4 (October, 1960), p. 345. ALso see H. W. Rodd, *The Story of the Service of Company E, and the Twelfth Wisconsin Regiment, Veteran Volunteer Infantry* (Milwaukee: Swain & Tate Co., 1893), p. 410.

14. William Miller diary, 28 Feb. 1865, William B. Miller Papers, INHS; Garret S. Byrne diary, 19 Feb. 1865, Garret S. Byrne Papers, Rutgers U.

15. George W. Pepper, *Personal Recollections of Sherman's Campaigns in Georgia and the Carolinas* (Zanesville, OH: Hugh Dunne, 1866), p. 500; Sebastian Duncan, Jr., to Father, 6 Apr. 1865, Sebastian Duncan, Jr., Papers, NJHS. Also see Hazen, *Narrative*, pp. 299 and 313.

16. Eli [Ricker] to Mary, 24 Jan. 1865, Edward G. Longacre, ed., " 'We Left a Black

Track in South Carolina:' Letters of Corporal Eli S. Ricker, 1865," *SCHM*, LXXXII, No. 3 (July, 1981), p. 218; William Miller diary, 29 Nov. 1864, William B. Miller Papers, INHS; Samuel Storrow diary, 13 Nov. 1864 and 24 Nov. 1864, Samuel Storrow Papers, MAHS. Also see William Pittenger diary, 31 Mar. 1865, William H. Pittenger Papers, OHS; James A. Connolly diary, 8 Dec. 1864, J. A. Connolly, Angle, ed. *Three Years*, p. 354; James T. Reeve diary, 8 Dec. 1864, James T. Reeve Papers, SHSW.

17. James C. Patten diary, 5 Sep. 1864, Robert G. Athearn, ed., "An Indiana Doctor Marches With Sherman: The Diary of James Comfort Patten," *INMH*, XLIX, No. 4 (December, 1953), p. 441; W. T. Sherman to John Sherman, 31 Dec. 1864, Rachel Sherman Thorndike, ed., *The Sherman Letters: Correspondence Between General and Senator Sherman from 1837 to 1891* (New York: Charles Scribner's Sons, 1894), pp. 241–42.

18. William Hemstreet, *MOLLUS–NY*, III, p. 164; Matthew Jamison journal, 12 Feb. 1865, Matthew Jamison, *Recollections of Pioneer and Army Life* (Kansas City, MO: Hudson Press, 1911), p. 306. Also see William E. Strong journal, 3 Feb. 1865, William E. Strong, "Reminiscences," p. 203, William E. Strong Papers, ILSHS; William H. Pittenger diary, 31 Mar. 1865, William H. Pittenger Papers, OHS.

19. Andrew Mc[Cormack] to ———, 8 Nov. 1864, Richard McMurry, "Sherman's Savannah Campaign," *CWTI*, XXI, No. 9 (January, 1983), p. 10; Harvey Reid diary-letter to Sister, 9 Feb. 1865, Harvey Reid Papers, SHSW. Also see Fergus Elliott diary, 23 Jan. 1865, Civil War Times Illustrated Collection, USMHI; John R. Boyle, *Soldiers True: The Story of the One Hundred Eleventh Regiment Pennsylvania Veteran Volunteers* (New York: Eaton & Mains, 1903), pp. 298–300; William B. Westervelt, *Lights and Shadows of Army Life As Seen By a Private Soldier* (Marlboro, NY: C. H. Cochrane, 1886), p. 88; Ashley Halsey, ed., *A Yankee Private's Civil War by Robert Hale Strong* (Chicago: Henry Regnery Co., 1961), p. 84.

20. See James C. Patten diary, 5 Sep. 1864, Athearn, ed., *INMH*, XLIX, pp. 409–10; Halsey, ed., *A Yankee Private's Civil War*, pp. 83–4; Records of Judge Advocate General (Army), RG 153, NA, NN 3937, trial of Henry M. Quinn.

21. John W. Bates diary, 2 Oct. 1864, Civil War Miscellaneous Collection, USMHI; Halsey, ed., *A Yankee Private's Civil War*, pp. 82 and 85. See also E. P. Failing diary, 10 Nov. 1864, Failing-Knight Papers, MAHS: Ephraim A. Wilson, *Memoirs of the War* (Cleveland: W. M. Bayne Printing Company, 1893), pp. 392–4; Isaac Roseberry diary, 2 Mar. 1865, Isaac Roseberry Papers, Bentley Library, UMI; Kilpatrick to Sherman, 24 Feb. 1865, OR I, XLVII, Pt. 2, p. 554; William H. McIntosh, "22nd Wisconsin," p. 183, William McIntosh Papers, SHSW.

22. Burke Wylie to Mother, 2 Apr. 1865, E. Burke Wylie Papers, IASHS; Arthur Sumner to Nina Hartshorn, Feb. 1865[?], Penn School Collection, SHC, UNC. For a statement opposing familiarity between officers and men, see Samuel Storrow diary, 8 Nov. 1864, Samuel Storrow Papers, MAHS.

23. Halsey, ed., *A Yankee Private's Civil War*, p. 82; Burke Wylie to Mother, 2 Apr. 1865, E. Burke Wylie Papers, IASHS; Matthew Jamison journal 12 Mar. 1865, M. Jamison, *Recollections*, p. 318. Also see F. M. McAdams, *Every-day Soldier* (Columbus, OH: Chas. M. Cott & Co., 1884), p. 136—F. M. McAdams journal, 14 Feb. 1865; Harvey Trumble journal, 10 Mar. 1865, Harvey M. Trumble, *History of the Ninety-Third Regiment Illinois Volunteer Infantry* (Chicago: The Blakely Printing Co., 1898), p. 180; Emory Sweetland diary, 26 Feb. 1865, Michael Winey Collection, USMHI; J. R. Kinnear, *History of the Eighty-Sixth Regiment Illinois Volunteer Infantry* (Chicago: Tribune Com-

pany's Book and Job Printing Office, 1866), p. 99. For an example of a soldier's reaction to a more bombastic officer, see William [Stevens] to Sister, 2 Apr. 1865, Stevens Family Papers, Bentley Library, UMI.

24. Bauer, ed., *Soldiering*, p. 249. See Appendix I for statistics. Also see [Lorenzo Pratt] to Perrants, 30 Sep. [1864], Civil War Miscellaneous Collection, USMHI.

25. Wilson, *Memoirs of the War*, p. 394; A. Ames to General   , 28 Mar. 1865, William H. Noble Papers, Duke U. Also see William H. H. Tallman, "Reminiscences," p. 47, Gregory Coco Collection, USMHI.

26. Harrison Pendergast journal, 19 Jan. 1865, Pendergast Papers, MNHS; Hedley, *Marching Through Georgia*, p. 258; Wilson, *Memoirs*, p. 394. Also see Edwin Hutchinson to Father, 29 Sep. 1864, Edwin Hutchinson Papers, LSU.

27. George W. Nichols journal, 5 Feb. 1865, George Ward Nichols, *The Story of the Great March* (New York: Harper & Brothers, 1866), p. 141; John E. Risendorph diary, 28 Feb. 1865, Risendorph Papers, MNHS; William Miller diary, 24 Mar. 1865, William B. Miller Papers, INHS. Also see Hinkley, *Service With the 3rd WI*, P. 170; Geo. S. Richardson to Father and Mother, 14 Dec. 1864, G. S. Richardson Papers, IASHS; [Lorenzo Pratt] to Perrants, 27 Jan. 1865, Civil War Miscellaneous Collection, USMHI.

28. Judson W. Bishop, *The Story of a Regiment* (St. Paul: Published by the Survivors of the Regiment, 1890), p. 196. Also see Unknown journal, 3 Feb. 1865, William Worth Belknap and Loren S. Tyler, *History of the Fifteenth Regiment Iowa Veteran Volunteer Infantry* (Keokuk, IA: R. B. Ogeen & Sons, 1887), pp. 447–48; Lucas, *99th in*, p. 169; OR I, XLVII, Pt. 1, p. 176; Halsey, ed., *A Yankee Private's Civil War*, pp. 106–7.

29. For two good stereotypical examples, see William Miller diary, 2/21/65, William B. Miller Papers, INHS, and Robert M. Rogers, *The 125th Regiment Illinois Volunteer Infantry* (Champaign, IL: Gazette Steam Print, 1882), p. 115.

30. See OR I, XLIV, pp. 19–25; Wm. F. Goodwin to Parents, 1 Oct. 1864, William F. Goodwin Papers, ILSHS. For a reaction to bad discipline, see OR I, XLIV, p. 338.

31. William H. H. Tallman, "Reminiscences," p. 118, Gregory Coco Collection, USMHI; Harvey Reid to Sisters, 18 Jan. 1865, Harvey Reid Papers, SHSW. See also Judson L. Austin to Wife, 4 Sep. 1864, Nina Ness Papers, Bentley Library, UMI; Halsey, ed., *A Yankee Private's Civil War*, pp. 83–84; William Grunert journal, 24 Jan. 1865 and 21 Feb. 1865, William Grunert, *History of the One Hundred and Twenty-Ninth Regiment Illinois Volunteer Infantry* (Winchester, IL: R. B. Dedman, 1866), pp. 159–60 and 198.

32. See OR I, XLIV, pp. 19–22 and 264; W. S. Fultz, "Reminiscences of Army Life," W. S. Fultz Papers, IASHS; Aten, *85th IL*, p. 243; John S. Cooper diary, 23 Jan. 1865, John S. Cooper Papers, Duke U; Hazen, *Narrative*, p. 299; Charles E. Wills diary, 7 Oct. 1864, 13 Oct. 1864, 27 Jan. 1865, and 12 Feb. 1865. Wills, ed., *Army Life*, pp. 307, 309–10, 337–38, and 345; H. H. Orendorff, et. al., *Reminiscences of the Civil War from Diaries of Members of the 103rd Illinois Volunteer Infantry* (Chicago: Press of J. F. Leaming & Co., 1904), p. 133; Allen Fahnestock diary, 7 Nov. 1864, Allen L. Fahnestock Papers, KMNP; Winther, ed. *With Sherman to the Sea*, pp. 151–52; Sherman to D. D. Porter, 17 Jan. 1865, OR I, XLVII, Pt. 2, p. 69; R. S. Finley to MAC, 18 Jan. 1865, R. S. Finley Papers, SHC, UNC; Reuben Sweet diary, 22-3 Oct. 1864, "Civil War Diary," in *Antigo Daily Journal*, 9 Mar. 1939 to 25 May, 1939; Burke Wylie to Mother, 2 Apr. 1865, Burke Wylie Papers, IASHS.

33. Daniel Oakey in Robert Underwood Johnson and Clarence Clough Buel, ed.,

Battles and Leaders of the Civil War (New York: The Century Co., 1888), IV, p. 671; Frederick Winkler to [Wife], 19 Dec. 1864, *Letters to Frederick C. Winkler, 1862 to 1865* (n.p., 1963), pp. 186–87; S. Duncan, Jr., to Mother, 26 Sep. 1864, Sebastian Duncan, Jr., Papers, NJHS. Also see William B. Miller diary, 21 Feb. 1865, William B. Miller Papers, INHS.

34. See Axel Reed diary, 21 Feb. 1865, Reed Papers, MNHS; Albion Tourgee, *The Story of a Thousand* (Buffalo: S. McGerald & Son, 1896), p. 377; James T. Reeves diary, 21 Feb. 1865, James T. Reeves Papers, SHSW; Bliss Morse diary, 11 Mar. 1865, Loren J. Morse, ed., *The Civil War Diaries of Bliss Morse* (Pittsburgh, KA: Pittcraft, Inc., 1964), p. 82; W. C. Johnson diary, 11 Mar. 1865, W. C. Johnson Papers, LC; William H. H. Tallman, "Reminiscences," p. 116, Gregory Coco Collection, USMHI; Mahlon H. Floyd diary, 13 Mar. 1865, Helen Floyd Carlin Papers, INHS; William Miller diary, 21 Feb. 1865, William B. Miller Papers, INHS.

35. William Miller diary, 21 Feb. 1865, William B. Miller Papers, INHS. Also see Charles W. McKay, "Reminiscences," in Michael Winey Collection, USMHI; A. C. Smith to beloved wife, 26 Sep. 1864, Abner C. Smith Papers, CTST Lib; Henry Clay Robbins, "Autobiography," Henry Clay Robbins Papers, SHSW; Hinkley, *Service with the 3rd WI*, p. 164; Joe [Brown] to Parents, Brothers & Sisters, 28 Mar. 1865, Civil War Times Illustrated Collection, USMHI; Bas to Brother Will, 31 Mar. 1865 Sebastian Duncan, Jr., Papers, NJHS.

36. See Appendix I. Also see OR I, XLIV, pp. 229–30, 264, and 311.

37. See Chas. S. Brown to Mother & Sister and all Browns, 23 Sep. 1864, Charles S. Brown Papers, Duke U; William Meffert diary, 20 Nov. 1864, William C. Meffert Papers, SHSW; Harrison Pendergast journal, 1 Dec. 1864, Pendergast Papers, MNHS.

38. Axel Reed diary, 4 Apr. 1865, Reed Papers, MNHS; Jesse Macy to Sister, 8 Nov. 1864, Jesse Macy Papers, IASHS. Also see Records of Judge Advocate General (Army) RG 153, NA, oo 548, trial of Emil Bartech.

39. Brown, *4th MN*, pp. 299–301; Charlie to Father, 16 Dec. 1864, and 5 Jan. 1865 [5], Charles S. Brown Papers, Duke U.

40. Sherman to Stanton, 13 Sep. 1864, OR I, XXXIX, Pt. 2, p. 370; Bishop, *Story of a Regiment*, p. 154. Also see Henry H. Wright, *A History of the Sixth Iowa Infantry* (Iowa City: State Historical Society of Iowa, 1923), pp. 338–39.

41. John Vail diary, 18 Nov. 1864, John Vail Papers, OHS. Also see Thomas T. Taylor diary, 6 Nov. 1864, Thomas T. Taylor Papers, LSU; Muster Rolls for October–December, 1864, 33rd Ohio Infantry and 47th Ohio Infantry, R.G. 94 NA; OR I, XLIV, pp. 229–30 and 264; Albert Wells to Dear Ones at Home, 23 Oct. 1864, Albert Wells Papers, GA Dept. of A & H; Rood, *Co. E and 12th WI*, pp. 357–8; William Meffert diary, 20 Nov. 1864, William C. Meffert Papers, SHSW.

42. Charley to Lucy, 21 Sep. 1864, Charles Peel Papers, Bentley Library, UMI; William Miller diary, 9 Nov. 1864, William B. Miller Papers, INHS; Charles F. Hubert, *History of the Fiftieth Regiment Illinois Volunteer Infantry* (Kansas City, MO: Western Veteran Publishing Company, 1894), pp. 377–78. Also see William Champion diary, entry after 25 Nov. 1864, *Civil War Diary of William Julius Champion* (Ann Arbor: University of Microfilms International, n.d.), n.p.; Lyman Widney to Parents, 8 Nov. 1864, Lyman S. Widney Papers, KMNP; William T. Dollison in E. Z. Hays, *History of the Thirty-Second Regiment Ohio Veteran Volunteer Infantry* (Columbus, OH: Cott & Evans, 1896), pp. 75 and 196.

43. Bishop, *Story of a Regiment*, pp. 154–57.

44. Dell to Anna, 18 Jan 1865, Adelbert M. Bly Papers, SHSW; Arthur Sumner to Nina Hartshorn, [Feb. 1865?], Penn School Collection, SHC, UNC.

45. Joe [Brown] to Parents, Brothers & Sisters, 28 Mar. 1864, Civil War Times Illustrated Collection, USMHI; Bas to Brother Will, 31 Mar. 1865, Sebastian Duncan, Jr., Papers, NJHS.

46. John Brobst to Mary, 2 Apr. 1865, Margaret Brobst Roth, ed., *Well Mary: Civil War Letters of a Wisconsin Volunteer* (Madison: University of Wisconsin Press, 1960), p. 128.

CHAPTER 2

1. Muster Rolls, October–December, 1864, RG 94 NA. See Appendix I.

2. Garrett S. Byrne diary, 21 Feb. 1865, Garrett S. Byrne Papers, Rutgers; Charles F. Morse to [members of family], 31 Jan. 1865, Charles F. Morse, *Letters Written During the Civil War, 1861–65* (Boston: Privately Printed, 1898), p. 211. Also see G. S. Bradley journal, 3 Feb. 1865, George S. Bradley, *The Star Corps* (Milwaukee: Jermain & Brightman, 1865), p. 256.

3. Jas. Sawyer to nancy, 25 Dec. 1864, James T. Sawyer Papers, SHSW; Emerson [Anderson] to Parents, 5 Sep. 1864, Civil War Papers, AAS; Allie Travis reminiscence in Richard Wheeler, *Sherman's March* (New York: Crowell, 1978), pp. 67–68; Levi D. Bryant to Wife, 28 Mar. 1865, Michael Winey Collection, USMHI; Magnus Brucker to Wife, 18 Sep. 1864, Magnus Brucker Papers, INHS. Also see John W. Storrs, *The Twentieth Connecticut* (Ansonia, CT: Press of the Naugatuck Valley Sentinel, 1886), p. 145; Chauncey to Brother, 15 Jul. 1863, and Chauncey to Mother, 28 July 1863, "Letters of a Badger Boy in Blue," *Wisconsin Magazine of History*, IV, No. 4 (June, 1921), pp. 449 and 455; Wm. C. Bennett to Doctor, 21 Jan. 1866, Noble C. Williams, *Echoes from the Battlefield* (Atlanta: The Franklin Printing and Publishing Company, 1902), p. 61; Lyman S. Widney to Parents, 15 Oct. 1864, Lyman S. Widney Papers, Keenesaw Mountain National Park; John Vail diary, 15 Jan. 1865, John Vail Papers, OHS; William M. Anderson, *They Died to Make Men Free: A History of the 19th Michigan Infantry in the Civil War* (Berrien Springs, MI: Hardscrabble Books, 1980), p. 165.

4. Benjamin Mabrey to wife, 23 Oct. 1864, Benjamin B. Mabrey Papers, INHS; C. R. Rey to Friend Lizzie, 24 Dec. 1864, and Rudolph Rey to Lizzie, 28 Mar. 1865, Rudolph Rey Papers, NYHS. Also see Michael H. Fitch, *Echoes of the Civil War As I Hear Them* (New York: R. F. Fenno & Company, 1905), p. 15; Charles E. Benton, *As Seen From the Ranks* (New York: G. P. Putnam's Sons, 1902), pp. 7–8; K. Jack Bauer, ed., *Soldiering: The Civil War Diary of Rice C. Bull, 123rd New York Volunteer Infantry* (San Rafael, CA: Presidio Press, 1977), p. 1; S. F. Fleharty, *Our Regiment: A History of the 102d Illinois Infantry Volunteers* (Chicago: Brewster & Hanscom, 1865), p. 7; Grunert, *129th Illinois*, p. 3; M. D. Gage, *From Vicksburg to Raleigh, or a Complete History of the Twelfth Regiment Indiana Volunteer Infantry* (Chicago: Clark & Co., 1865), p. ix.

5. Magnus Brucker to Wife, 18 Sep. 1864, Magnus Brucker Papers, INHS; Lyman S. Widney to Parents, n.d. [10 Sep. 1864?] Lyman S. Widney Papers, Kennesaw Mountain National Park. Also see Hedley, *Marching Through Georgia*, pp. 56–57; Lincoln to Horace Greeley, 8/22/62, John G. Nicolay and John Hay, eds. *Complete Works of Abraham Lincoln* (New York: Francis D. Tandy Company, 1895), VIII, pp. 154–56; A. M. Geer diary, 24 Sep. 1862. Mary Ann Andersen, ed., *The Civil War Diary of Allen*

Morgan Geer (New York: Cosmos Press, 1977), pp. 55–56; William Douglas Hamilton, *Recollections of a Cavalryman of the Civil War After Fifty Years, 1861–1865* (Columbus: F. J. Heer Printing Co., 1915), p. 10; Anderson, *They Died to Make Men Free*, pp. 164–65.

6. Samuel H. Hurst, *Journal-History of the Seventy-Third Ohio Volunteer Infantry* (Chillicothe, OH: n.p., 1866), p. 156; William Light Kinney, Jr., *Sherman's March—A Review* (Bennettsville, S.C.: Marlboro Herald-Advocate, 1963?), p. 224. See also M. Fitch to ———— 27 Mar. 1865, M. Fitch, *Echoes of the Civil War*, p. 269; Levi Green diary, 27 Jan. 1865. Green Papers, MNHS.

7. William Kephart diary, 10 Nov. 1864. William Kephart Papers, AL Dept. of A & H; Lyman D. Ames diary, 11 Nov. 1864. Lyman D. Ames Papers, OHS; Records of the Office of Judge-Advocate General (Army), RG 153, oo 209, trial of William G. Moore. Also see Records of the Office of Judge-Advocate General (Army) RG 153, oo 605, trial of Jacob Schroeder; LL 3072, trial of James Channon; MM 2049, trial of Jerome Patterson; MM 1933, trial of George Parry; MM 1879, trials of Julius W. Ulrich and John Watson; oo 3428, trial of Samuel Tomlinson, NA. John W. Bates diary, 2 Apr. 1865, Civil War Miscellaneous Collection, USMHI; John R. McBride, *History of the Thirty-Third Indiana Veteran Volunteer Infantry* (Palo Alto, CA: F. A. Stuart, 1906), pp. 236–37; Judson Austin diary, 24 Apr. 1865. Nina Ness Collection, Bentley Library, UMI; William Schaum diary, 17 Apr. 1865. William Schaum Papers, Duke U.

8. C. C. Babbitt to my dear loving wife, 19 Sep. 1864. Cyrus C. Babbitt Collection, WMIU; Frederic P. Kappelman to Parents, 31 Jan. 1865. Civil War Times Illustrated Collection, USMHI; Levi D. Bryant to Wife, 28 Mar. 1865., Michael Winey Collection, USMHI. Also see Albert S. Smith to Mother, 2 Nov. 1864, Sidney Smith Papers, Bentley Library, UMI.

9. James [Stallcop] to Cousin Kate, 3 Apr. 1865, "Letters of James Stallcop to Catherine Varner, Charlotte, Iowa, 1863–1865," *NDHQ*, IV, No. 2 (January, 1930), p. 139; W. C. Johnson diary, 3 Mar. 1865, W. C. Johnson Papers, LC; J. W. Bartness to Wife, 22 Jan. 1865, Donald F. Carmony, ed., "Jacob W. Bartness Civil War Letters," *INMH*, LII, No. 2 (June, 1956), p. 180. Also see William Bircher diary, 19 Apr. 1865, William Bircher, *A Drummer Boy's Diary* (St. Paul: St. Paul Book and Stationary Company, 1889), p. 183; William [Stevens] to Mother, 30 Mar. 1865, Stevens Family Papers, Bentley Library, UMI; Charles D. Kerr, "From Atlanta to Raleigh," *MOLLUS-MN*, I, p. 208; John L. Hostetter diary, 13 Dec. 1864, Edwin W. Payne, *History of the Thirty-Fourth Regiment of Illinois Volunteer Infantry* (Clinton, IA: Allen Printing Company, 1903), p. 173; S. Duncan, Jr., to Father, Sep. 1864, Sebastian Duncan, Jr., Papers, NJHS; Charles H. Spencer to Mother, 5 Jan. 1865, Charles H. Spencer Papers, SHSW; Charlie Albertson to Brothers, 17 Dec. 1864, Albertson Family, Georgia Historical Society; William B. Miller diary, 5 Nov. 1864, William B. Miller Papers, INHS; E. Woodman to Charlie, 3 Feb. 1865, Charles Butler Papers, Bentley Library, UMI; C. M. Smith to Father, 26 Oct. 1864, Charles M. Smith Papers, Keensaw Mountain National Park.

10. A. C. Smith to Wife, 5 Nov. 1864, Abner C. Smith Papers, CTST Lib; James A. Connelly diary, 3 Nov. 1864, J. A. Connolly, Angle, ed., *Three Years*, p. 289; Charles M. Smith to Father 21 Sep. 1864, Charles M. Smith Papers, Kennesaw Mountain National Park. Also see Sibley to Anna, 19 Sep. 1864, Sibley Papers, MNHS; John E. Hickman to friends at home, 9 Nov. 1864, Squire Family Papers, Bentley Library, UMI; E. D. L. to Parents, 18 Sep. 1864, Edwin D. Levings Papers, SHSW.

11. husband to wife, 18 Sep. 1864, J. A. Connolly, Angle, ed., *Three Years*, p. 262; Billings Sibley to Anna, 19 Sep. 1864, Sibley Papers, MNHS; John Herr to Sister, 2

Apr.[1865], John Herr Papers, Duke U. Also see William B. Miller diary, 2 Feb. 1865, William B. Miller Papers, INHS.

12. James C. Patten diary, 5 Sep. 1864, R. G. Athearn, ed., *INMH*, XLIX, p. 409; John Brobst to Mary, 27 Sep. 1864, Roth, ed., *Well Mary*, p. 93; Oscar to Parents, 11 Sep. 1864, E. O. Kimberley Papers, SHSW. Also see James C. Patten diary, 15 Sep. 1864 and 15 Oct. 1864, Athearn, ed., *INMH*, XLIX, pp. 409 and 415; Fred [Pimper] to Friend, 1 Sep. 1864, Pimper Manuscripts, Indiana U.; J. W. Garner to Father, 18 Sep. 1864, J. W. Garner Papers IASHS.

13. Henry Nurs to Father, 23 Oct. 1864, Henry Nurse Papers, ILSHS; Oscar to Parents, 11 Nov. 1864, E. O. Kimberley Papers, SHSW; S. Duncan, Jr., to Mother, 26 Sep. 1864, Sebastian Duncan Papers, NJHS; Laforest Dunham to Mr. & Mrs. Simeon H. Dunham, 1 Oct. 1864, Arthur H. De Rosier, Jr., ed., *Through the South With a Union Soldier* (Johnson City, TN: Publications of the East Tennessee State University Research Advisory Council, 1966), p. 153. Also see Rufus Mead to Folks at Home, 22 Sep. 1864, Rufus Mead Papers, LC.

14. Harvey Reid to Sisters, 30 Oct. 1864, Harvey Reid Papers, SHSW; William C. Meffert diary, 8 Nov. 1864, William C. Meffert Papers, SHSW; Orson B. Clinton to Carrie, 5 Nov. 1864, Orson B. Clinton Papers on microfilm, SHSW. Also see Wright, *6th Iowa*, p. 348; William Kephart diary, 24 Oct. 1864, William Kephart Papers, AL Dept. of A & H; E. D. L to Parents, 18 Sep. 1864, Edwin D. Levings Papers, SHSW.

15. Billings Sibley to Anna, 13 Sep. 1864, Sibley Papers, MNHS; John Brobst to Mary, 27 Sep. 1864, Roth, ed., *Well Mary*, p. 92. Also see Judson Austin to Wife, 25 Sep. 1864, Nina Ness Collection, Bentley Library, UMI.

16. E. S. [Emory Sweetland] to Good morning darling, 4 Sep. 1864, Michael Winey Collection, USMHI. Also see James to Cousin Kate, 20 Dec. 1864, "Letters of James Stallcop," *NDHQ*, IV, p. 132; Andrew Bush to Mary, 6 Nov. 1864 and 9 Nov. 1864, Andrew Bush Papers, INST Library; R. W. Henry to Wife, 6 Sep. 1864 and 10 Nov. 1864, R. W. Henry Papers, IASHS; R. N. Elder to Sister, 13 Sep. 1864, R. N. Elder Papers, OHS; Jesse Taft to wife and children, 8 Nov. 1864, Jesse Taft Papers, MISTU; J. W. Garner to Father, 18 Dec. 1864, J. W. Garner Papers, IASHS; Andrew W. Ingraham to Mother, 16 Sep. 1864, Henry R. Ingraham Papers, INHS; W. G. Eaton to Brother Rice, 23 Sep. 1864, Lola J. Warrick Collection, WMIU. For voting returns, see State of Wisconsin, Executive Department, Military Election Returns, Presidential Election, 1864, SHSW; *The Legislation Manual of the State of Wisconsin, 1865*, p. 191; Alfred H. Guernsey and Henry M. Alden, *Harper's Pictorial History of the Great Rebellion* (Chicago: McDonnell Bros., 1868), II, p. 669; State of Ohio Soldiers' Votes, 1864 Presidential Election, OHS; Department of State for Pennyslvania Bureau of Legislation and Elections, Soldiers' Votes, 1864, PA History and Museum Commission; *Cincinnati Enquirer*, 15 Nov. 1864, 16 Nov. 1864, and 21 Nov. 1864; *New York Times*, 12 Nov. 1864; *New York-Semi Weekly Tribune*, 25 Nov. 1864; *Chicago Tribune*, 17 Nov. 1864 and 4 Dec. 1864; *Daily Missouri Democrat*, 20 Nov. 1864 and 21 Nov. 1864; *Morning Cleveland Herald*, 16 Nov. 1864; *Cincinnati Daily Gazette*, 18 Nov. 1864; Harrison M. Keyes diary, 11 Sep. 1864, Harrisburg Civil War Round Table Collection, USMHI; William B. Miller diary, 8 Nov. 1864, William B. Miller Papers, INHS; William Grunert journal, 27 Oct. 1864, William Grunert, *129th Illinois*, pp. 115–16; H. H. Orendorff to Brother, 9 Nov. 1864, H. H. Orendorff Papers on microfilm, ILSHS; William H. H. Edderton diary, 30 Oct. 1864, E. W. Payne, *34th Illinois*, p. 162; John G. Brown reminiscence, A Committee of the Regiment, *The Story of the Fifty-Fifth Regiment Illinois Volunteer Infantry in the Civil War* (Clinton, MA: W. J. Coulter, 1887), p. 385; *Grand Rapids Daily Eagle*, 16

Nov. 1864; Abel C. Stelle, *Memoirs of the Civil War* (New Albany, IN: n.p., 1904), p. 17; G. S. Bradley to Home Friends, 11 Nov. 1864, Bradley, *The Star Corps*, p. 179; *Proceedings of Crocker's Iowa Brigade*, 1889, p. 156; OR I, XXXIX, Pt. 1, p. 655; John Boyle, *Soldiers True*, p. 252; D. Nichol to Father, 10 Oct. 1864, Harrisburg Civil War Round Table Collection, USMHI; William Thomas diary, 8 Nov. 1864, John W. Roswell, *Yankee Cavalrymen: Through the Civil War with the Ninth Pennsylvania Cavalry* (Knoxville: University of Tennessee Press, 1971), p. 199; William G. Dollison reminiscence, Hays, *32d Ohio*, p. 64; NcNeil, *Personal Recollections of Army Life* (Richwood, OH: n.p., n.d.), p. 58; J. Hamp. Se Cheverell, *Journal History of the Twenty-Ninth Ohio Veteran Volunteers, 1861–1865* (Cleveland: n.p., 1883), p. 127; N. L. Parmater diary, 9 Nov. 1864, N. L. Parmater Papers, OHS; OR I, XXXIX, Pt. 1, p. 672; J. H. Morse to Sister, 10 Nov. 1864, Bianca Morse Federico, ed., *Civil War Letters of John Holbrook Morse, 1861–1865* (Washington, D.C.: Published by Author, 1975), p. 159; Samuel Coble diary, 8 Nov. 1864, Samuel Coble Papers, INHS; Orville T. Chamberlain journal, 23 Nov. 1864, Joseph and Orville Chamberlain Papers, INHS; Nelson Purdum diary, 8 Nov. 1864, Nelson Purdum Papers, OHS; C. E. Estabrook, *Records and Sketches of Military Organization*, p. 644; *Roster of Wisconsin Volunteers* (for 17th Wisconsin), I, pp. 49–82; F. M. McAdams journal, 8 Nov. 1864, F. M. McAdams, *Every-Day Soldier Life*, p. 115. Those four states are Wisconsin, Iowa, Missouri, and Pennsylvania. The vote of the 15th Michigan also went to McClellan, although there is some doubt as to whether the returns were from the entire regiment. See Appendix III.

17. F. M. McAdams journal, 8 Nov. 1864, F. M. McAdams, *Every-Day Soldier Life*, p. 115; Frederick Winkler to [Wife], 8 Nov. 1864, *Letters of Frederick C. Winkler*, p. 179. Also see Frank Malcom to Wife, 8 Nov. 1864, James J. Robertson, Jr., *IJH*, LVIII, No. 4, p. 339; R. Mead to Folks at Home, 3 Nov. 1864, Rufus Mead Papers, LC.

18. Levi A. Ross to Parents, 3 Nov. 1864, Levi A. Ross Papers, ILSHS.

19. N. L. Parmater diary, 8 Nov. 1864, N. L. Parmater Papers, OHS.

20. Albert A. Champlin diary, 11 Oct. 1864, Alfred Mewett Papers, WRHS; E. D. Levings to Parents, 8 Nov. 1864, Edwin D. Levings Papers, SHSW; Levi A. Ross diary, 30 Oct. 1864, Levi A. Ross Papers, ILSHS. Also see C. W. Knapp to Parents, 4 Nov. 1864 and 9 Nov. 1864, Charles Webster Knapp Papers, SHSW; N. L. Parmater diary, 8 Nov. 1864, N. L. Parmater Papers, OHS; Nelson Perdum diary, 10 Nov. 1864, Nelson Perdum Papers, OHS; R. Mead to Folks at Home, 3 Nov. 1864, Rufus Mead Papers, LC.

21. R. M. Perry to Brother [Sep. or Oct. 1864?], R. Matthew Perry Papers, SHSW; Unknown soldier to Father, 23 Sep. 1864, Hubert, *50th Illinois*, p. 292; John H. Morse to Sister, 25 Oct. 1864, Federico, ed., *Letters*, p. 155. Also see W. S. Fultz, "Reminiscence of Army Life," W. S. Fultz Papers, IASHS; Boyle, *Soldiers True*, p. 251; Allen L. Fahnestock diary, 30 Oct. 1864, Allen L. Fahnestock Papers, KMNP.

22. Rudolph Rey to Lizzie, 28 Mar. 1865, Rudolph Rey Papers, NYHS.

23. See M. Gage, *From Vicksburg to Raleigh*, xi–xiii; Matthew Jamison diary, 17 Apr. 1865, M. Jamison, *Recollections of Pioneer and Army Life*, p. 327; Charlie to Mother & Etta, 18 Apr. 1865, Charles S. Brown Papers, Duke U.

24. Farnum to Wife, 17 Dec. 1864, Farnum Papers, MNHS; James C. Patten diary, 29 Dec. 1864, Athearn, ed., *INMH*, XLIX, p. 422; Richard Reeves diary, 18 Jan. 1865 and 30 Jan. 1865, Reeves Papers, MNHS; Bauer, ed., *Soldiering*, p. 196. Also see Martin Mock to wife, 25 Dec. 1864, Martin Mock Papers, OHS; Dresbach to Wife, 7 Jan. 1865, Dresbach Papers, MNHS.

25. George N. Compton diary, 4 Mar. 1865, George N. Compton Papers, ILSHS;

William C. Meffert diary, 18 Apr. 1865, William C. Meffert Papers, SHSW; William Strawn reminiscence, William Wirt Calkins, *The History of the One Hundred and Fourth Regiment of Illinois Volunteer Infantry* (Chicago: Donohue & Henneberry, 1895), p. 314; J. W. Hinkley to ———, 20 Apr. 1864[5], J. W. Hinkley, *Service in 3d Wisconsin*, pp. 174–75.

CHAPTER 3

1. Albert A. Champlin diary, 3 Dec. 1864, Alfred Mewett Papers, WRHS; Madame Sosnowski, "Burning of Columbia," in Mrs. Thomas Taylor et al., ed., *South Carolina Women in the Confederacy* (Columbia, S. C.: The State Company, 1903), pp. 267–68; John to Belle, 6 Apr. 1865, Federico, ed., *Civil War Letters of J. H. Morse*, p. 182; Isaac N. Carr diary, 8 Jan. 1865, Isaac N. Carr Papers, IASHS; John Henry Otto, "War Memories, 1864," p. 290, John Henry Otto Papers, SHSW; James Sawyer to Nancy, journal-letter, 26 Nov. 1864, James T. Sawyer Papers, SHSW; O. O. Winther, ed., *With Sherman to the Sea*, p. 136; Harrison Pendergast journal, 19 Nov. 1864, Pendergast Papers, MNHS.

2. Oscar L. Jackson diary, 8 Mar. 1865, Oscar Lewis Jackson, *The Colonel's Diary* (Sharon, PA: Published by his family, 1922), p. 193. Also see James Sawyer to Nancy, 26 Nov. 1864 letter-journal and 27 Dec. 1864, James Sawyer Papers, SHSW; Albert Champlin diary 8 Jan. 1865, Alfred Mewett Papers, WRHS.

3. Records of the Office of Judge Advocate General (Army), RG 153, NA, MM 1578, trial of Henry C. Clevinger; oo 281, trial of Robert Rabbitt, NA. Also see OR I, XLIV, Pt. 1, pp. 75 and 159; OR I, XLVII, Pt. 1, pp. 209 and 588. Rabbitt had his carbine resting over part of his saddle. He shifted the weapon, according to his testimony, and it discharged.

4. Van S. Bennett diary, 16 Oct. 1864, Van S. Bennett Papers, SHSW. Bennett believed the man was a member of the Twenty-third Corps. Also see Samuel Storrow diary, 4 Dec. 1864, Samuel Storrow Papers, MAHS; Records of the Office of Judge Advocate General (Army), RG 153, NA oo 281, trial of Robert Rabbitt; N. A.; Leon Litwack, *Been in the Storm So Long: The Aftermath of Slavery* (New York: Alfred A. Knopf, 1979), p. 128.

5. Edwin L. Lybarger diary, 6 Jan. 1865, Edwin L. Lybarger, *Leaves From My Diary* (Warsaw, OH: n.p., n.d.), n.p.; Dell Bly to Dear One, 6 Jan. 1865, Adelbert M. Bly Papers, SHSW; Richard Markle to Mother, 22 Jan. 1865, Richard Markle Papers, ILSHS; Arthur Sumner to Nina Hartshorn, Feb.?/65, Penn School Papers, SHC, UNC; Levi D. Bryant to Wife, 28 Mar. 1865, Michael Winey Collection, USMHI. Also see William S. Fultz, "11th Iowa," M. Throne, ed., IJH, LV, p. 83.

6. Oscar L. Jackson diary, 8 Mar. 1865, O. L. Jackson, *The Colonel's Diary*, p. 193; Stelle, *Memoirs of the Civil War*, pp. 23–24, Edwin E. Bryant, *History of the Third Regiment of Wisconsin Veteran Volunteer Infantry, 1861–1865* (Madison: Veteran Association of the Regiment, 1891), p. 196; Fleharty, *Our Regiment, 102nd Illinois*, p. 125.

7. William Schaum diary, 5 Apr. 1865, William Schaum Papers, Duke U; Records of the Office of Judge Advocate General (Army), RG 153, NA, MM 3937, trial of A. C. Warner, NA. Also see Fergus Elliott diary, 25 Nov. 1864, Civil War Times Illustrated Collection, USMHI; Leon F. Litwack, *North of Slavery: The Negro in the Free States, 1790–1860* (Chicago: University of Chicago Press, 1961), p. 93.

8. O. O. Winther, ed., *With Sherman to the Sea*, p. 149; Henry C. Laybourn diary,

23 Mar. 1865, Henry C. Laybourn Papers, U. of Iowa; William D. Evans diary, 11 Jan. 1865, William D. Evans Papers, WRHS. Also see Fredrick Pimper to Friend, 8 Jan. 1865, Pimper Manuscripts, Indiana U; George Drake to parents, 17 Jan 1865, Drake, ed., *The Mail Goes Through*, pp. 127–28; Wright, *6th Iowa*, p. 396; R. S. Finley to MAC, 18 Jan. 1865, R. S. Finley Papers, SHC, UNC; John S. Cooper diary, 30 Jan. 1865, John S. Cooper Papers, Duke U. Special Orders, No. 18. Fourth Division, Fifteenth Corps. 14 Feb. 1865. Letters and Endorsements Book, 110th U.S.C. Inf. Special Field Orders, No. 6. 110th US.C. Inf. 29 Mar. 1865. Special Field Orders Book, 110th U.S.C. Inf. R.G., NA. Muster Rolls, January–February 1865 for: 54th Massachusetts (Colored) Infantry; 3rd U.S. Colored Troops; 21st U.S. Colored Troops; 26th U.S. Colored Troops, 32nd U. S. Colored Troops; 33rd U.S. Colored Troops; 34th U.S. Colored Troops; 35th U.S. Colored Troops; 2nd U.S. Colored Light Artillery, Battery G. RG 393, NA.

9. See Williamson D. Ward journal, 28 Dec. 1864, W. D. Ward Papers on microfilm, INHS; Records of the Office of Judge Advocate General (Army), RG 153, NA oo 667, trial of James Cord, NA; Alfred Trego diary, 25 Nov. 1864, Alfred Trego Papers, Chicago HS.

10. Charles E. Wills diary, 15 Mar. 1865, C. E. Wills, *Army Life of an Illinois Soldier*, p. 362. Also see Records of the Office of Judge Advocate General (Army), RG 153, NN 3430, trial of William H. McMullen; MM 2436, trial of Hiram McCumber; oo 281, trial of Robert Rabbitt NA; Charles F. Hubert journal, 29 Nov. 1864, Hubert, *50th Illinois*, p. 326; Matthew Jamison diary, 2 May 1865, M. Jamison, *Recollections of a Pioneer and Army Life*, p. 331; Axel Reed diary, 29 Nov. 1864, Reed Papers, MNHS; Winther, ed., *With Sherman to the Sea*, pp. 135–36; F. M. McAdams journal, 19 Jan. 1865, McAdams, *Every-Day Soldier Life*, pp. 131–32; Benjamin F. Sweet, "War Record," Benjamin F. Sweet Papers, WHC–SHSMO; William Meffert diary, 4 Apr. 1865, William C. Meffert Papers, SHSW; David Bittle Floyd, *History of the Seventy-Fifth Regiment Indiana Infantry Volunteers* (Philadelphia: For the Author, 1893), p. 351; Marden Sabin, "Memoirs of Dr. Marden Sabin," INST Lib. The army had to continue its march and no one from the command knew whether the woman lived or died.

11. William B. Miller diary, 12 Feb. 1865 and 21 Jan. 1865, William B. Miller Papers, INHS; John R. Boyle, *Soldiers True*, p. 263. Also see S. Duncan, Jr., to Sister Nellie, 10 Jan. 1865, Sebastian Duncan, Jr., Papers, NJHS; Edward Oscar Kimberley, *Personal Recollections of the Colored Race During the Civil War, 1861, 1865*, p. 2; N. L. Parmater diary, 6 Dec. 1864, N. L. Parmater Papers, OHS; Charles D. Wills diary, 17 Nov. 1864, Charles D. Wills Papers, ILSHS; William Humphrey to Ma & Pa, 16 Dec. 1864, William T. Humphrey Papers, Chicago PL;; Peter Ege diary, 2 Dec. 1864, Peter Ege Papers, SHSW.

12. See Garret S. Byrne diary, 31 Jan. 1865, Garret S. Byrne Papers, Rutgers U; James A. Connolly diary, 20 Nov. 1864, J. A. Connolly, Angle, ed., *Three Years*, p. 313; J. R. Kinnear, *86th Illinois*, p. 81; Oscar [Kimberley] to Parents, 4 Apr. 1865, E. O. Kimberley Papers, SHSW.

13. Oscar L. Jackson diary, 13 Jan. 1865, O. L. Jackson, *The Colonel's Diary*, p. 175; David Nichol diary, 23 Mar. 1865, Harrisburg Civil War Round Table Collection, USMHI; Charles Smith to Father, 25 Jan. 1865, Charles M. Smith Paper, KMNP. Also see Matthew Jamison journal, 22 Feb. 1865, M. Jamison, *Recollection of Pioneer and Army Life*, p. 331; Oscar L. Jackson diary, 8 Mar. 1865, O. L. Jackson, *The Colonel's Diary*, p. 193; E. Hutchinson to Father, 15 Oct. 1864, Edwin Hutchinson Papers, LSU;

Ed Cort to Friends, 6 Apr. 1865, Helyn W. Tomlinson, ed., *"Dear Friends": The Civil War Letters and Diary of Charles Edwin Cort* (Helyn W. Tomlinson, 1962), pp. 187–88; William B. Miller diary, 3/24/65, William B. Miller Papers, INHS.

14. James Sawyer to Nancy, 25 Dec. 1864, James T. Sawyer Papers, SHSW; Frederick Winkler journal-letter to [Wife], 23 Nov. 1864, *Letters of Frederick C. Winkler*, pp. 180–81. Also see Sylvanus Crossly journal, 18 Feb. 1865, Sylvanus Crossly Papers, LC; Henry Hitchcock diary, 16 Nov. 1864 and 18 Nov. 1864, H. Hitchcock, *Marching with Sherman*, pp. 61 and 69–71; John Langhans to Brother, 9 Jun. 1865, Michael Winey Collection, USMHI; John C. Van Duzer diary, 17 Nov. 1864, John C. Van Duzer Papers, Duke U.; W. S. Schermerhorn to Children, 13 Mar. 1865, Winfield S. Schermerhorn Papers, IASHMA; William Strawn, "Reminiscence," in Calkins, *104th Illinois*, pp. 258–59.

15. Martin C. Short to Father & Mother, 18 Dec. 1864, Martin C. Short Papers, SHSW; Axel Reed diary, 6 Feb. 1865, Axel Reed Papers, MNHS; S. S. Farwell to Wife, 25 Mar. 1865, S. S. Farwell Papers, IASHS; Garret S. Byrne diary, 23 Nov. 1864, Garret S. Byrne Papers, Rutgers U; William T. Humphrey to Ma & Pa, 16 Dec. 1864, William T. Humphrey Papers, Chicago, PL. Also see James Sawyer to Nancy, 26 Nov. 1864 and 25 Dec. 1864, James T. Sawyer Papers, SHSW; Henry W. Slocum, "Reminiscence," in *Battles and Leaders of the Civil War*, IV, p. 689; Samuel Storrow diary, 4 Dec. 1864, Samuel Storrow Papers, MAHS; Oscar L. Jackson diary, 8 Mar. 1865, O. L. Jackson, *The Colonel's Diary*, pp. 192–93; Allen L. Fahnestock diary, 3 Dec. 1864, Allen L. Fahnestock Papers, KMNP; U. H. Farr, "Reminiscences," in Samuel Merrill, *The Seventieth Indiana Volunteer Infantry* (Indianapolis: The Bowen-Merrill Company, 1900), pp. 249–50; Hedley, *Marching Through Georgia*, p. 311; Harrison Pendergast journal, 9 Dec. 1864, Pendergast Papers, MNHS; William H. H. Enderton diary, 14 Dec. 1864, Payne, *34th Illinois*, p. 174; Special Field Orders, No. 120. HQ, Military Division of the Mississippi, 9 Nov. 1864, OR I, XXXIX, Pt. 3, p. 714; Sherman, *Memoirs*, II, p. 249; William Grunert journal, 23 Dec. 1864, W. Grunert, *129th Illinois*, p. 159; Levi Green diary, 17 Feb. 1865, Green Papers, MNHS; Axel Reed diary, 8 Feb. 1865, Reed Papers, MNHS.

16. Nelson Stauffer diary, 18 Nov. Stauffer, *Civil War Diary* (Northridge: California State University, 1976), n.p.; Halsey, ed., *A Yankee Private's Civil War*, pp. 113–14; W. S. Schermerhorn to children, 13 Mar. 1865, Winfield S. Schermerhorn Papers, IASHMA. Also see Potter, *Reminiscences of the Civil War*, pp. 109–11; N. Stauffer diary, 23 Feb. 1865, N. Stauffer, *Civil War Diary*, n.p.

17. O. D. Hormel, ed., *With Sherman to the Sea*, p. 217; Samuel Merrill to Emily, 15 Dec. 1864, Samuel Merrill Papers, INHS.

18. Bauer, ed., *Soldiering*, p. 178; James G. Essington diary, 19 Nov. 1864, James G. Essington Papers, INHS; Katharine Macy Noyes, ed., *Jesse Macy: An Autobiography* (Springfield, IL: Charles C. Thomas, 1933), pp. 60–61; H. G. Noble diary, 18 Dec. 1864, Henry G. Noble Papers, Bentley Library, UMI. Also see James to Wife and Children, 16 Jan. 1865, James R. Stillwell Papers, OHS; Pepper, *Personal Recollections*, p. 196; Edwin E. Marvin, *The Fifth Regiment Connecticut Volunteers: A History Compiled from Diaries and Official Reports* (Hartford: Wiley, Waterman & Eaton, 1899), pp. 354–55; H. Hitchcock diary, 17 Nov. 1864, H. Hitchcock, *Marching with Sherman*, p. 66; W. S. Schermerhorn to Brother & Sister, 12 Mar. 1865, Winfield S. Schermerhorn Papers, IASHMA; James Connolly diary, 29 Nov. 1864, J. A. Connolly, Angle, ed., *Three Years*, pp. 332–33; M. Jamison diary, 7 Mar. 1865, M. Jamison, *Recollections of Pioneer and Army Life*, p. 316.

19. Eugene [McWayne] to Mother & Sisters, 19 Dec. 1864, in R. M. McMurry, "Sherman's Savannah Campaign," *CWTI*, XXI, p. 12; C. C. Courtright journal, 30 Nov. 1864, Calkins, *104th Illinois*, p. 265; Dresbach to Wife, 30 Nov. 1864, Dresbach Papers, MNHS. Also see George B. McMillan diary, 6 Dec. 1864, George B. McMillan Papers, SHSW; William Schaum diary, 29 Jan. 1865 and 11 Apr. 1865, William Schaum Papers, Duke U.

20. Oscar L. Jackson diary, 7 Mar. 1865, O. L. Jackson, *The Colonel's Diary*, p. 191. Also see J. W. Bartmess to Companion, 13 Jan. 1865, D. F. Carmony, ed., *INMH*, LII, p. 179; Fergus Elliott diary, 13 Jan. 1865, Civil War Times Illustrated Collection, USMHI.

21. James H. Patton, "Reminiscences," Civil War Miscellaneous Collection, USMHI. Also see Frederick Sherwood journal, 27 Mar. 1865, Earl M. Hess Collection, USMHI; Matthew Jamison diary, 6 Mar. 1865, M. Jamison, *Recollections*, p. 316; George Hurlbut to Angie, 6 Jan. 1865, M. George Hurlbut Papers, KMNP.

22. Major S. H. M. Byers, *With Fire and Sword* (New York: The Neale Publishing Company, 1911), p. 148; Pepper, *Personal Recollections*, p. 245; Boyle, *Soldiers True*, p. 263. See also Sylvanus Crossly journal, 14–19 Feb. 1865, Sylvanus Crossly Papers, LC; Oscar L. Jackson diary, 8 Mar. 1865, O. L. Jackson, *The Colonel's Diary*, p. 193; Byers, *With Fire and Sword*, pp. 155–56; H. H. Tarr diary, 20 Nov. 1864, Storrs, *20th Connecticut*, p. 151; James H. Patton, "Reminiscences," Civil War Miscellaneous Collection, USMHI; J. H. Otto, "War Memories, 1864," pp. 243–44, John Henry Otto Papers, SHSW; L. A. Ross diary 18 Feb. 1865, L. A. Ross Papers, ILSHS; Bradley, *The Star Corps*, p. 258; H. C. Laybourn diary, 20 Nov. 1864, Henry C. Laybourn Papers, U. of Iowa; Hodgson journal, 26 Dec. 1864, Charles C. Jones, Jr., U. of Georgia; Sarah Jane Sams letter-diary to R, 15 Feb. 1865, Sarah Jane Sams, U. of South Carolina; [R. S. Cheves] to Husband, 18 Mar. 1865, Rachel Susan Cheves Papers, Duke U.

23. Philip Roesch journal-reminiscence, Philip Roesch Papers, SHSW.

24. Unidentified officer, Committee, *Ninety-Second Illinois Volunteers* (Freeport, IL: Journal Steam Publishing House and Bookbindery, 1875), pp. 199–200; Unknown diarist, 8 Dec. 1864, Committee, *92nd Illinois*, p. 197; Harrison Pendergast journal, 9 Dec. 1864, Pendergast Papers, MNHS. Also see William Strawn, "Reminiscences," Calkins, *104th Illinois*, p. 259; H. Pendergast journal, 9 Dec. 1864, Pendergast Papers, MNHS; James T. Reeve diary, 3 Dec. 1864 and 8 Dec. 1864, James T. Reeve Papers on microfilm, SHSW; William J. Gibson diary, 9–10 Dec. 1864, Tourgeé, *Story of a Thousand*, pp. 341–42; C. D. Kerr, *MOLLUS–MN*, I, p. 216; Unidentified diarist, 9 Dec. 1864, Committee, *92nd Illinois*, p. 198; Axel Reed diary, 9 Dec. 1864, Reed Papers, MNHS; Allen L. Fahnestock diary, 25 Nov. 1864, Allen Fahnestock Papers, KMNP; Michael Fitch diary, 4 Dec. 1864, M. Fitch, *Echoes of the Civil War*, p. 236. Davis did the same thing at Bear Creek two weeks earlier.

25. M. Fitch to ———, 27 Mar. 1865, M. Fitch, *Echoes of the Civil War*, p. 268; Pepper, *Personal Recollections*, p. 196. Also see Kinnear, *86th Illinois*, p. 81.

CHAPTER 4

1. See Dr. Thomas to Dr. Thrall, 20 Dec. 1864, Mildred Thrall, ed., "An Iowa Doctor in Blue: The Letters of Seneca B. Thrall, 1862–1864," *IJH*, LVIII, No. 2 (April, 1960), p. 187; Ezra Button diary, 17 Jan. 1865, John B. Tripp Papers, SHSW; Axel Reed diary, 10 Feb. 1865, Reed Papers, MNHS; Pepper, *Personal Recollections*, pp. 270–71.

2. H. H. Tarr diary, 18 Nov. 1864, Storrs, *20th Connecticut*, p. 150; William Grunert journal, 2 Feb. 1865, W. Grunert, *129th Illinois*, pp. 181–82; Jesse Bean diary, 1
Jan. 1865, Jesse S. Bean Papers, SHC, UNC; R. B. Hoadley to Cousin Em, 8 Apr.
1865, Robert Bruce Hoadley Papers, Duke U.

3. Rufus Mead, Jr., to Folks at Home, 4 Jan. 1865, Rufus Mead Papers, LC; B. F.
Heuston diary, 30 Oct. 1864, Benjamin Franklin Heuston Papers, SHSW; H. Hitchcock to Mrs. Hitchcock, 25 Apr. 1865, H. Hitchcock, *Marching with Sherman*, p. 314.
Also see Harvey Reid to Sisters, 30 Oct. 1864, Harvey Reid Papers, SHSW; L. A.
Ross, "Topography and Wealth of State," pp. 319–20, ILSHS; G. S. Bradley to ———,
12 Mar. 1865, G. S. Bradley, *The Star Corps*, p. 264; Matthew Jamison diary, 4 Mar.
1865, M. Jamison, *Recollections of Pioneer and Army Life*, p. 315; Roy Nichols journal,
2/25/65, G. W. Nichols, *The Story of the Great March*, pp. 185–86.

4. James Burkhalter diary, 13 Feb. 1865, Burkhalter Papers, ILSHS; Charles Wills
diary, 22 Feb. 1865, C. Wills, *Army Life of an Illinois Soldier*, p. 367; C. Stelle, *Memoirs
of the Civil War*, p. 33; S. F. Fleharty diary, 17 Nov. 1864, S. F. Fleharty, *Our Regiment: 102nd Illinois*, p. 110; John Risedorph diary, 25 Feb. 1865, Risedorph Papers,
MNHS. Also see Risedorph journal-reminiscences, 24–25 Feb. 1865, Risedorph Papers, MNHS; C. Wills diary, 11 Apr. 1865, C. E. Wills, *Army Life*, p. 368; Dr. Thomas
to Dr. Thrall, 20 Dec. 1864, M. Throne, ed., *IJH*, LVIII, No. 2, p. 187; Kinnear,
86th Illinois, p. 81; N. L. Parmater diary, 27 Feb. 1865, N. L. Parmater Papers, OHS;
No author [Green Southard] to Lyde, 13 Sep. 1864. Lyde Harriman Papers, OHS;
John Langhans to Brother, 9 Jun. 1865, Michael Winey Collection, USMHI; James A.
Connelly diary, 16 Nov. 1864, J. A. Connelly, Angle, ed., *Three Years*, p. 307. A Confederate soldier filed a similar complaint in letters H. Clay Reynolds to Mary, 4 Jan.
1865, and to Sweet Wife, 24 Jan. 1865, Henry Clay Reynolds Papers, AL Dept. of A
& H.

5. James Burkhalter diary, 13 Feb. 1865, Burkhalter Papers, ILSHS. Also see C. E.
Wills diary, 9 Feb. 1865, C. E. Wills, *Army Life*, p. 343; A. M. Geer diary, 28 Dec.
1864, Anderson, ed., *Diary of A. M. Geer*, p. 185.

6. B. H. Hill to The People of Georgia, 18 Nov. 1864, and G. T. Beauregard to the
People of Georgia, 18 Nov. 1864, OR I, XLIV, Pt. 1, p. 867; *Savannah Daily Morning
News*, 26 Nov. 1864, in McBride, *History of the 33rd Indiana*, p. 155; John L. Hostetter
diary, 12 Dec. 1864, Payne, *34th Illinois*, p. 172. Also see William B. Miller diary, 1
Dec. 1864, William B. Miller Papers, INHS; Appeal of G. T. Beauregard, 23 Dec.
1864 and Appeal of Z. B. Vance, 23 Dec. 1864, OR I, XLVII, Pt. 2, p. 1265.

7. George W. Gee to Clarence, 29 Mar. 1865, George W. Gee Papers, SHSW; Dr.
Thomas to Dr. Thrall, 20 Dec. 1864, M. Throne, ed., *IJH*, LVIII, No. 2, p. 188; C.
H. Brush to Father, 17 Dec. 1864, C. H. Brush Papers, ILSHS; W. C. Johnson diary,
4 Mar. 1865, W. C. Johnson Papers, LC; James Ghormley diary, 6 Mar. 1865, James
Ghormley Diary, SHSW. Also see L. A. Ross diary, 26 Nov. 1864, Levi A. Ross Papers, ILSHS; James Sawyer to Nancy, 18 Dec. 1864, James T. Sawyer Papers on microfilm, SHSW; A. W. Reese, "Recollections of the Civil War," pp. 90–91, A. W. Reese
Papers, WHC–SHSMO; James T. Reeve diary, 18 Nov. 1864, James T. Reeve Papers
on microfilm, SHSW; William C. Stevens to Dear Ones at Home, 5 Sep. 1864, Stevens
Family Papers, Bentley Library, UMI; Bryant, *3rd Wisconsin*, p. 286; J. R. M. Gaskill
diary, 22 Feb. 1865, James R. M. Gaskill Papers, Chicago HS.

8. S. S. Farwell to Wife, 15 Dec. 1864, S. S. Farwell Papers, IASHS; M. Dresbach
to Wife, letter-diary, 26 Feb. 1865, Dresbach Papers, MNHS. Also see J. H. Otto,

"War Memories, 1865," pp. 61–62, John Henry Otto Papers, SHSW; Mary Noble to Lelia, 20 Nov. 1864, Noble-Attaway Papers, SHC, UNC; L. L. Gates to Companion, 5 Sep. 1864, Luther L. Gates Papers, Emory U; Hinkley, *Service With the 3rd Wisconsin Infantry*, p. 141; William Meffert diary, 17 Nov. 1864, William C. Meffert Papers, SHSW; Hodgson Journal, 21 Dec. 1864, Charles C. Jones, Jr., Papers, U. of Georgia; E. P. Failing diary, 8 Jan. 1865, Failing-Knight Papers, MAHS; L. R. Ray diary, 19 Nov. 1864. A Confederate soldier who described the panic in Macon, Lavender Ray Papers in Georgia Division of the Daughters of the Confederacy Collection, GA Dept. of A & H.

9. M. Dresbach to Wife, letter-diary 26 Feb. 1865, Dresbach Papers, MNHS. Also see A. M. Geer diary, 7 Mar. 1865, Andersen, ed., *The Civil War Diary of A. M. Geer*, p. 202; T. M. Stevenson to Editor, 18 Jan. 1865, Thomas M. Stevenson, *History of the 78th Regiment* OVII (Zanesville, OH: Published by Hugh Dunne, 1865), p. 326.

10. Mrs. Randolph Sams to My Own Darling R, diary-letter, 8 Feb. 1865, Sarah Jane Sams Papers, U. of South Carolina; E. M. S[mith] to Eliza, 23 Mar. 1865, D. E. H. Smith et al., eds., *Mason Smith Family Letters, 1860–1868* (Columbia: University of South Carolina Press, 1950), p. 176.

11. James E. Edmonds diary, 20 Nov. 1864, James E. Edmonds Collection, USMHI; Unmailed letter, Mrs. William Moultrie Dwight to Capt. Henry A. Gaillard, 22 Feb. 1865, David Wyatt Aikin Papers, U. of South Carolina.

12. See Douglas Hapeman diary, 24 Nov. 1864, Douglas Hapeman Papers, ILSHS; Harry Dingam diary, 30 Nov. 1864, Federico, ed., *Civil War Letters of J. H. Morse*, p. 167; Axel Reed diary, 28 Nov. 1864, Reed Papers, MNHS; L. A. Ross diary, 28 Nov. 1864, Levi A. Ross Papers, ILSHS; Frank Putnam, *MOLLUS–WI*, III, p. 387; J. A. Connolly diary, 26 Nov. 1864, J. A. Connolly, Angle, ed., *Three Years*, p. 324.

13. Fanny Cohen diary, 24 Dec. 1864, S. B. King, Jr., ed., *GHQ*, XLI, p. 412; OTC[hamberlain] to Father, 21 Apr. 1865, Joseph and Orville Chamberlain Papers, INHS. Also see Elizabeth Georgia Basinger, "Reminiscence," W. S. Basinger Papers on microfilm, SHC, UNC; Imogene [Hoyle] to Ama, 28 Nov. 1864, Bomar/Killian Papers, Atlanta HS; G. S. Bradley diary, 16 Nov. 1864, G. S. Bradley, *The Star Corps*, p. 183.

14. William Grunert journal, 2 Feb. 1865, W. Grunert, *129th Illinois*, p. 182; Committee, *92nd Illinois*, p. 172; Axel Reed diary, 11 Feb. 1865, Reed Papers, MNHS; Garret S. Byrne diary, 21 Feb. 1865, Garret S. Byrne Papers, Rutgers U.

15. See Hinkley, *Service with the 3rd Wisconsin Infantry*, p. 165; Hodgson journal, 21 Dec. 1864 and 10 Jan. 1865, Charles C. Jones, Jr., Papers, U. of Georgia; W. W. Gordon diary, 24 Dec. 1864 and 7 Jan. 1865, W. W. Gordon Papers, SHC, UNC; Elizabeth Collier journal, 5 Apr. 1865, Elizabeth Collier Papers, SHC, UNC; Sherman, *Memoirs*, II, p. 236; Edward C. Anderson to Wife, 2 Jan. 1864[5], Edward C. Anderson Papers, SHC, UNC; Frederick Winkler to [Wife], journal-letter, 1 Dec. 1864, *Letters of Frederick C. Winkler*, p. 182; Alfred Trego diary, 29 Nov. 1864, Alfred Trego Papers, Chicago HS; Garret S. Byrne diary, 29 Nov. 1864, Garret S. Byrne Papers, Rutgers U; O. L. Jackson diary, 2 Dec. 1864, O. L. Jackson, *The Colonel's Diary*, p. 169; M. A. Emanuel to My Dear Friend, 18 Mar. 1865, M. A. Emanuel Papers, U. of South Carolina; William Stevens to Father, 1[3] May 1865, Stevens Family Papers, Bentley Library, UMI; Hamilton, *Recollections of a Cavalryman*, pp. 200–201; Elliott B. McKeever, "Atlanta to the Sea," Elliott B. McKeever Papers, WRHS; Wilbur F. Hinman, *The Story of the Sherman Brigade* (Alliance, OH: Published by the Author, 1897), p. 927.

16. Records of the House of Representatives on John Bass, 55th and 57th Congress RG 233, NA; Records of the U.S. Senate bill file S 2742, 57th Congress, RG 41, NA. See General Field Order, No. 36, Army of the Tennessee, 20 Dec. 1864, General Field Orders Book, Army of the Tennessee, RG 393, NA. Personal Service Records of John Bass, NA; Records of the Judge Advocate General (Army), RG 153, NA MM 3937, trial of Arthur W. McCarthy, NA; Your loving husband to Darling Mollie, 2 Apr. 1865, Charles B. Tompkins Papers, Duke U; William D. Evans diary, 3 Apr. 1865, William D. Evans Papers, WRHS; Edward E. Schweitzer diary, 2 Apr. 1865, Civil War Times Illustrated Collection, USMHI. A Confederate soldier claimed that some troops reported a Union soldier and a black kidnapped a woman in South Carolina, L. R. Ray to Brother, 9 Mar. 1865, Lavender Ray, GA Daughters of the Confederacy. GA Dept. of A & H.

17. See Oscar L. Jackson diary, 7 Mar. 1865, O. L. Jackson, *The Colonel's Diary*, p. 191; Halsey, ed., *A Yankee Private's Civil War*, p. 46; Samuel Merrill to Emily, 15 Dec. 1864, Samuel Merrill Papers, INHS; Kilpatrick to Wheeler, 23 Feb. 1865, OR I, XLVII, Pt. 1, p. 860.

18. Charles G. Michael diary, 23 Mar. 1865, Charles G. Michael Papers, INHS; Charles E. Belknap, "Christmas Day Near Savannah in Wartime," *MH*, VI, No. 4, pp. 591–96. Also see E. Hutchinson to Father, 15 Oct. 1864, Edwin Hutchinson Papers, LSU; S. M. Cort to dear friend, 22 Mar. 1865, Elisha Mitchell Papers, SHC, UNC; Daniel Sheehan diary, 25 Nov. 1864, Daniel W. Sheehan Papers, ILSHS; Mrs. Delia White Woodward, "Civil War Memorandum," Augustus White Long Papers, Duke U; Axel Reed diary, 10 Jan. 1865, Reed Papers, MNHS; Allen Fahnestock diary, 12 Nov. 1864, Allen L. Fahnestock Papers, KMNP; William P. Fulton diary, 12 Nov. 1864, William P. Fulton, KMNP.

19. S. S. Farwell to Wife, 26 Dec. 1864, S. S. Farwell Papers, IASHS. Also see C. E. Belknap, "Recollections of a Bummer," *MOLLUS–DC*, II, No. 28, pp. 8–10; McNeil, *Personal Recollections of Army Life*, pp. 69–70.

20. Winston Cheatham to Sister, 25 Dec. 1864, Cheatham Papers, MNHS; Isaac Carr diary, 21 Feb. 1865, Isaac N. Carr Papers, IASHS; Charles A. Willison, *Reminiscences of a Boy's Service With the 76th Ohio* (Menasha, WI: George Banta Publishing Company, 1908), p. 105; Frederick Sherwood to Mother, 6 Sep. 1864, Sherwood Family Papers, LSU; William H. Tallman "Reminiscences," p. 54, Gregory Coco Collection, USMHI; Farnum to Wife, 10 Nov. 1864, Farnum Papers, MNHS. Also see Unknown author diary, 3 Nov. 1864, Unknown diarist of Co. F, 9th Iowa, IASHA; William C. Bennett to Doctor, 21 Jan. 1866, Williams, *Echoes from the Battlefield*, p. 61; O. M. Poe to darling, 26 Dec. 1864, O. M. Poe Papers, LC; Ed to Nettie, 7 Jan. 1865, William Walton, ed., *A Civil War Courtship: The Letters of Edwin Weller from Antietam to Atlanta* (Garden City, NY: Doubleday & Company, 1980), p. 142; Halsey, ed., *A Yankee Private's Civil War*, p. 66; Edwin to Parents, 1 May, 1865, Edwin D. Levings Papers, SHSW; William [Stevens] to Sister, 2 Apr. 1865, Stevens Family Papers, Bentley Library, UMI.

21. James E. Edmonds diary, 17 Nov. 1864, James E. Edmonds Papers, USMHI; Sam to Maggie, 26 Mar. 1865, Samuel K. Harryman Papers, INST Library; Henry [Wright] to Folks at Home, 28 Mar. 1865, Howard Norman Monnett, ed., " 'The Awfulest Time I Ever Seen:' A Letter From Sherman's Army," *CWH*, VIII, No. 3 (September, 1962), p. 286. Also see Alfred Trego diary, 19 Nov. 1864, Alfred Trego Papers, Chicago HS; Charles Wills diary, 24 Nov. 1864, C. Wills, *Army Life*, p. 325.

22. William Miller diary, 5 Nov. 1864, William B. Miller Papers, INHS. Also see

Charles Spencer to Mother, 5 Jan. 1865, Charles H. Spencer Papers, SHSW; William Miller diary, 2 Nov. 1864, William B. Miller Papers, INHS; N. L. Parmater diary, 23 Sep. 1864, N. L. Parmater Papers, OHS; Charlie Albertson to Brothers, 17 Dec. 1864, Albertson Family Papers, GAHS; Allen Campbell to Father, 18 Dec. 1864, Campbell Family Papers, Michigan State U.

23. Two good examples are Henry Hitchcock diary and Joshua W. Williams diary. See H. Hitchcock diary, 16 Nov. 1864, and 1 Dec. 1864, H. Hitchcock, *Marching with Sherman*, pp. 62 and 125; Joshau Williams diary, 6 Nov. 1864 and subsequent entries, Indiana History Manuscripts, Indiana U.

24. Charles F. Morse to [members of his family], 2 Jan. 1865, C. F. Morse, *Letters Written during the Civil War*, p. 204; S. S. Farwell to Wife, 25 Mar. 1865, S. S. Farwell Papers, IASHS. Also see Bauer, ed., *Soldiering*, p. 193; Charles D. Wills diary, 20 Nov. 1864, Charles D. Wills Papers, ILSHS; W. C. Johnson diary, 13 Nov. 1864, Kerksis, ed., *The Atlanta Papers*, p. 808; William W. Campbell, "Reminiscences," William W. Campbell Papers on microfilm, SHSW; Boyle, *111th Pennsylvania*, p. 266; Pepper, *Personal Recollections*, p. 310; Aten, *85th Illinois*, pp. 261–62, Unknown author diary, 9/20/64, Unknown diarist, Co. F, 9th Iowa Papers, IASHS; J. H. Otto, "War Memories, 1865," p. 70, John Henry Otto Papers, SHSW; Byers, *With Fire and Sword*, p. 154; Perry Grubb "Reminiscences," Perry D. Grubb Papers, ILSHS. There was also a prison camp for officers in Columbia, SC.

25. G. S. Bradley journal, 3 Feb. 1865, G. S. Bradley, *The Star Corps*, p. 256; Lysander Wheeler to Parents, Bro and Sister, 2 Nov. 1864, Lysander Wheeler Papers, ILSHS; Charles F. Morse to [members of family], 31 Jan. 1865, C. F. Morse, *Letters Written during the Civil War*, p. 211; Hamilton, *Recollections of a Cavalryman*, pp. 154–55. Also see Lavender R. Ray to Sister, N. D. Lavender R. Ray Papers, Georgia Division of the Daughters of the Confederacy, GA Dept. of A & H.

26. E. D. Levings to Parents, 8 Nov. 1864, Edwin D. Levings Papers, SHSW; Harrison Pendergast journal, 13 Nov. 1864, Pendergast Papers, MNHS; Charley Smith to Father and Brother, 8 Dec. 1864, Charles M. Smith Papers, KMNP. Also see Lysander Wheeler to Parents, Bro and Sister, 29 Mar. 1865, Lysander Wheeler Papers, ILSHS; Minerva McClatchey diary, 15 Nov. 1864, McClatchey Family, GA Dept. of A & H.

27. Samuel Mahon to Lizzie, 22 Dec. 1864, John K. Mahon, ed., *IJH*, LI, No. 3, p. 258; Ed Cort to Friends, 16 Jan. 1865, H. W. Tomlinson, ed., *Dear Friends*, p. 179; Fred Marion to Sister, 24 Jan. 1865, Fred Marion Papers, ILSHS; John Herr to Sister, 5 Feb. 1865, John Herr Papers, Duke U; H. W. Slocum to My Dear Col., 6 Jan. 1865, J. Howland Papers, NYHS; Pepper, *Personal Recollections*, p. 330; Geo. M. Wise to Brother, 13 Mar. 1865, Wilfred W. Black, ed., "Civil War Letters of George M. Wise," *OHQ*, LXVI, No. 2 (April, 1957), 193. Also see William Grunert journal, 22 Dec. 1864, W. Grunert, *129th Illinois*, p. 158; Daniel Titus to Emeline Adams, 17 Jan. 1865, Civil War Miscellaneous Collection, USMHI; J. G. Berstler to Friend and Cousin, 2 Apr. 1865. Griffith Family Papers, IASHMA; Eli [Ricker] to Mother & Sister, 27 Mar. 1865, E. G. Longacre, ed., *SCHM*, LXXXII, p. 221; Mrs. L. Catherine Joyner "Reminiscence," in J. P. Carrol, "The Burning of Columbia, South Carolina," *SHSP*, VIII, No. 5 (May, 1880), p. 203; Oscar L. Jackson diary, 7 Mar. 1865, O. L. Jackson, *The Colonel's Diary*, p. 191; Frank H Putney, "Incidents of Sherman's March Through the Carolinas," *MOLLUS–WI*, III, pp. 382–83; Sherman to Halleck, 12 Dec. 1864, OR I, XLIV, Pt. 1, p. 702; M. Dresbach to Wife, 29 Jan. 1865, Dresbach Papers, MNHS; Isaac W. Muzzy to Wife Dosa, 26 Dec. 1864, Muzzy Papers, MNHS.

CHAPTER 5

1. F. H. Putney to Father, 14 Sep. 1864, Frank H. Putney Papers (microfilm), SHSW; Owen Stuart to Wife, 17 Dec. 1864, Civil War Times Illustrated Collection, USMHI; Emerson [Anderson] to Parents, 5 Sep. 1864, Civil War Papers, AAS.

2. See Jesse S. Bean diary, 26 Mar. 1865, Jesse S. Bean Papers, SHC, UNC; Rogers, *125th Illinois*, pp. 112–13; Jesse Taft to Wife & Children, 19 Oct. 1864, Jesse Taft Papers, MISTU.

3. Halsey, ed., *A Yankee Private's Civil War*, p. 182; [Levi Bryant] to Wife, 8 Nov. 1864, Michael Winey Collection, USMHI; Bliss Morse diary, 15 Jan. 1865, L. Morse ed., *Civil War Diary of Bliss Morse*, p. 75; W. C. Johnson journal, 20 Dec. 1864, Kerksis, ed., *Atlanta Papers*, pp. 828–29. Also see James F. Morrow diary, 12 Dec. 1864, Civil War Times Illustrated Collection, USMHI.

4. Laforest Dunham to Miss Hercey Dunham, 27 Sep. 1864, De Rosier, ed., *Through the South with a Union Soldier*, p. 151; William Grunert journal, 17 Jan., 1865, W. Grunert, *129th Illinois*, p. 174. Also see C. Hubert, *50th Illinois*, p. 342; H. P. Rugg diary, 28 Mar. 1865, H. P. Rugg Papers, CTST Lib.

5. See C. B. Tompkins to My Own Darling, 27 Mar. 1865, Charles B. Tompkins Papers, Duke U; Alonzo Miller to Sister, 19 Sep. 1864, Alonzo Miller Papers on microfilm, SHSW; Laforest Dunham to Miss Hercey Dunham, 27 Sep. 1864, De Rosier, ed., *Through the South with a Union Soldier*, p. 151; William Humphrey to Pa & Ma, 24 Dec. 1864, William T. Humphrey Papers, Chicago P.L.; M. W. Darling to Brother and Sister, 21 Jan. 1865, M. W. Darling Papers, U. of Iowa; Isaac N. Carr diary, 2 Jan. 1865, and 11 Jan. 1865, Isaac N. Carr Papers, IASHS.

6. Isaac N. Carr diary, 17 Jan. 1865, Isaac N. Carr Papers, IASHS; Eli [Ricker] to Mary, 8 Jan. 1865, E. G. Longacre, ed., *SCHM*, LXXXII, pp. 213–14. See also Isaac N. Carr diary, 10 Jan. 1865, Isaac N. Carr Papers, IASHS.

7. See J. C. Kirk to Isaac McMillan, 12 Mar. 1865, Wabash County Civil War Recollections, INST Library; OR I, XXXIX, Pt. 1, p. 677.

8. See OR I, XXXIX, Pt. 1, pp. 651–52; Henry Noble diary, 9 Nov. 1864, Henry G. Noble Papers, Bentley Library, UMI; Oliver Sanders journal, 28 Dec. 1864, Oliver Sanders Papers, WRHS.

9. R. R. Rockwood diary, 21–28 Oct. 1864, R. R. Rockwood Papers, WHC–SHSMO; Nelson Stauffer diary, 3 Apr. 1865, Stauffer, *Civil War Diary*, n.p. Also see M. Dresbach to Wife, 28 Dec. 1864, Dresbach Papers, MNHS; OR I, XXXIX, Pt. 1, p. 659; Billings Sibley to Sister, 29 May 1865, Sibley Papers, MNHS; J. W. Bartmess to Companion, 13 Jan. 1865, D. F. Carmony, ed., *INMH*, LII, p. 179; Jesse S. Bean diary, 7 Apr. 1865, Jesse S. Bean Papers, SHC, UNC; John D. Inskeep diary, 27 Mar. 1865 and 2 Apr. 1865, John D. Inskeep Papers, OHS; Samuel Mahon to Lizzie, 15 Jan. 1865, John K. Mahon, ed., "The Civil War Letters of Samuel Mahon, Seventh Iowa Infantry," *IJH*, LI, No. 3 (July, 1953), p. 259; Henry C. Laybourn diary, 16 Jan. 1865, Henry C. Laybourn Papers, U. of Iowa; Records of Judge Advocate General (Army), RG 153, NA oo 666, trial of Christopher McGee, NA; Henry Clay Robbins, "Autobiography," Henry C. Robbins Papers, SHSW.

10. See Records of Judge Advocate General (Army), RG 153, NA; Edgar S. Dudley, *Military Law and the Procedure of Courts-Martial* (New York: John Wiley & Sons, 1908); William Winthrop, *Military Law and Precedents* (Boston: Little, Brown and Company, 1896).

11. See Records of Judge Advocate General (Army), RG 153, NA, MM 1602, trials of Henry J. Sherman and Samuel Stiles; oo 674, trial of John B. Douglass; NN 3430, trials of William Cartwright and James ("Levi") Kennedy, oo 605, trial of Thomas Brooks.

12. See Records of Judge Advocate General (Army), RG 153, NA, MM 2496, trial of Josiah Todd; MM 1679, trial of James A. Webb; NN 3937, trial Arthur W. Mc-Carty. The army had no place to put convicted soldiers when it was in the Deep South, so it had to keep the men with the army but in confinement. Cargo space was at such a premium that they could not send the convicts north.

13. E. L. Lybarger diary, 24?Mar. 1865, Edwin L. Lybarger Papers, IASHMA. Also see William Bircher journal, 26?Mar. 1865, W. Bircher, *A Drummer Boy's Diary*, pp. 176–80; Records of Judge Advocate General (Army), RG 153, NA oo 3428, trial of James K. Preble, NA; Jack North to Mary, 2 Apr. 1865, Nina Ness Collection, Bentley Library, UMI; Wm. B. Miller diary, 31 Mar. 1865, William B. Miller Papers, INHS; John W. Bates diary, 31 Mar. 1865, Civil War Miscellany, USMHI; John Batchelor diary, 31 Mar. 1865, John Batchelor, ILSHS; Thomas H. Williams to Father, 2 Apr. 1865 (23 AC), Thomas H. Williams Papers, Bentley Library, UMI; Axel Reed diary, 1 Apr. 1865, Reed Papers, MNHS.

14. Farnum to Wife, 17 Dec. 1864, Farnum Papers, MNHS; Charley [Cox] to Katie, 2 Apr. 1865, Lorna Lutes Sylvester, ed., ' "Gone for a Soldier': The Civil War Letters of Charles Harding Cox," *INMH*, LXVIII, No. 3 (September, 1972), p. 233; Thos. Christie to Brother, 18 Dec. 1864, Christie Papers, MNHS; C. W. Knapp to Parents, 4 Nov. 1864, Charles Webster Knapp Papers, SHSW. Also see E. S. [Emory Sweetland] to Wife, 7 Sep. 1864, Michael Winey Collection, USMHI; Burke Wylie to Bro Robert, 25 Sep. 1864, Burke Wylie Papers, IASHS.

15. Jos. T. Smith to Nett, 4 Nov. 1864, Jos. Taylor Smith Papers, INHS. Also see O. M. Poe to Nell, 31 Oct. 1864 and 1 Nov. 1864, O. M. Poe Papers, LC; Thos. W. Christie to Brother, 10 Nov. 1864, Christie Papers, MNHS; C. M. Smith to Father, 7 Nov. 1864, Charles M. Smith Papers on microfilm, SHSW; C. C. Carpenter to Emmett Carpenter, 25 Dec. 1864, M. Throne, ed., *IJH*, LIII, pp. 86–87; Samuel Mahon to Lizzie, 5 Nov. 1864, Mahon, ed. *IJH*, LI, p. 257.

16. Edd Weller to Nettie, 25 Oct. 1864 and 11 Nov. 1864, Walton, ed., *A Civil War Courtship*, p. 125; Oscar to Parents, 26 Oct. 1864, E. O. Kimberley Papers, SHSW. Also see Fredrick to dear Friend, 14 Sep.[1864], Pimper Manuscripts, Indiana U.

17. Henry Clay Robbins, "Autobiography," Henry C. Robbins Papers, SHSW; Levi Ross to Parents, 15 Dec. 1864, Levi A. Ross Papers, ILSHS; Thaddeus H. Capron to ———, 13 Mar. 1865, Thaddeus H. Capron, ed., "War Diary of Thaddeus H. Capron," *Journal of the Illinois State Historical Society*, XII, No. 3 (October, 1919), p. 399. Also see A. S. W. [Williams] to Daughters, 27 Mar. 1865, Milo M. Quaife, ed, *From the Cannon's Mouth: The Civil War Letters of Alpheus S. Williams* (Detroit: Wayne State University Press, 1959), p. 377; William B. Miller diary 2 Nov. 1864 and 5 Nov. 1864, William B. Miller Papers, INHS; Jos. L. Locke to Miss Terry, 19 Apr. 1865, Joseph L. Locke Papers, ILSHS.

18. James A. Connolly diary, 11 Oct. 1864, J. A. Connolly, Angle, ed., *Three Years*, p. 274; William B. Miller diary, 5 Jan. 1865, William B. Miller Papers, INHS. Also see Charley [Cox] to dearest Sister, 14 Jan. 1865, L. L. Sylvester, ed., *INMH*, LXVIII, p. 224.

19. Chas. S. Brown to Mother, Etta, Lew, Fred, & all the rest, 15 Jan. 1865, Charles S. Brown Papers, Duke U; Frank Putney to Father, 10 Jan. 1865, Frank H. Putney

Papers on microfilm, SHSW. Also see C. S. Brown to Mother & Sister and all Browns, 23 Sep. 1864, Charles S. Brown Papers, Duke U.

20. George Baird (?) diary, 18 Dec. 1864, Brown, *4th Minnesota*, pp. 350–351; George B. McMillan diary, 17 Dec. 1864, George B. McMillan Papers, SHSW; Lyman S. Widney to Parents, 28 Sep. 1864, Lyman Widney Papers, KMNP. Also see W. H. Nugen to Sister Mary, 28 Sep. 1864, W. H. Nugen Papers, Duke U; John G. Brown reminiscence, Committee, *55th Illinois*, p. 429.

21. William H. H. Tallman, "Reminiscence," Gregory Coco Collection, USMHI. Also see John Cutter to Father, 20 Apr. 1865, Cutter Papers on microfilm, MNHS; Richard Reeves diary, 16 Apr. 1865, Reeves Papers, MNHS; Halsey, ed., *A Yankee Private's Civil War*, pp. 199–200.

22. Alfred Lamb journal, 13 Nov. 1864, Alfred Lamb, *My March with Sherman to the Sea*, (n.p.: Paddock Publications, 1951). Also see D. Nichol to Mother, 26 Oct. 1864, Harrisburg Civil War Round Table, USMHI: Jas. T. Sawyer to Nancy, 19 Sep. 1864, James T. Sawyer Papers, SHSW; George W. Gee to Clarence, 25 Oct. 1864, George W. Gee Papers, SHSW.

23. See Charles F. Hubert journal, 13 Dec. 1864, C. F. Hubert, *50th Illinois*, p. 337; E. P. Burton diary, 7 Dec. 1864, E. P. Burton, *Diary*, p. 46; J. H. Otto "Reminiscences, 1864," p. 296. John Henry Otto Papers, SHSW; Wm. T. Humphrey to Pa & Ma, 24 Dec. 1864, William T. Humphrey Papers, Chicago PL.; Anthony J. Baurdick diary, 10 Dec. 1864, Anthony J. Baurdick Papers, Emory U.

24. E. Hutchinson to Father, 29 Dec. 1864, Edwin Hutchinson Papers, LSU. Also see Willison, *Reminiscences of a Boy's Service with the 76th Ohio*, p. 105; Francis R. Baker "Reminiscences," p. 41, Francis R. Baker Papers, ILSHS; George Drake to Father, 22 Sep. 1864 and 18 Dec. 1864, J. A. Drake, ed., *The Mail Goes Through*, p. 114; Frank Putney to Father, 28 Dec. 1864, Frank H. Putney Papers on microfilm, SHSW; Richard Reeves diary, 22 Dec. 1864, Reeves Papers, MNHS; Pepper, *Personal Recollections*, p. 287; Henry Laybourn diary, 27 Dec. 1864 and 18 Jan. 1865, Henry C. Laybourn Papers, U. of Iowa; John Weissert to Mother & Children, 15 Jan. 1865, John Weissert Papers, Bentley Library, UMI.

25. Andrew Bush to Mary, 6 Nov. 1864, Andrew Bush Papers, INST Library. Also see Charles M. Smith to Father, 21 Sep. 1864, Charles M. Smith Papers, KMNP; George F. Shepherd to wife, 20 Sep. 1864 and 8 Oct. 1864, George F. Shepherd Papers on microfilm, SHSW; George B. McMillan diary, 29 Dec. 1864, George B. McMillan Papers, SHSW; Isaac N. Carr diary, 3 Jan. 1865, Isaac N. Carr Papers, IASHS; Charles H. Spencer to Father, 31 Dec. 1864, Charles H. Spencer Papers, SHSW; Henry C. Laybourn diary, 5 Jan. 1865, Henry C. Laybourn Papers, U. of Iowa; Isaac Kittinger diary, 6–26 Jan. 1865, Earl M. Hess Collection, USMHI; Bliss Morse diary, 17 Dec. 1864–17 Jan. 1865, L. J. Morse, ed., *The Civil War Diary of Bliss Morse*, pp. 74–75; J. W. Rumpel to Father, 25 Dec. 1864, H. E. Rosenberger, ed., "Ohiowa Soldier: The Letters of John Wesley Rumpel," *Annals of Iowa*, 3rd ser., XXXVI, No. 2 (Fall, 1961), p. 144. One ship ran the Savannah blockade only to find Sherman's army in control of the city.

26. C. H. Brush to Mother, 21 Dec. 1864, C. H. Brush Papers, ILSHS; Anthony J. Baurdick diary, 12 Dec. 1864, Anthony J. Baurdick Papers, Emory U; Nelson Stauffer diary, 29 Dec. 1864, N. Stauffer, *Civil War Diary*, n.p. Also see Halsey, ed., *A Yankee Private's Civil War*, p. 159; affectionate son [E. Wescott] to Mother, 11 Jan. 1865, Ebenezer Wescott Papers, SHSW; Isaac Roseberry diary, 25 Dec. 1864, Isaac Rose-

berry Papers on microfilm, Bentley Library, UMI; Ira Morrill diary, 13 Dec. 1864, Morrill Papers, MNHS.

27. C. C. Babbitt to my dear loving wife, 19 Sep. 1864, Cyrus C. Babbitt Collection, WMIU; James [Stallcop] to Cousin, 29 Mar. 1865, "Letters of James Stallcop," *NDHQ*, IV, p. 137; E. S. [Emory Sweetland] to Wife, 20 Jan. 1865, Michael Winey Collection, USMHI.

28. James T. Reeve diary, 30 Oct. 1864, James T. Reeve Papers on microfilm, SHSW. Also see S. S. Farwell to Wife, 9 Jan. 1865, S. S. Farwell Papers, IASHS; Grant Tuttle diary for October 1864, Mrs. Kathryn Hoppe Collection, WMIU; Jesse S. Bean diary, 5 Feb. 1865, Jesse S. Bean Papers, SHC, UNC; J. C. Bennett journal, 15 Apr. 1865, Merrill, *70th Indiana*, pp. 267–68.

29. Delos Lake to Brother, 17 Apr. 1865, Delos Lake Papers, Huntington Library. Also see McBride, *33rd Indiana*, pp. 215–16; Judson Austin to Wife, 2 Apr. 1865, Nina Ness Collection, Bentley Library, UMI; *Letter of Greeting and Record of the Christian Association of the Second Brigade, Third Division, Twentieth Corps* (Cincinnati: Printed at the Methodist Book Concern, 1865).

30. J. W. Bartness to Companion, 13 Jan. 1865, D. F. Carmony, ed., *INMH*, LII, p. 179; Jas. Greenalch to My Dear, 29 Oct. 1864, Knox Mellon, Jr., ed., "Letters of James Greenalch," *MH*, XLIV, No. 2 (June, 1960), p. 227. Also see Appendix II for specific data on venereal disease; Sam [Jarrett] to Cousin, 15 Jan. 1865, Jefferson Hartman Letters, Duke U; Edmund J. Cleveland diary, 6 Apr. 1865 (23 AC), Edmund J. Cleveland Papers, SHC, UNC.

31. L. A. Ross diary, 5 Nov. 1864, Levi A. Ross Papers, ILSHS; R. S. Finley to MAC, 18 Jan. 1865, R. S. Finley Papers, SHC, UNC; Frederick Sherwood to Mother, 3 Jan. 1865. Frederick Sherwood Papers, LSU; Williamson D. Ward journal, 25 Dec. 1864, Williamson D. Ward Papers, SHSW. Also see M. Dresbach to Wife, 7 Jan. 1865, Dresbach Papers, MNHS; Peter Ege diary, 14 Dec. 1864, Peter Ege Papers, SHSW; General Field Orders, No. 39, Army of the Tennessee, 27 Dec. 1864, ORI, XLIV, p. 822; J. H. Otto, "War Memories, 1864," pp. 367–68, John Henry Otto Papers, SHSW; E. S. [Emory Sweetland] to Wife, 20 Jan. 1865, Michael Winey Collection, USMHI; Matthew Jamison journal, 9 Jan. 1865, M. Jamison, *Recollections of Pioneer and Army Life*, p. 295; C. C. Platter diary, 11 Jan. 1865. C. C. Platter Papers, U. of Georgia. Records of Judge Advocate General (Army), RG 153, NA, LL 3072, trial of James W. Tate and trial of John W. Fields; oo 470, trial of Samuel McCray; oo 3543, trial of Hugh Alexander; oo 3632, trial of Greenburg B. Nevling, NA.

32. Laforest to Miss Hercey Dunham, 13 Sep. 1864, De Rosier, Jr., ed., *Through the South with a Union Soldier*, p. 149; Edwin E. Bryant, *3rd Wisconsin*, pp. 285–86. Also see Hinkley, *Service with the 3rd Wisconsin Infantry*, p. 150; Francis R. Baker "Reminiscence," p. 39, Francis R. Baker Papers, ILSHS; O. M. Poe to Nelly, 3 Apr. 1865, O. M. Poe Papers, LC; S. Jackson to Mother, 9 Apr. 1865, Smithfield Jackson Papers, KMNP.

33. John Vail diary, 2 Nov. 1864, John Vail Papers, OHS; Jas. Sawyer to Nancy, 4 Sep. 1864, James T. Sawyer Papers, SHSW; General Field Orders, No. 12, Army of the Tennessee, 5 Mar. 1865, ORI, XLVII, Pt. 2, p. 686. Also see John Vail diary, 4 Dec. 1864, John Vail Papers, OHS; George L. Childress diary, 7 Mar. 1865, George L. Childress Papers, ILSHS; *Veteran Banner*, OHS; William Miller diary, 29 Nov. 1864 and 28 Feb. 1865, William B. Miller Papers, INHS.

34. W. H. Brown to Emma, 30 Mar. 1865, Vivian C. Hopkins, ed., "Soldier of the

92nd Illinois: Letters of William H. Brown and His Fiancee, Emma Jane Frazey," *Bulletin of the New York Public Library*, LXXIII, No. 2 (February, 1969), p. 124; J. Bishop to Frank, 25 Dec. 1864, Bishop Papers, MNHS. Also see *Letter of Greetings from the Christian Association of the Second Brigade, Third Division, Twentieth Corps*, p. 4; Pepper, *Personal Recollections*, p. 197.

35. John W. Ludington to father Frances, 13 Jan. 1865, John W. Ludington Papers, IASHMA; Wm. F. Goodwin to Parents, 1 Oct. 1864, William F. Goodwin Papers, ILSHS. Also see Willie G. Baugh to Parents, 19 Oct. 1864, William G. Baugh Papers, Emory U; F. M. McAdams journal, 13 Sep. 1864 and 24 Feb. 1865, F. M. McAdams, *Every-Day Soldier Life*, pp. 107 and 139; Wm. Grunert journal, 17 Nov. 1864, Grunert, *129th Illinois*, pp. 124–25; H. D. Chapman diary, 10 Dec. 1864, Horatio Dana Chapman, *Civil War Diary* (Hartford: Allis, 1929), p. 106; Jesse Dawley diary, 29 Nov. 1864, Jesse Dawley Papers, U. of Iowa; Affidavits of Luke Murray and Aaron Riker, Dec. 1865, Luke Murray Papers, OHS; C. H. Dickinson diary, 8 Nov. 1864, Charles H. Dickinson Papers, SHSW; Philip Roesch diary, 4 Feb. 1865, Philip Roesch Papers, SHSW; Henry G. Noble diary, 26 Oct. 1864, Henry G. Noble Papers, Bentley Library, UMI. Records of Judge Advocate General (Army), RG 153, NA, LL 3060, trial of John W. Atherton; MM 1879, trial of John Ducey; MM 1933, trial of William Lewis; MM 1996, trial of J. N. Clampett; oo 548, trial of Rudolph Mueller, NA.

36. Richard Reeves diary, 3 Jan. 1865 and 4 Jan. 1865, Reeves Papers, MNHS; William B. Miller diary, 28 Dec. 1864, William B. Miller Papers, INHS; M. Dresbach to Wife, 22 Jan. 1865, Dresbach Papers, MNHS. Also see Thos. Christie to Father, 11 Jan. 1865, Christie Papers, MNHS; Harrison Walters diary, 26 Jan. 1865, Harrison Walters Papers, INHS; Winther, ed., *With Sherman to the Sea*, pp. 148–49 and 161–62.

37. Thos. D. Christie to Sister, 19 Oct. 1864, Christie Papers, MNHS. Also see Mahlon H. Floyd, "Sherman's March to the Sea," p. 13, speech delivered 18 Feb. 1889, Helen Floyd Carlin Papers, INHS; William [Stevens] to Dear Ones at Home, 8 Sep. 1864, Stevens Family Papers, Bentley Library, UMI; Henry Noble diary, 22 Oct. 1864, Henry G. Noble Papers, Bentley Library, UMI; Theodore Skinner to friends at home, 30 Apr. 1865 (23 AC), Civil War Miscellaneous Collection, USMHI; E. D. Levings to Parents, 22 Jan. 1865, Edwin D. Levings Papers, SHSW.

38. Grant W. Tuttle diary, 23 Dec. 1864, Mrs. Kathryn Hoppe Collection, WMIU; J. R. [Stillwell] to wife and little girls, 25 Jan. 1865, James R. Stillwell Papers, OHS. Also see William D. Evans diary, 26 Oct. 1864, William David Evans Papers, WRHS; William H. H. Tallman, "Reminiscences," Gregory Coco Collection, USMHI.

39. See Hedley, *Marching Through Georgia*, p. 290; Wm. Bircher diary, 24 Dec. 1864, W. Bircher, *A Drummer Boy's Diary*, pp. 154–55; Edwin Hutchinson to Father, 11 Oct. 1864, Edwin Hutchinson Papers, LSU; Payne, *34th Illinois*, p. 210; George Metz diary, 9 Apr. 1865, George P. Metz Papers, Duke U.

40. Charles D. Kerr, "From Atlanta to Raleigh," *MOLLUS–MN*, I, p. 208; Charles H. Dickinson diary, 29 Sep. 1864, Charles H. Dickinson Papers, SHSW; affectionate son [E. Wescott] to Mother, 11 Jan. 1865, Ebenezer Wescott Papers, SHSW. Also see Laforest Dunham to Hiram Dunham, 9 Sep. 1864, De Rosier, Jr., ed., *Through the South with a Union Soldier*, pp. 145–46; RSF to MAC, 22 Oct. 1864, R. S. Finley Papers, SHC, UNC; George Drake to parents, 31 Dec. 1864, J. A. Drake, ed., *The Mail Goes Through*, p. 126; C. C. B[abbitt] to dear wife and children, 24 Sep. 1864, Mrs. Ann Coffee Collection, WMIU; George McMillan diary, 11 Jan. 1865, George B. McMillan Papers, SHSW; Martin Mock to wife, 25 Dec. 1864, Martin Mock Papers, OHS; M.

Dresbach to Wife, 7 Jan. 1865, Dresbach Papers, MNHS; C. C. Carpenter to Emmett Carpenter, 25 Dec. 1864, M. Throne, ed., *IJH*, LIII, pp. 86–87; C. M. Smith to Father, 7 Nov. 1864, Charles M. Smith Papers on microfilm, SHSW; Thos. W. Christie to Brother, 10 Nov. 1864, Christie Papers, MNHS; Samuel Mahon to Lizzie, 5 Nov. 1864, J. K. Mahon, ed., *IJH*, LI, p. 257.

CHAPTER 6

1. Samuel Batchell to Wife, 3 Sep. 1864, Samuel Batchell Papers, Atlanta HS.

2. Minerva McClatchey diary, 9 Nov. 1864, McClatchey Family Papers, GA Dept. of A & H; E. P. Burton diary, 18 Jan. 1865, E. P. Burton, *Diary* (Des Moines: The Historical Record Survey, 1939), n.p.; Henry Hurter diary, 15 Nov. 1864, Civil War Times Illustrated Collection, USMHI. Also see Hedley, *Marching Through Georgia*, p. 245; Isaac Roseberry diary, 4 Nov. 1864, Isaac Roseberry Papers on microfilm at Bentley Library, UMI; W. C. Johnson diary, 29 Oct. 1864, Kerkis, ed., *Atlanta Papers*, p. 312; Winther, ed., *With Sherman to the Sea*, pp. 130–31; affectionate son to Mother, 24 Oct. 1864, Ebenezer Wescott Papers, SHSW; Axel Reed diary, 19 Jan. 1865, Reed Papers, MNHS; A. M. Geer diary, 24 Nov. 1864, M. A. Andersen, ed., *Diary of A. M. Geer*, p. 178; Sherman to J. D. Webster, 10 Oct. 1864, OR I, XXXIX, Pt. 3, p. 175; Special Field Orders, No. 114. Head Quarters Mil. Div. of Miss., 4 Nov. 1864. Special Field Orders Book, William T. Sherman Papers, RG 94, NA.

3. See Special Field Orders, Nos. 115, 119, and 120. HQ Mil. Div. of the Miss., 4 Nov. 1864, 8 Nov. 1864 and 9 Nov. 1864, OR I, XXXIX, Pt. 3, pp. 627, 701, and 713; Thos. Christie to Brother, 17 Dec. 1864, Christie Papers, MNHS; Owen Stuart to Wife, 20 Jan. 1864[5], Civil War Times Illustrated Collection, USMHI; Sherman to Slocum, 25 Feb. 1865, OR I, XLVII, Pt. 2, p. 573; Fleharty, *Our Regiment: 102d Illinois*, p. 144; Charles Lyman diary, 20 Feb. 1865, Charles N. Lyman Papers, IASHMA; General Field Orders, No. 11, Army of the Tennessee, 15 Feb. 1865, OR I, XLVII, Pt. 2, p. 429.

4. See W. S. Morris et al., *History: 31st Regiment Illinois Volunteers* (Evansville, IN: Keller Printing & Publishing Co., 1902), p. 132; OR I, XXV, Pt. 2, pp. 488–89; Hedley, *Marching Through Georgia*, pp. 263–65; Winther, ed., *With Sherman to the Sea*, p. 134; Mildred Throne, ed., "A History of Company D, Eleventh Iowa Infantry, 1861–1865 by William S. Fultz," *IJH*, LV, No. 1 (January, 1957), p. 71; William Grunert journal, 9 Nov. 1864, W. Grunert, *129th Illinois*, p. 120; [John E. Hickman] to friends at home, 4 Nov. 1864, Squire Family Papers, Bentley Library, UMI.

5. See J. C. Arbuckle, *Civil War Experiences*, p. 108; Oscar L. Jackson diary, 26 Nov. 1864, O. L. Jackson, *The Colonel's Diary*, p. 166; Thos. Christie to Brother, 17 Dec. 1864, Christie Papers, MNHS.

6. See Kinnear, *86th Illinois*, p. 80; OR I, XXV, Pt. 2, pp. 488–89.

7. See Frank L. Ferguson, "Sherman's March to the Sea," Civil War Times Illustrated Collection, USMHI.

8. See Hedley, *Marching Through Georgia*, p. 265; Circular HdQrs. Fifteenth Army Corps, 14 Nov. 1864, OR I, XLIV, Pt. 1, p. 453; Belknap et al., *15th Iowa*, p. 414; Special Field Orders, No. 120, HQ. Mil. Div. of the Miss., 9 Nov. 1864, OR I, XXXIX, Pt. 3, p. 713.

9. See William Bircher journal, 27 Feb. 1865, W. Bircher, *A Drummer Boy's Diary*,

pp. 167–68; Edward Mott Robbins, *Civil War Experiences, 1862–1865* (Privately Published, n.d.), p. 9; Westervelt, *Lights and Shadows*, p. 83.

10. Charles Wills diary, 1 Nov. 1864, C. E. Wills, *Army Life of an Illinois Soldier*, p. 317; Benjamin D. Dean, *Recollections of the 26th Missouri Infantry* (Lamar, MO: Southwest Missourian Office, 1892), p. 47. Also see John Risedorph diary, 13 Feb. 1865, Risedorph Papers, MNHS; Harrison Pendergast journal, 1 Dec. 1864, Pendergast Papers, MNHS; William Grunert journal, 15 Nov. 1864, W. Grunert, *129th Illinois*, p. 122; Sewall G. Randall diary, 7 Sep. 1864, 11 Sep. 1864, 21 Sep. 1864, and 3 Oct. 1864, Randall Papers, MNHS; H. H. Orendorff et al., *Reminiscences of the Civil War From Diaries of Members of the 103d Illinois Volunteer Infantry* (Chicago: Press of J. F. Leaming & Co., 1904), p. 144; OR I, XLIV, Pt. 1, p. 212.

11. Oscar L. Jackson diary, 13 Mar. 1865, O. L. Jackson, *The Colonel's Diary*, p. 197; R. Y. Woodlief diary, 2 Mar. 1865, R. Y. Woodlief Papers, U. of South Carolina. Also see Westervelt, *Lights and Shadows*, p. 83; Harrison Pendergast journal, 19 Nov. 1864, Pendergast Papers, MNHS; Charles Hubert journal, 20 Feb. 1865, C. F. Hubert, *50th Illinois*, p. 356; H. W. Rood, *Co. E and 12th Wisconsin*, p. 367; Ira S. Owen journal, 29 Aug. 1864, Ira S. Owens, *Greene County Soldiers in the Late War, Being a History of the Seventy-Fourth OVI* (Dayton, OH: Christian Publishing House Print, 1884), p. 83; William H. H. Tallman, "Reminiscences," Gregory Coco Collection, USMHI; Orendorff, et al., *103rd Illinois*, pp. 137–38; John Risendorph diary, 12 Mar. 1865, Risedorph Papers, MNHS; C. S. Brown to Father, Mother & Etta, 20 Oct. 1864, Charles S. Brown Papers, Duke U.

12. Cousin Bruce to Cousin Em, 18 Dec. 1864, Robert Bruce Hoadley Papers, Duke U; Nelson Stauffer diary, 3 Mar. 1865, N. Stauffer, *Civil War Diary*, n.p. Also see Kinnear, *86th Illinois*, p. 88; Richard Reeves diary, 16 Dec. 1864, Reeves Papers, MNHS; Ira Morrill diary, 13 Dec. 1864, Morrill Papers, MNHS; Dr. Thomas to Dr. Thrall, 20 Dec. 1864, M. Throne, ed., *IJH*, LVIII, No. 2, p. 188; W. C. Johnson diary, 14–20 Dec. 1864, Kerksis, ed., *Atlanta Campaign*, pp. 826–28; William H. H. Tallman, "Reminiscences," p. 96, Gregory Coco Collection, USMHI; Ezra Button diary, 21 Feb. 1865, John B. Tripp Papers, SHSW; Garret S. Byrne diary, 17 Mar. 1865, Garret S. Byrne Papers, Rutgers U; Halsey, ed., *A Yankee Private's Civil War*, p. 105; Alfred Lamb diary, 18 Dec. 1864, A. Lamb, *My March With Sherman to the Sea*, n.p.

13. Bryant, *History of the 3rd Wisconsin*, p. 281; Rood, *Co. E and the 12th Wisconsin*, p. 367. Also see Rudolph Rey to Lizzie, 28 Mar. 1865, Rudolph Rey Papers, NYHS; McBride, *33rd Indiana*, p. 239; William D. Evans diary, 3 Dec. 1864, William David Evans, WRHS; W. G. Putney, "Reminiscences," W. G. Putney, KMNP; Special Field Order, No. 175, HQ 3rd Div. 17th A.C., 16 Dec. 1864. Charles Reynolds Papers, LC; M. Fitch diary, 6 Dec. 1864, M. Fitch, *Echoes of the Civil War*, pp. 236–37; Garret S. Bryne diary, 14 Mar. 1865, Garret S. Byrne Papers, Rutgers U; Harlan Rugg diary, 25 Nov. 1864, Marvin, *5th Connecticut*, p. 356; Collins, *History of the 149th New York*, p. 293; William Gibson diary, 12 Nov. 1864–7 Dec. 1864, A. Tourgeé, *Story of a Thousand*, pp. 334–41; Hormel, ed., *With Sherman to the Sea*, p. 214; Levi Green diary, 27 Jan. 1865, Green Papers, MNHS; Unsigned to Mollie, 22 Jan. 1865, Charles B. Tompkins Papers, Duke U.

14. See Rood, *Co. E and the 12th Wisconsin*, pp. 366–67; George Campbell to Father, 30 Jan. 1865, Campbell Family Papers, Michigan State U; Bauer, ed., *Soldiering*, pp. 206 and 229; Ferdinand Sebring diary, 30 Nov. 1864, Wabash County Civil War Recollections, INST Library.

15. George N. Compton, "Reminiscences of the Georgia March," George N. Comp-

ton Papers, ILSHS; William [Stevens] to Mother, 30 Mar. 1865, Stevens Family Papers, Bentley Library, UMI. Also see C. F. Kimmel journal, 17 Nov. 1864, in 66th Illinois Collection, NYHS; L. A. Ross diary, 21 Nov. 1864, L. A. Ross Papers, ILSHS; Unknown diarist, 4 Dec. 1864, Unknown diary of Co. F, 9th Iowa, IASHS; Will Z. Corin to Sister, 6 Jan. 1865, Civil War Times Illustrated Collection, USMHI; Judson Bishop to Frank, 25 Dec. 1864, Bishop Papers, MNHS; C. C. Carpenter to wife, 16 Dec. 1864, M. Throne, ed., *IJH*, LIII, No. 1, p. 86.

16. Charley Smith to Father and Brother, 18 Dec. 1864, Charles M. Smith Papers on microfilm, SHSW and at KMNP; C. C. Platter diary, 17 Nov. 1864, C. C. Platter Papers, U. of Georgia; Allen Campbell to Father, 18 Dec. 1864, Campbell Family Papers, Michigan State U; Ed Cort to Friends, 20 Dec. 1864, Tomlinson, ed., *Dear Friends*, p. 175; J. W. Bartmess to Wife, 18 Dec. 1864, D. F. Carmony, ed., *INMH*, LII, p. 177; Nelson Stauffer diary, 15 Mar. 1865, N. Stauffer, *Civil War Diary*, n.p. Also see [John W. Reid] to William G., 27 Jan. 1865, William G. McCreary, Duke U; John M. Carr diary, 17 Nov. 1864, John M. Carr Papers, KMNP; Richard Reeves diary, 17 Nov. 1864, Reeves Papers, MNHS; William Meffert diary, 19 Nov. 1864 and 25 Nov. 1864, William C. Meffert Papers, SHSW; M. Dresbach to Wife, 14 Dec. 1864, Dresbach Papers, MNHS; J. H. Allspaugh diary, 23 Nov. 1864, J. H. Allspaugh Papers, U. of Iowa; Bliss Morse diary, 25 Nov. 1864, L. Morse, ed., *The Civil War Diary of Bliss Morse*, p. 70; Charles F. Morse diary, 3 Dec. 1864, Charles F. Morse, "Sherman's March to the Sea," *Twenty-Ninth Annual Meeting of the Second Regiment Mass. Infantry Ass'n.* (Lynn, MA: G.H. & A.L. Nichols, n.d.), p. 51; Edward Schweitzer diary, 28 Nov. 1864, Civil War Times Illustrated Collection, USMHI; George Drake to wife, 18 Dec. 1864, J. A. Drake, ed., *The Mail Goes Through*, p. 124; Allen Fahnestock diary, 4 Dec. 1864, Allen L. Fahnestock Papers, KMNP; Fred Marion to Sister, 15 Dec. 1864, Fred Marion Papers, ILSHS; Harvey Reid letter-diary to Sister, 14 Dec. 1864, Harvey Reid Papers, SHSW; John D. Inskeep diary, 6 Mar. 1865, John D. Inskeep Papers, OHS; William H. Lynch diary, 17 Feb. 1865, William H. Lynch Papers, WHC–SHSMO.

17. Harrison Pendergast journal, 16 Nov. 1864, Pendergast Papers, MNHS. Also see James T. Reeve diary, 22 Nov. 1864 and 23 Nov. 1864, James T. Reeve Papers, SHSW; W. B. Emmons diary, 9 Dec. 1864, W. B. Emmons Papers, U. of Iowa; James Sawyer to Nancy, 26 Nov. 1864, James T. Sawyer Papers, SHSW; James Connolly diary, 27 Nov. 1864, J. A. Connolly, Angle, ed., *Three Years*, p. 326; Garret S. Byrne diary, 9 Feb. 1865, Garret S. Byrne Papers, Rutgers U; J. H. Otto, "War Memories, 1864," p. 263, John Henry Otto Papers, SHSW; M. Fitch diary, n.d., M. Fitch, *Echoes of the Civil War*, p. 236; S. F. Fleharty diary, 19 Nov. 1864, S. F. Fleharty, *Our Regiment: 102nd Illinois*, p. 112; Jim to Cuz Sallie, 19 Dec. 1864, James M. Naylor Papers, OHS; James Burkhalter diary, n.d., James K. Burkhalter Papers, ILSHS.

18. Axel Reed diary, 27 Jan. 1865, Reed Papers, MNHS; Winther, ed., *With Sherman to the Sea*, pp. 151–52. Also see Woodson W. Brock, "Reminiscence," in C. T. De Velling, *History of the Seventeenth Regiment* (Zanesville, OH: E. R. Sullivan, 1889), p. 113; John D. Myers diary, 12 Mar. 1865, Sesqui Manuscripts, INHS; Halsey, ed., *A Yankee Private's Civil War*, p. 183; F. M. McAdams journal, 22 Feb. 1865, F. M. McAdams, *Every-Day Soldier Life*, pp. 138–39.

19. Alden B. Huntley diary, 28 Nov. 1864, Mr. & Mrs. Glover Shoudy Collection, WMIU; James Thompson journal, 14 Apr. 1865, James S. Thompson or microfilm, INHS.

20. Garret S. Byrne diary, 2 Feb. 1865, Garret S. Byrne Papers, Rutgers U; Allen

T. Underwood diary, 1 Feb. 1865, Allen T. Underwood Papers, IASHMA; James T. Reeve diary, 30 Jan. 1865, James T. Reeve Papers, SHSW. Also see Axel Reed diary, 28 Jan. 1865, Reed Papers, MNHS; OR I, XLIV, p. 59; OR I, XLVII, Pt. 1, p. 169; William B. Hazen diary, 3 Dec. 1864, W. B. Hazen, *Narrative*, p. 319; C. C. Platter diary, 16 Nov. 1864, C. C. Platter Papers, U. of Georgia; John C. Van Duzen diary, 9 Dec. 1864, John C. Van Duzen Papers, Duke U; Elias Perry diary, 17 Feb. 1865 and 4 Mar. 1865, Elias Perry Papers, WHC–SHSMO; Allen Fahnestock diary, 23 Mar. 1865, Allen L. Fahnestock Papers, KMNP; John D. Inskeep diary, 9 Mar. 1865, John D. Inskeep Papers, OHS; B. F. Sweet "Reminiscence," Benjamin F. Sweet Papers, WHC–SHSMO; William Evans diary, 9 Dec. 1864, William David Evans Papers, WRHS; OR I, XLVII, Pt. 1, p. 19.

21. Ezra Button diary, 7 Feb. 1865, John B. Tripp Papers, SHSW; A. C. Smith to Wife, 28 Jan. 1865, Abner C. Smith Papers, CTST Lib. Also see Collins, *149th New York*, pp. 313–18; George N. Compton diary, 21 Jan. 1865. George N. Compton Papers, ILSHS; George Drake to Sam 28 Mar. 1865, J. A. Drake, ed., *The Mail Goes Through*, pp. 136–37.

22. Harrison Pendergast Journal, 21 Nov. 1864, Pendergast Papers, MNHS. Also see Jesse Bean diary, 10 Apr. 1865 Jesse S. Bean Papers, SHC, UNC, Anthony J. Baurdick diary, 7 Feb. 1865, Anthony J. Baurdick Papers, Emory U.

23. Harrison Pendergast journal, 22 Nov. 1864, Pendergast Papers, MNHS, James R. M. Gaskill diary, 30 Jan. 1865, James R. M. Gaskill Papers, Chicago HS, Rufus Mead diary, 17–27 Jan. 1865, Rufus Mead Papers, LC, Roy Nichols journal, 10 Mar. 1865, G. W. Nichols, *Story of the Great March*, p. 229. Also see Daniel Oakey in *Battles and Leaders of the Civil War*, IV, p. 678, William Meffert diary, 15 Mar. 1865, William C. Meffert Papers, SHSW, J. H. Otto, "War Memories, 1864," p. 259, John Henry Otto Papers, SHSW, Chas. S. Brown to Mother & Sister Etta and all Browns, 23 Sep. 1864, Charles S. Brown Papers, Duke U; Francis R. Baker, "Reminiscences," p. 40, Francis R. Baker Papers, ILSHS. For Confederates with similar problems, see William E. Sloan diary, 19 Mar. 1865, William E. Sloan Papers, TNST Lib & A.

24. Frederick Sherwood diary, 17 Mar. 1865, Earl M. Hess Collection, USMHI, Bauer, ed., *Soldiering*, p. 228. Also see John Inskeep diary, 28 Feb. 1865, John D. Inskeep Papers, OHS, Bauer, ed., *Soldiering*, pp. 208 and 216.

25. Rufus Mead diary, 9 Mar. 1865, Rufus Mead Papers, LC. Also see Halsey, ed., *A Yankee Private's Civil War*, p. 101; OR I, LXIV, pp. 89 and 149; OR I, XLVII, Pt. 1, pp. 173–74, 209, 240, 384, and 588; Garret Byrne diary, 9 Feb. 1865, Garret S. Byrne Papers, Rutgers U; Allen Underwood diary, 11 Mar. 1865, Allen T. Underwood Papers, IASHMA; Alexander Downing diary, 27 Feb. 1865, O. B. Clark, ed., *Downing's Civil War Diary* (Des Moines: The Historical Department of Iowa, 1916), p. 257; William Schaum diary, 5 Feb. 1865, William Schaum Papers, Duke U; M. C. Short to Father & Mother, 21 Nov. 1864, Martin C. Short Papers, SHSW. The four corps and cavalry usually marched on different roads. That was why the number of miles of corduroy Sherman's troops laid was so high.

26. Alfred Lamb diary, 21 Nov. 1864, A. Lamb, *My March With Sherman to the Sea*. Also see OR I, XLVII, Pt. 1, p. 175; Sherman, *Memoirs*, II, p. 401, Wright, *6th Iowa*, p. 374; Judson Bishop to Sister, 6 Feb. 1865, Bishop Papers, MNHS; Rood, *Co. E and 12th Wisconsin*, p. 413; H. Hitchcock diary, 30 Nov. 1864, H. Hitchcock, *Marching With Sherman*, p. 118; M. C. Short to Father & Mother letter-diary, 25 Nov. 1864, Martin C. Short Papers, SHSW, Official Diary of the Army of the Tennessee, 16 Nov. 1864, Sladen Family Collection, USMHI.

27. W. C. Johnson diary, 27 Feb. 1865, W. C. Johnson Papers, LC. Also see OR I, XLVII, Pt. 1, p. 229, Oscar L. Jackson diary, 5 Mar. 1865, O. L. Jackson, *The Colonel's Diary*, p. 190; William Sloan diary, 19 Feb. 1865, William E. Sloan Papers, TNST Lib & A, discusses the same problems from the Confederate side.

28. C. C. Platter diary 2 Dec. 1864, C. C. Platter Papers, U. of Georgia; Ole Kittelson diary, 24 Nov. 1864, Ole Kittelson Papers, SHSW. Also see William Gibson diary, 7 Dec. 1864, Tourgeé, *Story of a Thousand*, p. 341, Wm. A. Schofield to Father, 22 Jan. 1865, William A. Schofield Papers, GAHS; George McMillan diary, 1 Dec. 1864, George B. McMillan Papers, SHSW, Axel Reed diary, 12 Dec. 1864, Reed Papers, MNHS.

29. Garret Byrne diary, 23 Jan. 1865, Garret S. Byrne Papers, Rutgers U; Jacob Allspaugh diary, 6 Feb. 1865, J. H. Allspaugh Papers, U. of Iowa; Ezra Button diary, 6 Feb. 1865, John B. Tripp Papers, SHSW; T. S. Howland to sister, 30 Mar. 1865, Howland Papers, MAHS; M. Griffin to Glyde Swain, 1 Apr. 1865, Samuel G. Swain Papers, SHSW. Also see Richard Reeves diary, 19–21 Jan. 1865, Reeves Papers, MNHS; Tom H. Colman to Parents, 12 Jan. 1865, Coleman-Hayter Papers, WHC–SHSMO; Benjamin F. Sweet, "War Record." Benjamin F. Sweet, WHC–SHSMO; William Hazen diary, 12 Feb. 1865, W. Hazen, *Narrative*, p. 345, Wm. H. McIntosh, "22nd Wisconsin," p. 180, William H. McIntosh Papers, SHSW; William H. H. Minot diary, 12 Feb. 1865, William H. H. Minot Papers, U. of Alabama; Robinson, *Civil War Experience, 1862–1865*, p. 10; Edward E. Schweitzer diary, 12 Feb. 1865, Civil War Times Illustrated Collection, USMHI; Lyman Widney reminiscence, Lyman Widney Papers, KMNP; Philip Roesch journal, 8 Feb. 1865, Philip Roesch Papers, SHSW; Ezra Button diary, 12 Feb. 1865, John B. Tripp Papers, SHSW; Oscar L. Jackson diary, 16 Feb. 1865, O. L. Jackson, *The Colonel's Diary*, p. 182; J. H. Otto, "War Memories, 1864," p. 299, John Henry Otto Papers, SHSW; Bauer, ed., *Soldiering*, pp. 208–209.

30. F. M. Behymer, "Reminiscence," in Hubert, *50th Illinois*, p. 361.

31. Jos. L. Locke to Miss Terry, 19 Apr. 1865, Joseph L. Locke Papers, ILSHS. Also see Levi Green diary, 10 Feb. 1865, Green Papers, MNHS; Alfred Trego diary, 28 Nov. 1864, Alfred Trego Papers, Chicago HS; Harrison Pendergast journal, 26 Nov. 1864, Pendergast Papers, MNHS; W. S. Fultz, "Reminiscences of Army Life," W. S. Fultz Papers, IASHS; Halsey, ed., *A Yankee Private's Civil War*, p. 108; Bliss Morse diary, 14 Feb. 1865, L. Bliss, ed., *Diaries of Morse Bliss*, p. 79; OR I, XLIV, p. 134; Special Orders, No. 58. HQ, Third Division, Seventeenth Army Corps, 12 Mar. 1865, OR I, XLVII, Pt. 2, p. 798; Ezra Button diary, 23 Feb 1865, John B. Tripp Papers, SHSW; James Reeve diary, 6 Mar. 1865, James T. Reeve Papers, SHSW; W. C. Johnson diary, 8 Dec. 1864, Kerkiss, ed. *Atlanta Papers*, p. 823.

32. William Meffert diary, 24 Mar. 1865, William C. Meffert Papers, SHSW; son to Mother, 9 Apr. 1865, Ebenezer Wescott Papers, SHSW. Also see S. A. McNeil, *Personal Recollections*, p. 63; George B. McMillan diary, 13 Dec. 1864, George B. McMillan Papers, SHSW; Frederick Sherwood diary, 17 Dec. 1864, Earl M. Hess Papers, USMHI; Philip Roesch, "Reminiscence," Philip Roesch Papers, SHSW; Alonzo Miller to Sister and the Rest, 12 Mar. 1865, Alonzo Miller Papers, SHSW; E. P. Burton diary, 15 Nov. 1864, E. P. Burton, *Diary*, n.p.; Axel Reed diary, 28 Jan. 1865, Reed Papers, MNHS; Billings Sibley to Anna, 29 Jan. 1865, Sibley Papers, MNHS.

33. John Cutter to Father, 2 Feb. 1865, Cutter Papers on microfilm, MNHS; John E. Risedorph diary, 25 Feb. 1865, Risedorph Papers, MNHS. Also see Halsey, ed., *A Yankee Private's Civil War*, p. 143, J. H. Otto, "War Memories, 1865," p. 114, John Henry Otto Papers, SHSW; Nixon B. Stewart, *Dan McCook's Regiment. 52nd OVI* (Al-

liance OH: Published by the Author, 1900), p. 156,; B. F. Heuston to Dearly Cherished Wife, 14 Mar. 1865, Benjamin Franklin Heuston Papers, SHSW; John G. Brown, "Reminiscence," Committee, *55th Illinois*, p. 427; Report of Inspector General of the Seventeetnh Army Corps in William E. Strong journal, 24 Mar. 1865, p. 279, William E. Strong Papers, ILSHS; Michael Dresbach to Wife, 28 Dec. 1864, Dresbach Papers, MNHS; Allen L. Fahnestock diary, 5 Mar. 1865, Allen L. Fahnestock Papers, KMNP; Alonzo Miller to Sister and the Rest, 12 Mar. 1865, Alonzo Miller Papers, SHSW; OR I, XLVII, Pt. 1, p. 409; William Pittenger diary, 17 Mar. 1865, William H. Pittenger Papers, OHS; Oscar L. Jackson diary, 11 Mar. 1865, O. L. Jackson, *The Colonel's Diary*, p. 195.

34. Alexander Downing diary, 6 Dec. 1864, Clark, ed., *Downing's Civil War Diary*, p. 235; John E. Risedorph diary, 18 Mar. 1865, Risedorph Papers, MNHS. Also see Halsey, ed., *A Yankee Private's Civil War*, p. 102.

35. George Drake to Parents, 30 Oct. 1864, J. A. Drake, ed., *The Mail Goes Through*, p. 120; E. Woodman to Charlie, 3 Feb. 1865, Charles Butler Papers, Bentley Library, UMI; Jesse Macy to Parents, 14 Dec. 1864, Jesse Macy Papers, IASHS; Charlie to Mollie, 15 Mar. [1865]. Charles B. Tompkins Papers, Duke U; John W. Reid to Will, 29 Mar. 1865, William G. McCreary Papers, Duke U; C. M. Smith to Father, 7 Jan. 1865, Charles M. Smith Papers, SHSW. Also see W. C. Johnson diary, 23 Mar. 1865, W. C. Johnson Papers, LC; John W. Geary to Mary, 10 Dec. 1864, John W. Geary Papers, Atlanta HS; Young Powell to Ellen 27 Mar. 1865, Ellen Aumack Papers, Duke U; George T. Spaulding to Wife, 13 Mar. 1865, George T. Spaulding Papers, SHSW; Geo. S. Richardson to Father and Mother, 14 Dec. 1864, George S. Richardson Papers, IASHS; [Lorenzo Pratt] to Perrants, 27 Jan. [1865], Civil War Miscellaneous Collection, USMHI; John H. Morse to Sister Belle, 27 Sep. 1864, Federico, ed., *Civil War Letters of J. H. Morse*, p. 153; Charley to Parents, 15 Dec. 1864, Charles Webster Knapp Papers, SHSW; OR I, XLVII, Pt. 1, p. 441; Eli S. Ricker to Mary, 6 Jan. 1865, E. G. Longacre, ed., *SCHM*, LXXXII, p. 212; "Autobiography of Dr. Henry Clay Robbins," Henry Clay Robbins Papers, SHSW; Frank Malcom to Wife, 6 Apr. 1865, J. J. Robertson, Jr., *IJH*, LVIII, pp. 349–50; E. P. Burton diary,. 10 Mar. 1865, E. P. Burton, *Diary*, n.p.; Judson Bishop to Mother, 13 Dec. 1864, Bishop Papers, MNHS; OR I, XLIV, p. 103; Nelson Stauffer diary, 23 Jan. 1865, N. Stauffer, *Civil War Diary*, n.p.; Address of H. C. McArthur, 23 Sep. 1891, *Proceedings of Crocker's Iowa Brigade*, p. 80; Thos. Christie to Sandy, 6 Jan. 1865, Christie Papers, MNHS; Burke Wylie to Mother, 14 Jan. 1865, Burke Wylie Papers, IASHS; Sherman, *Memoirs*, II, p. 241; W. S. Fultz, "11th Iowa," M. Throne, ed., *IJH* LV, p. 82.

36. Dell to Annie, 8 Apr. 1865, Adelbert M. Bly Papers, SHSW; Burke Wylie to Mother, 14 Jan. 1865, Burke Wylie Papers, IASHS; J. H. Otto, "War Memories, 1865," p. 2, John Henry Otto Papers, SHSW; "diary" of a Veteran Volunteer of Co. E, 29th Ohio, probably N. L. Parmater, N. L. Parmater Papers, OHS. Also see Joshua Comfort to father and Mother, 28 Mar. 1865, Joshua & Merritt Comfort, Duke U; Isaac W. Muzzy to Wife, 15 Dec. 1864, Muzzy Papers, MNHS; Dresbach to Wife, 15 Dec. 1864, Dresbach Papers, MNHS.

CHAPTER 7

1. Ed. Hutchinson to Mother, 16 Dec. 1864, Edwin Hutchinson Papers, LSU; Frank Putney, *MOLLUS–WI*, III, p. 384; Halsey, ed., *A Yankee Private's Civil War*, p. 100. Also see W. C. Johnson diary, 23 Nov. 1864, Kerksis, ed., *Atlanta Papers*, p. 811.

2. Taylor, *Lights and Shadows*, p. 20. Also see Westervelt, *Lights and Shadows*, p. 80; Minerva McClatchey diary, 7/3/64, McClatchey Family Papers, GA Dept. of A. & H; Halsey, ed., *A Yankee Private*, pp. 42 and 45; Henry Hurter diary, 16 Oct. 1864, Civil War Times Illustrated Collection, USMHI; Albert A. Champlin diary, 14 Oct. 1864, Alfred Mewett Papers, WRHS; B. Wiley, *Billy Yank*, pp. 234–36. For Confederates see General Orders, No. 21, Ross's Cavalry Brig. Jackson's Div., OR I, XXXIX, Pt. 2, p. 830; W. W. Gordon, "Reminiscences," pp. 13–14, J. Frederick Waring Papers, GAHS; *Raleigh Daily Conservative*, 29 Mar. 1865 and 30 Mar. 1865, Editorial; Imogene Hoyle to Ama Bomar, 1 Jan. 1865, Bomar Family Papers, Emory U; A. J. Jackson journal, 9 Oct. 1864, Co. G. 2nd Regiment Infantry Georgia State Line Papers, GA Dept. of A. & H; Lawrence W. Taylor, "Boy Soldiers of the Confederacy," p. 6, Franklin Harper Elmore Papers, SHC, UNC; Williamson Ward journal, 7 Sept. 1864, Williamson D. Ward Plapers, INHS; W. S. Penniman, "Reminiscences of Personal Experiences During the Civil War," W. S. Penniman Papers, SHC, UNC; OR I, XLIV, p. 412.

3. W. T. Sherman to Ellen, 21 Oct. 1864, Howe, ed., *Home Letters*, pp. 313–14; Geo. S. Richardson to Father and Mother, 22 Oct. 1864, George S. Richardson Papers, IASHS; Daniel F. Griffin to ———, 22 Oct. 1864, Arville L. Funk, *A Hoosier Regiment in Dixie: A History of the Thirty-Eighth Indiana Volunteer Infantry Regiment* (Chicago: Adams Press, 1978), p. 80; Joshua Comfort to Father and Mother, 30 Oct. 1864, Joshua and Merritt Comfort, Duke U; F. W. Tupper to Father, 31 Oct. 1864, F. W. Tupper Papers, ILSHS. Also see Lyman Widney reminiscences, Lyman S. Widney Papers, KMNP; J. H. Allspaugh diary, 18–9 Oct., 1864 J. H. Allspaugh Papers, U. of Iowa; Michael Dresbach to Wife, 30 Oct. 1864, Dresbach Papers, MNHS; W. C. Johnson diary, 16 Oct. 1864 and 21 Oct. 1864, Kerksis, ed., *Atlanta Papers*, p. 806; Fred Marion to Sister, 23 Oct. 1864, Fred Marion Papers, ILSHS; A. W. Reese, "Recollections of the Civil War," pp. 88–89, A. W. Reese Papers, WHC–SHSMO; John Batchelor diary, 20 Oct. 1864, John Batchelor Papers, ILSHS; Warren Akin to Sir, 31 Oct. 1864, Warren Akin Papers, Atlanta HS; Reuben Sweet diary, 22 Oct. 1864, R. Sweet, "Civil War Diary," *Antigo Daily Journal*, 9 Mar.–25 May 1939; Andrew Bush to Mary, 22 Oct. 1864, Andrew Bush Papers, INST Lib; Alonzo Miller to Sister, 31 Oct. 1864, Alonzo Miller Papers, SHSW; Ed Cort to Friends, 25 Oct. 1864, Tomlinson, ed., *Dear Friends*, p. 166; A. C. Smith to Wife, 28 Oct. 1864, Abner C. Smith Papers, CTST Lib; OR I, XXXIX, Pt. 1, pp. 650 and 680–81; Alex Campbell to Brother, 16 Oct. 1864, Campbell Family Papers, Michigan St. U; Horatio D. Chapman diary, 20 Sep. 1864 and 16–18 Oct. 1864, Chapman, *Civil War Diary*, pp. 95–6: Sherman to Slocum, 23 Oct. 1864, OR I, XXXIX, Pt. 3, p. 406; Hinkley, *Service with the 3rd Wisconsin*, p. 144.

4. Special Field Orders, No. 120, HQ. Mil. Div. of the Miss. 9 Nov. 1864, OR I, XXXIX, Pt. 3, p. 713.

5. See Circular, Hdqrs. Fourth Div., Fifteenth A.C. OR I, XLIV, p. 480; Sherman to Grant, 16 Dec. 1864, OR I, XLIV, p. 727; OR I, XLIV, pp. 199–200 and 233; Aten, *85th Illinois*, pp. 257–58.

6. See Special Field Orders, No. 46, Army of the Tennessee, 22 Feb. 1865, Hazen to Woodhull, 22 Feb. 1865, OR I, XLVII, Pt. 2, pp. 528–30; Alonzo Cady to Wife, 31 Jan. 1865, Cady-Randolph Papers, MNHS; Samuel Mahon, MOLLUS–IA, II, p. 193.

7. OR I, XLIV, p. 152. Also see Bauer, ed., *Soldiering*, p. 181; Samuel Toombs reminiscence, 14 Feb. 1865, S. Toombs, *Reminiscences of War*, p. 203; Halsey, ed., *A Yankee Private*, p. 49; Alonzo Cady to Wife, 31 Jan. 1865, Cady-Randolph Papers, MNHS; Charles A. Booth to ———, 27 Mar. 1865, Bradley, *The Star Corps*, pp. 275–76; Mah-

lon H. Floyd speech, "Sherman's March to the Sea," 2/12/89, Helen Floyd Carlin Papers, INHS; Special Field Orders, No. 14. Fourth Division, 15 AC, 11 Feb. 1865, Special Field Orders Book, Fourth Division, 15 AC, RG 393, NA.

8. Thos. Christie to David, 28 Mar. 1865, Christie Papers, MNHS; Chester to Brother Asa, 28 Mar. 1865, Chester M. Slayton Papers, Bentley Library, UMI; David P. Conyngham, *Sherman's March Through the South* (New York: Sheldon and Company, 1865), p. 314; M. F. Force, *MOLLUS–OH*, I, p. 12; Dean, *Recollections of the 26th Missouri*, p. 50. Also see Charles A. Hopkins, "The March to the Sea," *Soldiers and Sailors Historical Society of Rhode Island: Personal Narratives*, ser. III, No. 12, p. 16; Wayne E. Morris to Companion, 4 Sep. 1864, Wayne E. Morris Papers, Bentley Library, UMI; Pepper, *Personal Recollections*, p. 276; M. T. Reeves to W. S. Fultz, 29 Aug. 1887, W. S. Fultz Papers, IASHS; William D. Evans diary, 4 Mar. 1865, William D. Evans Papers, WRHS; Sherman, *Memoirs*, II, pp. 273–74; Hedley, *Marching Through Georgia*, p. 271; Halsey, ed., *A Yankee Private*, p. 47.

9. See C. E. Benton, *As Seen From the Ranks*, pp. 224–26; Harvey Reid journal, 20 Nov. 1864, Harvey Reid Papers, SHSW; Harrison Pendergast journal, 19 Dec. 1864, Pendergast Papers, MNHS.

10. Henry Nurs to Mother, 18 Dec. 1864, Henry Nurse Papers, ILSHS. Also see Michael Dresbach, "Reminiscences of Sherman's Campaign through Georgia and the Carolinas," p. 10, Dresbach Papers, MNHS; William T. Humphrey diary, 4 Feb. 1865, William T. Humphrey Papers, Chicago PL; Dean, *Recollections of the 26th Missouri*, p. 50; Thos. Christie to Dave, 28 Mar. 1865, Christie Papers, MNHS; General Orders, No. 25, HQ. Fourth Division, Seventeenth A.C., 17 Nov. 1864, Special Field Orders, No. 12, First Division, Fourteenth A.C., 17 Nov. 1864, Orders, Twentieth A.C. 17 Nov. 1864, Circular, Third Cavalry Division, 17 Nov. 1864, OR I, XLIV, pp. 482–85; A. M. Geer diary, 8 Dec. 1864, Andersen, ed., *Diary of A. M. Geer*, p. 181; William Sharpe journal, n.d., Merrill, *70th Indiana*, p. 221; N. L. Parmater diary, 23 Oct. 1864, N. L. Parmater Papers, OHS; Jesse Dawley diary, 7 Dec. 1864, Jesse Dawley Papers, U. of Iowa; Peter Ege diary, 19 Nov. 1864, in Payne, *34th Illinois*, p. 164, and Peter Ege Papers, SHSW; Isaac N. Carr diary, 30 Jan. 1865, Isaac N. Carr Papers, IASHS.

11. Sam to Maggie, 18 Dec. 1864, Samuel K. Harryman Papers, INST Lib; William E. Strong journal, 9 Feb. 1865, "Reminiscences," p. 219, William E. Strong Papers, ILSHS; OR I, XLIV, p. 14. Also see Lyman Widney reminiscence, Lyman S. Widney Papers, KMNP; John Risedorph diary, 23 Feb. 1865, Risedorph Papers, MNHS; Grace P. J. Beard, "A Series of True Incidents Connected with Sherman's March to the Sea," p. 9, Grace P. J. Beard Papers, SHC, UNC; William E. Strong, "Reminiscences of the March to the Sea," pp. 26–27, William E. Strong Papers, ILSHS; Joseph R. Stanford to Lt. Col. J. K. Scott, 27 Feb. 1865, Jefferson K. Scott Papers, INHS; Special Field Orders, No. 46, Army of the Tennessee, 22 Feb. 1865, Hazen to Maj. Max Woodhull, 22 Feb. 1865, OR I, XLVII, Pt. 2, pp. 528–30; Charles A. Booth to ———, 27 Mar. 1865, Bradley, *The Star Corps*, pp. 275–76; B. F. Heuston diary, 21 Feb. 1865, Benjamin Franklin Heuston Papers, SHSW; Erza Button diary, 21 Feb. 1865, John B. Tripp Papers, SHSW; Trimble, *93rd Illinois*, p. 176; Harvey to Sisters, 24 Oct. 1864, Harvey Reid Papers, SHSW; William White to Sister, 8 Nov. 1864, Mills Lane, ed., *"Dear Mother: Don't grieve about me. If I get killed, I'll only be dead."* (Savannah: Beehive Press, 1977), pp. 333–34.

12. John Van Duzen journal-letter, 6 Dec. 1864, C. J. Brockman, Jr., ed., *GHQ*,

LIII, p. 233; composite diary, 25 Nov. 1864, Orendorff et al., *103rd Illinois*, pp. 158–59; Jas. Sawyer to Nancy, 18 Dec. 1864, James T. Sawyer Papers, SHSW; Frank Putney, *MOLLUS–WI*, III, p. 384. Also see J. H. Otto, "War Memories, 1864," pp. 329–30, "War Memories, 1865," p. 60, John Henry Otto Papers, SHSW; James E. Morrow diary, 27 Nov. 1864, Civil War Times Illustrated Collection, USMHI; Halsey, ed., *A Yankee Private*, p. 50–51; Garret S. Byrne diary, 16 Nov. 1864 and 18 Mar. 1865, Garret S. Byrne Papers, Rutgers U; Doc to Sister Ann, 27 Mar. 1865. R. N. Elder Papers, OHS; Eugne [McWayne] to Mother & Sisters, 19 Dec. 1864, in R. M. McMurry, "Sherman's Savannah Campaign." *CWTI*, XXI, p. 12; Sarah Jane Sams to Darling R, letter-diary, 4 Feb. 1865, Sarah Jane Sams Papers, U. of South Carolina; G. D. Kerr, *MOLLUS–MN*, I, pp. 211–12; Alexander, *97th Indiana*, pp. 23–24.

13. Garret S. Byrne diary, 11 Feb. 1865, Garret S. Byrne Papers, Ruters U. Also see unknown journal, 25 Feb. 1865, Brown, *4th Minnesota*, pp. 380–81; Kinnear, *86th Illinois*, p. 86; Fleharty, *Our Regiment: 102nd Illinois*, pp. 139–40.

14. See Sherman to Grant, 29 Jan. 1865, OR I, XLVII, Pt. 2, p. 156; Sherman *Memoirs*, II, p. 191; Orders, HQ. Left Wing, Army of Georgia, 23 Nov. 1864, OR I, XLIV, p. 532; Special Orders, No. 57, HQ. Seventeenth Army Corps, 3 Mar. 1865, OR I, XLVII, Pt. 2, p. 667; Committee, *92nd Illinois*, p. 198; Johnston to Lee, 1 Mar. 1865, OR I, XLVII, Pt. 1, p. 1051; Bauer, ed., *Soldiering*, p. 198; J. H. Otto, "War Memories, 1865," p. 65, John Henry Otto Papers, SHSW; Judson Bishop to Sister, 31 Jan. 1865, Bishop Papers, MNHS.

15. William Miller diary, 17 Dec. 1864, William B. Miller Papers, INHS; Woodson W. Brock reminiscence, De Velling, *17th Ohio*, p. 114. See also H. H. Tarr diary, 20 Nov. 1864, Storrs, *20th Connecticut*, p. 151, Dunkelman and Winey, *The Hardtack Regiment*, p. 139; Leslie Anders, *The Eighteenth Missouri* (Indianapolis: The Bobbs-Merrill Company, 1968), p. 277; William Miller diary, 18 Nov. 1864, William B. Miller Papers, INHS; William H. H. Enderton diary, 25 Nov. 1864, Payne, *34th Illinois*, p. 165; Joseph Hoffhines to Wife, 11 Nov. 1864, Joseph Hoffhines Papers, OHS; C. C. Platter diary, 11 Nov. 1864, C. C. Platter Papers, U. of Georgia; L. A. Ross diary, 30 Nov. 1864, L. A. Ross Papers, ILSHS; OR I, XLIV, pp. 197–98; O. T. C. to Charley, 17 Dec. 1864. Joseph and Orville Chamberlain Papers, INHS; Lyman Widney to Parents, 27 Dec. 1864, Lyman Wideny Papers, KMNP; F and L Elliott to Father and Mother, 19 Dec. 1864, Civil War Times Illustrated Collection, USMHI; Stelle, *Memoirs of the Civil War*, p. 19; Charles S. Gaylord diary, 2 Dec. 1864, William H. H. Enderton diary, 6 Dec. 1864, John L. Hostetter diary, 8 Dec. 1864, Payne, *34th Illinois*, pp. 168–70; G. S. Bradley diary, 4 Dec. 1864, G. S. Bradley, *The Star Corps*, p. 205; Levi Green diary, 26 Jan. 1865, Green Papers, MNHS; William H. H. Tallman, "Reminiscences," p. 77, Gregory Coco Collection, USMHI; OR I, XLVII, Pt. 1, p. 683; Boyle, *Soldiers True*, p. 277; W. H. Chamberlain, *History of the Eighty-First Regiment Ohio Infantry Volunteers* (Cincinnati: Gazette Steam Printing House, 1865), p. 158; R. Y. Woodlief diary, 10 Feb. 1865, R. Y. Woodlief Papers, U. of South Carolina; J. W. Cushing reminiscence of 13 Feb. 1865, Committee, *92nd Illinois*, p. 335; Kilpatrick to Wheeler, 22 Feb. 1865, James Moore, *Kilpatrick and Our Cavalry* (New York: W. J. Widdleton, 1865), pp. 220–21; Williamson Ward diary, 21–2 Feb. 1865, Williamson D. Ward Papers, INHS; Oscar Jackson diary, 23–4 Feb. 1865, O. L. Jackson, *The Colonel's Diary*, pp. 186–87; Official Diary of the Army of the Tennessee, 24 Feb. 1865, Sladen Family Collection, USMHI; John Risedorph diary, 24 Feb. 1865, Risedorph Papers, MNHS; Kilpatrick to Sherman, 24 Feb. 1865, OR I, XLVII, Pt. 2, pp. 554–55; OR I, XLVII, Pt. 1, pp.

318–19; William T. Clark to S. M. Budlong, 25 Feb. 1865, OR I, XLVII, Pt. 1, pp. 327–28.

16. Circular, HQ. Army of the Tennessee, 25 Feb. 1865, OR I, XLVII, Pt. 2, p. 566; Kilpatrick to L. M. Dayton, 22 Feb. 1865, OR I, XLVII, Pt. 2, p. 533; Unknown journal, 25 Feb. 1865, Brown, *4th Minnesota*, p. 380; John W. Bates diary, 1 Mar. 1865, Civil War Miscellaneous Collection, USMHI; George Drake to Parents, 17 Dec. 1864, J. A. Drake, ed., *The Mail Goes Through*, p. 123. Also see Sherman to Howard, 23 Feb. 1865, OR I, XLVII, Pt. 2, p. 537; Alexander Downing diary, 14 Mar. 1865, Clark, ed., *Downing's Civil War Diary*, p. 261; Robert Oliver journal, 19 Mar. 1865, Committee, *55th Illinois*, p. 425; David Nichol diary, 17 Mar. 1865, Harrisburg Civil War Round Table, USMHI; Henry Noble diary, 30 Nov.–6 Dec. 1864, Henry G. Noble Papers, Bentley Library, UMI; Hinkley, *Service with the 3rd Wisconsin*, pp. 167–68; Peter Dinger reminiscence in W. W. Caulkins, *104th Illinois*, p. 336; J. H. Otto, "War Memories, 1865," p. 7, John Henry Otto Papers, SHSW; Charles S. Brown to Etta, 26 Apr. 1865, Charles S. Brown Papers, Duke U; Q. A. Brown to Esteemed Brother, 3 Apr. 1865, Earl M. Hess Collection, USMHI; Frank Malcom to Wife, 29 Mar. 1865, J. J. Robertson, Jr., ed., *IJH*, LVIII, No. 4, p. 349; Oscar L. Jackson diary, 2 Mar. 1865, O. L. Jackson, *The Colonel's Diary*, p. 189; Trimble, *93rd Illinois*, p. 177; *Adjutant General's Report of the State of Illinois*, IV, p. 288; H. Hitchcock diary, 3 Dec. 1864, H. Hitchcock, *Marching With Sherman*, p. 136; Halsey, ed., *A Yankee Private's Civil War*, p. 53; OR I, XLIV, pp. 148, 152, 203, 233–34, and 388; C. C. Walton, ed., *Behind the Guns: The History of Battery I, 2nd Regiment, Illinois Light Artillery by Sgt. Thaddeus C. S. Brown, Sgt. Samuel J. Murphy, and Bugler William G. Putney* (Carbondale: Southern Illinois University Press, 1965), pp. 132–33; George Metz diary, 31 Oct. 1864, George P. Metz Papers, Duke U; General Warren McCain, *A Soldier's Diary or The History of Company "L" Third Indiana Cavalry* (Indianapolis: William A. Patton, 1885), p. 40; Williamson D. Ward diary, 11 Sep. 1864, Williamson D. Ward Papers, INHS; Hays, *32nd Ohio*, pp. 62–63; William Meffert diary, 20 Oct. and 6 Nov. 1864, William C. Meffert Papers, SHSW; Aten, *85th Illinois*, pp. 247–48; OR I, XLVII, Pt. 1, pp. 327–28; Charles H. Warren to Jos. W. Roberts, 27 Feb. 1865, OR I, XLVII, Pt. 1, p. 332; Sherman Leland diary, 26 Feb. 1865, Calkins, *104th Illinois*, p. 291; William Grunert journals, 26 Feb. 1865, W. Grunert, *129th Illinois*, p. 202; Dresbach to Wife, journal-letter, 26 Feb. 1865, Dresbach Papers, MNHS; Charles F. Hubert journal, 28 Feb. 1865, C. F. Hubert, *50th Illinois*, pp. 362–63; Cornelius Cadle, "An Adjutant's Recollections," *MOLLUS–OH*, V, p. 398; Special Orders, No. 56, HQ. Seventeenth Army Corps, 2 Mar. 1865, OR I, XLVII, Pt. 2, pp. 649–50; Williamson Ward diary, 7 Mar. 1865, Williamson D. Ward Papers, INHS; Official Diary of the Army of the Tennessee, 11 Mar. 1865, Sladen Family Collection, USMHI: Peter Dinger reminiscence in Calkins, *104th Illinois*, pp. 336–37; Henry C. Laybourn diary, 14 Mar. 1865, Henry C. Laybourn Papers, U. of Iowa; W. H. Forbis reminiscence of 16 Mar. 1865, Tourgeé, *Story of a Thousand*, p. 364; John R. McBride journal, 23 Mar. 1865, J. R. McBride, *33rd Indiana*, pp. 174–5; William D. Evans diary, 11 and 22 Mar. 1865, William D. Evans Papers, WRHS; Charles Hubert journal, 22 Mar. 1865, C. F. Hubert, *50th Illinois*, p. 374.

17. See Halsey, ed., *A Yankee Private*, p. 53; Peter Dinger, reminiscence, Calkins, *104th Illinois*, p. 336; Hinkley, *Service with the 3rd Wisconsin*, pp. 167–68; Henry G. Noble diary, 30 Nov.–6 Dec. 1864, Henry G. Noble Papers, Bentley Library, UMI; Alexander G. Downing diary, 14 Mar. 1865, Clark, ed., *Downing's Civil War Diary*, p. 261; Samuel Mahon, *MOLLUS–IA*, II, p. 195; Michael Dresbach, "Reminiscences of

Sherman's Campaign through Georgia and the Carolinas," p. 10, Dresbach Papers, MNHS; Dr. Thomas to Dr. Thrall, 20 Dec. 1864, M. Throne, ed., *IJH*, LVIII, p. 187; Harvey Reid letter-diary, 20 Nov. 1864, Harvey Reid Papers, SHSW; G. K. Collins, *149th New York*, p. 293; David Nichol diary, 20 Feb.[1865], Harrisburg Civil War Round Table Collection, USMHI; Charles S. Brown to Etta, 26 Apr. 1865, Charles S. Brown Papers, Duke U; Wilson, *Memoirs of the War*, p. 392.

18. See OR I, XLIV, pp. 152, 203, 233–34, and 388; David Nichol diary, 17 Mar. 1865, Harrisburg Civil War Round Table Collection, USMHI; John D. Inskeep diary, 25 Feb. 1865, John D. Inskeep Papers, OHS.

19. Frederick Smith journal, 24 Nov. 1864, Cyrus Kingsbury Remington, *A Record of Battery I, First N.Y. Light Artillery Vols.* (Buffalo: Press of the Courier Company, 1891), p. 117. Also see Orders, HQ. Left Wing, Army of Georgia, 23 Jan. 1865, OR I, XLIV, p. 532; George Nichols journal, n.d., G. W. Nichols, *Story of the Great March*, p. 51; Samuel Storrow diary, 21 Nov. 1864, Samuel Storrow Papers, MAHS; W. C. Johnson diary, 22 Nov. 1864, Kerksis, ed., *Atlanta Papers*, p. 812; Michael Dresbach diary, 22 Nov. 1864, Dresbach Papers, MNHS; Charles H. Spencer to Brother, 6 Nov. 1864, Charles H. Spencer Papers, SHSW; Benton, *As Seen From the Ranks*, pp. 234–35; Ole Kittelson diary, 27 Nov. 1864, Ole Kittelson Papers, SHSW; W. H. H. Enderton diary, 27 Nov. 1864, Payne, *34th Illinois*, p. 166; L. A. Ross diary, 1 Dec. 1864, L. A. Ross Papers, ILSHS; John J. McKee diary, 29 Nov. 1864, John J. McKee Papers, IASHS; Benjamin Sweet, "War Record," Benjamin F. Sweet Papers, WHC–SHSMO; Arbuckle, *Civil War Experiences*, p. 107; Eli S. Ricker to Abigail, 5 Apr. 1865, E. G. Longacre, ed., *SCHM*, LXXXII, p. 224; Henry O. Marcy, *MOLLUS–MA*, II, pp. 332, 340, and 343; Philip Roesch reminiscence of 18 Nov. 1864, Philip Roesch Papers, SHSW; L. A. Ross diary, 6 Dec. 1864, L. A. Ross Papers, ILSHS; Special Field Order, No. 167, 6 Dec. 1864, Charles Reynolds Papers, LC. Foraging parties usually pushed deep into the countryside for provender and left the area near the road to foragers on the hook.

20. See Henry Hunter diary, 6 Dec. 1864, Civil War Times Illustrated Collection, USMHI; Hedley, *Marching Through Georgia*, p. 273; Isaac N. Carr diary, 12 Mar. 1865, Isaac N. Carr Papers, IASHS.

21. See W. H. Forbis reminiscence, Tourgeé, *Story of a Thousand*, pp. 358–59; Ferd Boltz diary, 21 Feb. 1865, Ferd F. Bolt Papers, Duke U; John Wesley Daniels diary, 21 Feb. 1865, John Wesley Daniels Papers, Bentley Library, UMI; Allen T. Underwood diary, 21 Feb. 1865, Allen T. Underwood Papers, IASHMA; William Miller diary, 3 Mar. 1865, William B. Miller Papers, INHS; Ezra Button diary, 11 Mar. 1865, John B. Tripp Papers, SHSW; Joel Hansberger & Henry Rea reminiscence, De Velling, *17th Ohio*, p. 118; W. C. Johnson diary, 11 Mar. 1865, W. C. Johnson Papers, LC; Mahlon Floyd diary, 13 Mar. 1865, Helen Floyd Carlin Papers, INHS; W. H. H. Tallman, "Reminiscences," p. 116, Gregory Coco Collection, USMHI.

22. See OR I, XLIV, pp. 65, 75–76, 78, 159, 166–67, 210–11, and 367; OR I, XLVII, Pt. 1, pp. 178–79, 209, 437, 443, 589, 873, 877, 891, 898, and 902.

23. W. C. Johnson diary, 22 Nov. 1864, Kerksis, ed., *Atlanta Papers*, p. 811; H. D. Chapman diary, 25 Oct. 1864, H. D. Chapman, *Civil War Diary*, p. 98; M. Dresbach to Wife, 15 Dec. 1864, Dresbach Papers, MNHS; Bliss Morse diary, 16 Dec. 1864, L. Morse, ed., *The Civil War Diary of Bliss Morse*, p. 73; Francis R. Baker, "Reminiscences," p. 40, Francis R. Baker Papers, ILSHS; Farnum to Wife, 19 Dec. 1864, Farnum Papers, MNHS; Dresbach to Wife, 5 Mar. 1865, Dresbach Papers, MNHS. Also see

[Rufus Mead] to Folks at Home, 28 Dec. 1864, Rufus Mead Papers, LC; Willie G. Baugh to Parents, 19 Oct. 1864, William G. Baugh Papers, Emory U; Isaac Kittinger diary, 31 Dec. 1864, Earl M. Hess Collection, USMHI; John Potter, *Reminiscences of the Civil War in the United States* (Oskaloosa, IA: The Globe Press, 1897), p. 115; J. W. Rumpel to Father, 25 Dec. 1864, H. E. Rosenberger, ed., *Annals of Iowa*, XXXVI, p. 144; Isaac N. Carr, 4 Mar. 1865, Isaac N. Carr Papers, IASHS; William Meffert diary 13–5 Dec. 1864, William C. Meffert Papers, SHSW; Halsey, ed., *A Yankee Private*, p. 102; Garret Byrne diary, 20 Nov. 1864, Garret S. Byrne Papers, Rutgers U; OR I, XLIV, pp. 177–78 and 211.

24. W. H. Cassidy parody, F. M. McAdams journal, 7 Feb. 1865, F. M. McAdams, *Every-day Soldier Life*, pp. 134–35. Also see Collins, *Memoirs*, p. 293.

25. R. B. Satterlee to Wife, 30 Mar. 1865, Richard B. Satterlee Papers, SHSW; Oscar [Baxter] to Sister, 19 Oct. 1864, Larry Martin Collection, WMIU; John Risedorph diary, 28 Feb. 1865, Risedorph Papers, MNHS; Allen T. Underwood diary, 19 Feb. 1865, Allen T. Underwood Papers, IASHMA; Farnum to Wife, 19 Dec. 1864, Farnum Papers, MNHS. Also see John Stevens, "Account of Sherman's Raid," Civil War Times Illustrated Collection, USMHI; William H. H. Minot diary, 25–7 Feb. 1865, William H. H. Minot Papers, U. of Alabama; L. A. Ross, "Sherman's System of Foraging," p. 13, L. A. Ross Papers, ILSHS; Nelson Stauffer diary, 15 Dec. 1864, N. Stauffer, *Civil War Diary*, n.p.; L. A. Ross diary, 27 Nov. 1864, L. A. Ross Papers, ILSHS; James Sawyer to Nancy, 5 Nov. 1864, James Sawyer to Nancy, 8 Dec. 1864, James T. Sawyer Papers, SHSW; H. H. Tarr diary, 17 Nov. 1864, Storrs, *20th Connecticut*, p. 150; [Rufus Mead] to Folks at Home, 28 Dec. 1864, Rufus Mead Papers, LC; Wm. A. Schofield to Father, 2 Feb. 1865, William A. Schofield Papers, GAHS; Hamilton, *Recollections of a Cavalryman*, pp. 154–55.

CHAPTER 8

1. Henry Hitchcock diary, 24 Nov. 1864, H. Hitchcock, *Marching With Sherman*, p. 89. Also see Levi Ross diary, 12 Nov. 1864, Levi A. Ross Papers, ILSHS.

2. E. Hutchinson to Father, 15 Oct. 1864, Edwin Hutchinson Papers, LSU; H. H. Orendorff to Brother, 22 Jan. 1865, H. H. Orendorff papers, ILSHS; Sherman to Halleck, 24 Dec. 1864, OR I, XLIV, p. 799.

3. James A. Connolly diary, 13 Nov. 1864, J. A. Connolly, Angle, ed., *Three Years*, p. 298; Hedley, *Marching Through Georgia*, p. 255; P. B. Buckingham to Wife, 18 Dec. 1864, Philo Buckingham Papers, AAS; William H. Pittenger diary, 14 Feb. 1865, William H. Pittenger Papers, OHS; Alonzo Miller to Sister, 14 Mar. 1865, Alonzo Miller Papers, SHSW. Also see H. Hitchcock diary, 23 Nov. 1864, H. Hitchcock, *Marching With Sherman*, p. 86.

4. S. S. Farwell to Wife, 15 Dec. 1864, S. S. Farwell Papers, IASHS; W. G. Eaton to Brother Rice, 6 Jan. 1865, Lola J. Warrick Collection, WMIU; Styles Porter diary, 22 Feb. 1865, Styles W. Porter Papers, OHS; Alonzo Miller to Sister, 14 Mar. 1865, Alonzo Miller Papers, SHSW. Also see George T. Spaulding to Wife, 13 Mar. 1865, George T. Spaulding Papers, SHSW; Thomas McCormick to Friend Maggie, 26 Dec. 1864, Margaret Stanford Collection, WMIU; P. B. Buckingham to Wife, 18 Dec. 1864, Philo Buckingham Papers, AAS; *Raleigh Daily Conservative*, 25 Mar. 1865; William Champion diary, 13 Feb. 1865, *Civil War Diary of William Julius Champion*, n.p.; W. C. Johnson diary, 15 Nov. 1864, Kerksis, ed., *Atlanta Papers*, p. 809; Daniel Titus to Eme-

line Adams, n.d., from *Yankee Magazine* (October, 1972), p. 97, in Civil War Miscellaneous Collection, USMHI; C. C. Platter diary, 15 Nov. 1864, C. C. Platter Papers, U. of Georgia; I. W. Avery, *The History of the State of Georgia From 1850 to 1881* (New York: AMS Press, 1972), p. 331.

5. Charles Berry Senior diary, 11 Feb. 1865, Charles Berry Senior Papers, IASHS; W. P. Howard to Joseph E. Brown, 7 Dec. 1864, Franklin M. Garrett, *Atlanta and Environs* (New York: Lewis Historical Publishing Company, Inc., 1954), I, p. 653. Also see W. H. Hanks to Col. F. L. Childs, 3 Apr. 1865, Frederick L. Childs Papers, U. of South Carolina; King, Jr., ed., *The War-Time Journal of a Georgia Girl*, pp. 45–46; John Gay diary, 19 Nov. 1864, John Gay Papers, IASHS; OR I, XLVII, Pt. 1, pp. 84 and 318; Ezra Button diary, 6 Mar. 1865, John B. Tripp Papers, SHSW; Charles E. Wills diary, 6 Mar. 1865, C. E. Wills, *Army Life*, p. 358; Alexander G. Downing diary, 20 Feb. 1865, Clark, ed., *Downing's Civil War Diary*, p. 255; Arbuckle, *Civil War Reminiscence*, p. 137; William Meffert diary, 6 Mar. 1865, William C. Meffert Papers, SHSW; Charles F. Hubert journal, 6 Mar. 1865, C. F. Hubert, *50th Illinois*, p. 365; W. C. Jacobs diary, 6 Mar. 1865, Chamberlain, *81st Ohio*, p. 161; Jesse Bean diary, 19 Feb. 1865, Jesse S. Bean Papers, SHC, UNC; James T. Reeve diary, 5 Nov. 1864, James T. Reeve Papers, SHSW; OR I, XLVII, Pt. 1, pp. 209, 588, and 864; OR I, XLIV, pp. 76, 159, 211, and 367; James L. Watkins, *King Cotton: A Historical and Statistical Review, 1790 to 1908* (New York: Negro Universities Press, 1969), p. 30; Wm. A. Scofield to Father, 22 January 1865, William A. Scofield Papers, GAHS; Special Field Orders, No. 8, Headquarters, Fourth Division. Fifteenth Corps, 18 Nov. 1864, OR I, XLIV, p. 487; Hinkley, *Service With the 3rd Wisconsin*, pp. 151–52; Oscar L. Jackson diary, 7 Mar. 1865, O. L. Jackson, *The Colonel's Diary*, p. 192; Collins, *Memoirs*, p. 296; Smith D. Atkins reminiscence of 26 Nov. 1864, Smith D. Atkins, "With Sherman's Calvalry," *MOLLUS–IL*, II, p. 390; William Evans diary, 23 Feb. 1865, William D. Evans Papers, WRHS; Alonzo Miller to Sister, 18 Dec. 1864, Alonzo Miller Papers, SHSW; Mahlon H. Floyd, "Sherman's March to the Sea," speech of 12 Feb. 1889, pp. 15–16, Helen Floyd Carlin Papers, INHS; Horatio Chapman diary, 19 Nov. 1864, Horatio D. Chapman, *Civil War Diary*, p. 101; Halsey, ed., *A Yankee Private's Civil War*, p. 200; George S. Bradley diary, 19 Nov. 1864, G. S. Bradley, *The Star Corps*, pp. 185–86; Rufus Mead diary, 12 Apr. 1865, Rufus Mead Papers, LC.

6. J. F. Gilmer to James A. Seddon, 3 Jan. 1865, OR I, XLIV, pp. 1012–13. Also see OR I, XLIV, pp. 75–76, 166–67, 210–11, and 367; OR I, XLVII, Pt. 1, pp. 240, 384, 588, and 864; Roy Nichols Journal, 3 Dec. 1864, R. Nichols, *The Story of the Great March*, p. 80.

7. See Hedley, *Marching Through Georgia*, p. 255; Winther, ed., *With Sherman to the Sea*, pp. 123–24; C. C. Platter diary, 13 Nov. 1864, C. C. Platter Papers, U. of Georgia; Minerva McClatchey diary, 15 Nov. 1864, McClatchey Family Papers, GA Dept. of A & H; Harrison Pendergast journal, 13 Nov. 1864, Pendergast Papers, MNHS; Jacob Allspaugh diary, 21 Feb. 1865, J. H. Allspaugh Papers, U. of Iowa; Axel Reed diary, 13 Nov. 1864, Reed Papers, MNHS; Joseph M. Strickling, "Reminiscence," p. 37, Joseph Mitchell Strickling Papers, OHS; OR I, XLIV, p. 60; John Henry Otto, "War Memories, 1864," p. 255. John Henry Otto Papers, SHSW; Bauer, ed., *Soldiering*, p. 184; Sherman to Slocum, 9 Feb. 1865, OR I, XLVII, Pt. 2, p. 364; William Duncan, "Through the Carolinas With the Army of the Tennessee," *MOLLUS–MN*, IV, p. 330; Sherman to Slocum, 18 Nov. 1864, OR I, XLIV, p. 489; William E. Strong, "Reminiscences of the March to the Sea," p. 9, William E. Strong Papers, ILSHS; G.

W. Southwick to J. W. Lathrop, 1 Feb. 1865, G. W. Southwick Papers, ILSHS; Judson W. Bishop, *The Story of a Regiment*, p., 158; Hartwell Osborn, *Trials and Triumphs, the Record of the Fifty-Fifth Ohio Volunteer Infantry* (Chicago: A. C. McClurg & Co., 1904), p. 177.

8. See Halsey, ed., *A Yankee Private's Civil War*, pp. 132–33; W. F. Eaton to Whiting, 14 Jan. 1865, American Missionary Association Papers, Armistad Research Center; F. F. Freeman diary, 28 Mar. 1864, J. K. Bettersworth, ed., *Mississippi in the Confederacy. As They Saw It* (Baton Rouge: Louisiana State University Press, 1961), pp. 212–13; William L. Nugent to Wife, 13 Mar. 1864, William M. Cash and Lucy Somerville Howorth, ed., *My Dear Nellie: The Civil War Letters of William L. Nugent to Eleanor Smith Nugent* (Jackson: University of Mississippi Press, 1977), pp. 160–61; Henry O. Marcy, "Sherman's Campaign in the Carolinas," *MOLLUS–MA*, II, p. 332; John S. Cooper diary, 23 Jan. 1865, John S. Cooper Papers, Duke U; Winther, ed., *With Sherman to the Sea*, p. 142.

9. See Joshua to J. R. Crew, 23 Oct. 1864, J. R. Crew Papers, Atlanta HS; Michael Dresbach to Wife, 1 Nov. 1864, Dresbach Papers, MNHS; Bliss Morse diary, 12 Nov. 1864, L. Morse, ed., *The Civil War Diaries of Bliss Morse*, p. 69; James A. Connolly diary, 13 Nov. 1864, J. A. Connolly, Angle, ed., *Three Years*, p. 298; W. C. Johnson diary, 13 Nov. 1864, Kerksis, ed., *Atlanta Papers*, p. 808; Hedley, *Marching Through Georgia*, p. 256.

10. Sherman to Poe, 11 Nov., 1864, OR I, XXXIX, Pt. 3, p. 741; Axel Reed diary, 15 Nov. 1864, Reed Papers, MNHS; Samuel Storrow diary, 11 Nov. 1864, Samuel Storrow, MAHS; Allen Campbell to Father, 21 Dec. 1864, Campbell Family Papers, Michigan State U. Also see W. P. Howard to Joseph E. Brown, 7 Dec. 1864, Garrett, *Atlanta and Environs*, I, p. 653; Harrison Pendergast diary, 15 Nov. 1864, Pendergast Papers, MNHS; W. C. Johnson diary, 15 Nov. 1864, Kerksis, ed., *Atlanta Papers*, p. 809; Winther, ed., *With Sherman to the Sea*, p. 133; James T. Reeve diary, 11 Nov. 1864 and 16 Nov. 1864, James T. Reeve Papers, SHSW. In July 1864 Lt. Gen. Jubal Early burned two-thirds of Chambersburg after its citizens refused to pay a ransom.

11. See Cicular, Headquarters. Fourteenth Army Corps, 18 Nov. 1864, OR I, XLIV, p. 489; Howard to Sherman, 23 Nov. 1864, OR I, XLIV, p. 67; General Field Orders No. 26, Headquarters. Department and Army of the Tennessee, 22 Nov. 1864, OR I, XLIV, p. 521; J. W. Hinkley diary, 25 Nov. 1864, J. W. Hinkley Papers, SHSW; M. Dresbach to Wife, 14 Dec. 1864, Dresbach Papers, MNHS; W. C. Johnson diary, 28 Nov. 1864, Kerksis, ed., *Atlanta Papers*, pp. 816–17; John Rziha diary, 28 Nov. 1864, David J. de Laubenfels, ed., "With Sherman Through Georgia," *GHQ*, XLI, No. 3 (September, 1957), p. 297; William Miller diary, 9 Dec. 1864, William B. Miller Papers, INHS; James C. Bonner, "Sherman at Milledgeville in 1864," *JSH*, XXII, No. 3 (August, 1956), p. 280; OR I, XLIV, p. 256; Henry Hitchcock diary, 3 Dec. 1864 and 8 Dec. 1864, H. Hitchcock, *Marching With Sherman*, pp. 133 and 157; Halsey, ed., *A Yankee Private's Civil War*, p. 46; OR I, XLIV, p. 408; John Jackman journal, 13 Jan. 1865, John S. Jackman Papers, LC.

12. W. C. Johnson diary, 5 Feb. 1865, W. C. Johnson Papers, LC; George B. McMillan diary, 30 Jan. 1865, George B. McMillan Papers, SHSW; Willison, *Reminiscences of a Boy's Service With the 76th Ohio*, p. 116; A. S. W[illiams] to Dear Daughter, 12 Mar. 1865, Quaife, ed., *From the Cannon's Mouth*, p. 373; [Sebastian Duncan] to Mother, 1 Feb. 1865, Sebastian Duncan, Jr., Papers, NJHS; John Risedorph diary, 5 Mar. 1865, Risedorph Papers, MNHS; William D. Evans diary, 13 Feb. 1865, William David Ev-

ans Papers, WRHS; W. F. Eaton to Whiting, 14 Jan. 1865, American Missionary Association Papers, Armistad Research Center. See also Willison, *Reminiscences of a Boy's Service*, pp. 108–9; James C. Patten diary, 18 Dec. 1864, R. G. Athearn, ed., *INMH*, XLIX, p. 420; William H. H. Tallman, "Reminiscences," p. 76, Gregory Coco Collection, USMHI.

13. John H. Morse to Sister, 25 Mar. 1865, Federico, ed., *Civil War Letters of J. H. Morse*, p. 178; Garret S. Byrne diary, 3 Feb. 1865, Garret S. Byrne Papers, Rutgers U. Also see W. H. Forbis reminiscence, Tourgeé, *The Story of a Thousand*, p. 358; W. C. Olds to Alice, 5 Apr. 1865, Civil War Miscellany, from *The Collector*, XLV, No. 2 (December, 1930), p. 14, Barker Research Center, U. of Texas.

14. Ed Cort to Friends, 16 Jan. 1865, Tomlinson, ed., *Dear Friends*, p. 179. Also see John H. Roberts to Eleanor, 1 Feb. 1865, John H. Roberts Papers, SHSW; James R. Stillwell to dear wife and children, 12 Mar. 1865, James R. Stillwell Papers, OHS; Ferd F. Boltz diary, 10 Feb. 1865, Ferd F. Boltz Papers, Duke U; John W. Reid to Wife, 29 Mar. 1865, William G. McCreary Papers, Duke U; E. P. Burton diary, 17 Mar. 1865, E. P. Burton, *Diary*, n.p.; George S. Bradley diary, 29 Jan. 1865, G. S. Bradley, *The Star Corps*, p. 252; C. Emerson Allen diary, 30 Jan. 1865, C. Emerson Allen Papers, Bentley Library, UMI; James K. Burkhalter diary, 12 Feb. 1865, James Burkhalter Papers, ILSHS; [Lorenzo Pratt] to the dear Old folks at Home, 31 Mar. 1865, Civil War Miscellaneous Collection, USMHI.

15. J. Taylor Holmes journal, 10 Feb. 1865, J. T. Holmes, *52d Ohio Volunteer Infantry, Then and Now* (Columbus, OH: Berlin Print, 1898), p. 20; R. Y. Woodlief diary, 6 Feb. 1865, R. Y. Woodlief Papers, U. of South Carolina. Also see J. Taylor Holmes journal, 8 Feb. 1865, J. T. Holmes, *52d Ohio*, p. 20; J. P. Carroll, "The Burning of Columbia, South Carolina—Report of the Committee of Citizens Appointed to Collect Testimony," *Southern Historical Society Papers*, VIII, No. 5 (May 1880), p. 203; James W. Davidson, "Who Burned Columbia—A Review of General Sherman's Version of the Affair," *SHSP*, VII, No. 4 (April, 1879), p. 190; Samuel Toombs, *Reminiscences of the War* (Orange, NJ: Printed at the Journal Offiice, 1878), p. 201; OR I, XLVII, Pt. 1, pp. 222, 678, 720, and 731; Pepper, *Personal Recollections*, p. 347; Mrs. Rosa J. Meetye of Lexington, S.C., reminiscence, U. R. Brooks, *Stories of the Confederacy* (Columbia, SC: The State Company, 1912), p. 332; Dunkelman and Winey, *The Hardtack Regiment*, p. 133; S. F. Fleharty reminiscence of 8 Feb. 1865, S. F. Fleharty, *Our Regiment: 102nd Illinois*, p. 136; W. C. Johnson diary, 7–8 Feb. 1865 and 10 Feb. 1865, W. C. Johnson Papers, LC; Michael Dresbach, "Reminiscences of Sherman's Campaign Through Georgia and the Carolinas," pp. 15–16, Dresbach Papers, MNHS; Official Diary of the Army of the Tennessee, 12 Feb. 1865, Sladen Family Papers, USMHI; George McMillan diary, 12–4 Feb. 1865, G. B. McMillan Papers, SHSW; Garret S. Byrne diary, 6 Feb. 1865, Garret S. Byrne Papers, Rutgers U; Jacob Allspaugh diary, 11 Feb. 1865, J. H. Allspaugh Papers, U. of Iowa; John W. Bates diary, 14 Jan. 1864[5], Civil War Miscellaneous Collection, USMHI; William H. Lynch diary, 17 Feb. 1865, William H. Lynch Papers, WHC–SHSMO.

16. C. C. Platter, 17 Feb. 1865, C. C. Platter Papers, U. of Georgia; W. Baugh to Father, n.d. [March, 1865]. William G. Baugh Papers, Emory U; Jesse S. Bean, "Note on the Burning of Columbia," Jesse S. Bean Papers, SHC, UNC; Arbuckle, *Civil War Reminiscences*, p. 133; William D. Evans diary, 17 Feb. 1865, William D. Evans Papers, WRHS; Edwin D. Levings to Parents, 12 Mar. 1865, Edwin D. Levings Papers, SHSW; George B. McMillan diary, 17 Feb. 1865, George B. McMillan Papers, SHSW; E. H.

King diary, 18 Feb. 1865, Civil War Miscellaneous Collection, USMHI; Anthony J. Baurdick diary, 19 Feb. 1865, Anthony J. Baurdick Papers, Emory U. Also see Official Diary of the Army of the Tennessee, 17–8 Feb. 1865, Sladen Family Papers, USMHI; John G. Brown reminiscence, Committee, *55th Illinois*, p. 407; Wright, *6th Iowa*, pp. 404–5; Mary Darby de Treville, "Extracts from the Letters of a Confederate Girl to a Cousin in Virginia, From 1860 to 1866," and Catherine Prioleau Ravenel, "Personal Recollections and Experiences During the Burning of Columbia, S.C." Mrs. T. Taylor et al., *South Carolina Women in the Confederacy* (Columbia, SC: The State Company, 1903), II, pp. 147 and 179; Eli Sherlock diary, 17 Feb. 1865, Eli Sherlock Papers, INHS; Winther ed., *With Sherman to the Sea*, pp. 152–54; Samuel Snow to Parents, 28 Mar. 1865, Snow Family Papers, Duke U; H. C. McArthur, "The Burning of Columbia, SC," p. 9, H. C. McArthur diary, 17 Feb. 1865, H. C. McArthur Papers, IASHMA; C. R. Woods to Max. Woodhull, 17 Feb. 1865, OR I, XLVII, Pt. 2, pp. 457–58; Levi Green diary, 17 Feb. 1865, Green Papers, MNHS; Oliver Kindley diary, 17 Feb. 1865, Oliver C. Kindley Papers, IASHMA; S. S. Farwell to Wife, 25 Mar. 1865, S. S. Farwell Papers, IASHS; John J. Hardin to Father & Mother, 29 Mar. 1865, Sesqui Manuscripts, INHS; J. G. Jannicke reminiscence of 17 Feb. 1865, George Baird diary, 17 Feb. 1865, Unidentified officer's diary, 18 Feb. 1865, Brown, *4th Minnesota*, pp. 376–78; Jesse L. Dozer diary, 17 Feb. 1865, W. W. Black, ed., *GHQ*, LII, p. 465; Unknown reminiscences, "Recollections of the Great March" by Edwin Levings, Edwin D. Levings Papers, SHSW; Jesse S. Bean diary, 17 Feb. 1865, Jesse S. Bean Papers, SHC, UNC; Willison, *Reminiscences of a Boy's Service*, p. 116; John E. Risedorph diary, 17–8 Feb., 1865 Risedorph Papers, MNHS; William Champion diary, 17 Feb. 1865, *Civil War Diary of William J. Champion*, n.p.; Orendorff, H. H., to Maggie Orendorff, 27 Mar. 1865, H. H. Orendorff Papers, ILSHS; George Keckler to Henry C. Packhurst, 17 Feb. 1915, Henry C. Packhurst Papers, IASHS; William E. Strong journal, 17 Feb. 1865, "Reminiscences," pp. 246–51, William E. Strong Papers, ILSHS; Pepper, *Personal Recollections*, p. 311; Isaac Carr diary, 17–19 Feb. 1865, Isaac N. Carr Papers, IASHS; Henry [Wright] to Folks at Home, 28 Mar. 1865, H. N. Monnett, ed., *CWH*, VIII, p. 285; Winston Cheatham to Sister, 27 Mar. 1865, Cheatham Papers, MNHS; Marion B. Lucas, *Sherman and the Burning of Columbia* (College Station: Texas A & M University Press, 1976), p. 128; OR I, XLVII, Pt. 1, p. 310; [Robert Wilson] to Robert, 1 Mar. 1865, Robert Wilson Papers, U. of South Carolina; Willie Baugh to Parents, 27 Mar. 1865, William G. Baugh Papers, Emory U; John Gay diary, 17 Feb. 1865, John Gay Papers, IASHS; Rea P. J. Shand recollections, Brooks, *Stories of the Confederacy*, p. 339; Edward E. Schweitzer diary, 17 Feb. 1865, Civil War Times Illustrated Collection, USMHI; Order of Bvt. Maj. Genl. John M. Corse, 19 Feb. 1865, Joseph T. Zealy Papers, U. of South Carolina; Hazen, *Narrative*, p. 353; T. M. S[tevenson] to Editor, n.d., T. M. Stevenson, *78th Ohio*, p. 331.

17. D. Nichol to Father, 14 Mar. 1865, Harrisburg Civil War Round Table Collection, USMHI; Charley to Father, 31 Mar. 1865, Charles Webster Knapp Papers, SHSW; Charles E. Wills diary, 7 Mar. 1865, C. E. Wills, *Army Life*, p. 358. Also see I. M. Logan to Father & Mother Brothers & Sisters, n.d. (11th Georgia Cav, CSA), I. M. Logan Papers, GA Dept. of A & H; Aten, *85th Illinois*, p. 270; Hamilton, *Recollections of a Cavalryman*, p. 154; James E. Morrow diary, 18 Nov. 1864, Civil War Times Illustrated Collection, USMHI; W. F. Eaton to Bro. Whiting, 14 Jan. 1865, American Missionary Association Papers, Armistad Research Center; Garret Byrne diary, 20 Feb. 1865, Garret S. Byrne Papers, Rutgers U; Bauer, ed., *Soldiering*, p. 214; William H. H. Tallman, "Reminiscences," p. 81, Gregory Coco Papers, USMHI; N. L. Parmater

diary, 21 Feb. 1865, N. L. Parmater Papers, OHS; Sam to Maggie, 26 Mar. 1865, Samuel K. Harryman Papers, INST Lib; OR I, XLVII, Pt. 1, p. 583; David A. Flateley diary, 7 Mar. 1865, David A. Flateley Papers, INHS; John to Friend Kate, 28 Mar. 1865, "Letters of John Adams," *NDHQ*, IV, p. 268; Maria L. Haynsworth to Mother, letter-diary, 28 Apr.–6 May 1865, Maria L. Haynsworth Papers, SHC, UNC.

18. Special Orders, No. 63, Headquarters, Seventeenth Army Corps, 10 Mar. 1865, OR I, XLVII, Pt. 2, pp. 760–61; William D. Evans diary, 11 Mar. 1865, William D. Evans Papers, WRHS. Also see Levi D. Bryant to Wife, 28 Mar. 1865, Michael Winey Collections, USMHI; Billings Sibley to Sister and Mother, 26 Mar. 1865, Sibley Papers, MNHS; Sherman to Slocum, 6 Mar. 1865, A. M. Van Dyke to Logan, 7 Mar. 1865, Blair to A. M. Van Dyke and Blair to Howard, 7 Mar. 1865, General Orders No. 8, Headquarters, Army of Georgia, 7 Mar. 1865, Sherman to Kilpatrick, 7 Mar. 1865, OR I, XLVII, Pt. 2, pp. 704, 714–15, 717, 719, and 721; John D. Inskeep diary, 13 Mar. 1865, John D. Inskeep Papers, OHS; Elizabeth Collier journal, 27 Mar. 1865, Elizabeth Collier Papers, SHC, UNC.

19. Thomas T. Taylor diary, 17 Nov. 1864, Thomas T. Taylor Papers, LSU; Jacob Allspaugh diary, 22 Feb. 1865, J. H. Allspaugh Papers, U. of Iowa; S. Jack North to Mary, 2 Apr. 1865, Nine Ness Collection, Bentley Library, UMI. Also see Lyman Widney reminiscences, Lyman S. Widney Papers, KMNP; Chas. S. Brown to Folks, n.d. Charles S. Brown Papers, Duke U; Martin C. Short to Father & Mother, diary-letter, 17 Nov. 1864, Martin C. Short Papers, SHSW; Alfred Trego diary, 20 Nov. 1864, Alfred Trego Papers, Chicago HS; Levi Green diary, 31 Jan. 1865, Green Papers, MNHS; John Batchelor diary, 11 Feb. 1865, John Batchelor Papers, ILSHS; Special Orders, No. 17, Headquarters, Third Brigade, Fourth Division, Fifteenth Army Corps. 5 Mar. 1865, Special Field Orders, No. 56, Headquarters, Department and Army of the Tennessee, 8 Mar. 1865, OR I, XLVII, Pt. 2, pp. 689 and 728; Sherman to Wheeler, 8 Feb. 1865, OR I, XLVII, Pt. 2, p. 342; Wheeler to Hardee, 24 Dec. 1864, and H. W. Feilden to Wheeler, 25 Dec. 1864, OR I, XLIV, pp. 986 and 988; Circular, Headquarters, Twenty-third Army Corps, 12 Apr. 1865, OR I, XLVII, Pt. 3, pp. 188–89; Oscar L. Jackson diary, 12 Apr. 1865, O. L. Jackson, *The Colonel's Diary*, p. 196; OR I, XLVII, Pt. 1, p. 687. Confederates also destroyed property of Unionists and their own railroads. See Norman D. Brown, ed., *One of Cleburne's Command: The Civil War Reminiscences and Diary of Capt. Samuel T. Foster, Granbury's Texas Brigade, CSA* (Austin: University of Texas Press, 1980), p. 140; J. A. Connolly diary, 15 Oct. 1864, J. A. Connolly, Angle, ed., *Three Years*, p. 278; Tom H. Coleman to Parents, 1/12/65, Thomas H. Coleman Papers, WHC–SHSMO; J. H. Otto, "War Memories, 1865," pp. 13–14, John Henry Otto Papers, SHSW.

20. Levi Ross diary, 22 Oct., 1864, Levi A. Ross Papers, ILSHS; W. C. Johnson diary, 24 Nov. 1864, Kerksis, ed., *Atlanta Papers*, p. 813–14. Also see Garret Byrne journal, 23 Nov. 1864, Garret S. Byrne Papers, Rutgers U; OR I XLIV, p. 212; OR I, XLVII, Pt. 1, p. 195; Kinnear, *86th Illinois*, p. 108; Oscar L. Jackson diary, 8 Mar. 1865, O. L. Jackson, *The Colonel's Diary*, pp. 193–94; Mahlon H. Floyd, "Sherman's March to the Sea," p. 12, Speech of 12 Feb. 1889. Helen Floyd Carlin Papers, INHS; Jacob Allspaugh diary, 28 Nov. 1864, J. H. Allspaugh Papers, U. of Iowa; Emma Le Conte diary, 18 Feb. 1865, Earl S. Miers, ed., *When the World Ended: The Diary of Emma Le Conte* (New York: Oxford University Press, 1957), p. 48. Records of the Judge Advocate General (Army) RG 153, NA, MM 1856, trial of Isaac Williams, NN 3588, trial of Henry Mooney.

21. T. S. Howland to sister, 30 Mar. 1865, Thomas S. Howland Papers, MAHS;

Elliott B. McKeever, "Atlanta to the Sea," Elliott B. McKeever Papers, WRHS; John E. Hickman to Friends at Home, 30 Mar. 1865, Squire Family Papers, Bentley Library, UMI. Also see J. W. Rumpel to Father, 25 Dec. 1864, H. E. Rosenberger, ed., *Annals of Iowa*. 3rd ser. XXXVI, No. 2, p. 144; Garret Byrne diary, 13 Mar. 1865, Garret S. Byrne Papers, Rutgers U; William Grunert journal, 24 Jan. 1865, W. Grunert, *129th Illinois*, p. 177; A. S. W[illiams] to Dear Pitt, 21 Apr. 1865, Quaife, ed., *From the Cannon's Mouth*, p. 385; F. M. McAdams journal, 6 Dec. 1864, F. M. McAdams, *Every-Day Soldier Life*, p. 122; Marden Sabin, "Memoirs of Dr. Marden Sabin," p. 39, Marden Sabin Papers, INST Lib; Stelle, *Memoirs of the Civil War*, pp. 27–28.

22. Charles S. Brown to Etta, 26 Apr. 1865, Charles S. Brown Papers, Duke U; Styles W. Porter diary, 28 Nov. 1864, Styles W. Porter Papers, OHS; Dresbach to Wife, 15 Dec. 1864, Dresbach Papers, MNHS; Willison, *Reminiscences of a Boy's Service With the 76th Ohio*, pp. 114–15; John E. Risedorph diary, 26 Feb. 1865, Risedorph Papers, MNHS. Also see Kinnear, *86th Illinois*, p. 108; Charles Berry Senior diary, 14 Feb. 1865, Charles Berry Senior Papers, IASHS; E. P. Burton diary, 17 Feb. 1865, E. P. Burton *Diary*, n.p.; Thomas T. Taylor diary, 23 Nov. 1864, Thomas T. Taylor Papers, LSU; Dr. Thomas to Dr. Thrall, 20 Dec. 1864, M. Throne, ed., *IJH*, LVIII, No. 2, pp. 187–88; James T. Reeve diary, 24 Nov. 1864, James T. Reeve Papers, SHSW; Ezra Button diary, 22 Feb. 1865, John B. Tripp Papers, SHSW; Ella Anderson Clark reminiscence, pp. 119–20, James Osgood Andrew Clark Papers, Emory U; Michael Dresbach, "Reminiscences of Sherman's Campaign Through Georgia and the Carolinas," p. 11, Dresbach Papers, MNHS; Ria Gaillard to Cousin, 17 Mar. 1865, Dwight Wyatt Aikin Papers, U. of South Carolina; Garret S. Byrne diary, 6 Feb. 1865, Garret S. Byrne Papers, Rutgers U: Howard to Sherman, 29 Nov. 1864, OR I, XLIV, p. 67; Sherman, *Memoirs*, II, pp. 182–83; ? to Major George Pomutz, 10 Feb. 1865, Elisha Leaming Papers, IASHMA; Mrs. Randolph Sams to My Own Darling R, letter-diary, 9 Feb. 1865, Sara Jane Sams Papers, U. of South Carolina; OR I, XLVII, Pt. 1, p. 551; Dave N[ichol] to Sister, 4 Sep. 1864, Harrisburg Civil War Round Table Collection, USMHI; Mary Leverette to Caroline, 18 Mar. 1865, Mary Leverette Papers, U. of South Carolina; Oscar L. Jackson diary, 24 Nov. 1864, O. L. Jackson, *The Colonel's Diary*, p. 165; R. W. Henry to Wife, 13 Mar. 1865, R. W. Henry Papers, IASHS; Thos. Christie to brother, 18 Dec. 1864, Christie Papers, MNHS; [Robert Wilson] to Robert, 1 Mar. 1865, Robert Wilson Papers, U. of South Carolina; Charles F. Morse to [members of family], 31 Jan. 1865, Morse, *Letters Written During the Civil War*, p. 210; Harvey Reid diary-reminiscence, 18 Nov. 1864, Harvey Reid Papers, SHSW; Henry Hitchcock diary, 29 Nov. 1864, H. Hitchcock, *Marching With Sherman*, pp. 114–15; Fleharty, *102nd Illinois*, p. 140; Jacob Allspaugh diary, 23 Mar. 1865, J. H. Allspaugh Papers, U. of Iowa; Joshua W. Williams diary, 10 Nov. 1864, Indiana History Manuscripts, Indiana U, Charles D. Kerr, *MOLLUS–MN*, I, pp. 211–12.

23. Charles F. Hubert journal, 20 Feb. 1865, C. F. Hubert, *50th Illinois*, p. 356; J. H. Roberts to Brother, 7 Jan. 1865, John H. Roberts Papers, SHSW; Manning F. Force, "Marching Across Carolina," *MOLLUS–OH*, I, p. 15. See also Horatio Chapman diary, 25 Oct. 1864, H. D. Chapman, *Civil War Diary*, p. 98; Garret S. Byrne diary, 11 Feb. 1865, Garret S. Byrne Papers, Rutgers U; Willison, *Reminiscences of a Boy's Service*, pp. 102–3; William Strawn reminiscence, Calkins, *104th Illinois*, p. 295; J. M. Wills diary, 22 Nov. 1864, Merrill, *70th Indiana*, p. 219; Oscar [Kimberley] to Parents, 5 Apr. 1865, E. O. Kimberley Papers, SHSW; William Baugh to Parents, 14 Mar. 1865, William G. Baugh Papers, Emory U; Charley to Father, 12 Mar. 1865, Charles M. Smith Papers, SHSW; Charley to Father, 31 Mar. 1865, Charles Webster Knapp Papers, SHSW.

24. C. Cadle, Jr., to Col. George E. Spencer, 20 Nov. 1864, OR I, XLIV, pp. 504–5; Special Field Orders, No. 44, Department and Army of the Tennessee, 20 Feb. 1865, OR I, XLVII, Pt. 2, p. 502. Also see O. O. Howard to Soldiers of the Army of the Tennessee, 16 Oct. 1864, OR I, XXXIX, Pt. 3, pp. 308–9. General Field Orders, No. 18, 13 Sep. 1864. General Field Orders, No. 23, 21 Sep. 1864. Headquarters, Department and Army of the Tennessee, OR I, XXXIX, Pt. 2, pp. 833 and 860–61; OR I, XLIV, pp. 201 and 226; Howard to Kilpatrick, 21 Nov. 1864. OR I, XLIV, pp. 508–9; Special Field Orders, No. 172, 19 Nov. 1864. General Field Orders, No. 26, 22 Nov. 1864. Headquarters Department and Army of the Tennessee, OR I, XLIV, pp. 493 and 521; OR I, XLVII, Pt. 1, p. 656; Howard to Blair, 10 Jan. 1865, and Howard to Logan and Blair, 20 Feb. 1865, OR, I, XLVII, Pt. 2, pp. 33 and 505–6; General Field Orders, No. 3, 11 Jan. 1865, General Field Orders, No. 7, 30 Jan. 1865. General Field Orders, No. 9, 9 Feb. 1865, Headquarters, Department and Army of the Tennessee, OR I, XLVII, Pt. 2, pp. 34–35, 171, and 360; General Orders, No. 10, Fourth Division, Seventeenth Army Corps, 30 Jan. 1865, OR, I, XLVII, Pt. 2, pp. 173–74; Circular, Headquarters, Twentieth Army Corps, 31 Jan. 1865 and 1 Feb. 1865, OR I, XLVII, Pt. 2, pp. 184–85 and 199–200; Special Orders, No. 38, Headquarters, Fifteenth Army Corps, 7 Feb. 1865, OR, I, XLVII, Pt. 2, p. 331; George Bargus diary, 25 Nov. 1864, Civil War Times Illustrated Collection, USMHI; Charles W. Wills diary, 25 Nov. 1864, 13 Feb. 1865, 24 Feb. 1865, 28 Feb. 1865, 12 Apr. 1865, C. E. Wills, *Army Life*, pp. 326, 345, 352, 355, and 369; A. M. Geer diary, 30 Aug. 1864, Andersen, ed., *Diary of A. M. Geer*, p. 159; Peter Knudson Brye to Peter Olsen Brye, 26 Dec. 1864, Peter Knudson Brye Papers, SHSW; Nicholas De Graff diary-reminiscence, 31 Mar. 1865 and 4/3–5/65, Civil War Times Illustrated Collection, USMHI; Orville T. Chamberlain diary, 24 Nov. 1864, Joseph and Orville Chamberlain Papers, INHS; Thomas T. Taylor diary, 5–6 Dec. 1864 and 11–2 Dec. 1864, Thomas T. Taylor Papers, LSU; Isaac Roseberry diary, 17 Oct. 1864, Isaac Roseberry Papers on microfilm, Bentley Library, UMI; Matthew Jamison diary-reminiscence, 5 Dec. 1864, M. Jamison, *Recollections*, p. 285; Henry Hitchcock diary, 20 Nov. 1864. H. Hitchcock, *Marching with Sherman*, pp. 76–77; Levi Green diary, 27 Jan. 1865 and 6 Mar. 1865, Green Papers, MNHS; John Bates diary, 18 Mar. 1865, Civil War Miscellaneous Collection, USMHI; H. M. Keyes diary, 17–8 Dec. 1864, Harrisburg Civil War Round Table Collection, USMHI; George B. McMillan diary, 7 Jan. 1865 and 1 Apr. 1865, George B. McMillan Papers, SHSW; Regimental Muster and Descriptive Rolls, 32nd Infantry, 1862–1865, Wisconsin Adjutant General's Office, SHSW; Hazen, *Narrative*, pp. 415–16; Records of the Judge Advocate General (Army), RG 153, NA, trial of O. H. P. Ewing, NN 3837; trial of Michael Reid and Patrick Ryan, MM 1879 and NN 3973, trial of Sidney W. Woodward, MM 1854, trial of John W. Atherton, LL 3060, NA; George P. Metz diary, 25, Apr. 1865, George P. Metz Papers, Duke U; James Louis Matthews diary, 24 Sep. 1864, R. C. Hackett, ed., *INMH*, XXIV, p. 312; Marcus Pratt diary, 7 Mar. 1865, Marcus A. Pratt Papers, SHSW; Garret S. Byrne diary, 11 Feb. 1865, Garret S. Byrne Papers, Rutgers U; Harvey Reid to Sisters, 31 Jan. 1865, Harvey Reid Papers, SHSW; Nelson Stauffer diary, 2–3 Apr. 1865, N. Stauffer, *Civil War Diary*, n.p., Jesse Bean diary, 7 Apr. 1865, Jesse S. Bean Papers, Duke U.

25. Garret Byrne diary, 1 Feb. 1865, Garret S. Byrne Papers, Rutgers U. Also see Numa Barned to Parents, 1 Apr. 1865, Schoff Collection, Clements Library, UMI, Perry D. Grubb reminiscence, Perry D. Grubb Papers, ILSHS; Harry Mahler diary, 25 Oct. 1864, Henry Mahler Papers, IASHS; William H. Duncan, "With the Army of the Tennessee through the Carolinas," *MOLLUS–MN*, IV, pp. 521 and 528; Henry C.

Laybourn diary, 24 Mar. 1865, Henry C. Laybourn Papers, U. of Iowa; William E. Sloan diary, 17 Apr. 1865, William E. Sloan Papers, TNST L & A; OR I, XLIV, pp. 280 and 310; R. H. Robertson to J. E. Johnston, 17 Mar. 1865, OR I, XLVII, Pt. 2, p. 1421; R. E. Lee to Vance, 9 Mar. 1865, OR I, XLVII, Pt. 2, pp. 1353–54; Hampton to Johnston, 31 Mar. 1865, OR I, XLVII, Pt. 3, p. 729; Pepper, *Personal Recollections*, p. 172; W. L. Nugent to Nellie, 14 Oct. 1864, Cash and Howorth, eds., *Dear Nellie*, p. 219; Noble C. Williams, *Echoes from the Battlefield or Southern Life During the War* (Atlanta: Franklin Printing and Publishing Company, 1902), p. 46; Axel Reed diary, 4 Sep. 1864, Reed Papers, MNHS; R. Mead, Jr., to Folks at Home, 8 Sep. 1864, Rufus Mead Papers, LC; Imogene [Hoyle] to Ama, 28 Nov. 1864, Bomar/Killian Papers, Atlanta HS; C. C. Platter diary, 21 Dec. 1864, C. C. Platter Papers, U. of Georgia; John J McKee diary, 21 Dec. 1864, John J. McKee Papers, IASHS; William A. Fletcher, *Rebel Private, Front and Rear* (Austin: University of Texas Press, 1954), p. 143; Garret Byrne diary, 13 Mar. 1865, Garret S. Byrne Papers, Rutgers U; J. A. Keller to Col. John M. Obey, 16 Mar. 1865, J. A. Keller Papers, U. of South Carolina; W. W. Gordon diary, 12 Apr. 1865, W. W. Gordon Papers, SHC, UNC; Committee, *92nd Illinois*, p. 239; Musa V. Crowe to Miss S. V. W., 25 Feb. 1865, Musa V. Crowe Papers, GA Dept. of A & H; Robert D. Smith diary, 7 Feb. 1865, J. K. Garrett, ed., *Confederate Diary of Robert D. Smith* (Columbia, TN: Capt. James Madison Sparkman Chapter, United Daughters of the Confederacy, 1975), p. 84.

26. Will [Nugent] to darling Nellie, 26 Sep. 1864, Cash and Howorth, *Dear Nellie*, p. 211; Augustine T. Smythe to Mother, 11 Dec. 1864, Augustine T. Smythe Papers, SHC, UNC; R. B. Hardman to Ma, 12 Jan. 1865, R. B. Hardman, AL Dept. of A & H; H. Clay Reynolds to Mary, 4 Jan. 1865, Henry Clay Reynolds Papers, AL Dept. of A & H; Wm. E. Stanton to Cousin, 30 Mar. 1865, William E. Stanton Papers, Barker Research Center, U. of Texas. Also see Margaret Crawford Clarkson, "Recollections of Sherman's Raid through South Carolina, February, 1865," Taylor, *South Carolina Women in the Confederacy*, II, p. 201; T. C. B. to *Confederate Veteran*, 1919. *Confederate Veteran* Miscellaneous Papers, Duke U; John G. Brown reminiscence in Committee, *55th Illinois*, p. 419; T. M. S. to Editor, nd., T. M. Stevenson, *78th Ohio*, p. 335; Charles E. Wills diary, 20 Nov. 1864, C. E. Wills, *Army Life*, p. 321; L. R. Ray to Father, 5 Dec. 1864, Lavender R. Ray Papers, Georgia Division of the Daughters of the Confederacy, GA Dept of A & H; R. Amos Jarman, "History of Co. K, 27 Mississippi Infantry," p. 39, R. Amos Jarman Papers, MS Dept of A & H; B. S. Williams story in Hampden, South Carolina Newspaper, February 20, 1921, B. S. Williams Papers, Emory U; Bromfield Ridley, *Battles and Sketches of the Army of Tennessee* (Mexico, MO: Missouri Printing & Publishing Co., 1906), p. 459, J. H. Cornish diary, 10 Feb. 1865, J. H. Cornish Papers, SHC, UNC; W. T. Ward to Lt. Colonel Perkins, 4 Jan. 1865, OR I, XLVII, Pt. 2, p. 15; Beauregard to Cooper, 23 Dec. 1864, and Wheeler to Bragg, 28 Dec. 1864, OR I, XLIV, pp. 979 and 998; Circular, Jos. Wheeler, 10 Dec. 1864, OR I, XLIV, pp. 946–47; General Orders, No. 7, Headquarters, Cavalry Corps, 'Joseph Wheeler, 29 Dec. 1864, OR I, XLIV, p. 1002; D. H. Hill to Wheeler, 2/13/65, OR I, XLVII, Pt. 2, p. 1177; Albert Porter diary, 12 Feb. 1865, Albert Quincy Porter Papers, Confederate Miscellany, Emory U; W. W. Gordon, "Reminiscence," p. 12, J. Frederick Waring Papers, GAHS; Lyman Widney to Parents, 27 Dec. 1864, Lyman Widney Papers, KMNP; Charles F. Hubert journal, 18 Mar. 1865, C. F. Hubert, *50th Illinois*, pp. 369–70; Alfred Roman, Inspection Report of Wheeler's Cavalry, 22 Jan. 1865, Alfred Roman Papers, LC; D. N. Couch to J. A. Campbell, 27 Mar. 1865, OR

I, XLVII, Pt. 3, p. 37; James W. Albright diary, 16 Apr. 1865, James W. Albright Papers, SHC, UNC; Mary Noble to Lelia, 20 Nov. 1864, Noble-Attaway Papers, SHC, UNC; John M. Oliver to G. Lofland, 28 Mar. 1865, OR I, XLVII, Pt. 3, p. 46.

27. King, Jr., ed., *The War-Time Journal of a Georgia Girl*, pp. 30–31; L. R. Ray to Brother, 9 Mar. 1865, Lavender R. Ray Papers, Georgia Division of the Daughters of the Confederacy, GA Dept. of A & H; Tom H. Colman to Sister Cassie Bro Bob & Henry, 3 Mar. 1865, Thomas H. Colman Papers, WHC–SHSMO. Also see Will [Nugent] to darling wife, 1 Dec. 1864, Cash and Howorth, *Dear Nellie*, p. 224; Enoch D. John to parents, diary-letter, 18 Dec. 1864; Paul Scott, ed., "With Tears in Their Eyes," *CWTI*, XXI, p. 29; S. W. Ferguson, "Memoirs," Chapter 5, p. 3, S. W. Ferguson Papers, SHC, UNC; Roy Nichols journal, 12 Mar. 1865,, R. Nichols, *The Story of the Great March*, p. 239; L. R. Ray to Brother, 9 Mar. 1865, L. R. Ray diary, 3–4 Mar. 1865, Lavender R. Ray Papers, Georgia Division of the Daughters of the Confederacy, GA Dept. of A & H; H. W. Barcalay reminiscence, H. W. Barclay Papers, Barker Research Center, U. of Texas. Some Federals believed Confederates had a right to bushwack. Q. A. Brown to Esteemed Brother, 3 Apr. 1865, Earl M. Hess Collection, USMHI; Jacob Allspaugh diary, 11 Nov. 1864, J. H. Allspaugh Papers, U. of Iowa; William Miller diary, 16 Mar. 1865, William B. Miller Papers, INHS; Charles S. Brown to Etta, 26 Apr. 1865, Charles S. Brown Papers, Duke U.

28. See OR I, XXXIX, Pt. 1, pp. 648–49; Sherman to John E. Smith 11/8/64, L. M. Dayton to Davis, 9 Nov. 1864, OR I, XXXIX, Pt. 3, pp. 703 and 717; OR I, XLIV, p. 57; Kilpatrick to Sherman, 30 Nov. 1864, and L. M. Dayton to J. Kilpatrick, 1 Dec. 1864, OR I, XLIV, pp. 585–86 and 601; OR I, XLVII, Pt. 1, pp. 318–19 and 683; Special Field Orders, No. 12, Headquarters, Military Division of the Mississippi, 14 Jan. 1865, OR I, XLVII, Pt. 2, p. 50; Kilpatrick to L. M. Dayton, 22 Feb. 1865, Sherman to Howard, 23 Feb. 1865, and Sherman to Kilpatrick, 23 Feb. 1865, OR, I, XLVII, Pt. 2, pp. 533, 537 and 544; Sherman to Hampton, 24 Feb. 1865, and Hampton to Sherman, 27 Feb. 1865, OR I, XLVII, Pt. 2, pp. 546 and 596–97; Wm. T. Clark to S. M. Budlong, 25 Feb. 1865, and Chas H. Warren to Capt. Jos. W. Roberts, 27 Feb. 1865, OR I, XLVII, Pt. 2, pp. 327–28 and 332; Woodhull to Corse, Woods, Hazen & Smith, 25 Feb. 1865, OR I, XLVII, Pt. 2, p. 570; Special Orders, No. 52, Headquarters, Seventeenth Army Corps, 25 Feb. 1865, OR I, XLVII, Pt. 2, p. 572; Special Orders, No. 56, Headquarters, Seventeenth Army Corps, 2 Mar. 1865, OR I, XLVII, Pt. 2, pp. 649–50; Official Diary of the Army of the Tennessee, 24 Feb. 1865, Sladen Family Papers, USMHI; John Risedorph diary, 24 Feb. 1865, Risedorph Papers, MNHS; Roy Nichols journal, 14 Apr. 1865, G. W. Nichols, *The Story of the Great March*, p. 295; E. W. Allen, "Two Days with Sherman Army in South Carolina," *Union and Confederate Annals*, I, No. 1 (January, 1884), pp. 44–45; George McMillan diary, 2 Mar. 1865, George B. McMillan Papers, SHSW; J. H. Otto, "War Memories, 1864," pp. 234 and 288–89, and "War Memories, 1865," pp. 77–78, John Henry Otto Papers, SHSW; Henry Hitchcock diary, 5 Dec. 1864, H. Hitchcock, *Marching With Sherman*, p. 143; R. Y. Woodlief diary, 4 Feb. 1865, R. Y. Woodlief Papers, U. of South Carolina; James Thompson diary, 15 Oct. 1864, James S. Thompson Papers, INHS; Pepper, *Personal Recollections*, p. 330; John C. Van Duzer diary, 25 Nov. 1864, John C. Van Duzer Papers, Duke U; Halsey, ed., *A Yankee Private's Civil War*, pp. 53–54 and 164; Charles F. Hubert journal, 2/28/65, C. F. Hubert, *50th Illinois*, pp. 362–63; Wm. C. Stevens to Family, 25 Sep. 1864, Stevens Family, Bentley Library, UMI; Williamson Ward journal, 21–2 Feb. 1865, Williamson D. Ward Papers, INHS; Harvey Reid to

Sister, letter-diary, 9 Feb. 1865, Harvey Reid Papers, SHSW; Lyman Widney to Parents, 27 Dec. 1864, Lyman Widney Papers, KMNP; William D. Evans diary, 11 Mar. 1865 and 22 Mar. 1865, William D. Evans Papers, WRHS; John Harvey to Frances Harvey, 27 Feb. 1928, Frances Harvey Papers, Barker Research Center, U. of Texas; Chas. S. Brown to all Brown's and any other man, 3 Feb. 1865, Chas. S. Brown Papers, Duke U; unknown journalist, 25 Feb. 1865, A. Brown, *4th Minnesota*, p. 380; Trimble, *93rd Illinois*, p. 177; *Report of Adjutant-General of the State of Illinois* (Springfield: H. W. Rokker, State Printer and Binder, 1866), IV, p. 288; William Miller diary, 11 Nov. 1864, William B. Miller Papers, INHS; James A. Congleton journal, 13 Apr. 1865, James A. Congleton Papers, LC; Charles N. Lyman diary, 5 Feb. 1865, Charles N. Lyman Papers, IASHMA. Bushwackers and Confederates seemed to get a fair trial. Records of the Judge Advocate General (Army), RG 153, NA, trial of Charles Winslow, IL 3233, trial of James S. Randle, MM 1836, trial of Theodore Coe, oo 579, NA. Confederates hung bushwackers. R. F. Bunting to the Houston Telegraph, 18 Oct. 1864, R. F. Bunting Papers, Barker Research Center, U. of Texas; O. P. Hargis, 'First-Person Story of Wheeler's Cavalrymen," *CWTI*, VII, No. 8 (December, 1968), p. 37.

29. Emma Le Conte diary, 23 Feb. 1865, Miers, ed. *When the World Ended*, p. 66; Elizabeth Collier diary, 25 Apr. 1865, Elizabeth Collier Papers, SHC, UNC; Margaret Crawford Adams, "Tales of a Grandmother," Taylor et al., *South Carolina Women in the Confederacy*, I, p. 225; Eliza C. Clay to Mrs. Smith, 16 Jan. 1865, Thomas Butler Papers, SHC, UNC. Also see Elizabeth Colier diary, 27 Mar. 1865, Elizabeth Collier Papers, SHC, UNC; Emma Le Conte diary, 18 Feb. 1865, Miers, ed., *When the World Ended*, p. 49; Harriette C. Keatings, "Reminiscence," p. 8, Harriette Keatings Papers, LC; [Robert Wilson] to Robert, 1 Mar. 1865, Robert Wilson Papers, U. of South Carolina; Bessie Reese Cornwall, "Stoneman's and Sherman's Visit to Jasper County," p. 12, Confederate Miscellany, Emory U; Unmailed letter, Mrs. Wm. Moultrie Dwight to Capt. Henry A. Gaillard, 22 Feb. 1865, David Wyatt Aikin Papers, U. of South Carolina; Will [Nugent] to Nellie, 14 Oct. 1864, Cash and Howorth, *Dear Nellie*, p. 219; Mrs. W. B. Dunlap, "Reminiscences of the Confederate War," Taylor et al. *South Carolina Women in the Confederacy*, I, p. 232; William J. McNeill, "The Stress of War; The Confederacy and William Tecumseh Sherman During the Last Year of the Civil War," dissertation at Rice University, 1973.

30. Arthur P. Ford, *Life in the Confederate Army* (New York: Neale Publishing Co., 1905), p. 44; "Memoirs of Charles H. Olmstead," ed. L. M. Hawes, *GHQ*, XLV, pp. 150–53; R. E. Lee to Z. B. Vance, 24 Feb. 1865, OR I, XLVII, Pt. 2, pp. 1270–71. Also see W. S. Penniman, "Reminiscences of Personal Experiences During the Civil War," pp. 89–90, W. S. Penniman Papers, SHC, UNC; Mallery King to dearest sister, 28 Jan. 1865, Thomas Butler Papers, SHC, UNC; Alfred Ayer to Father, 6 Jan. 1864[5], Lewis Malone Ayer Papers, U. of South Carolina; J. A. Moor to Wife, 16 Dec. 1864, James A. Moor Papers, AL Dept. of A & H; Sarah Jane Sams to Darling R[andolph Sams], letter-diary, 8 Feb. 1865, Sarah Jane Sams Papers, U. of South Carolina; H. P. Rugg diary, 10 Dec. 1864, H. P. Rugg Papers, CTST Lib; Breckinridge to Vance, 1 Mar. 1865, Vance to Lee, 2 Mar. 1865, and Bragg to R. E. Lee, 2 Mar, 1865, OR I, XLVII, Pt. 2, pp. 1296, 1312, and 1314; James M. Mullen, "Last Days of Johnston's Army," *SHSP*, XVIII (January–December, 1896), p. 103.

CHAPTER 9

1. See Unknown author's journal, 3 Feb. 1865, Belknap and Tyler, *15th Iowa*, pp. 447–48; Halsey, ed., *A Yankee Private's Civil War*, pp. 106–7.

2. See Elliot B. McKeever, "Atlanta to the Sea," Elliot B. McKeever Papers, WRHS.

3. Winther, ed., *With Sherman to the Sea*, p. 157. Also see Bishop, *The Story of a Regiment*, pp. 196–97; Unknown author in Lucas, *99th Indiana*, p. 169; Rice in Dean, *Recollections of the 26th Missouri*, p. 73; Charles F. Hubert journal, 4 Sep. 1864 C. F. Hubert, *50th Illinois*, p. 290; Boatner, *Civil War Dictionary*, p. 397.

4. Rice in Dean, *Recollections of the 26th Missouri*, p. 73; James A. Congleton journal, 15 Mar. 1865, James A. Congleton Papers, LC; Henry Clay Robbins, "Reminiscences," Henry Clay Robbins Papers, SHSW; OR I, XLVII, Pt. 1, p. 176.

5. See Unknown author, Lucas, *99th Indiana*, p. 169.

6. L. A. Ross diary, 29 Nov. 1864, L. A. Ross Papers, ILSHS; Hitchcock to Mrs. Hitchcock, 12 Mar. 1865, Hitchcock, *Marching With Sherman*, p. 266; George W. Gee to Clarence, 29 Mar. 1865, George W. Gee Papers, SHSW. Also see Thos. Christie to Brother, diary-letter, 5 Dec. 1864, Christie Papers, MNHS; J. H. Otto, "War Memories, 1865," p. 7, John Henry Otto Papers, SHSW.

7. James A. Connolly diary, 4 Dec. 1864, J. A. Connolly, Angle, ed., *Three Years*, p. 345; A. Baird to Davis, 3 Dec. 1864, OR I, XLIV, p. 618; James A. Connolly diary, 30 Nov. 1864, Connolly, Angle, ed., *Three Years*, p. 333; Ed Cort to Friends, 20 Dec. 1864, Tomlinson, ed., *Dear Friends*, p. 174.

8. OR I, XLIV, pp. 365 and 409; OR I, XLIV, p. 363; Journal of the Third Division (Cavalry), 4 Dec. 1864, OR I, XLIV, p. 55; J. Kilpatrick to Capt. E. B. Beaumont, 3 Jan. 1865, OR I XLIV, p. 361; OR I XLIV, p. 409. Also see OR I, XLIV, p. 15, 365–67, 370–71, 380–81, 408–9, and 411.

9. Dean, *Recollections*, p. 44; Charles E. Wills diary, 11 Nov. 1864, C. E. Wills, *Army Life*, p. 324. Also see Charles E. Wills diary, 16 Nov. 1864, C. E. Wills, *Army Life*, p. 320; A. J. Jackson journal, 22 Nov. 1864, Co. G, 2nd Regiment Infantry Georgia State Line Papers, GA Dept. of A & H; Winther, ed., *With Sherman to the Sea*, pp. 136–37; Charles D. Wills diary, 22 Nov. 1864, Charles D. Wills Papers, ILSHS; OR I, XLIV, pp. 97–98, 107, and 414; Muster Rolls, October to December, 1864, NA, of 12th Indiana, RG 94, NA: Thos. S. Christie to Sandy, letter-diary of 10 Dec. 1864, Christie Papers, MNHS; W. C. Johnson diary, 5 Feb. 1865, W. C. Johnson Papers, LC; Sherman, *Memoirs*, II, p. 194; Reeve diary, 24 Nov. 1864, James T. Reeve Papers, SHSW; Potter, *Reminiscences of the Civil War*, p. 126; Frank Malcom to his Wife, 17 Dec. 1864. Robertson, ed., *IJH*, LVIII, p. 341; R. B. Satterlee to Wife, 27 Jan. 1865. Richard B. Satterlee Papers, SHSW; Davis to Cobb, 18 Nov. 1864, and Beauregard to Seddon, 18 Nov. 1864, OR I, XLIV, pp. 865–66.

10. William Grunert journal, 22 Nov. 1864, W. Grunert, *129th IL*, p. 128; P. Steketee to Brother George Steketee, 24 Oct. 1864, Peter Steketee Papers, Bentley Library, UMI; M. C. Short to Father & Mother, 18 Dec. 1864, Martin C. Short Papers, SHSW. Also see Halsey, ed., *A Yankee Private's Civil War*, pp. 128–29; Garret S. Byrne diary, 5 Mar. 1865, Garret S. Byrne Papers, Rutgers U; James A. Connolly diary, 2 Dec. 1864, J. A. Connolly, Angle, ed., *Three Years*, pp. 338–39; Axel Reed diary, 4 Dec. 1864, Reed Papers, MNHS; Ed Cort to Friends, 20 Dec. 1864, Tomlinson, ed., *Dear Friends*, p. 173; John H. Otto, "War Memories, 1864," pp. 291–92, John Henry Otto Papers, SHSW; Emerson [Anderson] to Parents, 17 Oct. 1864, Civil War Papers, AAS;

Henry Hitchcock diary, 9 Dec. 1864, H. Hitchcock, *Marching With Sherman*, p. 165; James Congleton journal, 8 Apr. 1865, James A. Congleton Papers, LC; C. C. Platter diary, 12 Feb. 1865, C. C. Platter Papers, U. of Georgia; Ed. to Libbie, 25 Jan. 1865, Edward Webb Papers, WRHS; Sherman to Grant, 29 Jan. 1865, OR I, XLVII, Pt. 2, p. 156; C. H. Brush to Mother, 28 Jan. 1865, C. H. Brush Papers, ILSHS; Alonzo Miller to Sister, 25 Jan. 1865, Alonzo Miller Papers, SHSW; John Cutter to Father, 2 Feb. 1865, Cutter Papers, MNHS; George W. Gee to Clarence, 29 Mar. 1865, George W. Gee Papers, SHSW; Richard Reeves diary, 5–6 Feb. 1865 and 11–12 Féb. 1865, Reeves Papers, MNHS.

11. Bauer, ed., *Soldiering*, p, 191; Billings Sibley to Anna, 30 Dec. 1864, Sibley Papers, MNHS; Owen E. Bennett to Mother, 6 Nov. 1864, Owen Bennett Papers, INHS; Bauer, ed., *Soldiering*, p. 232. Also see William E. Stanton to Cousin, 30 Mar. 1865, William E. Stanton Papers, Barker Research Center, U. of Texas; William B. Miller diary, 16 Dec. 1864, William B. Miller Papers, INHS; G. S. Bradley diary, 2 Dec. 1864, G. S. Bradley, *The Star Corps*, p. 200; S. S. Farwell to Wife, 25 Mar. 1865, S. S. Farwell Papers, IASHS; John L. Hostetter diary, 19 Mar. 1865, Payne, *34th IL*, p. 208; Official Diary of the Army of the Tennessee, 22 Mar. 1865, Sladen Family Collection, USMHI.

12. John Langhans to Brother, 22 Jan. 1865, Michael Winey Collection, USMHI; Edwin Levings to Cousin Hattie, 18 Jan. 1865, Edwin D. Levings Papers, SHSW; Richard S. Reeves diary, 7 Feb. 1865, Reeves Papers, MNHS; Also see Ezra Button diary, 1 Mar. 1865, John B. Tripp Papers, SHSW; Jesse Taft to daughters Jennette and Sarah, 23 Jan. 1865, Taft Family Papers, MI ST U.

13. Charles Smith to Father, 25 Jan. 1865, Charles M. Smith Papers, KMNP; E. A. Wilson, *Memoirs of the War*, p. 398. Also see George Spaulding to Fida, 9 Oct. 1864, George T. Spaulding Papers, SHSW; William B. Miller diary, 20 Mar. 1865, William B. Miller Papers, INHS.

14. James H. Gardner reminiscence in De Velling, *17th OH*, pp. 7–8; Willison, *Reminiscences of a Boy's Service*, p. 126; Cornelius Cradle, *MOLLUS–OH*, V, pp. 389–90. Also see John N. Coulter to Nan, 6 Nov. 1864, John N. Coulter Papers, IASHMA.

15. Willison, *Reminiscences of a Boy's Service*, p. 126; Charles H. Spencer to Mother, 22 Oct. 1864, Charles H. Spencer Papers, SHSW. Also see Chas. S. Brown to Mother & Etta, 16 Dec. 1864, Charles S. Brown Papers, Duke U; George Nichols journal, 5 Feb. 1865, Nichols, *Story of the Great March*, p. 143; George Drake to parents, 29 Mar. 1865, Drake, ed., *The Mail Goes Through*, p. 138; Sherman, *Memoirs*, II, p. 395.

16. William Meffert diary, 16 Mar. 1865, William C. Meffert Papers, SHSW. Also see Matthew Jamison journal, 8 Feb. 1865, M. Jamison, *Recollections of Pioneer and Army Life*, p. 303; William Miller diary, 3/11/65, William B. Miller Papers, SHSW; Chas. S. Brown to Mother & Etta, 16 Dec. 1864, Charles S. Brown Papers, Duke U; Owen Stuart to Wife, 17 Dec. 1864, Civil War Times Illustrated Collection, USMHI.

17. Thos. Christie to Sandy, 5 Jan. 1865, Christie Papers, MNHS; Winther, ed., *With Sherman to the Sea*, p. 151. Also see Willie Baugh to Lizzie, 9 Nov. 1864, William G. Baugh Papers, Emory U, Benton, *As Seen From the Ranks*, pp. 238–39.

18. Aten, *85th IL*, pp. 225–26; Owen Stuart to Wife, 17 Dec. 1864, Owen Stuart Papers, ILSHS. Also see OR I, XLIV, pp. 61, 95, and 110; Farnum to Wife, 17 Dec. 1864, Farnum Papers, MNHS; Williamson D. Ward journal, 21 Dec. 1864, Williamson D. Ward Papers, INHS; William E. Strong, "Reminiscences of the March to the Sea," p. 48, William E. Strong Papers, ILSHS; Jno A. Lair to Father & Mother, 2 Jan. 1865,

John A. Lair Papers, LC; Unknown diarist of 9th Iowa, 14 Dec. 1864, and Unknown diarist of Co. F, 9th Iowa, IASHS; William C. Marlatt diary, 13 Dec. 1864, in possession of Mr. James J. McDonald, Madison, WI.

19. Thomas McCormick to Friend Maggie, 26 Dec. 1864, Margaret Stanford Collection, WMIU. Also see Halsey, ed., *A Yankee Private's Civil War*, p. 146; Official Diary of the Army of the Tennessee, 18–20 Dec. 1864, Sladen Family Collection, USMHI; OR I, XLIV, pp. 100, 128, 150–51, and 337; Wm. Belknap to Mac, 22 Dec. 1864, H. C. McArthur Papers, IASHMA; Lyman Widney reminiscence, Lyman Widney Papers, KMNP; OR I, XLIV, pp. 309–10 and 315; Jacob Allspaugh diary, 21 Dec. 1864, J. H. Allspaugh Papers, U. of Iowa; George Bargus diary, 21 Dec. 1864, Civil War Times Illustrated Collection, USMHI; George McMillan diary, 21 Dec. 1864, George B. McMillan Papers, SHSW. A number of soldiers knew the Confederate were evacuating. C. C. Platter diary, 21 Dec. 1864, C. C. Platter Papers, U. of Georgia; Official Diary of the Army of the Tennessee, 20 Dec. 1864, Sladen Family Collection, USMHI; J. W. Hinkley diary, 20 Dec. 1864, John W. Hinkley Papers, SHSW; Winther, ed., *With Sherman to the Sea*, pp. 141–42.

20. Laforest Dunham to Mr. & Mrs. Simeon H. Dunham, 30 Mar. 1865, De Rosier, ed., *Through the South*, pp. 168–69. Also see OR I, XLVII, Pt. 1, pp. 63–66, 789, and 869; Osborn, *Trials and Triumphs*, p. 199; Halsey, ed., *A Yankee Private's Civil War*, p. 186; Sherman, *Memoirs*, II, p. 301; D. M. Tedder, "Fort Sumter to Bentonville," p. 14, D. M. Tedder Papers, SHC, UNC; Boatner, *Civil War Dictionary*, p. 35.

21. Charles S. Brown to Etta, 26 Apr. 1865, Charles S. Brown Papers, Duke U. Also see James T. Reeve, "Memorandum of 3/19/65," James T. Reeve Papers, SHSW; William Meffert diary, 19 Mar. 1865. William C. Meffert Papers, SHSW; John Wesley Daniels diary, 19 Mar. 1865, John Wesley Daniels Papers, Bentley Library, UMI; OR I, XLVII, Pt. 1, pp. 450 and 468; G. R, Kellams to Lt. A. Gentry, 21 Mar. 1865, Gibson County Civil War Papers, INHS; Alexander McClurg, "The Last Chance of the Confederacy," *Atlantic Monthly*, (September, 1882), pp. 392–93; J. L. Keller in S. S. Canfield, *History of the 21st Regiment Ohio Volunteer Infantry* (Toledo: Vrooman, Anderson & Bateman, 1893), p. 183.

22. Benton, *As Seen From the Ranks*, p. 269; William Meffert diary, 19 Mar. 1865, William C. Meffert Papers, SHSW; Benton, *As Seen From the Ranks*, p. 270. Also see Chas. S. Brown to Folks, n.d., Charles S. Brown Papers, Duke U; James Burkhalter diary, 20 Mar. 1865, Burkhalter Papers, ILSHS.

23. Will Robinson to Father, 24 Mar. 1865, William C. Robinson Papers, ILSHS. Also see Frank L. Ferguson, "Battle of Bentonville, N. Carolina," Civil War Times Illustrated Collection, USMHI; F. M., McAdams journal, 19 Mar. 1865, McAdams, *Every-Day Soldier Life*, p. 144; A. C. McClurg, *Atlantic Monthly*, L, p. 394; OR I, XLVII, Pt. 1, pp. 534–35; James Burkhalter diary, 19 Mar. 1865. Burkhalter Papers, ILSHS.

24. Lt. Col. G. W. Grummond Report, OR I, XLVII, Pt. 1, p. 504; F. M. McAdams journal, 19 Mar. 1865, F. M. McAdams, *Every-Day Soldier Life*, p. 145.

25. See OR I, XLVII, Pt. 1, pp. 526 and 826; Storrs, *20th CT*, p. 164–66; Underwood, *33rd MA*, pp. 283–84; Hurst, *73rd OH*, pp. 175–77; Nixon B. Stewart, *Dan McCook's Regiment, 52d O.V.I.*, p. 161; John Batchelor diary, 19 Mar. 1865, John Batchelor Papers, ILSHS; Lyman Widney reminiscence, Lyman S. Widney Papers, KMNP.

26. See Ezra Button diary, 19 Mar. 1865, John B. Tripp Papers, SHSW; Halsey, ed., *A Yankee Private's Civil War*, p. 190; William T. Humphrey diary, 19 Mar. 1865, William T. Humphrey Papers, Chicago PL; William Meffert diary, 19 Mar. 1865, Wil-

liam C. Meffert Papers, SHSW; Charles S. Dickinson diary, 19 Mar. 1865, Charles H. Dickinson Papers, SHSW.

27. See John Risedorph diary, 22 Mar. 1865, Risedorph Papers, MNHS; Levi S. Green diary, 21 Mar. 1865, Green Papers, MNHS; Charles Berry Senior to Father, 29 Mar. 1865, Charles Berry Senior Papers, IASHS; C. C. Platter diary, 20 Mar. 1865, C. C. Platter Papers, U. of Georgia; Winther, ed., *With Sherman to the Sea*, p. 160; A. M. Bly to Anna, 29 Mar. 1865, Adelbert M. Bly Papers, SHSW; OR I, XLVII, Pt. 1, pp. 67–76 and 1060; W. C. Johnson diary, 22 Mar. 1865, W. C. Johnson Papers, LC.

28. Jas Sawyer to nancy, 27 Jan. 1865, James T. Sawyer Papers, SHSW; Lyman Hardman diary, 13 Dec. 1864, Lyman Hardman Papers, WRHS. Also see John Van Duzer to Capt., letter-diary of 9 Dec. 1864, John Van Duzer Papers, Duke U; William Pittenger diary, 2 Feb. 1865, William H. Pittenger Papers, OHS; Fergus Elliott diary, 9 Jan. 1865, Civil War Times Illustrated Collection, USMHI; Philip Roesch reminiscence, Philip Roesch Papers, TNST Lib & A.

29. E. Woodman to Charlie, 18 Apr. 1865, Charles Butler Papers, Bentley Library, UMI, OR I, XLVII, Pt. 1, p. 442. Also see E. Woodman to Charlie, 18 May 1865, Charles Butler Papers, Bentley Library.

30. F. W. Tupper to Parents, 24 Dec. 1864, F. W. Tupper Papers, ILSHS; Thos. T. Taylor to Wife, 20 Dec. 1864, Thomas T. Taylor Papers, OHS and LSU; Abner C. Smith to Wife, 23 Mar. 1865, Abner C. Smith Papers, CTST Lib. Also see Chas. N. Lyman to Mrs. Abner C. Smith 2nd, 29 Mar. 1865, Abner C. Smith Papers, CTST Lib.; Hormel, *With Sherman to the Sea*, pp. 194–5 and 215.

31. Robert M. Atkinson to mother, 29 Jan. 1864[5], Robert M. Atkinson Papers, OHS; Charles S. Brown to Etta, 26 Apr. 1865, Charles S. Brown Papers, Duke U; Winther, ed., *With Sherman to the Sea*, p. 143; W. H. Brown to Emma, 30 Mar. 1865, Vivian C. Hopkins, ed., "Soldier of the 92nd Illinois: Letters of William H. Brown and His Fiancee, Emma Jane Frazey," *Bulletin of New York Public Library*, LXXIII, No. 2 (February, 1969), pp. 123–24. Also see Sewall G. Randall, 5 Oct. 1864, Randall Papers, MNHS; Lyman D. Ames diary, 26 Sep. 1864, Lyman D. Ames Papers, OHS; G. W. Pepper, *Personal Recollections*, p. 187; I. Thayer to Wife, 1/24–5/65, I. Thayer Papers, U. of South Carolina; R. B. Hoadley to Cousin Em, 8 Apr. 1865, Robert Bruce Hoadley Papers, Duke U; James to Cousin Kate, 3 Apr. 1865, "Letters of Jas. Stallcop," *NDHQ*, IV, p. 139; Chas. N. Lyman to Mrs. Abner C. Smith 2nd, 29 Mar. 1865, Abner C. Smith Papers, CTST Lib.

32. John L. Hostetter, 13 Dec. 1864, Payne, *34th IL*, p. 173; Hedley, *Marching Through Georgia*, p. 266. Also see George Hurlbut to Angie, 11 Sep. 1864, George Hurlbut Papers, KMNP; J. G. Berstler to Friend and Cousin, 2 Apr. 1865, Griffith Family Papers, IASHMA; Young [Powell] to Ellen, 27 Mar. 1865, Ellen Aumack Papers, Duke U; husband to wife, 11 Sep. 1864, James A. Connolly, Angle, ed., *Three Years*, p. 258.

CHAPTER 10

1. Young [Powell] to Ellen, 27 Mar. 1865, Ellen Aumack Papers, Duke U; J. G. Berstler to Friend and Counsin, 2 Apr. 1865, Griffith Family Papers, IASHMA. Also see Logan and Blair, 26 Mar. 1865, Howard, 27 Mar. 1865, and Sherman, 1 Apr. 1865, OR I, XLVII, Pt. 3, pp. 28–29.

2. John D. Inskeep diary, 9 Apr. 1865, John D. Inskeep Papers, OHS; Billings Sib-

ley to Anna, 19 Apr. 1865, Sibley Papers, MNHS; Alonzo Cady to Wife, 16 Apr. 1865, Cady-Randolph Papers, MNHS. Also see J. W. Hinkley to Friend Wells, 7 Apr. 1865, J. W. Hinkley Papers, SHSW; Axel Reed diary, 8 Apr. 1865, Reed Papers, MNHS; Laforest Dunham to Mr. & Mrs. Simeon H. Dunham, 9 Mar.[Apr.] 1865, De Rosier, ed., *Through the South*, p. 166; Dr. Henry Clay Robbins autobiography, Henry Clay Robbins Papers, SHSW; S. Duncan to   , 12 Apr. 1865, Sebastian Duncan, Jr., Papers, NJHS; I. Shoger to Wife, 16 Apr. 1865, Federal Soldiers' Letters, SHC, UNC; Special Field Orders, No. 54, Headquarters, Mil. Div. of the Miss., 12 Apr. 1865, OR I, XLVII, Pt. 3, p. 180; OR I, XLVII, Pt. 1, pp. 30–31; Fred Marion to Sister, 28? Apr. 1865, Fred Marion Papers, ILSHS.

   3. John H. Morse to Belle, 21 Apr. 1865, Federico, ed., *Civil War Letters of J. H. Morse*, p. 184. Also see Winther, ed., *With Sherman to the Sea*, p. 167; John Weissert to Mother and Children, 19 Apr. 1865, John Weissert Papers, Bentley Library, UMI; Samuel Mahon to Lizzie, 19 Apr. 1865, Mahon, ed., *IJH*, LI, No. 3, p. 261; Matthew Jamison diary, 17 Apr. 1865, M. Jamison, *Recollections*, p. 327; Charlie to Mother & Etta, 18 Apr. 1865, Charles S. Brown Papers, Duke U. Several soldiers cheered Lincoln's assassination and were arrested for it. Record of Judge Advocate General (Army), RG 153, NA, trial of Frederick Bodmer, MM 1997, NA; J. Swisher, "Sketches and Recollections" in McAdams, *Every-Day Soldier Life*, p. 341; Alexander Downing diary, 17 Apr. 1865, Clark, ed., *Downing's Civil War Diary*, p. 268; Ira S. Owens journal, 26 Apr. 1865, I. S. Owens, *Greene County—74th Ohio*, p. 26; Mahlon Floyd diary, 28 Apr. 1865, Helen Floyd Carlin Papers, INHS; Andrew J. Johnson diary, 4 May 1865, Andrew J. Johnson Papers, INHS.

   4. Thomas C. Fitzgibbon to Judge, 8 Apr. 1865, Thomas W. Sherman Papers, Bentley Library, UMI; Hezekiah McCorkle diary, 30 Apr. 1865, Hezekiah McCorkle Papers, GA Dept. of A & H; John Brobst to Mary, 22 Apr. 1865, Roth, ed., *Well Mary*, pp. 135–36; William Miller diary, 28 Apr. 1865, William B. Miller Papers, INHS; A. M. Geer diary, 16 Apr. 1865, Andersen, ed., *Civil War Diary of A. M. Geer*, p. 214; J. W. Hinkley to   , 20 Apr. 1864[5], Hinkley, *Service With the 3rd Wisconsin*, p. 174; W. G. ? to George Hall, 22 Apr. 1865, George Hall Papers, IASHS. Also see Oscar L. Jackson diary, 21 Apr. 1865, O. L. Jackson, *The Colonel's Diary*, pp. 208–9; William [Stevens] to Father, 26 Apr. 1865, Stevens Family Papers, Bentley Library, UMI; John Cutter to Father, 20 Apr. 1865, Cutter Papers, MNHS; William Grunert journal, 18 Apr. 1865, W. Grunert, *129th Illinois*, p. 235; R. B. Satterlee to Wife, 23 Apr. 1865, Richard B. Satterlee Papers, SHSW; Jos. L. Locke to Miss Terry, 19 Apr. 1865, Joseph L. Locke Papers, ILSHS; L. R. Ray diary, 22 Apr. 1865, Lavender R. Ray Papers, Georgia Dvision of the Daughters of the Confederacy, GA Dept. of A & H; Lyman Ames diary, 20–1 Apr. 1865, Lyman D. Ames Papers, OHS; Owen Stuart to Wife, 21 Apr. 1865, Civil War Times Illustrated Collection, USMHI; Hitchcock to Mrs. Hitchcock, 7 Apr. 1865, H. Hitchcock, *Marching With Sherman*, p. 291; Joseph Hoffhines to Wife, 9 Apr. 1865 and 25 Apr. 1865, Joseph Hoffhines Papers, OHS; William Bircher journal, 28 Apr. 1865, W. Bircher, *A Drummer Boy's Diary*, p. 185; Charles H. Spencer to Mother, 23 Apr. 1865, Charles H. Spencer Papers, SHSW; Edward E. Schweitzer diary, 21 Apr. 1865, Civil War Times Illustrated Collection, USMHI; James Reid Jones reminiscence, James Reid Jones Papers, GA Dept. of A & H.

   5. Wright, *6th Iowa*, p. 396; James T. Reeve diary, 27 Nov. 1864, James T. Reeve Papers, SHSW; Merrill, *70th Indiana*, p. 234. Aslo see D. R. Lucas diary, 2 May 1865, D. R. Lucas, *99th Indiana*, p. 78

6. William H. Pittenger diary, 5 May 1865, William H. Pittenger Papers, OHS; Styles W. Porter diary, 7 May 1865, Styles W. Porter Papers, OHS. Also see John Cutter to Sister, 22 May 1865, Cutter Papers, MNHS; Samuel Mahon to Lizzie, 8 May 1865, Mahon, *IJH*, LI, No. 3, p. 262; Fred Marion to Sister, 9 May 1865, Fred Marion Papers, ILSHS; John Batchelor diary, 11 May 1865, John Batchelor Papers, ILSHS; Charles W. McKay reminiscence in *National Tribune Scrap Book*, p. 156, Michael Winey Collection, USMHI; Halsey, ed., *A Yankee Private*, p. 203; E. P. Burton diary, 3 May 1865, 6 May 1865, and 17 May 1865, E. P. Burton, *Diary*, n.p.; Charles Berry Senior diary, 17 May 1865, Charles Berry Senior Papers, IASHS; William H. H. Enderton diary, 7 May 1865, Payne, *34th Illinois*, p. 213; John D. Inskeep diary, 6 May 1865, John D. Inskeep Papers, OHS.

7. Charlie to Darling Wife, 7 Apr. 1865, Charles B. Tompkins Papers, Duke U; Sibley to Anna, 20 May 1865, Sibley Papers, MNHS; A. M. Geer diary, 12 May 1865, Andersen, ed., *Civil War Diary of A. M. Geer*, p. 220; Charles H. Spencer to Mother, 11 May 1865, Charles H. Spencer Papers, SHSW. Also see Dresbach to Wife, 28 Mar. 1865, Dresbach Papers, SHSW; R. S. Finley to Miss MAC, 18 Jan. 1865, R. S. Finley Papers, SHC, UNC; Isaac N. Carr diary, 10 May 1865, Isaac N. Carr Papers, IASHS; John to Sister, 27 May 1865, Federico, ed., *Civil War Letters of J. H. Morse*, p. 191; Winther, ed., *With Sherman to the Sea*, pp. 170–72; Frank Malcom to Wife, 25 May 1865, J. J. Robertson, ed., *IJH*, LVIII, No. 4, p. 355; M. Griffin to Glyde Swain, 1 Apr. 1865, Samuel G. Swain Papers, SHSW; H. H. Orendorff to Brother, 2 Apr. 1865, H. H. Orendorff Papers, ILSHS; Halsey, ed., *A Yankee Private's Civil War*, p. 205.

8. Sibley to Sister, 29 May 1865, Sibley Papers, MNHS; Edwin D. Levings to Parents, 29 May 1865, Edwin D. Levings Papers, SHSW; F. H. Putney to Father, 25 May 1865, Frank H. Putney Papers, SHSW; Burke Wylie to Brother, 25 May 1865, Burke Wylie Papers, IASHS. Also see Rufus Mead diary, 24 May 1865, Rufus Mead Papers, LC; James Sawyer to Nancy, 2 Oct. 1864, James T. Sawyer Papers, SHSW; Burke Wylie to Mother, 2 Apr. 1865, Burke Wylie Papers, IASHS; OR I, XLVII, Pt. 1, p. 793.

9. See Samuel Mahon to Lizzie, 8 May 1865, Mahon, ed., *IJH*, LI, No. 3, p. 262; William Fulton diary, 4 Jul. 1865, William P. Fulton Papers, KMNP; Sam Snow to Parents, 29 May 1865, Snow Family Papers, Duke U; Halleck to Stanton, 26 Apr. 1865, OR I, XLVII, Pt. 3, pp. 311–12; General Orders, No. 1, Hdqrs. Mil. Division of the James, 22 Apr. 1865, OR I, XLVI, Pt. 3, p. 891; Halleck to Meade, 27 Apr. 1865, OR I, XLVI, Pt. 3, p. 968; OR I, XLVII, Pt. 1, pp. 36–37; Gideon Wells diary, 21–5 Apr. 1865, *Diary of Gideon Wells* (Boston: Houghton Mifflin Company, 1911), II, pp. 195–97; Benjamin P. Thomas and Harold M. Hyman, *Stanton: The Life and Times of Lincoln's Secretary of War* (New York: Alfred A. Knopf, 1962), p. 408. *New York Times*, 24 Apr. 1865. One member of Sherman's army who did not support his commander was C. C. Carpenter to Wife, 12 May 1865, M. Throne, ed., *IJH*, LIII, No. 1, pp. 87–88.

10. Laforest Dunham to Mr. & Mrs. Simeon H. Dunham, 18 Oct. 1864, De Rosier, ed., *Through the South*, p. 157; Willie G. Baugh to Parents, 7 Nov. 1864, William G. Baugh Papers, Emory U; John L. Hostetter diary, 13 Dec. 1864, Payne, *34th Illinois*, p. 173; J. M. Scott to Liz, 17 Apr. 1865, James M. Scott Papers, OHS. Also see Ira S. Morrill diary, 23 Nov. 1864, 14 Dec. 1864, and 17–9 Dec. 1864. Morrill Papers,

MNHS; William A. Scofield to Father, 29 Apr. 1865, William A. Scofield Papers, GAHS; John Langhans to Brother, 28 May 1865, Michael Winey Collection, USMHI.

11. Fitch, *Echoes of the Civil War*, p. 334. Aslo see Will Barlow to Jennie, 6 Apr. 1865, Jennie Safford Smith Papers, Emory U; Orville to Father, 3 Jan. 1865, Joseph and Orville Chamberlain Papers, INHS.

12. Charley [Cox] to Sister, 24 Jan. 1865. L. L. Sylvester, ed., *INMH*, LXVIII, p. 227; Emerson [Anderson] to Parents, 5 Sep. 1864, Civil War Papers, AAS; Charles M. Smith to Father, 21 Sep. 1864, Charles M. Smith Papers, KMNP; R. S. Finley to MAC, 30 Mar. 1865, R. S. Finley Papers, SHC, UNC; Frank L. Ferguson, "Sherman's March to the Sea," Civil War Times Illustrated Collection, USMHI. Also see Isaac N. Carr diary, 27 Jan. 1865, Isaac N. Carr Papers, IASHS; Frederick Sherwood to Mother, 29 Mar. 1865, Frederick Sherwood Papers, LSU; Judson Austin to Wife, 24 Apr. 1865, Nina Ness Papers, Bentley Library, UMI.

13. Richard Reeves diary, 27 May 1865, Reeves Papers, MNHS; Bauer, ed., *Soldiering*, p. 249. Also see William P. Fulton diary, 4 Jul. 1865, William P. Fulton Papers, KMNP; Special Field Orders, No. 76. HQ. Mil. Div. of the Miss., 30 May 1865, OR I, XLVII, Pt. 1, pp. 45–46; John to Belle, 6 Apr. 1865, Federico, ed., *Civil War of J. H. Morse*, p. 182; William H. H. McIntosh, "The 22nd Wisconsin," p. 169, William H. McIntosh Papers, SHSW; John Langhans to Brother, 9 Jun. 1865, Michael Winey Collection, USMHI.

Bibliography

MANUSCRIPTS

Alabama Department of Archives and History, Montgomery, AL
    M.J. Blackwell:
        George
    Newton H. Davis:
        Newton H. Davis
        H. H. Halbert
    Finch Family:
        James H. Finch
    Benjamin Robert Glover
    Bolling Hall:
        James A. Hall
        J. M. Tolly
    Charles Terrell Hardman
    William G. Kephart
    W. E. Matthews
    Richard Calvin McCalla
    David L. Mitchell
    Henry Clay Reynolds
    I. J. Rogers
    David Alexander Green Ross
    L. N. Story:
        W. C. Athey
        G. W. Athey
    Samuel King Vann
    War Manuscripts:
        Joseph Baumer
        Thomas Warrick

American Antiquarian Society, Worcester, MA
    John E. Anderson
    Philo Buckingham
Armistad Research Center, New Orleans, LA
    American Missionary Association:
        James P. Blake
        W. F. Eaton
        W. J. Richardson
Atlanta Historical Society, Atlanta, GA
    Warren Akin
    Lewis H. Andrews
    Tom Barnett
    Samuel Batchell
    Bomar-Kilian:
        Ama Bomar
    Calhoun Family:
        James Calhoun
    James Porter Crane:
        James Porter Crane
        Clinton(?)
    J. R. Crew
    John M. Davidson
    John W. Geary
    Cornelius R. Hanleiter
    A. Holliday
    Benjamin T. Hunter
    John Keely
    James G. Lam
    McClatchey Family:
        Penn (?) McClatchey
    Emma J. Slade Prescott
Chemung County Historical Society, Elmira, NY
    "Sherman's Foragers and Bummers," unknown author
Chicago Historical Society, Chicago, IL
    George W. Brent
    James R. M. Gaskill
    Alfred H. Trego
Chicago Public Library, Chicago, IL
    William T. Humphrey
Columbia University, New York, NY

U.S. Civil War Collection
    Martha Avriett
    T. J. Trimnal
Connecticut State Library, Hartford, CT
    W. W. Packer
    Harlan P. Rugg
    Abner C. Smith
Cornell University, Ithaca, NY
    Jane and Gilbert Krueger:
        Edwin Obriham
Perkins Library, Duke University, Durham, NC
    A. Ames
    Ellen Aumack:
        Young J. Powell
    Alonzo G. Beardsley:
        B. A. Dunbar
    Ferd F. Boltz
    Charles S. Brown
    Ellison Capers
    Rachel Susan Cheves:
        J. K. Cheves
        Joseph Cheves Haskell
    Joshua & Merritt Comfort:
        Joshua Comfort
    John S. Cooper
    CSA Archives Miscellaneous Papers:
        Thomas Carpenter
        David ——
        R. Gilmer
        W.A.R.
    Confederate Veteran Unpublished Miscellaneous Papers:
        T.C.B. [otherwise unidentified]
    Peter Eltinge
    John Herr
    Robert Bruce Hoadley
    Augustus White Long:
        Mrs. Delia White Woodward
    Hugh Mac Rae:
        Alex Mac Rae, Jr.
        Donald Mac Rae

A. J. McBride
William G. McCreary:
    John W. Reid
William E. Merritt
George P. Metz
William H. Nugen
Palmer Family:
    B. F. Darling
William Schaum
Snow Family:
    Samuel Snow
Ella Gertrude Thomas
Sara Ann Tillinghast
Charles Brown Tompkins
U.S. Army Miscellaneous Letters:
    R. G. Maryandye (?)
John C. Van Duzer
Joseph Wheeler
Benjamin S. Williams:
    W. H. D.
    Benjamin S. Williams
Woodruff Library, Emory University, Atlanta, GA
John H. Ash
William T. Baugh
Anthony J. Baurdick
James A. Blackshear
Ama Bomar
William A. Chunn
James Osgood Andrew Clark:
    Ella Anderson Clark
Confederate Miscellany:
    James Albert Beasley
    Mrs. Campbell Bryce
    Bessie Reese Cornwell
    Ervin Godfrey
    John S. Lightfoot
    Albert Quincy Porter
    Alfred Shuler
Mumford H. Dixon

Tomlinson Fort
Luther L. Gates
Gourdin-Young:
      Robert Newman Gourdin
Cornelius R. Hanleiter
William Harden
John L. Hoster
R. B. Jett
Chawncey W. Mead
Jennie Safford Smith:
      William W. Barlow
James W. Watkins
Benjamin S. Williams
Georgia Department of Archives and History, Atlanta, GA
      Augustus S. Avant
      John Major Baker
      J. H. Booker
      James Welsman Brown
      Company G, 2nd Regiment Infantry Georgia State Line:
            Alphonza J. Jackson
      John W. Crabb
      Wendell D. Croom
      Musa V. Crowe
      Z. T. De Loach
      Dickey Family:
            William J. Dickey
            John C. Reynolds
            W. H. Reynolds
      Robert O. Douglass
      Washington L. Dunn
      J. J. Eckles
      Henry Greene Edenfield
      Forty-Sixth Georgia Regiment Volunteer Infantry:
            Gus McGee (or McGehee)
      Adolphus S. Fowler
      Georgia Division, Daughters of the Confederacy:
            Mrs. Kirby-Smith Anderson
            Mrs. B. T. Cole
            Wesley W. De Haven

Henry Graves
Iverson D Graves
Joseph J. Hardee
C. M. Hardy
T. J. Marshall
W. M. McCaslan
Lavender R. Ray
Willie Hunt Smith
L. P. Thomas
T. D. Tinsley
Horatio Goss
Tully Graybill
O. P. Hargis
Edward Harper
William Brown Henslee
G. B. Holcomb
H. T. Howard
G. C. Johnson
John A. Johnson
George Jones:
    George Jones
    John W. Fisher
James Reid Jones
J. Gadsden King
I. M. Logan
James L. Lynch
J. J. Mackay
W. H. Malone
Benjamin Franklin Mason
McClatchey Family:
    Penn McClatchey
    Minerva Leah Rowles McClatchey
A. S. McCollum
Hezekiah McCorkle
George M. McKinnon
Montgomery Family:
    James T. Branan
    Vincent Montgomery
    William K. Watson
James A. Moor

I. V. Moore
Charles Hart Olmstead
E. J. Simpson
Lois Johnson Stewart
Jasper Turner
Twelfth Wisconsin:
    Unknown diarist
Milton C. Wade, Sr.
Albert Wells
Thomas Williams White
Williams-Hix Papers:
    Sarah E. Hix
J. W. Wooten
J. A. Wynn
Perry W. Zeigler
Georgia Historical Society, Savannah, GA
Charlie Albertson
J. H. Everett:
    Divine
E. D. Fennell
David Boston Morgan
Edwin Rhodes
William H. Scofield
Telfair Family:
    No author
J. Frederick Waring:
    W. W. Gordon
    Joseph Frederick Waring
Henry E. Huntington Library, San Marino, CA
Delos Lake
Illinois State Historical Society, Springfield, IL
Samuel D Atkins
Francis R Baker
Abiel M. Barker
John Batchelor
C. H. Brush
James K. Burkhalter
Nicholas C. Buswell
George L. Childress
George N. Compton

Joseph R. Cox
Willard A. Dickerman
James R. M. Gaskill
Perry D. Grubb
Douglas Hapeman
Joseph L. Locke
Bichard Markle
Frederick Marion
Henry Nurs[e]
Henry H. Orendorff
Goerge Reid
Joshua D. Rilea
William C. Robinson
Levi Adolphus Ross
Daniel W. Sheehan
Charles E. Smith
G. W. Southwick
William E. Strong
Owen Stuart
F. W. Tupper
Lysander Wheeler
Charles D. Wills
Indiana Historical Society, Indianapolis, IN
James Adams
Robert F. Bence
Owen E. Bennett
Magnus Brucker
Helen Floyd Carlin:
    Mahlon H. Floyd
Jonathan J. Carter
Aden G. Cavins
Joseph and Orville Chamberlain:
    Orville T. Chamberlain
Samuel Coble
John R. Copeland
James G. Essington
David A. Fateley
William Fifer
John Fritz
Gibson County Civil War Papers:
    Gideon R. Kellams

Burton Gillespie
William P. Hobbs
Henry R. Ingraham:
    Andrew W. Ingraham
Andrew J. Johnson:
    Andrew J. Johnson
    Nathaniel L. Johnson
Charles P. Lesh:
    John A. Wilkens
Benjamin B. Mabrey
John D. Martin
Charles G. Michael
William B. Miller
Jefferson K. Scott
Sesqui:
    John H. Hardin
    John D. Myers
Eli Sherlock
Joseph Taylor Smith
Edward P Stanfield
Jocob Stoler
James S. Thompson
Brumfield Turner
Augustus Van Dyke
Harrison Walters
Williamson D. Ward
Amos C. Weaver:
    Sylvester S. Wills
Elizah T. Zenor
Indiana State Library, Indianapolis, IN
    Andrew Bush
    Daniel E. Bruce
    John M. Godown
    Samuel K. Harryman
    Will H. Judkins
    Samuel Merrill
    Marden Sabin
    Wabash County Civil War Recollections:
        Isaac McMillan
        Ferdinand Sebring
    Aurelius M. Willoughby

Lilly Library, Indiana University, Bloomington, IN
    Indiana History:
        Henry Johnson
        Joshua W. Williams
    Frederick E. Pimper
    Woodburn:
        John D. Alexander
Iowa State Historical Museum and Archives, Des Moines, IA
    Alonzo Abernathy
    Nathaniel M. Baughman
    William M. Blair
    William Christy
    Samuel F. Cooper
    John Newton Coulter
    Alexander G. Downing
    Levi N. Green
    Griffith Family:
        J. G. Berstler
    S. B. Humbert
    Oliver C. Kinley
    Elisha Leaming
    John W. Ludington
    Edwin L. Lybarger
    Charles N. Lyman
    H. C. McArthur
    Robert E. McCrellis
    James Norman
    Winfield S. Schermerhorn
    Oliver Shibley
    Ralph Tripp
    Loren S. Tyler
    Allen T. Underwood
    Albert Utterback
    Hiram Wayne
    James A. Williamson
Iowa State Historical Society, Iowa City, IA
    Isaac N. Carr
    Henry M. Farr
    S. S. Farwell
    William S. Fultz
    J. W. Garner

John Gay
Joseph F. Growe
Greig Harmanson:
    George Hall
Robert W. Henry
Jesse Macy
Harry Mahler
John J. McKee
Henry Clinton Parkhurst
George S. Richardson
Charles Berry Senior
Seventh Iowa Regiment, Co. G
Seneca B. Thrall
Unknown Diary, Co. F, 9th Iowa Infantry
E. Burke Wylie
Kennesaw Mountain National Park, Marietta, GA
John Barnett
Martin D. Bushnell
John M. Carr
Allen L. Fahnestock
William P. Fulton
George Hurlbut
Smithfield Jackson
James W. Langley
W. G. Putney
Charles M. Smith
D. J. Spencer
Lyman S. Widney
Library of Congress, Washington, D.C.
Alston Family:
    Jacob M. Alston
James D. Barbee and David R. Barbee:
    R. Herbert Jones
    F. A. Olds
Wimer Bedford
James A. Congleton
John Cope:
    John Cope
    John F. Oglevee (?)
    Laird Singer
J. Dexter Cotton

Sylvanus Crossly
Louis Elseffer:
    Harry S. Elseffer
James H. Goodnow
John S. Jackman
W. C. Johnson
Harriette C. Keatinge
John A. Lair
Rufus Mead
John S. Newton
Henry W. Perkins
O. M. Poe
Alfred Roman
Charles Reynolds
Department of Archives and Manuscripts, Louisiana State University, Baton l
LA
John Bass
William H. Ellis
Edwin Hutchinson
Levi Lytle
Maria McKinne Winter Robertson
Frederick Sherwood
P. D. Stephenson
Thomas T. Taylor
Massachusetts Historical Society, Boston, MA
Thomas S. Howland
Knight-Failing:
      E. P. Failing
Samuel Storrow
University Archives, Michigan State University, East Lansing, MI
Campbell Family:
    Alex Campbell
    Allen Campbell
Jesse Taft
Minnesota Historical Society, St. Paul, MN
Judson W. Bishop
Alonzo D. Cady
James M. Cheatham
Thomas D. Christie
John Cutter
Michael Dresbach

Reuben Farnum
Levi Nelson Green
Ira Newell Morrill
Isaac W. Muzzy
Timothy Harrison Pendergast
Sewall G. Randall
Axel Hayford Reed
Richard S. Reeves
John E. Risedorph
Billings D. Sibley
Mississippi Department of Archives and History, Jackson, MS
W. R. Barry
Marion Frances Baxter
Joseph J. Hunter
R. Amos Jarman
John D. Rendall
H. Clay Sharkey
Thomas T. Smith
National Archives, Washington, D.C.
Record Group 94:
W. T. Sherman's Orders and Letter Books
Muster Rolls for Regiments in the 14, 15, 17, and 20 AC
and 3rd Cavalry Division, Military Division of the Mis-
sissippi
Record Group 393:
Abstract of Letters Received, 14 AC
Letters Received, 15 AC, Inspector General
Letters Sent by Inspector General, 20 AC
Letters Sent, 15 AC
Letters Sent, 14 AC Commissary of Musters
List of Federal Prisoners in Charge of Provost Marshal, 17
AC
Order Book, 15 AC
Provost Marshall, Beaufort, SC
Special Field Orders Book, Military Division of the Missis-
sippi
Special Field Orders Book, Circulars Book, General Orders
Book, and Abstracts of Orders Book, 15 AC
Special Field Orders Book, General Orders Book, and Spe-
cial Orders Book, Fourth Division, 15 AC
Descriptive Books, Muster Rolls, Morning Reports, Special

Field Orders Book, and Order Books, 110th U.S. Colored Infantry.

Muster Rolls for January–February 1865 for the 54th Mass (Colored) Infantry; 3rd U.S. Colored Troops; 21st U.S. Colored Troops; 26th U.S. Colored Troops; 32nd U.S. Colored Troops; 33rd U.S. Colored Troops; 34th U.S. Colored Troops; 35th U.S. Colored Troops; 2nd U.S. Colored Light Artillery, Battery G.

Record Group 153:

Register of the Records of the Proceedings of the U.S. Army General Courts-Martial, 1809–1890

Proceedings of the U.S. Army General Courts-Martial, 1809–1890

–LL 2761,   Richard Springer
–LL 3022,   Frederick Sudderman
–LL 3023,   John B. Riggs
–LL 3031,   Henry Broderick
–LL 3060,   John W. Atherton
–LL 3072,   John W. Fields, Norman Maybe, James W. Tate, James Channon
–LL 3073,   Pren Metham
–LL 3100,   John Hupp, N. H. Whitterman
–LL 3157,   Milton Young
–LL 3233,   Charles Winslow
–MM 1578, Henry Clevinger, Alphonso Dickey, James Palmer
–MM 1602, William H. Clemmens, Henry Beales, Henry J. Sherman, Samuel Stiles
–MM 1679, James Webb
–MM 1733, John Mercer
–MM 1759, William Loeb
–MM 1801, Charles H. Jackson
–MM 1832, Daniel McMullen
–MM 1836, James S. Randle
–MM 1854, Sidney Woodward
–MM 1879, John Ducey, Michael Reid, Patrick Ryan, Julius W. Ulrich, John Watson
–MM 1933 William Lewis, George Parry
–MM 1996, J. N. Clampett
–MM 1997, Fred Bodmer

–MM 2409, Jerome Patterson
–MM 2436, John Armentrout, Dallas Cross, Hiram Mc-
Cumber, B. F. Riggs, L. H. Sanders
–MM 2496, William Eason
–MM 3115, Charles A. Henderson
–NN 3374, James A. McAuley, William Wyatt
–NN 3396, Samuel Cottrell, Cornelius Johnson
–NN 3414, John W. Wheeler
–NN 3421, Michael Rabble
–NN 3430, William Cartwright, James "Levi" Kennedy, Wil-
liam C. Lake, John McDonough, William H.
McMullen
–NN 3466 Henry H. Huddleston, Robert S. Emerson
–NN 3543, Hugh Alexander
–NN 3588, Henry J. Mooney
–NN 3632, Greenburg B. Nevling
–NN 3937, O. H. P. Ewing, Henry Holtz, Arthur McCarty,
Henry Quinn, A. C. H. Warner
–NN 3959, Linas L. Larringer
–NN 3973, Grant J. Ross, Michael Reid, Patrick Ryan
–OO 209, Cornelius Cronan, William D. Moore
–OO 281, Isaac P. Griffith, John D. Gibson, Robert Rabbitt
–OO 407 James H. Waddell
–OO 470, Milon Hopkins, Soloman H. Hopper, Samuel
McCray, William H. Raney, James H. Waddle
–OO 548, Emil Bartech, Lyman H. Jones, Rudolph Mueller
–OO 579, Theodore Coe
–OO 605 Thomas Brooks, Alexander God, Daniel Herrin,
David Ollinger, Jacob Shroeder, Samuel Tomlin-
son, Henry Westerman, Salathiel Wheeler, Wil-
liam W. Zuel
–OO 666, Christopher McGee
–OO 667, James Cord
–OO 674, John B. Douglas, Robert McNary
–OO 704, William L. Speering, John Thomas
–OO 3428, James K. Preble
New Jersey Historical Society, Newark, NJ
Ezra A. Carman
Sebastian Duncan, Jr.
New York Historical Society, New York, NY

James Chesnut
Rudolph Rey
Sixty-Sixth Illinois:
    Charles F. Kimmel
Henry W. Slocum in Thomas S. Howland
Alfred Baker Smith
Wright Family:
    Edward Bingham Wright
New York Public Library, New York, NY
    Joseph G. Canning
    John Leland Jordan
Ohio Historical Society, Columbus, OH
    Lyman D. Ames
    Robert M. Atkinson:
        Robert M. Atkinson
        George W. Duffield
    J. W. Baldwin
    John Beiser
    R. N. Elder
    John W. Griffith
    Lyde Harriman:
        Green Southard
        Wesley Southard
    Samuel Baker Herrington
    George H. Hildt:
        Daniel G. Hildt
        George H. Hildt
    Joseph Hoffhines
    John D. Inskeep
    William Joslin
    Lewis Family:
        Harry Lewis
    Martin Mock
    Luke Murray:
        Luke Murray
        Aaron D. Riker
    James M. Naylor
    Robert Norris
    N. L. Parmater
    William H. Pittenger

Styles W. Porter
Nelson Purdum
James M. Scott
Robert K. Scott
James H. Smith
James R. Stillwell
Joseph Mitchell Strickling
Lynne Starling Sullivant
Thomas T. Taylor:
    S. P. Bonner
    Thomas T. Taylor
John Vail
Veteran Banner

Soldiers' Votes, 1864 Presidential Election

Pennsylvania History and Museum Commission, Harrisburg, PA
    Department of State, Bureau of Legislation and Elections
        Soldiers' Votes, 1864
In the Private Possession of Mr. James J. McDonald
    William C. Marlatt
Rutgers University, New Brunswick, NJ
    Garret S. Byrne
State Historical Society of Wisconsin, Madison, WI
    J. Allen Barber
    Van S. Bennett
    William Smith Bloom
    Adelbert M. Bly
    Peter Knudson Brye
    William W. Campbell
    Orson P. Clinton
    Richard Robert Crowe
    Charles H. Dickinson
    Peter Ege
    William Fay
    George W. Gee
    James Ghormley
    Thomas Hatchford
    William I. Henry
    Benjamin Franklin Heuston

Julian W. Hinkley
Ole Kittelson
Charles Webster Knapp
Edwin D. Levings:
    Edwin D. Levings
    Homer Levings
William H. McIntosh
George B. McMillan
William C. Meffert
Alonzo Miller
Levi H. Nickel
John Henry Otto
R. Matthew Perry
Marcus S. Pratt
James K. Proudfit
Frank H. Putney
James T. Reeve
Harvey Reid
Henry Clay Robbins
John H. Roberts
Philip Roesch
Richard Baxter Satterlee
James F. Sawyer
George F. Shepherd
William T. Sherman
Martin C. Short
Charles M. Smith
George T. Spaulding
Charles H. Spencer
Samuel G. Swain:
    M. Griffin
John B. Tripp:
    Ezra W. Button
M. Ebenezer Wescott

*Executive Department: Military Votes, 1864 General Election
    Service Records of the 32nd Wisconsin Infantry*

Tennessee State Library and Archives, Nashville, TN
    Carroll H. Clark

Carmichael Dibble
Philip Roesch
William E. Sloan
United States Army Military History Institute, Carlisle Barracks, PA
    Solon Carter
    Civil War Miscellaneous:
        John W. Bates
        John Barrett
        David C. Bradley
        Henry Bryan
        Ensign H. King
        John W. Latimer
        George B. Lower
        Robert Major
        James H. Patton
        Lorenzo N. Pratt
        Chauncey B. Reese
        Theodore W. Skinner
        Daniel Titus
        Unidentified diarist, Schofield's command
    Civil War Times Illustrated:
        Lyman Daniel Ames
        George Bargus
        Marion Francis Baxter in Lionel Baxter
        N. Blackwell in Lionel Baxter
        Joseph J. Brown
        William H. Brown
        Alex Caldwell in Caldwell Family
        William Z. Corbin
        Nicholas De Graff
        Fergus Elliott
        Lewis Elliott in Fergus Elliott
        Orin Ellis
        James Farson
        Frank L. Ferguson
        William Augustus Fleming
        John Porter Fort
        Abraham Gibble
        James Griffin
        Henry Hurter

Friedrick P. Kappelman
James E. Morrow
Isaac C. Nelson
Ario C. Pardee, Jr.
Joseph Parkinson
Thomas E. Pierce
Edward E. Schweitzer
Joseph J. Scroggs
Daniel Sterling
John Stevens
Owen Stuart
James W. Turner in Joseph Shreve
Unknown Soldier, Tenth Army Corps, J.C.
Gregory Coco:
William H. H. Tallman
James E. Edmonds
Halstead-Mans Family:
Benton Halstead
Harrisburg Civil War Round Table:
Elgin and the Civil War
Harrison Keyes
David Nichol
William R. Talley
Earl M. Hess:
Quincy A. Brown
Leonidas M. Jordan
Isaac Kittinger
Frederick Sherwood
James Washburn
John S. Miles
Benjamin Milikin
Hubbard T. Minor
John W. Rathburn:
J. H. Case
Sladen Family:
Joseph Sladen
Michael Winey:
Levi D. Bryant
Guy C. in Martin D. Bushnell
Milton J. Griswold

William D. Harper
John Langhans
George J. Mason
Dick McCadden in Soldiers of the 154th NYSV
Charles W. McKay
Emory Sweetland
William Stanley Hoole Special Collections Library, University of
Alabama, University, AL
H. D. Clayton
Harden Perkins Cochrane
James Montgomery Lanning
William H. H. Minot
University of Georgia, Athens, GA
Jeremy F. Gilmer
Frances Hodgson Heidler:
S. C.
Charles Colcock Jones, Jr:
Charles Colcock Jones, Jr.
Hodgson
Francis H. Nash
C. C. Platter
Thirty-Eighth Indiana
Robert Williams:
Lawson (?) Williams
University of Iowa, Iowa City, IA
Jacob Harrison Allspaugh
Marcellus W. Darling
Jesse Dawley
W. B. Emmons
James Giauque
Henry C. Laybourn
Philip J. Wiliams
Wendell D. Wiltsie
Bentley Historical Library, University of Michigan, Ann Arbor, MI
C. Emerson Allen
Ira K. Bailey:
Lewis J. Rice
Curtis Buck
Charles Butler:
Edson Woodman

William J. Carroll
John Wesley Daniels
David P. Ingraham
Robert Blake Minor
Wayne E. Morris
Nina Ness:
    Judson L. Austin
    Alphonzo Covey
    William Fifer
    S. Jack North
Henry G. Noble
Charles Peel
Alfred S. Richards
Isaac Roseberry
Thomas W. Shearman:
    Thomas Fitzgibbon
Chester M. Slayton
Sligh Family:
    James M. Sligh
Sidney Smith:
    Albert S. Smith
Oliver L. Spaulding
Squire Family:
    John E. Hickman
Stanard Family:
    William B. Stanard
Peter Steketee
Stevens Family:
    William C. Stevens
John Weissert
Thomas H. Williams
Ellen Wilson:
    Ebenezer Post
William L. Clements Library, University of Michigan, Ann Arbor, MI
    Schoff:
        Numa Barned
        Adam Cosner
Western Historical Collection, University of Missouri and State Historical Society of Missouri, Columbia, MO

John T. Buegel
Coleman-Hayter:
    Tom H. Colman
Company C, Twenty-Third Missouri Infantry Volunteers:
    Albert D. Hampshire
William H. Lynch
Elias Perry
A. W. Reese
R. R. Rockwood
Henry Harrison Sawyer
Benjamin F. Sweet
Lot Dudley Young
Southern Historical Collection, University of North Carolina, Chapel
    Hill, NC
James W. Albright
Edward C. Anderson
Arnold-Screven:
    John Screven
Mrs. George J. Baldwin
David Alexander Barnes
W. S. Basinger:
    Elizabeth Georgia Basinger
Jesse S. Bean
Grace Pierson James Beard
Taylor Beatty
J. C. C. Black
William Kennedy Blake
Boykin:
    Rev. Robert Wilson
Thomas Butler:
    Eliza Clay
    Mallery King
William Calder
Duncan G. Campbell
Chisolm Family:
    (?) Chisolm
Edmund J. Cleveland
Elizabeth Collier
Confederate Miscellaneous:
    W. A. Harris

J. H. Cornish
Joseph B. Cumming
Henderson Deans
Zaccheus Ellis
Franklin Harper Elmore:
    Lawrence W. Taylor
    Mrs. Sally Elmore Taylor
Grace B. Elmore
Joseph Espey
Federal Soldiers' Letters:
    I. Shoger
Robert Stuart Finley
Gordon Family:
    W. W. Gordon
Graves Family:
    Henry Graves
    Iverson D. Graves
Meta Morris Grimball
G. W. F. Harper
Maria L. Hayneworth
Heyward-Ferguson:
    S. W. Ferguson
Emma E. Holmes
Aristide Hopkins
Robert Philip Howell
Charles Woodward Hutson
Cadwallader Jones:
    Annie I. Jones
Jones Family:
    Alex C. Jones
Elisha Mitchell:
    S. M. Coit
Thomas J. Myers
Noble-Attaway:
    Mary W. Noble
Charles H. Olmstead
Penn School:
    Arthur Summer
W. S. Penniman
C. S. Powell

Benedict Joseph Semmes
Augustus T. Smythe
D. M. Tedder:
    Daniel Miles Tedder
    Andrew Woodley
Terry Family:
    Joseph Green Terry
Samuel Thompson:
    John Thompson
    Joseph S. Thompson
Louis H. Webb
N. W. Wilson
Francis D. Winston:
    E. B. Lane
Jonathan Worth:
    W. H. Bagley
    Jonathan Worth
University of South Carolina, Columbia, SC
    Dwight Wyatt Aikin:
        Mrs. William Moultrie Dwight
        Mrs. R. E. Ellison
        Ria Gaillard
    E. C. Anderson
    Lewis Malone Ayer:
        Alfred Ayer
    I. T. Bleckley
    Frederick L. Childs:
        Frederick L. Childs
        W. H. Hanks
    Mrs. Emily Caroline Ellis
    N. A. Emanuel
    W. F. Fain
    Octavia Chaires Greenhow
    Greenville Ladies Association
    George Huggins
    William H. Johnson
    J. A. Keller
    Edward Henry Kellers
    Mary Leverette
    S. M. McCain

    Thomas Jefferson McKie
    John R. Niernsee
    Ellen Maria Ravenell
    Benjamin Rawls
    Sarah Jane Sams
    William A. Scofield
    William T. Sherman
    Harriet Hyrne Simons
    Madame Sosnowski
    Alexander Ross Taylor
    J. Thayer
    W. H. Thomas
    Moultrie Reid Wilson
    Robert Wilson
    John Henry Winder
    R. Y. Woodlief
    Joseph T. Zealy
Barker Texas History Center, University of Texas, Austin, TX
    H. W. Barclay
    Archivald Allen Black
    F. F. Bunting
    Civil War Miscellany:
        W. C. Olds
    James R. Cole
    Thomas Hampton
    Joseph B. Hart
    Frances Harvey:
        John Harvey
    William Nicholsen
    Horace Reed
    Mrs. E. M. Schwety
    William E. Stanton
    C. Irvine Walker
Western Michigan University, Kalamazoo, MI
    Mrs. Ann Coffee:
        Cyrus C. Babbitt
    Allan M. Giddings:
        Byron E. Churchill
    Mrs. Clarissa and Stanley Oswalt Haas:
        Herschel A. Foster

Mrs. Kathryn Hoppe:
    Grant M. Tuttle
Mr. & Mrs. Robert F. Keefer:
    John Keefer
Larry Martin:
    Oscar M. Baxter
Mr. and Mrs. Glover Shoudy:
    Alden B. Huntley
Margaret Stanford:
    Thomas McCormick
Mrs. Paul H. Todd, Sr.:
    Lebeus Chapin
Don E. Truax:
    Abram Pelig Woodward
Lola J. Warrick:
    Willard G. Eaton
Western Reserve Historical Society, Cleveland, OH
    William David Evans
    Joseph W. Gaskill
    Lyman Hardman
    John A. McIntosh
    Elliott B. McKeever
    Alfred Mewett:
        Albert A. Champlin
    Regimental Papers of the Civil War:
        Peter Murphy, 137th NY
    Oliver Sanders
    Edward A. Webb
    Laurens W. Wolcott
Yale University, New Haven, CT
    Arthur B. Carpenter
    David Herrick Gile

PUBLISHED PRIMARY SOURCES

SOLDIERS

Abernathy, Alonzo. "Incidents of an Iowa Soldier's Life, or Four Years in Dixie." *Annals of Iowa*, 3rd Series, XII, No. 6 (October, 1920), 401–28.

Alexander, John D. *History of the Ninety-Seventh Regiment of Indiana Volunteer Infantry*. Terre Haute, IN: Moore & Langen, 1891.

Allen, E. W. "Two Days With Sherman's Army in South Carolina." *Union and Confederate Annals*, I, No. 1(January, 1884), 42–45.

Ambrose, D. Lieb. *History of the Seventh Regiment Illinois Volunteer Infantry*. Springfield, IL: Illinois Journal Compnay, 1868.

Andersen, Mary Ann, ed. *The Civil War Diary of Allen Morgan Geer*. New York: Cosmos Press, 1977.

Angle, Paul M., ed. *Three Years in the Army of the Cumberland: The Letters and Diary of Major James A. Connolly*. Bloomington: Indiana University Press, 1959.

Arbuckle, John C. *Civil War Experiences of a Foot-Soldier Who Marched with Sherman*. Columbus, OH: n.p., 1930.

Aten, Henry J. *History of the 85th Illinois Volunteers*. Hiawatha, KA: Regimental Association, 1901.

Athearn, Robert G., ed. "An Indiana Doctor Marches with Sherman: The Diary of James Comfort Pattern." *Indiana Magazine of History*, XLIV, No. 4 (December, 1953), 405–22.

Atkins, Smith D. "With Sherman's Cavalry." *MOLLUS–Illinois*, II, 382–98.

Barker, "Len." *Military History of Company "D" 66th Illinois*. Reed City, MI: n.p., 1915.

Barnard, George N. *Photographic Views of Sherman's Campaign*. New York, n. d.

Bates, Marcus W. "Battle of Bentonville." *MOLLUS–Minnesota*, V, 136–51.

Bauer, K. Jack, ed. *Soldiering: The Civil War Diary of Rice C. Bull, 123rd New York Volunteer Infantry*. San Rafael, CA: Presidio Press, 1977.

Beall, John B. *In Barrack and Field*. Nashville: M. E. Church, South, 1893.

Belknap, Charles E. "Bentonville: What a Bummer Knows About It." *MOLLUS–District of Columbia*, I, War Papers 12.

——. "Christmas Day Near Savannah in Wartime." *Michigan History Magazine*, VI, No. 4, 591–96.

——. "Recollections of a Bummer." *MOLLUS–District of Columbia*, II, War Papers No. 28.

Belknap, William Worth, and Tyler, Loren S. *History of the Fifteenth Regiment, Iowa Veteran Volunteer Infantry*. Keokuk, IA: R. B. Ogden & Son, 1887.

Bell, John T. *Tramps and Triumphs of the Second Iowa Infantry*. Omaha: Gibson, Miller, & Richardson, 1886.

Benton, Charles E. *As Seen From the Ranks*. New York: G. P. Putnam's Sons, 1902.

Bettersworth, J. K., ed. *Mississippi in the Confederacy, As They Saw It*. Baton Rouge: Louisiana State University Press, 1961.

Bevens, W. E. *Reminiscences of a Private*. 1913 (?).

Bircher, William. *A Drummer Boy's Diary*. St. Paul: St. Paul Book and Stationery Company, 1889.

Bishop, Judson W. *The Story of a Regiment*. St. Paul: Published by the Survivors of the Regiment, 1890.

Black, John Logan. *Crumbling Defenses*. Macon, GA: Eleanor D. McSwain, 1960.

Black, Wilfred W., ed. "Civil War Letters of George M. Wise." *Ohio Historical Quarterly*, LXV, No. 1 (January, 1956), 53–81, and LXVI, No. 2 (April, 1957), 187–95.

——. "Marching With Sherman Through Georgia and the Carolinas." *Georgia Historical Quarterly*, LII, Nos. 3 and 4 (September 1968–December, 1968), 308–36 and 451–79.

Blackburn, J. K. P. *Reminiscences of the Terry Rangers*. Austin: University of Texas, 1919.

Boyle, John Richard. *Soldiers True: The Story of the One Hundred and Eleventh Regiment Pennsylvania Veteran Volunteers*. New York: Eaton & Mains, 1903.

Bradley, George S. *The Star Corps*. Milwaukee: Jermain & Brightman, 1865.

Bratton, J. R. "Letter of a Confederate Surgeon on Sherman's Occupation of Milledgeville." *Georgia Historical Quarterly*, XXXII, No. 3 (September, 1948), 231–32.

Brockman, Charles J., Jr., ed. "The John Van Duzer Diary of Sherman's March from Atlanta to Hilton Head." *Georgia Historical Quarterly*, LIII, No. 2 (June, 1969), 220–40.

Brooks, R. P., ed. "Howell Cobb Papers." *Georgia Historical Quarterly*, VII, No. 4 (December, 1922), 355–94.

Brooks, U. R. *Stories of the Confederacy*. Columbia, S.C.: The State Company, 1912.

Brown, Alonzo L. *History of the Fourth Regiment of Minnesota Infantry Volunteers*. St. Paul: The Pioneer Press Company, 1892.

Brown, Norman D., ed. *One of Cleburne's Command: The Civil War*

Reminiscences and Diary of Capt. Samuel T. Foster, Granbury's Texas Brigade, C.S.A. Austin: University of Texas Press, 1980.

Bruce, Foster, and Lynch, William O. "Daniel E. Bruce, Civil War Teamster." *Indiana Magazine of History*, XXXIII, No. 2 (June, 1937), 187–98.

Bryant, Edwin E. *History of the Third Regiment of Wisconsin Veteran Volunteer Infantry, 1861–1865.* Madison: Veteran Association of the Regiment, 1891.

Burton, E. P. *Diary of E. P. Burton.* Des Moines: The Historical Record Survey, 1939.

Byers, Major S. H. M. *With Fire and Sword.* New York: The Neale Publishing Company, 1911.

Byrne, Frank L., ed. *The View from Headquarters: Civil War Letters of Harvey Reid.* Madison: The State Historical Society of Wisconsin, 1965.

Cadle, Cornelius. "An Adjutant's Recollections." *Military Order of the Loyal Legion of the United States—Ohio*, V, 384–401.

Calkins, William Wirt. *The History of the One Hundred and Fourth Regiment of Illinois Volunteer Infantry.* Chicago: Donohue & Henneberry, 1895.

Canfield, S. S. *History of the 21st Regiment Ohio Volunteer Infantry.* Toledo: Vrooman, Anderson & Bateman, 1893.

Capron, Thaddeus H. "War Diary of Thaddeus H. Capron." *Journal of the Illinois State Historical Society*, XII, No. 3 (October, 1919), 330–406.

Carlin, William P. "The Battle of Bentonville." *Military Order of the Loyal Legion of the United States—Ohio*, III, 231–51.

Carlisle, James C. *Documents of the Assembly of the State of New York*, XI, No. 148. Albany: Printing House of C. Van Benthuysen & Sons, 1868.

Carmen, E. A. "General Hardee's Escape from Savannah." *Military Order of the Loyal Legion of the United States—District of Columbia*, I, War Papers No. 13.

Carmony, Donald F., ed. "Jacob W. Bartness Civil War Letters." *Indiana Magazine of History*, LII, No. 2 (June, 1956), 157–86.

Cash, William M., and Howorth, Lucy Somerville, eds. *My Dear Nellie: The Civil War Letters of William L. Nugent to Eleanor Smith Nugent.* Jackson: University of Mississippi Press, 1977.

Chamberlain, W. H. *History of the Eighty-First Regiment Ohio Infantry Volunteers.* Cincinnati: Gazette Steam Printing House, 1865.

Chapman, Horatio Dana. *Civil War Diary.* Hartford: Allis, 1929.

Civil War Diary of William Julius Champion. Ann Arbor: University Microfilms International, n.d.

Clark, Olynthus B., ed. *Downing's Civil War Diary.* Des Moines: The Historical Department of Iowa, 1916.

Clark, Walter A. *Under the Stars and Bars.* Augusta: Chronicle Printing Company, 1900.

Cluett, William W. *History of the 57th Regiment Illinois Volunteer Infantry.* Princeton, IL: Lessee Republican Job Department, 1886.

Coffman, Edward M., ed. "Henry M. West's Political Letter." *Filson Club Quarterly*, XXX, No. 4 (October, 1956), 340–42.

Collins, George K. *Memoirs of the 149th Regiment New York Volunteer Infantry.* Syracuse: Published by the Author, 1891.

——. *Record 149th New York Volunteer Regiment Infantry, 1861–1865.* Syracuse: Onondaga Historical Association, 1928.

Collins, R. M. *Chapters from the Unwritten History of the War Between the States.* St. Louis: Nixon-Jones Printing Co., 1893.

Committee. *Ninety-Second Illinois Volunteers.* Freeport, IL: Journal Steam Publishing House and Bookbindery, 1875.

A Committee of the Regiment. *The Story of the Fifty-Fifth Regiment Illinois Volunteer Infantry in the Civil War.* Clinton, MA: W. J. Coulter, 1887.

Compton, James. "Some Incidents Not Recorded in the Rebellion Records." *Military Order of the Loyal Legion of the United States—Minnesota*, VI, 251–58.

Cook, S. G., and Benton, Charles E., eds. *The "Dutchess County Regiment" in the Civil War: Its Story As Told by its Members.* Danbury, CT: The Danbury Medical Printing Co., Inc., 1907.

Cox, Jacob D. "The Surrender of Johnston's Army and the Closing Scenes of the War in North Carolina." *Military Order of the Loyal Legion of the United States—Ohio*, II, 247–76.

Croom, Wendell D. *The War History of Company "C," Sixth Georgia Regiment.* Fort Valley, GA: Survivors of the Company, 1879.

Cuttino, George Peddy, ed. *Saddle Bags and Spinning Wheels.* Macon: Mercer University Press, 1981.

Dacus, Robert H. *Reminiscences of Company "H," First Arkansas Mounted Rifles.* Dardanelle, AR: Post-Despatch Print, 1897.

Davidson, James Wood. "Who Burned Columbia—A Review of General Sherman's Version of the Affair." *Southern Historical Society Papers*, VII, No. 4 (April, 1879), 185–92.

Dean, Benjamin D. *Recollections of the 26th Missouri Infantry*. Lamar, MO: Southwest Missourian Office, 1892.

de Laubenfels, David J., ed. "With Sherman Through Georgia." *Georgia Historical Quarterly*, XLI, No. 3 (September, 1957), 288–300.

De Rosier, Arthur H., Jr., ed. *Through the South With a Union Soldier*. Johnson City, TN: Publications of the East Tennessee State University Research Advisory Council, 1966.

De Velling, C. T. *History of the Seventeenth Regiment*. Zanesville, OH: E. R. Sullivan, 1889.

Diary of Capt. Henry C. Dickinson, C.S.A. Denver: Williamson-Haffner Co., n.d.

Donahower, Jeremiah Chester. "The Constitution of 1789." *Military Order of the Loyal Legion of the United States—Minnesota*, VI, 238–50.

Dougall, Allen H. "Bentonville." *Military Order of the Loyal Legion of the United States—Indiana*, 212–19.

Drake, Julia A., ed. *The Mail Goes Through or The Civil War Letters of George Drake (1846–1918)*. San Angelo, TX: Anchor Publishing Co., 1964.

Duncan, William. "The Army of the Tennessee Under Major-General O. O. Howard." *Military Order of the Loyal Legion of the United States—Minnesota*, IV, 164–75.

——. "Through the Carolinas With the Army of the Tennessee." *Military Order of the Loyal Legion of the United States—Minnesota*, IV, 329–36.

——. "With the Army of the Tennessee Through the Carolinas." *Military Order of the Loyal Legion of the United States—Minnesota*, IV, 517–30.

Dunlap, Leslie W., ed. *"Your Affectionate Husband, J. F. Culver."* Iowa City: Friends of the University of Iowa Libraries, 1978.

Eaton, Clement, ed. "Diary of an Officer in Sherman's Army Marching Through the Carolinas." *Journal of Southern History*, IX, No. 2 (May, 1943), 238–54.

Federico, Bianca Morse, ed. *Civil War Letters of John Holbrook Morse, 1861–1865*. Washington, D.C.: Published by the Author, 1975.

Fitch, Michael H. *Echoes of the Civil War As I Hear Them*. New York: R. F. Fenno & Company, 1905.

Fleharty, S. F. *Our Regiment: A History of the 102d Illinois Infantry Volunteers*. Chicago: Brewster & Hanscom, 1865.

Fletcher, William Andrew. *Rebel Private: Front and Rear*. Austin: University of Texas Press, 1954.

Floyd, David Bittle. *History of the Seventy-Fifth Regiment Indiana Infantry Volunteers*. Philadelphia: For the Author, 1893.

Force, Manning F. "Marching Across Carolina." *Military Order of the Loyal Legion of the United States—Ohio*, I, 1–18.

Ford, Arthur P. *Life in the Confederate Army*. New York: The Neale Publishing Company, 1905.

Franklin, John Hope, ed. *The Diary of James T. Ayers*. Springfield: Published by the Illinois State Historical Society, 1947.

Fryer, D. F. *History of the Eightieth Ohio Veteran Volunteer Infantry, 1861 to 1865*. Newcomerstown, OH: n.p., 1904.

Funk, Arville L. *A Hoosier Regiment in Dixie: A History of the Thirty-Eighth Indiana Volunteer Infantry Regiment*. Chicago: Adams Press, 1978.

Gage, M. D. *From Vicksburg to Raleigh, or a Complete History of the Twelfth Regiment Indiana Volunteer Infantry*. Chicago: Clark & Co., 1865.

Garrett, Franklin M. *Atlanta and Environs*, I. New York: Lewis Historical Publishing Company, Inc., 1954.

Garrett, Jill K., ed. *Confederate Diary of Robert D. Smith*. Columbia, TN: Capt. James Madison Sparkman Chapter, United Daughters of the Confederacy, 1975.

Gleason, Levi. "The Experiences on Observations of a Drafted Man in the Civil War." *Military Order of the Loyal Legion of the United States—Minnesota*, VI, 545–56.

Goodloe, Albert Theodore. *Confederate Echoes*. Nashville: M. E. Church, South, 1893.

Goodrell, W. H. "The Burning of Columbia, S.C." *Iowa Historical Record*, IV, No. 3 (July, 1888), 125–28.

Grant, U. S. *Personal Memoirs*. 2 vols. New York: Charles L. Webster & Company, 1885.

Grecian, J. *History of the Eighty-Third Regiment, Indiana Volunteer Infantry*. Cincinnati: John F. Uhlhorn, 1865.

Griffith, Lucille, ed. *Yours Till Death: Civil War Letters of John W. Cotton*. University: University of Alabama Press, 1951.

Grigsby, Melvin. *Smoked Yank*. Sioux Falls, ND: Dakota Bell Publishing Co., 1888.

Grubbs, George W. *The Fortunate Regiment*. An Address at the 28th Annual Reunion, 70th Indiana Regiment, 1902.

Grunert, William. *History of the One Hundred and Twenty-Ninth Regiment Illinois Volunteer Infantry*. Winchester, IL: R. B. Dedman, 1866.

Hackett, Roger C., ed. "Civil War Diary of Sergeant James Louis

Matthews." *Indiana Magazine of History*, XXIV, No. 4 (December, 1928), 306–16.

Halsey, Ashley, ed. *A Yankee Private's Civil War by Robert Hale Strong*. Chicago: Henry Regnery Company, 1961.

Hamilton, William Douglas. *Recollections of a Cavalryman of the Civil War After Fifty Years, 1861–1865*. Columbus, OH: F. J. Heer Printing Co., 1915.

Hargis, O. P. "First-Person Story of Wheeler's Cavalryman." *Civil War Times Illustrated*, VII, No. 8 (December, 1968), 37–42.

Harwell, Richard, ed. *A Confederate Marine: A Sketch of Henry Lea Graves with Excerpts from the Graves Family Correspondence, 1861–1865*. Tuscaloosa, AL: Confederate Publishing Company, Inc., 1963.

Havens, L. C. *Historical Sketch of the 136th New York Infantry, 1862–1865*. 1934.

Hawes, Lilla Mills, ed. "The Memoirs of Charles H. Olmstead." *Georgia Historical Quarterly*, XLV, No. 2 (June, 1961), 137–55.

Hays, E. Z., ed. *History of the Thirty-Second Regiment Ohio Volunteer Infantry*. Columbus: Cott & Evans, 1896.

Hazen, William B. *A Narrative of Military Service*. Boston: Ticknor and Company, 1885.

Head, Thomas A. *Campaigns and Battles of the Sixteenth Regiment Tennessee Volunteers*. Nashville: Cumberland Presbyterian Publishing House, 1885.

Hedley, F. Y. *Marching Through Georgia: Pen-Pictures of Everyday Life*. Chicago: Donohue, Henneberry & Co., 1890.

Hemstreet, William. "Little Things About Big Generals." *Military Order of the Loyal Legion of the United States—New York*, III, 148–66.

Hermann, I. *Memoirs of a Veteran*. Lakemont, GA: CSA Press, 1974.

Hinkley, Julian Wisner. *Service With the Third Wisconsin Infantry*. Madison: Wisconsin History Commission, 1912.

Hinman, Wilbur F. *The Story of the Sherman Brigade*. Alliance, OH: Published by the Author, 1897.

Historical Sketch of Co. "D," 13th Regiment N.J. Vols. New York: D. H. Gildersleeve & Co., 1875.

History of Company B, 40th Alabama Regiment Confederate States Army from the Diary of Elbert D. Willett. Anniston, AL: Norwood, 1902.

History of the 37th Regiment O.V.V.I. Toledo: Montgomery & Vrooman, Printers, 1890.

Holmes, J. Taylor. *52nd O.V.I., Then and Now*. Columbus: Berlin Print, 1898.

Hopkins, Charles A. "The March to the Sea." *Soldiers and Sailors His-*

torical Society of Rhode Island: Personal Narratives, Series III, No. 12.

Hopkins, Vivian C., ed. "Soldier of the 92nd Illinois: Letters of William H. Brown and His Fiancee, Emma Jane Frazey." *Bulletin of the New York Public Library*, LXXIII, No. 2 (February, 1969), 114–36.

Hormel, Olive Deane. *With Sherman to the Sea: A Drummer's Story of the Civil War as Related by Corydon Edward Foote*. New York: The John Day Company, 1960.

Horrall, S. F. *History of the Forty-Second Indiana Volunteer Infantry*. Chicago: Published by the Author, 1892.

Howard, Oliver Otis. *Autobiography*. 2 vols. New York: The Baker & Taylor Company, 1907.

Howard, Wiley C. *Sketch of Cobb Legion Cavalry*. 1901.

Howe, M. A. De Wolfe, ed. *Home Letters of General Sherman*. New York: Charles Scribner's Sons, 1909.

——. *Marching with Sherman: Passages From the Letters and Campaign Diaries of Henry Hitchcock, Major and Assistant Adjutant General of Volunteers, November 1864–May 1865*. New Haven: Yale University Press, 1927.

Hubert, Charles F. *History of the Fiftieth Regiment Illinois Volunteer Infantry*. Kansas City, MO: Western Veteran Publishing Company, 1894.

Hurst, Samuel H. *Journal-History of the Seventy-Third Ohio Volunteers Infantry*. Chillicothe, OH: np, 1866.

In Memoriam. H. W. Slocum. Albany: State of New York, 1904.

Jackson, Harry F., and O'Donnell, Thomas F., eds. *Back Home in Oneida: Herman Clark and His Letters*. Syracuse: Syracuse University Press, 1965.

Jackson, Oscar Lewis. *The Colonel's Diary*. Sharon, PA: Published by his Family, 1922.

Jamison, Matthew H. *Recollections of Pioneer and Army Life*. Kansas City, MO: Hudson Press, 1911.

Johnson, L. M. "A Night With Bushwackers." *Blue and Gray*, II, No. 4 (October, 1893), 328–31.

Johnson, Robert Underwood, and Buel, Clarence Clough, eds. *Battles and Leaders of the Civil War*, IV. New York: The Century Co., 1888.

Johnson, W. C. "The March to the Sea." *Atlanta Papers*. Dayton: Morningside Press, 1980.

Jones, Charles C., Jr. *General Sherman's March From Atlanta to the Coast: An Address Delivered Before the Confederate Survivors' Association*. Augusta: By Order of the Association, 1884.

Joyner, F. B. "With Sherman in Georgia—A Letter From the Coast."

Georgia Historical Quarterly, XLII, No. 4 (December, 1958), 440–41.

Kerr, Charles D. "From Atlanta to Raleigh." *Military Order of the Loyal Legion of the United States—Minnesota*, I, 202–23.

Keyes, John R. "An Interrupted Cavalry Charge." *Blue and Gray*, II, No. 2 (August, 1893), 141–42.

Kimberley, Edward O. *Personal Recollections of the Colored Race During the Civil War, 1861, 1865*. N.p., n.d.

Kinnear, J. R. *History of the Eighty-Sixth Regiment Illinois Volunteer Infantry*. Chicago: Triubune Company's Book and Job Printing Office, 1866.

Kinney, William Light, Jr., ed. *Sherman's March—A Review*. Bennettsville, S.C.: Marlboro Herald-Advocate, 1963 (?).

Kirwan, A. D., ed. *Johnny Green of the Orphan Brigade, the Journal of a Confederate Soldier*. Lexington: University of Kentucky Press, 1956.

Lamb, Alfred. *My March With Sherman to the Sea*. n.p.: Paddock Publications, 1951.

Lane, Mills, ed. *"Dear Mother: Don't Grieve about me. If I get killed, I'll only be dead."* Savannah: Beehive Press, 1977.

Landstrom, Russel C. "Civil War Experiences of John McAllister." Reprinted from *Cedar Rapids Republican*, April 10, 1927, in *Annals of Iowa*, XXXIX, No. 4 (Spring, 1968), 314–20.

Leggett, M. D. "The Military and the Mob." *Military Order of the Loyal Legion of the United States—Ohio*, I, 188–97.

Letter of Greeting and Record of the Christian Association of the Second Brigade, Third Division, Twentieth Army Corps. Cincinnati: Printed at the Methodist Book Concern, 1865

Letters of Frederick C. Winkler, 1862 to 1865. 1963.

"Letters of James Stallcop to Catherine Varner, Charlotte, Iowa, 1863–1865." *North Dakota Historical Quarterly*, IV, No. 2 (January, 1930), 116–42.

"Letters of John Adams to Catherine Varner, 1864–1865." *North Dakota Historical Quarterly*, IV, No. 4 (July, 1930), 266–70.

"Letters Written by Dr. James R. Zearing to His Wife Lucinda Helmer Zearing During the Civil War, 1861–1865." *Transactions of the Illinois State Historical Society*. 1921.

Lloyd, Frederick. "War Memories." *Iowa Historical Record*, XIV, No. 1 (January, 1898), 218–21.

Longacre, Edward G., ed. " 'We Left a Black Track in South Carolina': Letters of Corporal Eli S. Ricker, 1865." *South Carolina Historical Magazine*, LXXXII, No. 3 (July, 1981), 210–24.

Lucas, D. R. *History of the 99th Indiana Infantry.* Lafayette, IN: Rossert, Spring, 1985.

Lybarger Edwin L. *Leaves From My Diary.* Warsaw, OH, n.d.

Mackintosh, Robert Harley,Jr., ed. *Dear Martha.* Columbia, S.C.: R. L. Bryan Company, 1976.

Mahon, John K., ed. "The Civil War Letters of Samuel Mahon Seventh Iowa Infantry." *Iowa Journal of History*, LI, No. 3 (July, 1953), 233–66.

Mahon, Samuel. "The Forager in Sherman's Last Campaigns." *Military Order of the Loyal Legion of the United States—Iowa*, 188–200.

Marcy, Henry O. "Sherman's Campaign in the Carolinas." *Military Order of the Loyal Legion of the United States—Massachusetts*, II, 331–48.

Marshall, R. V. *An Historical Sketch of the Twenty-Second Regiment Indiana Volunteers.* Madison, IN: Courier Co., 1877.

Marvin, Edwin E. *The Fifth Regiment Connecticut Volunteers: A History Compiled from Diaries and Official Reports.* Hartford: Wiley, Waterman & Eaton, 1889.

McAdams, F. M. *Every-Day Soldier Life.* Columbus: Chas. M. Cott & Co., 1884.

McArthur, H. C. *The Capture and Destruction of Columbia, South Carolina, February 17, 1865: Personal Experiences and Recollections.* Np., 1911.

McCain, General Warren. *A Soldier's Diary or The History of Company "L" Third Indiana Cavalry.* Indianapolis: Warren A. Patton, 1885.

McClurg, Alexander. "The Last Chance of the Confederacy." *Atlantic Monthly*, L (September, 1882), 389–400.

McCrory, W. "Early Life and Personal Reminiscences of General William T. Sherman." *Military Order of the Loyal Legion of the United States—Minnesota*, III, 310–46.

McMurry, Richard. "Sherman's Savannah Campaign." *Civil War Times Illustrated*, XXI, No. 9 (January, 1983), 8–25.

McNeil, S. A. *Personal Recollections of Service.* Richwood, OH, n.d.

Mellon, Knox, Jr., ed. "Letters of James Greenalch." *Michigan History* XLIV, No. 2 (June, 1960), 188–240.

Merrill, Samuel. *The Seventieth Indiana Volunteer Infantry.* Indianapolis: The Bowen-Merrill Company, 1900.

Miller, James Cooper. "We Scattered the Rebels." *Civil War Times Illustrated*, VIII, No. 5 (August, 1969), 42–48.

———. "With Sherman Through the Carolinas." *Civil War Times Illustrated*, VIII, No. 6 (October, 1969), 35–44.

Mims, Wilbur F. *War History of the Prattville Dragoons.* Thurber, TX: Journal Printery, n.d.

Mitchell, Enoch L., ed. "Letters of a Confederate Surgeon in the Army of Tennessee to His Wife." *Tennessee Historical Quarterly*, V, No. 2 (June, 1946), 142–81.

Monnett, Howard Norman, ed. " 'The Awfulest Time I Ever Seen': A Letter From Sherman's Army." *Civil War History*, VIII, No. 3 (September, 1962), 283–89.

Moore, James. *Kilpatrick and Our Cavalry.* New York: W. J. Widdelton, 1865.

Morris, W. S., Hartwell, L. D., and Kuykendall, J. B. *History: 31st Regiment Illinois Volunteers.* Evansville, IN: Keller Printing & Publishing Co., 1902.

Morse, Charles Fessenden. *Letters Written During the Civil War, 1861–1865.* Boston: Privately Printed, 1898.

——. "Sherman's March to the Sea." *Twenty-Ninth Annual Meeting of the Second Regiment Mass. Infantry Ass'n.* Lynn, MA: G.H. & A.L. Nichols, n.d.

Morse, Loren J., ed. *Civil War Diaries of Bliss Morse.* Pittsburg, KA: Pittcraft, Inc., 1964.

Mullen, James M. "Last Days of Johnston's Army." *Southern Historical Society Papers*, XVIII (January–December, 1890), 97–113.

Nichols, George Ward. *The Story of the Great March.* New York: Harper & Brothers, 1866.

Nicolay, John G., and Hay, John, eds. *Complete Works of Abraham Lincoln*, VIII. New York: Francis D. Tandy Company, 1895.

Nourse, Henry S. "The Burning of Columbia, S.C., February 17, 1865." *Papers of the Military Historical Society of Massachusetts*, IX, 417–48.

Noyes, Katharine Macy, ed. *Jesse Macy: An Autobiography.* Springfield, IL: Charles C. Thomas, 1933.

Orendorff, H. H., et al. *Reminiscences of the Civil War From Diaries of Members of the 103d Illinois Volunteer Infantry.* Chicago: Press of J. F. Leaming & Co., 1904.

Osborn, Hartwell, et al. *Trials and Triumphs: The Record of the Fifty-Fifth Ohio Volunteer Infantry.* Chicago: A. C. McClurg & Co., 1904.

Owens, Ira S. *Greene County Soldiers in the Late War, Being a History of the Seventy-Fourth O.V.I.* Dayton, OH: Christian Publishing House Print, 1884.

Palfrey, John C. "General Sherman's Plans After the Fall of Atlanta." *Atlanta Papers.* Dayton, OH: Morningside Press, 1980, 163–97.

Payne, Edwin W. *History of the Thirty-Fourth Regiment of Illinois Volunteer Infantry.* Clinton, IA: Allen Printing Company, 1903.

Pepper, George W. *Personal Recollections of Sherman's Campaigns in Georgia and the Carolinas.* Zanesville, OH: Hugh Dunne, 1866.

Perry, Henry Fales. *History of the Thirty-Eighth Regiment Indiana Volunteer Infantry.* Palo Alto, CA: F. A. Stuart, 1906.

Potter, John. *Reminiscences of the Civil War in the United States.* Oskaloosa, IA: The Globe Press, 1897.

Proceedings of Crocker's Iowa Brigade at the Fifth Biennial Reunion and Sixth Biennial Reunion. Des Moines: Kenyon's Press, 1892.

Putney, Frank H. "Incidents of Sherman's March Through the Carolinas." *Military Order of the Loyal Legion of the United States—Wisconsin,* III, 381–88.

Quad, M. "Sherman's March to the Sea, As Seen by a Northern Soldier." *Southern Historical Society Papers,* X, Nos. 8–9 (August–September, 1882), 410–15.

Quaife, Milo M., ed. *From the Cannon's Mouth: The Civil War Letters of Alpheus S. Williams.* Detroit: Wayne State University Press, 1959.

Quint, Alonzo. *The Record of the Second Massachusetts Infantry.* Boston: James P. Walker, 1867.

Remington, Cyrus Kingsbury. *A Record of Battery I, First N.Y. Light Artillery Vols.* Buffalo: Press of the Courier Company, 1891.

Ridley, Bromfield L. *Battles and Sketches of the Army of Tennessee.* Mexico, MO: Missouri Printing & Publishing Co., 1906.

Rieger, Paul E., ed. *Through One Man's Eyes.* Mount Vernon, OH: Paul E. Rieger, 1974.

Robbins, Edward Mott. *Civil War Experiences, 1862–1865.* Privately Published, n.d.

Robertson, James J., Jr., ed. "Such Is War: The Letters of an Orderly in the 7th Iowa Infantry." *Iowa Journal of History,* LVIII, No. 4 (October, 1960), 321–56.

Rogers, Robert M. *The 125th Regiment Illinois Volunteer Infantry.* Champaign, IL: Gazette Steam Print, 1882.

Rood, H. H. *History of Company "A," Thirteenth Iowa Veteran Infantry.* Cedar Rapids, IA: Daily Republican, 1889.

——. "Sketches of the Thirteenth Iowa." *Military Order of the Loyal Legion of the United States—Iowa,* I, 115–56.

Rood, H. W. *Story of the Service of Company E, and the Twelfth Wisconsin Regiment, Veteran Volunteer Infantry.* Milwaukee: Swain & Tate Co., 1893.

Rosenberger, H. E., ed. "Ohiowa Soldier: The Letters of John Wesley Rumpel." *Annals of Iowa,* 3rd Series, XXXVI, No. 2 (Fall, 1961), 111–48.

Roth, Margaret Brobst, ed. *Well Mary: Civil War Letters of a Wisconsin Volunteer.* Madison: University of Wisconsin Press, 1960.

Rugeley, H. J. H. *Batchelor–Turner Letters, 1861–1864.* Austin: Steck Co., 1961.

Ryan, Harriet Fitts, ed. "The Letters of Harden Perkins Cochrane, 1862–1864." *Alabama Review,* VIII, No. 4 (October, 1955), 277–90.

Ryder, John J. *Reminiscences of Three Years' Serivce in the Civil War.* New Bedford, MA: Reynolds Printing, 1928.

Scott, Paul, ed. " 'With Tears in Their Eyes.' " *Civil War Times Illustrated,* XXI, No. 9 (January, 1983), 26–29.

Se Cheverell, J. Hamp. *Journal History of the Twenty-Ninth Ohio Veteran Volunteers, 1861–1865.* Cleveland, 1883.

Seeley, N. B. *Some Stories of the Civil War in Prose and Poem.* 1905.

Sharland, George. *Knapsack Notes of Gen. Sherman's Grand Campaign Through the Empire State of the South.* Springfield, IL: Johnson & Bradford, 1865.

Sherlock, E. J. *Memorabilia of the Marches and Battles in Which the One Hundredth Regiment of Indiana Infantry Took an Active Part.* Kansas City, MO: Gerard-Woody Printing Co., 1896.

Sherman, William T. *Memoirs of W. T. Sherman By Himself.* 2 vols. New York: Charles L. Webster & Co., 1891.

Shingleton, Royce, ed. " 'With Loyalty and Honor As a Patriot': Recollections of a Confederate Soldier by Claude Lee Hadaway." *Alabama Historical Quarterly,* XXXIII, Nos. 3 and 4 (Fall–Winter, 1971), 240–63.

Simmons, Slann L. C., ed. "Diary of Abram W. Clement, 1865." *South Carolina Historical Magazine,* LIX, No. 1 (January, 1958), 78–83.

Simpson, Col. Harold B. *The Bugle Blows Softly: The Confederate Diary of Benjamin M. Seaton.* Waco, TX: Texian Press, 1965.

Sligh, Charles R. *History of the Services of the First Regiment Michigan Engineers and Mechanics.* Grand Rapids, MI: n.p., 1921.

Smith, Charles H. *The History of Fuller's Ohio Brigade.* Cleveland: A. J. Watt, 1909.

Smith, Daniel E. Huger, et al., eds. *Mason Smith Family Letters, 1860–1868.* Columbia: University of South Carolina Press, 1950.

Smith, Frank. "A Maine Boy in the Tenth Ohio Cavalry." *The Maine Bugle.* Campaign IV (January, 1897), 11–21.

Stauffer, Nelson. *Civil War Diary.* Northridge, CA: California State University, 1976.

Stelle, Abel C. *Memoirs of the Civil War*. New Albany, IN: n.p., 1904.

Sterkx, H. E., ed. "Autobiography and Civil War Letters of Joel Murphree of Troy, Alabama, 1864–1865." *Alabama Historical Quarterly*, XIX, No. 1 (Spring, 1957), 170–208.

Stevenson, Thomas M. *History of the 78th Regiment O.V.V.I.* Zanesville, OH: Published by Hugh Dunne, 1865.

Stewart, Nixon B. *Dan McCook's Regiment. 52nd O.V.I.* Alliance, OH: Published by the Author, 1900.

Stone, Sylvanus Whipple to Dear Wife, 24 Dec. 1864. Documents. *North Dakota Historical Quarterly*, I, No. 2 (January, 1927), 64–66.

Storrs, John W. *The Twentieth Connecticut*. Ansonia, CT: Press of the Naugatuck Valley Sentinel, 1886.

Sweet, Reuben. "Civil War Diary" in *The Antigo Daily Journal*, March 9–May 25, 1939.

Sylvester, Lorna Lutes, ed. " 'Gone for a Soldier': The Civil War Letters of Charles Harding Cox." *Indiana Magazine of History*, LXVIII, No. 3 (September, 1972), 181–239.

Taylor, J. C. *Lights and Shadows In the Recollections of a Youthful Volunteer in the Civil War*. Ionia, MI: Sentinel Standard, n.d.

Taylor, John S. *Sixteenth South Carolina Regiment, CSA From Greenville County, SC*. 1963.

Thomas, L. P. "Their Last Battle." In W. L. Calhoun, ed. *History. 42d Regiment Georgia Volunteers*. University, AL: Confederate Publishing Co., 1977.

Thorndike, Rachel Sherman, ed. *The Sherman Letters: Correspondence Between General and Senator Sherman from 1837 to 1891*. New York: Charles Scribner's Sons, 1894.

Throne, Mildred, ed. "A Commissary in the Union Army: Letters of C. G. Carpenter." *Iowa Journal of History*, LIII, No. 1 (January, 1955), 59–88.

——. "A History of Company D, Eleventh Iowa Infantry, 1861–1865 by William S. Fultz." *Iowa Journal of History*, LV, No. 1 (January, 1957), 35–90.

——. "An Iowa Doctor in Blue: The Letters of Seneca B. Thrall, 1862–1864." *Iowa Journal of History*, LVIII, No. 2 (April, 1960), 97–188.

Tomlinson, Helyn W., ed. *"Dear Friends": The Civil War Letters and Diary of Charles Edwin Cort*. n.p.: Helyn W. Tomlinson, 1962.

Tooms, Samuel. *Reminiscences of the War*. Orange, NJ: Printed at the Journal Office, 1878.

Tourgeé, Albion W. *The Story of a Thousand*. Buffalo: S. McGerald & Son, 1896.

Trimble, Harvey M. *History of the Ninety-Third Regiment Illinois Volunteer Infantry*. Chicago: The Blakely Printing Co., 1898.

Underwood, Adin B. *The Three Years' Service of the Thirty-Third Mass. Infantry Regiment, 1862–1865*. Boston: A Williams & Co., 1881.

Vandiver, Frank E., ed. *Narrative of Military Operations by Joseph E. Johnston*. Bloomington, IN: Indiana University Press, 1959.

Waddle, Angus L. *Three Years with the Armies of the Ohio and the Cumberland*. Chillicothe, OH: Scioto Gazette Book and Job Office, 1889.

Walker, C. I. *Rolls and Historical Sketch of the Tenth Regiment So. Ca. Volunteers*. Charleston: Walker, Evans & Cogswell, 1881.

Walker, P. R. "*Address.*" *92d Ill. Volunteers 5th Triennial Reunion*. Freeport, IL: Journal Printing Co., 1879.

Wallace, William. "Operations of the Second South Carolina Regiment in Campaigns of 1864 and 1865." *Southern Historical Society Papers*, VII, No. 3 (March, 1879), 128–31.

Walton, Clyde C., ed. *Behind the Guns: The History of Battery I, 2nd Regiment, Illinois Light Artillery by Sgt. Thaddeus C. S. Brown, Sgt. Samuel J. Murphy and Bugler William G. Putney*. Carbondale: Southern Illinois University Press, 1965.

Walton, William, ed. *A Civil War Courtship: The Letters of Edwin Weller from Antietam to Atlanta*. Garden City, NY: Doubleday & Company, 1980.

Welch, Spencer Glasgow. *A Confederate Surgeon's Letters to his Wife*. New York: The Neale Publishing Company, 1911.

Welles, E. L. "Hampton at Fayetteville." *Southern Historical Society Papers*, XIII (January–December, 1885), 144–48.

——. "A Morning Call on General Kilpatrick." *Southern Historical Society Papers*, XII, No. 3 (March, 1884), 123–30.

Westervelt, William B. *Lights and Shadows of Army Life, As Seen By a Private Soldier*. Marlboro, NY.: C. H. Cochrane, Printer, 1886.

Williams, Noble C. *Echoes From the Battlefield*. Atlanta: The Franklin Printing and Publishing Company, 1902.

Willison, Charles A. *Reminiscences of a Boy's Service with the 76th Ohio*. Menasha, WI: George Banta Publishing Company, 1908.

Wills, Charles, ed. *Army Life of an Illinois Soldier: Letters and Diary of the Late Charles W. Wills*. Washington, D.C.: Mary E. Kellogg, 1906.

Wilson, Ephraim A. *Memoirs of the War*. Cleveland: W. M. Bayne Printing Co., 1893.

Wilson, James. "Late Provost Marshal, Army of the Tennessee." *Iowa Historical Record*, III, No. 3 (July, 1887), 481–96.

Winther, Oscar Osburn, ed. *With Sherman to the Sea: The Civil War Letters, Diaries and Reminiscences of Theodore F. Upson.* Bloomington: Indiana University Press, 1958.

Woodhull, Maxwell Van Zandt. "A Glimpse of Sherman Fifty Years Ago." *Military Order of the Loyal Legion of the United States—District of Columbia*, IV, War Papers No. 97.

Wright, Henry H. *A History of the Sixth Iowa Infantry.* Iowa City: State Historical Society of Iowa, 1923.

CIVILIANS

Bonner, James C., ed. *The Journal of a Milledgeville Girl, 1861–1867.* Athens: University of Georgia Press, 1964.

Botume, Elizabeth Hyde. *First Days Amongst the Contrabands.* New York: Arno Press, 1968.

Bryan, T. Conn, ed. "A Georgia Woman's Civil War Diary: The Journal of Minerva Leah Rowles McClatchey." *Georgia Historical Quarterly*, LI, No. 1 (June, 1967), 197–216.

Carrol, J. P. "The Burning of Columbia, South Carolina—Report of the Committee of Citizens Appointed to Collect Testimony." *Southern Historical Society Papers*, VIII, No. 5 (May, 1880).

Conyngham, David P. *Sherman's March Through the South.* New York: Sheldon and Company, 1865.

Crabtree, Beth G., and Patton, James W., eds. *"Journal of a Secesh Lady": The Diary of Catherine Ann Devereux Edmondston, 1860–1866.* Raleigh: North Carolina Division of Archives and History, 1979.

Durham, Roger S., ed. "Personal Narrative of Sherman's Raid in Liberty County, Georgia Atrocities of the Enemy, ETC. by John Stevens." *Civil War Times Illustrated*, XXI, No. 9 (January, 1983), 15–25.

"An Eye-Witness Account of the Occupation of Mt. Pleasant." *South Carolina Historical Magazine*, LXVI, No. 1 (January, 1965), 8–14.

Gatell, Frank Otto, ed. "A Yankee Views the Agony of Savannah." *Georgia Historical Quarterly*, XLIII (December, 1959), 428–31.

Gay, Mary A. H. *Life in Dixie During the War.* Atlanta: Foote & Davies, 1901.

Hickerson, Thomas Felix, ed. *Echoes of Happy Valley: Letters and Diaries.* Durham: Published by the Author, 1962.

Holland, Rupert Sargent, ed. *Letters and Diary of Laura M. Towne.* Cambridge, MA: Riverside Press, 1912.

Holmes, Charlotte R., ed. *The Burckmeyer Letters, March 1863–June 1865.* Columbia, S.C.: The State Company, 1926.

Jones, Katharine M., ed. *Heroines of Dixie.* Indianapolis: The Bobbs-Merrill Company, Inc., 1955.

King, Spencer B., Jr., ed. "Fanny Cohen's Journal of Sherman's Occupation of Savannah." *Georgia Historical Quarterly*, XLI, No. 4 (December, 1957), 407–16.

——. *The War-Time Journal of a Georgia Girl.* Macon: The Ardivan Press, 1960.

MacLean, Clara D. "The Last Raid." *Southern Historical Society Papers*, XIII (January–December, 1885), 466–76.

Martin, Josephine Bacon, ed. *Life on a Liberty County Plantation: The Journal of Cornelia Jones Pond.* Darien, GA: Privately Printed, 1974.

McGee, Charles M., Jr., and Lander, Ernest M., Jr., eds. *A Rebel Came Home.* Columbia: University of South Carolina Press, 1961.

Miers, Earl Schenck, ed. *When the World Ended: The Diary of Emma Le Conte.* New York: Oxford University Press, 1957.

Monroe, Haskell, ed. *Yankees A' Coming: One Month's Experience During the Invasion of Liberty County, Georgia, 1864–1865 by Mary Sharpe Jones and Mary Jones Mallard.* Tuscaloosa, AL: Confederate Publishing Company, Inc., 1959.

Oates, John A. *The Story of Fayetteville and the Upper Cape Fear.* Charlotte, N.C., 1950.

Pearson, Elizabeth Ware, ed. *Letters from Port Royal, 1862–1868.* New York: Arno Press, 1969.

Poe, Clarence, ed. *True Tales of the South at War.* Chapel Hill: University of North Carolina Press, 1961.

Porter, A. Toomer. *Led On! Step by Step.* New York: G. P. Putnam's Sons, 1898.

Street, Julian, ed. *A Woman's Wartime Journal: The Diary of Dolly Sumner Lunt.* Macon: The J. W. Burke Co., 1927.

Taylor, Mrs. Thomas, et al., ed. *South Carolina Women in the Confederacy.* Columbia, SC: The State Company, 1903.

Two Diaries: Journals Kept by Miss Susan R. Jervey and Miss Charlotte St. J. Ravenel. Pinopolis, SC: St. John's Hunting Club, 1924.

Underwood, J. L. *The Women of the Confederacy.* New York: The Neale Publishing Company, 1906.

Williams, Ben Ames, ed. *A Diary From Dixie by Mary Boykin Chesnut.* Boston: Houghton Mifflin Company, 1949.

Windler, Penny Nichols. *Placid.* Warwick, VA: High-Iron Publishers, 1961.

Wood, W. Kirk, ed. *A Northern Daughter and a Southern Wife*. Augusta: Richmond County Historical Society, 1976.

GOVERNMENT PUBLICATIONS

Annual Report of the Adjutant General of Missouri, 1863 and 1866.

Bates, Samuel P. *History of Pennsylvania Volunteers*. 4 vols. Harrisburg: B. Singerly, State Printer, 1869.

Catalogue of Connecticut Volunteer Organizations. Hartford: Brown & Gross, 1869.

Estabrook, Charles E., et al. *Records and Sketches of Military Organizations*. Madison, WI: Published by the State, 1914.

The Executive Documents to the House of Representatives, 39th Congress, 1st Session, 1865–6. Washington, D.C.: Government Printing Office, 1866.

The Legislation Manual of the State of Wisconsin, 1865. Madison: Atwood & Rublee, State Printers, 1865.

Massachusetts Soldiers, Sailors, and Marines in the Civil War. 8 vols. Norwood, MA: Norwood Press, 1931.

The Medical and Surgical History of the War of the Rebellion. Washington, D.C.: Government Printing Office, 1870–88.

Message and Annual Reports for 1864. Pt. 1. Columbus: Richard Nevins, State Printer, 1865.

Minnesota in the Civil and Indian Wars. St. Paul: Pioneer Press Company, 1891.

New York in the War of the Rebellion, 1861 to 1865. 5 vols. Albany: J. R. Lyon Company, State Printers, 1912.

Official Roster of the Soldiers of the State of Ohio in the War of the Rebellion. 12 vols. Cincinnati: Wilstach, Baldwin & Co., 1886.

Record of Service of Michigan Volunteers in the Civil War. Kalamazoo: Ahling Bros. & Everard, 1905 (?).

Register of the Commissioned Officers and Privates of the New Jersey Volunteers. Jersey City: Printed by John H. Lyon, 1863.

Report of the Adjutant General of the State of Illinois. 9 vols. Springfield: H. W. Rokker, State Printer and Binder, 1866.

Report of the Adjutant General of the State of Indiana. 8 vols. Indianapolis: Alexander H. Conner, State Printer, 1869.

Robertson, Jno. *Michigan in the War*. Lansing: W. S. George & Co., State Printers and Binders, 1882.

Roster and Record of Iowa Soldiers in the War of the Rebellion. 6 vols. Des Moines: Emory H. English, State Printer, 1908.

Roster of Wisconsin Volunteers, War of the Rebellion, 1861–1865. Madison: Democrat Printing Company, 1886.

The War of the Rebellion: A Compilation of the Official Records of the Union and Confederate Armies. Washington, D.C.: Government Printing Office.

NEWSPAPERS

Chicago Tribune
Cincinnati Daily Gazette
Cincinnati Enquirer
Coffee Cooler (Sturgis, MI)
Daily Missouri Democrat
Grand Rapids Daily Eagle
Harper's Weekly
Hillsborough Recorder
Leslie's Illustrated Weekly Magazine
Morning Cleveland Herald
New York Semi-Weekly Tribune
New York Times
New York Tribune
Raleigh Daily Conservative
Savannah Republican

SECONDARY SOURCES

Adams, George Worthington. *Doctors in Blue: The Medical History of the Union Army in the Civil War.* New York: Henry Schuman, 1952.

Adamson, A. P. *Brief History of the Thirtieth Georgia Regiment.* Griffin, GA: The Mills Printing Company, 1912.

Ambrose, Stephen A. *Halleck: Lincoln's Chief of Staff.* Baton Rouge: Louisiana State University, 1962.

Anders, Leslie. *The Eighteenth Missouri.* Indianapolis: The Bobbs-Merrill Company, 1968.

Anderson, William M. *They Died to Make Men Free: A History of the 19th Michigan Infantry in the Civil War.* Berrien Springs, MI: Hardscrabble Books, 1980.

Avery, I. W. *The History of the State of Georgia From 1850 to 1881.* New York: AMS Press, 1972.

Barnard, Harry Vollie. *Tattered Volunteers: The Twenty-Seventh Ala-*

bama Infantry Regiment, C.S.A. Northport, AL: Hermitage Press, 1965.

Barrett, John G. *The Civil War in North Carolina.* Chapel Hill: University of North Carolina Press, 1963.

——. *Sherman's March Through the Carolinas.* Chapel Hill: University of North Carolina Press, 1956.

Benton, Josiah H. *Voting in the Field.* Boston: Privately Printed, 1915.

Blackburn, John W. *Gray Jackets with Blue Collars.* Beaver Dam, KY: The Embry Newspapers, Inc., 1963.

Bonner, James C. "Sherman at Milledgeville in 1864." *Journal of Southern History,* XXII, No. 3 (August, 1956), 273–91.

Breeden, James O. "A Medical History of the Latter Stages of the Atlanta Campaign." *Journal of Southern History,* XXXV, No. 1 (February, 1969), 31–59.

Bryan, T. Conn. *Confederate Georgia.* Athens: University of Georgia Press, 1953.

Calhoun, W. L. *History: 42d Regiment Georgia Volunteers.* University, AL: Confederate Publishing Co., 1977.

Castel, Albert. "The Guerrilla War, 1861–1865." *Civil War Times Illustrated* (October, 1974).

Clark, John B., Jr. "Fire Protection in the Old South." 2 vols. Dissertation, University of Kentucky, 1957.

Clauss, Errol MacGregor. "Sherman's Failure at Atlanta." *Georgia Historical Quarterly,* LIII, No. 3 (September, 1969), 321–29.

Cochran, Hamilton, *Blockade Runners of the Confederacy.* Indianapolis: Bobbs-Merrill, Inc., 1958.

Colier, Major Calvin L. *First In—Last Out: The Capitol Guards, Ark. Brigade.* Little Rock: Pioneer Press, 1961.

Cook, Harvey T. *Sherman's March Through South Carolina in 1865.* Greenville, SC: n.p., 1938.

Davis, William C. *The Orphan Brigade.* Garden City, NY: Doubleday & Company, Inc., 1980.

Dodson, W. C., ed. *Campaigns of Wheeler and His Cavalry, 1862–1865.* Atlanta: Hudgins Publishing Company, 1899.

Drago, Edmund L. "How Sherman's March Through Georgia Affected the Slaves." *Georgia Historical Quarterly,* LVIII, No. 3 (Fall, 1973), 361–75.

Dudley, Edgar S. *Military Law and the Procedure of Courts-Martial.* New York: John Wiley & Sons, 1908.

Dunkelman, Mark H., and Winey, Michael J. *The Hardtack Regiment:*

An Illustrated History of the 154th Regiment New York State Infantry Volunteers. Rutherford, NJ: Fairleigh Dickinson University Press, 1980.

Dyer, John P. *Fightin' Joe Wheeler.* Baton Rouge: Louisiana State University Press, 1941.

Eisenschimel, Otto, and Newman, Ralph. *The Civil War: The American Iliad as Told by Those Who Lived It,* I. New York: Grosset & Dunlap, Inc., 1956.

Frederickson, George M. *The Black Image in the White Mind: The Debate on Afro-American Character and Destiny, 1817–1914.* New York: Harper & Row, 1965.

Geary, Mary de Forest. *A Giant in Those Days.* Brunswick, GA: Coastal Printing Company, 1980.

Gibson, John M. *Those 163 Days: A Southern Account of Sherman's March From Atlanta to Raleigh.* New York: Coward-McCann, Inc., 1961.

Gould, B. A., and Baxter, Col. J. H. "Personal Characteristics of the Union Volunteers." *The National Tribune Library,* I, No. 3 (December 14, 1895), 6–12.

Gray, Tom S., Jr. "The March to the Sea." *Georgia Historical Quarterly,* XIV, No. 2 (June, 1930), 111–38.

Guernsey, Alfred H., and Alden, Henry M. *Harper's Pictorial History of the Great Rebellion,* II. Chicago: McDonnell Bros., 1868.

Harmon, George D. "The Military Experiences of James A. Peifer." *North Carolina Historical Review,* XXXII, No. 4 (October, 1955), 544–72.

Henderson, Lindsey P., Jr. *The Oglethorpe Light Infantry.* Savannah: The Civil War Centennial Commission of Savannah and Chatham County, 1961.

Herd, E. Don, Jr. *The South Carolina Upcountry, 1540–1980,* II. Greenwood, S.C.: Attic Press, 1982.

Hoole, William Stanley. *Alabama Tories.* Tuscaloosa, AL: Confederate Publishing Company, Inc., 1960.

Hughes, Nathaniel Cheairs, Jr. *General William J. Hardee: Old Reliable.* Baton Rouge: Louisiana State University, 1965.

Jeffries, C. C. *Terry's Rangers.* New York: Vantage Press, 1961.

Jordan, Winthrop. *White Over Black: American Attitudes toward the Negro, 1550–1812.* Chapel Hill: University of North Carolina Press, 1968.

Keegan, John. *The Face of Battle.* London: Jonathan Cape, 1976.

Lawrence, Alexander A. *A Present for Mr. Lincoln.* Macon: The Ardivan Press, 1961.

Leeper, Wesley Thurman. *Rebels Valiant: Second Arkansas Mounted Rifles.* Little Rock: Pioneer Press, 1964.

Lewis, Lloyd. *Sherman, Fighting Prophet.* New York: Harcourt, Brace and Company, 1932.

Liddell Hart, B. H. *Sherman: Soldier, Realist, American.* New York: Dodd, Mead & Company, 1929.

Litwack, Leon F. *Been in the Storm So Long: The Aftermath of Slavery.* New York: Alfred A. Knopf, 1979.

——. *North of Slavery: The Negro in the Free States, 1790–1860.* Chicago: University of Chicago Press, 1961.

Lucas, Marion Brunson. *Sherman and the Burning of Columbia.* College Station: Texas A & M University Press, 1976.

Luvaas Jay. "Bentonville—Johnston's Last Stand." *North Carolina Historical Review,* XXXIII, No. 3 (July, 1956), 332–58.

McInvale, Morton R. " 'All That Devils Could Wish For': The Griswoldville Campaign, November, 1864." *Georgia Historical Quarterly,* LX, No. 2 (Summer, 1976), 117–30.

McMurry, Richard M. "Confederate Morale in the Atlanta Campaign of 1864." *Georgia Historical Quarterly,* LIV, No. 2 (Summer, 1970), 226–43.

McNeill, William J. "The Stress of War: The Confederacy and William Tecumseh Sherman During the Last Year of the Civil War." Dissertation, Rice University, 1973.

——. "A Survey of Confederate Soldier Morale During Sherman's Campaign Through Georgia and the Carolinas." *Georgia Historical Quarterly,* LV, No. 1 (Spring, 1971), 1–25.

McPherson, James M. *The Negro's Civil War.* New York: Vantage Books, 1965.

Miers, Earl Schenck. *The General Who Marched to Hell: William Tecumseh Sherman and His March to Fame and Infamy.* New York: Alfred A. Knopf, 1951.

Oates, John A. *The Story of Fayetteville and the Upper Cape Fear.* Charlotte, NC: The Dowd Press, 1950.

Quiner, E. B. *The Military History of Wisconsin: A Record of the Civil and Military Patriotism of the State in the War for the Union.* Chicago: Clarke & Co., 1866.

Rogers, George A., and Saunders, R. F., Jr. "The Scourge of Sherman's Men in Liberty County, Georgia." *Georgia Historical Quarterly,* LX, No. 4 (Winter, 1976), 356–69.

Rose, Willie Lee. *Rehearsal for Reconstruction: The Port Royal Experiment.* New York: Vantage Books, 1964.

Roswell, John W. *Yankee Cavalrymen: Through the Civil War with the Ninth Pennsylvania Cavalry*. Knoxville: University of Tennessee Press, 1971.

Sefton, James E. *The United States Army and Reconstruction, 1865–1877*. Baton Rouge: Louisiana State University Press, 1967.

Semkins, Francis Butler, and Patton, James Welch. *The Women of the Confederacy*. Richmond: Garrett and Massie, 1936.

Stanard, David E., ed. *Death in America*. Philadelphia: University of Pennsylvania Press, 1975.

Taylor, A. Reed. "The War History of Two Soldiers: A Two-Sided View of the Civil War." *The Alabama Review*, XXIII, No. 2 (April, 1970), 83–109.

Thomas, Benjamin P., and Hyman, Harold M. *Stanton: The Life and Times of Lincoln's Secretary of War*. New York: Alfred A. Knopf, 1962.

Walters, John Bennett. "General William T. Sherman and Total War." *Journal of Southern History*, XIV, No. 4 (November, 1948), 447–80.

Watkins, James L. *King Cotton: A Historical and Statistical Review, 1790 to 1908*. New York: Negro Universities Press, 1969.

Wiley, Bell I. "The Common Soldier of the Civil War." *Civil War Times Illustrated*, XII, No. 4 (July, 1973), 1–64.

——. *The Life of Billy Yank: The Common Soldier of the Union*. Indianapolis: Bobbs-Merrill Company, 1952.

——. *The Life of Johnny Reb: The Common Soldier of the Confederacy*. Indianapolis: Bobbs-Merrill Company, 1943.

——. "Southern Reaction to Federal Invasion." *Journal of Southern History*, XVI, No. 4 (November, 1950), 491–510.

Williams, Harry T. *McClellan, Sherman and Grant*. Wesport, CT: Greenwood Press, 1976.

Williamson, Joel *After Slavery: The Negro in South Carolina During Reconstruction, 1861–1877*. New York: W. W. Norton & Company, Inc., 1965.

Winthrop, William. *Military Law and Precedents*. Boston: Little, Brown and Company, 1896.

Index